Best Practice

Best Practice
Process Innovation Management

Edited by
Mohamed Zairi

OXFORD   AUCKLAND   BOSTON   JOHANNESBURG   MELBOURNE   NEW DELHI

Butterworth-Heinemann
Linacre House, Jordan Hill, Oxford OX2 8DP
225 Wildwood Avenue, Woburn, MA 01801-2041
A division of Reed Educational and Professional Publishing Ltd

A member of the Reed Elsevier plc group

First published 1999

British Library Cataloguing in Publication Data
A catalogue record for this book is available from the British Library

ISBN 0 7506 3953 9

Composition by Genesis Typesetting, Rochester, Kent
Printed and bound in Great Britain by Biddles Ltd. Guildford

FOR EVERY TITLE THAT WE PUBLISH, BUTTERWORTH-HEINEMANN
WILL PAY FOR BTCV TO PLANT AND CARE FOR A TREE.

Contents

Contributors

Pervaiz Ahmed
Unilever Lecturer in Innovation Management, University of Bradford.

Sattam Alshammri
King Saud University, Kingdom of Saudi Arabia.

Patrick Allen
Teaching Fellow in Marketing, University of Bradford.

Dr Kate Blackmon
Research Fellow, Centre for Operations Management, London Business School.

Brian Cumming
Senior Engineer, Ford Motor Co.

Professor Richard Duggan
Senior Adviser on Innovation, Innovation Unit, Department of Trade and Industry.

D. M. Ginn
Program Manager, Conix Corporation.

Phil Hanson
Practice Leader in Manufacturing Excellence, IBM Consulting Group.

Dr M. F. Trueman
Lecturer in Marketing and Innovation, University of Bradford Management Centre.

Professor Chris Voss
BT Professor of Total Quality Management, London Business School.

Frances Wilson
Consultant in the E-Business Practice, IBM Consulting, Warwick.

Professor Mohamed Zairi
Professor of Best Practice Management, European Centre for TQM, University of Bradford.

Foreword

The first authoritative definition of innovation in the context of commerce and industry was provided in 1967 by Robert L. Charpie in his influential report to the US Department of Commerce. In this submission, 'Technological Innovation: its Environment and Management', innovation is seen as: 'The successful bringing to market of new or improved products, processes or services'.

This captures the same concept of innovation as the more succinct definition adopted in 1992 by the working party of the Confederation of British Industry and the Department of Trade and Industry which has now become widely accepted throughout the UK: 'Innovation is the successful exploitation of new ideas'.

In the period between the formulation of these alternative definitions, innovation has moved rapidly up the agendas of all involved in trade and commerce.

> 'Innovation is the central issue of competitiveness in the 1990s.'
>
> *Professor Michael Porter*

> 'Innovation must be the driving force behind the entire business policy, both downstream and upstream of the actual production of goods and services .... Innovation can be successful if all of the skills of the firm are mobilized. Conversely it will fail when this cohesion is lacking .... One of Europe's major weaknesses lies in its inferiority in terms of transforming the results of technological research and skills into innovations and competitive advantages.
>
> *Edith Cresson,*
> *European Commissioner, Green Paper on Innovation, 20 December 1995*

Within the rapidly growing body of literature on innovation, the role of this volume is to bring together academic, public sector and industrial perspectives; and provide a holistic view of the many facets which must be successfully balanced if ideas and inventions are to be transformed into innovations. Equally importantly, the book balances contributions which portray innovation as a 'procedural' process which can be successfully accomplished if all pre-planned stages are successfully executed with the behavioural concept of innovation.

In the latter approach innovation is regarded primarily as a culture which, at its most productive, provides a fertile environment within which the innate creativity of the human resource can provide a constant stream of incremental improvements, interposed with periodic paradigm shifts.

As an experienced, hardened veteran of many attempts to introduce innovation in products, processes and services into international markets during the past thirty-five years, I welcome this pluralistic view. Innovation is a hard and demanding process, where failure is the likely outcome and success the elusive prize.

Would-be innovators encountering early setback, seem frequently to draw comfort from the observations of that early student of change mangement:

'There is nothing more difficult to carry out,
   nor more doubtful of success,
   nor more dangerous to handle
 than to institute a new order of things.'

Machiavelli

Mastery of procedure and behaviour, backed by a sound grasp of both theory and practice of innovation provides a prescription for beating the odds in successfully exploiting ideas. This book, I hope, will provide a sound basis for those striving for such mastery.

Richard Duggan
Senior Adviser on Innovation to the Innovation Unit, DTI

Introduction

What is best practice innovation management?

What makes some organizations more highly admired and innovative than others may not be as obvious as we think. The power of innovativeness that best in class organizations exhibit on a sustainable basis is not always attributed to the same factors. The widely quoted 3M, for instance, is known for its insistence on teamwork, the spirit of intrapreneurship, the 15 per cent rule, among many others. Other organizations such as Cadillac, Rank Xerox and IBM rely on the use of total quality management (TQM) engineering tools and techniques, and the application of simultaneous engineering, and so on.

A benchmarking investigation conducted by the author on a selective group of highly innovative and commercially successful organizations has revealed that they each enjoy many unique attributes as the core to their business success. A wide range of perspectives is presented below.

D2D

- **Vendor partnerships** – joint improvement projects with vendors – regular monitoring and review of vendor performance.
- **Vendors supporting corporate goals** – integrated role in the planning or inventory requirements and the achievements of set targets for time to market and the overall cost reductions necessary for maintaining high customer satisfaction levels.
- **Integrated supply chain management system** – based on the use of information technology (IT) and which captures value added throughout the chain in line with the desired corporate targets.
- **Comprehensive use of IT** – IT drives the supply chain and other functions, particularly linking D2D with its major suppliers through EDI.
- **The development of an innovation culture** – this is done through the encouragement of benchmarking and high interest in technological

exploitation. The external focus, networking and sharing for learning is considered crucial for success at D2D.

- **A formal innovation process** – this gets used for product and process development and through a discipline of design for manufacturability (DFMA) time to market is made possible. People are trained to use the process at all levels, and the employee appraisal system includes the need to be trained for using the process.
- **Idea generation process** – various mechanisms in place for idea generation including visits, conferences, research, collaborative projects with other partners and the use of a corporate system, DELTA.
- **Heavy reliance on performance measurement** – measures in all areas of value added and the development of a culture which is committed to continuous improvement.
- **Tools and techniques** – extensive use of tools such as quality function deployment (QFD), DFMA, simultaneous engineering, Taguchi, statistical process control (SPC), among others.
- **TQM** – a culture of quality which led D2D to win the European Quality Award (EQA).

Rover Group

- **Supplier partnerships** – critical to Rover, total partnerships with key suppliers have been achieved through an evolutionary process which took many years.
- **Time to market** – achieved through interlinking all the activities and goal congruence.
- **Scheduling processes** – computerized systems, which trigger the need for procurement on a local basis rather than in a centrally controlled fashion as used to be the case.
- **Project management policy (PMP)** – this is the complete routemap for managing projects throughout the whole cycle which includes decision and planning phase, delivery phase and post-launch phase. The PMP system includes stages, activities, deliverables, reviews and measures.
- **A culture of research and technology management** – technology is researched continuously: it has to be proven in terms of its technical performance, it has to lead to clear benefits and then it has to maintain high standards of quality, manufacturability and reliability.
- **Tools and techniques** – a whole range of tools are used including DFMA, Taguchi, failure mode, effects analysis (FMEA), Poka Yoke, SPC, QFD among many others.
- **TQM** – Rover is a learning organization where quality management has brought about a radical transformation within the company.

IBM (UK) Ltd

- **TQM** – use of TQM in the form of an approach which is dedicated to total customer satisfaction, and called market-driven quality.
- **Tools and techniques** – use of tools and techniques such as QFD, DFMA, benchmarking, 6 Sigma Design, concurrent engineering.
- **Supplier partnerships** – through commitment to zero defect and 'six sigma performance'.
- **Teamwork** – wider employee involvement and management by a multifunctional, team-based approach.
- **Technology** – plays a key role in innovation through product and process design and implementation.
- **Integrated product development process** – a comprehensive system which includes various stages of design and implementation, monitoring and review development.

3M

- **Teamwork** – characterizes the whole culture of the organization.
- **Ideas** – ideas can come from anywhere within the organization and everyone can sponsor an idea (known as *intrapreneuring*).
- **Innovation steering committee** – to protect, encourage and monitor the development of a culture of innovation.
- **Recognition for innovation** – no reprimand or blame but high praise and reward.
- **Corporate dependence on innovation** – innovation is the business and not just part of the business.
- **Technological exploitation** – technological transfer and successful application and implementation.

Ford

- **Engineering skills** – people equipped with skills to make concurrent engineering and parallel working work.
- **People skills** – communication and interpersonal skills to make the interface between *socio* and *technical* systems effective.
- **Tools and techniques** – a wide variety of tools used at different levels including Taguchi Methods, SPC, design of experiments, QFD, FMEA, problem-solving.
- **TQM** – the use of a comprehensive quality system referred to as quality operating system (QOS).

AT&T

- **The Pace innovation process** – a comprehensive gate-based process for innovation.
- **Tools and techniques** – various modern tools and techniques used, including DFMA, QFD, ISO 9001 among others.
- **Project management** – an effective way of successfully managing projects, based on teamwork and cross-functional involvement.

Phillips BCS

- **Product release procedure** – a comprehensive system with procedures and guidelines for new product development.
- **Stages of new product development (NPD)** – various stages in the product life cycle, all clearly defined, including concept, feasibility, development, introduction, distribution and end of life.

Cadillac

- **Simultaneous engineering** – an entire structure of simultaneous engineering (reversed pyramid) including SEE Steering Committee, vehicle systems management teams, product development and improvement teams, all focusing on the end customers and dealers.
- **Product programme management process (PPMP)** – a four-phase innovation process based on gates and gatekeepers geared for achieving time to market.
- **TQM** – comprehensive use of quality management, in-process quality is assessed at every stage of the new idea development (NID) process and there is a five-step problem-solving process for conducting continuous improvement.
- **Supplier partnerships** – suppliers are assessed against excellence criteria and partnerships are achieved through a commitment to supplier training and development.

Hewlett Packard

- **TQM** – dedication to total quality management with a deployment approach from the top.
- **Quality innovation delivery chain** – the approach used for achieving time to market.
- **Product generation team** – used to promote product evolution as a transdivisional partnership throughout the organization.
- **Teamwork** – research, development, production teams working closely together for a shared goal of product and process innovation and improvement.

SmithKline Beecham

- **Measurement** – emphasis on corporate-wide measurement and inter-activity linkages.

Rank Xerox

- **Product delivery process (PDP)** – an integrated approach to NPD, where planning, engineering, manufacturing, marketing work in harmony to manage projects, overseen by gatekeepers at appropriate levels.
- **PDP stages** – seven stages involved, including pre-concept (Idea phase), concept, design, demonstration, production, launch, maintenance.
- **TQM** – comprehensive TQM programme called leadership through quality, used to drive PDP.
- **Tools and techniques** – comprehensive use of tools such as QFD, benchmarking, SPC, problem-solving and FMEA, among others.
- **Measurement** – emphasis on total measurement and a problem-solving approach.
- **Teamwork** – proper project planning and execution.
- **Integration** – proper matrices used to correlate deliverables to responsibilities – where people could be required to provide an input, where input can be optional.

ICI–Imagedata

- **New product scheme** – based on gates and gatekeepers through six phases. Deliverables at feasibility stage include the involvement of all major activities, including supply chain.

Exxon Chemical

- **Product innovation process (PIP)** – five-stage process-based approach to innovation.
- **Measurement** – great emphasis is placed on measurement, in particular on process measures to ensure the discipline of using PIP and its effectiveness.
- **Project management** – structure is based on having senior sponsorships, team leadership, cross-functional team involvement and the use of satellite contributions.
- **Tools and techniques** – comprehensive use of tools and techniques such as QFD, NEWPROD, marketing techniques, experience curves.

- **TQM** – quality is used to ensure that PIP is optimized through continuous improvement activity. Quality improvement teams are put together to investigate ways for ensuring that PIP is made more robust and used more widely.
- **Effective implementation of PIP** – many reasons led to the effective implementation of PIP using comprehensive awareness programmes, videos, pocket guides, trend setters, away days and stewardship meetings, technical transfer teams and process optimization teams, and so on.
- **Gatekeeping** – effective gatekeeping through cross-functional and multi-level representation to ensure that projects are in line with corporate objectives and to steer them towards success.

Kodak Ltd

- **Integrated innovation process** – represented by four stages, used for the creation of customer *value*, using multifunctional teams working on projects and using continuous improvement and a process-disciplined approach.
- **Tools and techniques** – comprehensive tools utilization including for instance QFD, Customer Oriented Product Conceptualization (COPC), seven planning tools, seven problem-solving tools, Taguchi techniques, project management course, project leadership tool, benchmarking, value engineering, value analysis.
- **Project management** – based on multifunctional teams, using functional skills and expertise, effective project leadership, having a project sponsor, using project performance goals and relying on an integrated project planning.

Cadbury

- **Innovation process** – based on a series of phases and two gates using three different routes: *Mainstream, Fast-track, Repeat.*
- **Product change management (PCM)** – integrated, computerized approach to project management, system developed on a mainframe computer, leads to high success rate through extensive market testing.
- **Talking about time to market** – for insurance, speed, breakthrough launches requires a radically new and different approach to innovative activity.

The vision for this book was put together using an all-encompassing, integrated, current and effective model of innovation management. It was deemed to be considered necessary to broaden the theme of innovation management by doing the following:

- Taking a process-based perspective and discussing innovation in terms of market-related issues and customer-focused outcomes and measured by commercial benefits.
- Widening the scope so that innovation is not described only in terms of technological exploitation and product launches. This reflects a major departure from all approaches addressed hitherto and a change from all texts published so far.
- Taking a balanced view of how innovation is and ought to be managed by reflecting front-end and back-end issues, aspects of links and integration between various key disciplines, placing emphasis on the balance between having creative phases and productive phases, demonstrating the importance of relying on modern tools and techniques for managing projects etc.
- Demonstrating that innovation management is not a mechanistic approach but rather a dynamic one by showing the importance of feedback through continuous learning, continuous improvement and the emphasis on performance improvement.
- Sustainability of effective innovation management comes from the way culture is managed, how it evolves and more importantly how it is steered and guided for repeated success and world-class competitive performance.
- Having a direct link between the engagement of businesses in their totality and having a vision of market orientation and a very clear focus on customers globally and on how world-class business performance can be achieved.

Structure and logic of the book

The key pillars in the development of this book include:

- market orientation and customer focus
- the triad of technology, product and process vision
- creative phase (ideation and design)
- productive phase (integrated supply chain)
- partnerships (customer/suppliers)
- emphasis on measurement
- having a strong culture of innovation.

The richness of this debate is reflected in the text and the structure, the contributions and the ideas and the concepts and examples of best practice that have been incorporated.

We have not elaborated on each of the aspects representing the main pillars of process innovation management as we currently understand it, and how they would impact on organizational future competitiveness, but only to how others have emphasized the importance of these individual components.

The importance of R&D and technology management

As an article in *Technology Strategies*, October 1996, reports: 'It is not possible to predict when discontinuities will occur, but an intelligent view on what is and is not likely will enable you to predict the future better than the competition, thus gaining a significant competitive advantage.

Research and development (R&D) and *Technology Strategies* have to be detached from the present. They have to look at needs, future requirements and emerging technological opportunities for the future. It will, however, always be important to have a balanced technology portfolio by analysing the market, developing the vision and putting together the means for implementing the vision.

Greenwald and Rudolph (1996) suggest a multifunctional process with three steps, as follows:

1 The creation of alternative scenarios, which describe the future business environment.
2 The development of a 'working vision', which articulates the future scope and position of the firm.
3 The development of a 'pathway' to achieve that vision.

The harnessing of technology and R&D management for continuous and sustainable commercial outcomes can perhaps be seen from the way Japanese organizations scan technological opportunities, assess cost and complexity issues for development and manufacturing, evaluate market/customer receptability and predict related commercial outcomes.

Harryson (1997) reports on the experience of Sony and Canon whose philosophy is, on the whole, based on sourcing specialized technologies externally and using the internal R&D competitiveness for commercial exploitation of technology.

In Sony and Canon, the emphasis is on education, training, cross-functionalism and the adoption of a continuous and seamless process of innovation. This process flows from research through design and to manufacturing.

- Research is focused on building and trying prototypes until they are optimised.
- Design involves the development of the product and process for ease of manufacturability.

Manufacturing

Trials and optimization in terms of quality, cost and time ensure optimum sums to support the innovation process that Canon and Sony use. Harryson (1997) highlights three supporting initiatives:

1 The strategic training and rotation of engineers so that each member of the innovation process gains a holistic understanding of the seeds of technology, the needs of the market and the requirements of manufacturing.
2 A focus on prototyping at the research stage to encourage researchers to exchange knowledge with manufacturing at the outset. In other words, research activity gets approved only if there is a commercial application in mind.
3 The direct transfer of researchers to the factory floor in order to drive technological competence into production processes and products.

Further, all personnel involved in R&D activities are required to have good marketing and sales skills, and they are expected to lead projects with marketing and sales responsibilities. One of Canon's representatives quoted in Harryson (1997) describes the approach as follows: 'We don't have many company members with business school backgrounds. Instead, we let our engineers move into planning and marketing divisions to gain experience. These engineers are better at bringing back knowledge from the market.'

Customer/supplier partnerships

It is widely agreed that some of the critical success factors for future competitiveness tend to relate closely to factors of quality, delivery, flexibility and responsiveness. The prediction is that cost/price factors will not be dominant in the next few years. The advent of technologies such as electronic data interchange (EDI) and computer-assisted design (CAD) will greatly influence and shape the nature and competitiveness. What will be very significant is that the links for close partnership will manifest themselves in in-bound and out-bound logistics, up and down the value chain, to optimize aspects of quality, delivery, speed and cost. Further, it is anticipated that at a more strategic level, more collaboration on design and new product development will also take place.

Electronic data interchange (EDI), for instance, is very persuasive in many industries and its benefits have been widely reported. This is not to say that its implementation is not full of challenges and dogma. In its basic terms, EDI is defined by Lynch (1995) as: 'the exchange of information, in a standard format between one organization's computer and another, using electronic means'.

Lynch (1995) argues that EDI is not the penultimate mother of all tools for electronic commerce. It has to be considered as one of many tools and has to be introduced to reflect the vision and strategic direction of the business concerned. Part of the reason why partnerships were difficult to forge is because EDI was not linked to the business intentions. As Lynch (1995) states: 'many implementations "fail" to make the most technical activity of EDI with its business application, i.e. instead of stepping back to look at their business, they concentrate too much on the technology, and simply try to replace all their current manual transactions with EDI'.

In addition to obvious and tangible benefits such as improved accuracy, precision timing, lower transaction costs, improved cash flow and improved accountability, Lynch claims that the real benefits are those which are often 'hidden' and those that can lead to strategic benefits, such as:

- more effective use of human resources
- closer trading partner relationships
- driving business process change
- competitive advantage.

Process/product management/idea generation

It is often recognized that innovation comes through 10 per cent inspiration and 90 per cent perspiration. Most of the literature tends to focus more on the 'hard' aspects of innovation, those often associated with aspects of design, manufacturing and project management. According to Deschamps (1995) innovation has to be divided into an upstream process (sensing and creating opportunities) and a downstream process (converting selected opportunities into winning products). The upstream process is essentially the creative phase of innovation management and is described as having three stages:

- Fertilization – to envision the opportunities.
- Seeding – to generate and manage the idea flow.
- Incubation – to manage precursor projects.

As far as downstream aspects are concerned, these include technical and commercial feasibility, manufacturability, producibility and selectability, among others. On the whole, this approach needs to reflect fluidity and dynamism in terms of managing the process of new product development on a micro basis, in terms of managing individual projects. Wealleans (1996) refers to this parallel, simultaneously based approach by arguing that:

in order to create effective product design programs with modern needs for speed and innovation, companies can no longer afford to have design specification and design implementation as serial events. The final brief for the design has to be generated while development work is being carried out. This results in faster design programs producing more exciting products. The mark of those companies that can make it work will be that they will produce tomorrow's best and most up-to-date new products today.

On the approach to innovation process management, Deschamps (1995) argues that: 'the innovation process cannot be allowed to remain random and undirected. While there are a number of ways an organisation can choose to nurture and manage product innovation, and several approaches for allocating responsibility, there must be commitment from senior management to set up a structure for the process to succeed.'

The management of design

Design as a 'function' is the critical link in the innovation chain. It is the opportunity of linking customer *wants* into the organizational *hows*. As described by Peters (1995): 'Design is not just about drawing shapes and colours, it is a very practical discipline which also demands vision – seeing into the future. Whereas all other disciplines relevant to market, such as production, distribution and R&D are the products of intense specialization, design takes what it needs from the specialists and applies imagination.'

Peters (1995) goes on to say: 'Design is a moulding process, in which the material of information and technology is squeezed often painfully into a practical, possible shape. The conflict is creative.'

Modern design uses a wide variety of tools for creativity, optimization and building-in engineering robustness. One of the tools growing in application is rapid prototyping. This powerful tool can enable designers to develop complex prototypes with speed, accuracy and minimum cost. These factors are, of course, very important for time to market new product launches and therefore effective competitiveness.

Chait (1996) describes rapid prototyping as: 'the direct conversion of a computer-aided design (CAD) image to any physical model or prototype'. He reports that users of this tool are already reaping major benefits in terms of cost savings, quality enhancements and speed reductions. It is likely that rapid prototypes will have a major impact on building design capability and enhancing the culture of innovation in any organization. The predictions according to Chait and others are that:

- all data will be highly mobile and access to rapid prototyping will be decentralized

- manipulation of data will be humanized (pictorial, speed, pen, tactile)
- physical realization of ideas will become nearly instantaneous (i.e. dreamware)
- potential may develop for direct production
- desktop prototyping machines are likely to be found in every manufacturing company within the next ten years.

The culture of innovation

The culture of innovation is perhaps a difficult area to address, as culture is a unique characterization of organizations, describing how they define, manage and sustain a spirit of innovativeness and a discipline of continuity and persistence to survive and prosper in the marketplace. One of the problems that organizations encounter in defining innovation and building a positive and ongoing climate and spirit of creativity is whether innovation is what should be pushed out into the marketplace in terms of new products, new technologies and new services, or whether it has to be reflected by pulling in customer and market needs.

It is reported that 70 per cent of US shareholder reports include statements on huge commitments to innovation and excellent performance outcomes for the companies represented. A recent survey has disclaimed that figure, however, and reported that only about 7 per cent of the public interviewed knew or cared about innovation (Schwarz, 1996). Schwarz (1996) argues that these results are due to the fact that, 'the general public were being promised innovation while actually receiving tired, old formulas'. He goes on to say: 'Innovation is any form of value creation, both internally and in the market place. Most of the time it is quantifiable, but sometimes it can be only a perception of value creation.' This statement is arguably of critical importance. Innovative organizations are not necessarily those that can be characterized by high levels of complexity and sophistication, but those that leave a lasting impression on the customer.

In order to further elaborate on this important point, the following examples, all of different industries and backgrounds, reflect unique cultures of innovation, which impact immensely on customers.

Kodak

Kodak has been serving its customer base for over 155 years. It claims that the spirit of customer satisfaction was initiated by its founder, George Eastman.

- Kodak uses the Worldwide Innovation Network (WIN).
- WIN links together innovation and quality (IQ).

- Ideas are received from all over the globe and, by using a filtering process, the big ideas are pursued vigorously.
- WIN plays a key role at the front end for the generation, prescreening and enhancment of ideas.
- Kodak places emphasis on stakeholder benefits, realistic quantifications and professional proposals.

As Schwarz (1996) puts it: 'Encouragement by leaders to all employees to join the innovation process is the most effective fuel to set the process in motion. There is never a shortage of creative solutions to problems, but it takes leaders and visionaries to nurture ideas from a seed into a giant sequoia.'

Nordstrom

Created in 1901 as one of the leading fashion retailers in the USA, Nordstrom offers a variety of quality apparel, shoes and accessories for everyone (Lavere and Kleiner, 1997).

Gap was launched in 1969 and is known for the famous Levi Strauss product range.

Body Shop was launched by Anita Roddick, using the famous slogan 'Reuse, Refill, Recycle'. They soon established themselves and are seen as caring for environmental and social issues.

The Table I.1 compares and contrasts the three different cultures, using some key factors.

Structure of the book

The structure of the book is perhaps better understood through Figure I.1. The various contributions are intended to reflect the different and critical aspects of process innovation management. Simulating each component of process innovation and its management will present the reader with individually based analyses, rich in terms of theory and concept and supported throughout by a huge catalogue of examples and case studies of best practice applications.

All the chapters together are intended to provide a comprehensive and total coverage of innovation management as it stands now and as it affects academics and practitioners alike, now and in the future.

Chapter 1

This chapter looks at the meaning of the word *innovation* and how it evolved to incorporate elements of successful commercialization. The criteria that

Table I.1 *Comparison of three retailing cultures*

Company names

Factor	Nordstrom	Gap	Body Shop
Leadership	Promotes only from within Top management communicate by personal visits Employees are encouraged to speak directly to top managers Quarterly issued newsletter updates on business issues and used to reinforce values of company Employees are encouraged to have an input on strategy and policy	CEO is known to be very communicative He encourages management to implement their own ideas Promotes only from within	Total alignment to company values and principles Clear and strong business philosophy Everyone has the same commitment to environmental causes
Quality and service	Retailing is not just for selling but also for forging relationships Philosophy is always to look for ways to improve products and services Uses a decentralized approach to buying Buyers can team up with suppliers to produce jointly developed products Strong commitment to delighting the customer	Committed to quality and using the motto: 'down-to-earth Gap basis' A casual approach to serving the customer with total dedication	Committed to quality through observing impact on environment Customer service is inherent in culture of service to humanity Employees are ready and willing to connect with and educate the customer while selling
Empowerment and reward structures	Employees are praised in large corporate meetings Use of cash and other incentives Use of all-star awards for exemplary service	Use salaried staff only Internal promotions opportunity ladder Managers committed to training and coaching their staff Use of recognition and praise	Similar to GAP

Source: Adapted from: Lavere and Kleiner (1997)

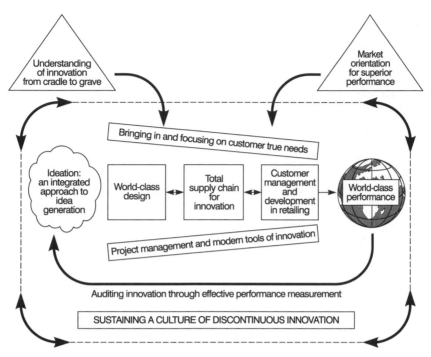

Figure I.1 *Structure of this book*

support creativity and innovation are reviewed, as is the important role that innovation has played in the development of the human race.

The chapter discusses how a good idea alone does not necessarily mean that an innovation will take place; very often the idea will have to wait for other enabling technologies to become available to support the development of the creative thought into a successful application. The nature of these enabling features is discussed and the continuous central role that materials development has had in this process is illustrated.

The chapter proposes that, as a constant source of potential change, other technologies evolve alongside materials and mature to provide incremental opportunity for innovation to take place. The microcomputer enables this incremental boost to innovation.

Process innovation is reviewed in the context of changes occurring in engineering development, and the way in which the application of computer technology is opening up the route to this change is discussed.

Some key factors that resist innovation and change are also discussed and the proposal is made that these factors, which are increasing in influence, in combination with the effects of engineering process innovations, may result in the suppression of product innovation.

Chapter 2

This chapter addresses several questions:

1 What is meant by market orientation?
2 What effect does a market orientation have on business performance?
3 What are the prerequisites for the application of market orientation?
4 What are the consequences of exhibiting a market-oriented strategy?
5 Is there any link between market orientation, quality, customer satisfaction and business profitability?

In answering the above questions, an intensive review of the literature and empirical works was undertaken. A model was developed and tested in a service context. The findings revealed significant and positive relationships between the degree of market orientation and level of customer satisfaction, relative service quality, employee organizational commitment, and profitability. Furthermore, the findings suggest that adopting a market orientation in an organization depends on senior management characteristics (emphasis, leadership, professionalism). Market orientation, in turn, leads to profitability through satisfied customers and committed employees moderated by competition intensity, market turbulence and technology turbulence. Some examples of best practice firms, derived from the application of market orientation, are included. Finally, a guide and recommendations for applying market orientation are presented.

Chapter 3

This chapter examines tools and techniques for promoting creativity within business organizations. It begins with an extensive review of the creative process. First, the role of the individual as a creative entity is made, followed by a discussion of creativity within and between teams. The range of tools and techniques that can be used to enhance creative performance are highlighted. Coverage of creative problem techniques for the individual includes morphological analysis and problem redefinition and at the team level includes synectics, hitchhiking, creative listening and Taguchi techniques. The chapter also provides suggestions on how to run effective creative sessions, and addresses implementation. Illustrative examples and cases are widely used to enrich the discussion.

Chapter 4

There is a growing awareness that design is an important factor in industrial competitiveness but a full implementation of this resource is often hampered by a lack of understanding about its true value and potential. This phenomenon is of growing significance in the light of intense global competition since, for many small and medium-sized companies (SMEs), design represents a tool which is at best used only in a limited way. This work provides a fresh look at the meaning and value of design. It examines a wide range of design attributes in a hierarchical framework for new product development central to company strategy. These attributes are grouped together at four levels, which represent a focus as well as control of projects in terms of their *value, image, process* and *production*. This analysis is illustrated with examples of some leading companies, which have used design as a strategic resource to facilitate and improve their competitive performance. It also applies the typology and framework in two case studies of deliberately contrasting SMEs.

Chapter 5

This chapter focuses on how a very successful quality function deployment (QFD) team within Ford of Europe has adapted to the new Ford 2000 culture to become an example of best practice in ascertaining customer true needs. Within seven years, the Emissions QFD team matured into an Emissions Quality Forum co-ordinating all the emissions-related quality, robustness and systems engineering subsystem team activities within the globalized Ford Automotive Operations. The Emissions QFD and Quality Forum have produced excellent results in terms of improved quality, timing and cost criteria, by focusing in on true customer needs.

This team has developed its own proforma for integrating a comprehensive toolbox of customer-driven quality techniques within the company-wide product development process. It has also shown flexibility in customizing existing tools, especially QFD and robustness engineering. In doing so, the team has assisted the continuous improvement of the company-wide quality process.

The chapter is divided into eight sections starting with a brief introduction to three of the fundamental themes of the chapter: the needs of the customer; the needs of the automotive industry and the need for QFD. This is followed by a detailed look at the four key components of bringing in and focusing on customer true needs by looking at a definition of the customer within the Ford 2000 perspective. To reinforce all these arguments, the sixth section identifies a best practice case study from within Ford that demonstrates how a QFD team became a world-wide quality forum. The criteria of success within the case study is then correlated with the results of an internal Ford benchmarking survey corroborated by a Massachusetts Institute of Technology (MIT) survey to assess effective QFD. The chapter concludes by bringing together all the arguments discussed into a coherent strategy for bringing in and focusing on customer true needs, with an emphasis on deployment.

Chapter 6

This chapter looks at project management in the modern innovation context, highlighting the characteristics of successful project management and project leadership. It goes on to elaborate how cultures of effective project management can be built and sustained by examining examples of best practice. Case studies of Rover, IBM, 3M, Ford and Kodak are used to illustrate and develop theory. A review of tools for effective project management is also presented.

Chapter 7

This chapter discusses the role of the supply chain within innovation. The chapter highlights the necessity of having an integrated approach to the supply chain if the process is to be effective in producing successful innovation outcomes. The chapter uses case study evidence to highlight key issues of supply chain management. Many cases are discussed in detail, including Nissan, Kodak, Rank Xerox, ICL(D2D), the National Roads and Motorists Organisation (NRMA), Cadillac Motors, Zytec and Texas Instruments. The chapter ends by proposing a model of best practice on the basis of evidence collected from a benchmarking exercise.

Chapter 8

This chapter examines the nature of relationships between retailers and their suppliers, and the effect these relationships have on customer management techniques. The chapter begins by introducing the retailing environment, and examining the types of relationships that can be formed. Contrast is also made with the Japanese practice of relationship building before drawing out key elements of relationship building and maintenance. Discussion of relationships within the context of category management is made in detail. The evolution of efficient consumer response (ECR) and its implications for current and future development of retailers is also covered. Case examples are provided to back up the discussion.

Chapter 9

This chapter highlights the fundamental importance of continuously measuring and tracking innovation. It reviews various methodologies of measurement and presents a case for adopting an integrated perspective to the total process of innovation. Specific criteria of measurement are presented for both process and product-based assessments of innovation effectiveness. The chapter highlights best practice through discussion of Hewlett Packard, Exxon

Chemicals, Rank Xerox, D2D, Kodak, Mercury, M&M Mars group, and others to highlight the form and format of assessment and audit. The chapter also indicates how QFD and the McKinsey 7Ss model can be used as holistic tools of measurement.

Chapter 10

This chapter examines how the competitiveness of manufacturing companies has typically been assessed using high-level financial and economic measures, which are proxies for managerial inputs and outputs. An alternative method is to examine the operational practices and performances that are driving the competitiveness of individual manufacturers. These practices and performances need to be referenced to a so-called 'world-class' scale against which manufacturing companies can be benchmarked and towards which they must progress if they are to be competitive in the global market of the late twentieth century.

World-class manufacturing is considered as a point at which a certain standard of practice and performance has been obtained, equalling or surpassing the very best of the international competitors in every area of a company's business, such that the company has achieved international leadership and success.

The components of a model for benchmarking world-class status, developed by IBM and London Business School (LBS) and drawing on the ethos of the European Foundation for Quality Management (EFQM), Baldrige and so-called 'Japanese' manufacturing, are presented, the central hypothesis being that the implementation of best practice leads to superior business performance and customer satisfaction.

The chapter illustrates how the technique of 'best practice benchmarking' can offer a significant insight into the workings of an individual site as well as the competitiveness of sector and national manufacturing capability, the latter through European manufacturing studies in which the model is applied. For individual sites, the critical factors necessary for achieving world-class status are dependent on a company's current practice and performance.

The chapter also shows that, because the goal of achieving and maintaining world-class manufacturing capability is a continuously moving target, it is essential to examine every element of the model of 'best practice' to ensure that it reflects the true state of the art.

Chapter 11

This chapter focuses upon the 'softer' dimension of innovation, namely that of innovation cultures and innovation climates. The chapter presents a case arguing that, despite the fact that the softer side of innovation is often ignored, possession of a culture and organizational climate of innovation underpins long-term competitive success. The chapter looks at how climates and cultures of innovation can be built and sustained. Evidence is also presented to define the parameters necessary for organizational cultures to be effective, and the types of norms that need to be put in place to create innovative behaviour by employees.

Individual motivations and characteristics are also discussed in relation to their impact upon innovation and creativity within the organization. The key role that leadership and employee empowerment play within innovation is also highlighted, while characteristics that define innovation climates and cultures are identified. The theoretical discussion is supplemented by case studies to illustrate theoretical issues.

References

Chait, A. L. (1996) The business implications of developing technologies. *Technology Strategies*, January, 11–13.

Deschamps, P. (1995) Nurturing and managing product innovation, *Technology Strategies*, October, 16–19.

Greenwald, G. and Rudolph, S. (1996) Scenarios and long-term technology strategy. *Technology Strategies*, October, 6–8.

Harryson, S. (1997) Lessons in R&D from Canon and Sony. *Technology Strategies*, June, 24–6.

Lavere, S. and Kleiner, B. H. (1997) Key success factors from leading innovative retailers. *Technology Strategies*, April, 23–5.

Lynch, G. (1995) The EDI challenge. *Technology Strategies*, October, 7–10.

Peters, I. M. (1995) Design for the Future. *Technology Strategies*, October, 21–3.

Schwarz, W. (1996) Letting the customer drive innovation. *Technology Strategies*, January, 27–8.

Wealleans, D. C. (1996) Losing control of design definition. *Technology Strategies*, October, 8–10.

1 Understanding innovation from cradle to grave

Brian Cumming

This chapter looks at the meaning of the word *innovation* and how it evolved to incorporate elements of successful commercialization. The criteria that support creativity and innovation are reviewed, as is the important role that innovation has played in the development of the human race.

The chapter discusses how a good idea alone does not necessarily mean that an innovation will take place; very often the idea will have to wait for other enabling technologies to become available to support the development of the creative thought into a successful application. The nature of these enabling features is discussed and the continuous central role that materials development has had in this process is illustrated.

The chapter proposes that, as a constant source of potential change, other technologies evolve alongside materials and mature to provide incremental opportunity for innovation to take place. The microcomputer enables this incremental boost to innovation.

Process innovation is reviewed in the context of changes occurring in engineering development, and the way in which the application of computer technology is opening up the route to this change is discussed.

Some key factors that resist innovation and change are also discussed and the proposal is made that these factors, which are increasing in influence, in combination with the effects of engineering process innovations, may result in the suppression of product innovation.

Innovation is ... about maintaining the highest rate of change that the organization and the people within it can stand. (Sir John Harvey-Jones, former Chairman, ICI)

Introduction

This chapter looks at the process of innovation, and its importance to society. The automobile industry mainly is used to illustrate various points, because this is the author's background and the automobile industry is a good subject for the study of innovation.

Key elements of effective innovation management

What is innovation?

Many authors have provided definitions for the word *innovation*, and each has its own nuance.

In 1968, the Zuckerman Committee defined innovation as 'a series of technical, industrial and commercial steps' (Robertson, 1974). In 1969, Marquis defined innovation as 'a unit of technological change', quoting Schmookler's definition of technical change as 'an enterprise producing goods or services or using a method or input that is new to it' (Marquis, 1969). Important to this definition is the concept that it is only the first enterprise to adopt the change that executes innovation; subsequent adopters are imitators, not innovators.

In 1973, Tinnesand published the results of a study into the definition of innovation gleaned from a review of 188 publications (Tinnesand, 1973). His findings were as follows:

The introduction of a new idea	36 per cent
A new idea	16 per cent
The introduction of an invention	14 per cent
An idea different from existing ideas	14 per cent
The introduction of an idea disrupting prevailing behaviour	11 per cent
An invention	9 per cent

In 1985, Kuhn suggested that 'creativity forms something from nothing' and that innovation 'shapes that something into products and services' (Kuhn, 1985), while three years later, Badawy wrote 'creativity brings something new into being' and that 'innovation brings something new into use' (Badawy, 1988).

Also in 1988, Urabe wrote 'innovation consists of the generation of a new idea and its implementation into a new product, process, or service, leading to the dynamic growth of the national economy and the increase of employment as well as the creation of pure profit for the innovative business enterprise' (Urabe, 1988) and in 1990 Udwadia defined innovation as 'the successful creation, development and introduction of new products, processes or services' (Udwadia, 1990).

In 1992, Twiss stated that 'for an invention to become an innovation it must succeed in the marketplace' (Twiss, 1992) and in 1996, the CBI/DTI Innovation Unit stated that innovation is 'the process of taking new ideas effectively and profitably through to satisfied customers' (DTI, 1996).

It can be seen, therefore, how the definition of the word 'innovation' has subtly changed over the last thirty years. In the 1960s and 1970s innovation was thought of as a process; the introduction of change. Some, apparently, regarded innovation as simply the generation of a new idea. In the Tinnesand data, for example, the second, fourth and sixth categories all seem to be very similar, as they relate merely to the generation of a new concept, and when totalled, represent a sizeable 39 per cent of the understanding of the meaning of the term innovation.

Most authors now agree that this process of idea generation is *creativity*, and although creativity is an important precursor to innovation, the two terms are not synonymous.

Since the late 1960s, the meaning of the term innovation seems to have been refined. The implication that a new concept had to be brought into use before innovation could be said to have taken place became widely accepted.

Latterly, this definition has been further refined to encapsulate the concept of success: a new concept must be brought into successful use before innovation has taken place. This is reflected in the words *effectively, profitably* and *satisfied customers* used in the Innovation Unit paper. This hardening of the understanding of the word innovation to include the concept of successful commercialization is probably a result of the increase in business competitiveness and developing customer focus that have occurred in the last thirty years.

Summarizing all these ideas, perhaps the most succinct definition of innovation that meets current thinking, and covers the broadest range of applications, is that innovation is *the first successful application of a product or process*.

Managerial and environmental elements required for innovation

There have been many studies on the important elements required for achieving the successful application of a new idea (i.e. innovation), and there tends to be broad agreement on the important criteria.

Many of these studies include analyses of the creative process that is an important precursor to innovation. This is a logical inclusion since, without creativity, innovation cannot take place. Using this premise, there are three basic steps to be considered – idea generation, the successful development of that idea into a usable concept, and the successful application of that concept. Figure 1.1 summarizes factors gleaned from the literature that have a positive effect on each of the three steps.

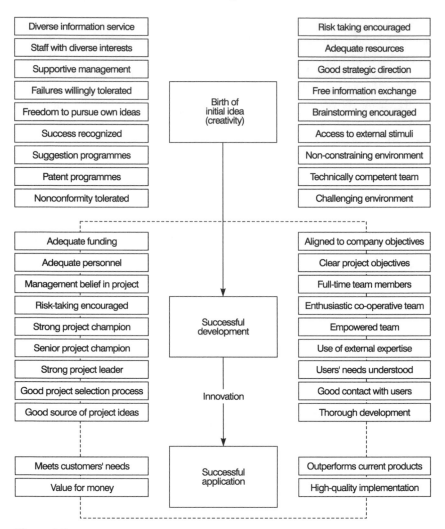

Figure 1.1

At the invention stage, previous researchers have highlighted the importance of correct managerial attitudes and working conditions in facilitating a
creative environment. Critical to this are:

- freedom of the employee to think and act according to his or her own ideas
  rather than following strict management plans
- the encouragement of risk-taking
- the non-critical acceptance of any failures that result

- access to a diverse range of stimuli and ideas
- the recognition of success.

The development phase of this process is where the new concept is refined to ensure that it meets all the needs of the end user, in all respects, and that it functions correctly with other parts of the system into which it will be integrated. This is where the details and specifications are derived for the proposed application. The most often quoted issues here are the provision of adequate resources, strong support and direction from the company, the use of appropriate external expertise, good co-operation within the team, and close contact with the end user.

The third phase is 'successful application'. This is the acid test: 'will the customer adopt the new concept?' This is the last stage of the process, but it is an area that must be considered early in the development programme. Many researchers have highlighted the need to understand exactly what the end user wants at an early stage in the development process, and there are many cases quoted where a failure to understand the customer's perspective have led to the failure of a seemingly good idea. This point is well illustrated by Robertson (1974) who cites the case of a food-processing firm that invested substantial sums in developing a process for freeze-drying food, only to be overtaken by the increasing use of domestic refrigerators, which provided a more acceptable and convenient method of preserving food. They had failed to take a broad view of what the customer really wanted at the outset of their development, and became focused solely on one solution, a solution that, in the end, the customer decided was not the correct one.

With hindsight, it is always easy to see the correct solution, and there is no guarantee that gaining a good understanding of the customers' needs will lead to a successful implementation of the product. However, the reverse is almost certainly true: failing to understand what the customer wants will almost certainly work against the success of the project or product.

If we are considering innovation that relates to a marketable product, then there are clearly many other marketing-related factors that play a part in successful adoption. These factors include, for example, effective advertising and the effects of branding. Their omission from Figure 1.1 should not imply that they are considered to be unimportant; these factors do not have a direct bearing on the technical development of a particular new product, which is why they have been omitted. In other words, how a product should be advertised will not affect the derivation of the design, whereas the end customers' perspective of value for money will be central to the development process.

The limitation of product innovation

A useful way to view these criteria is to look at innovation as a process, and to analyse the parameters involved using a 'P' diagram. This is a tool designed

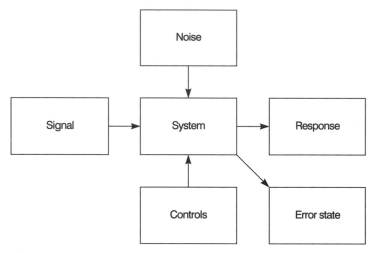

Figure 1.2 *The 'P' diagram*

for the analysis of engineering systems, and it uses the concept of energy flow to focus on the processes within that system. It is used to provide an understanding of the parameters involved in the function of that system. Figure 1.2 shows the configuration of the 'P' diagram.

In Figure 1.2, the system is shown as having three parameters acting upon it – Signal, Controls and Noise – and it has two potential outputs – Response and Error state. Each of these is defined as follows:

- **Signal** – This is the basic input into the system, the 'trigger' that causes the system to function. In a simple example this might be the action of switching on a lighting system.
- **Controls** – These are the features of the system that are readily open to control. In the lighting system example this could be the power of the bulb, the position of the lamp, and the distance of the lamp from the subject.
- **Noise** – These are parameters that can affect the system but over which control is difficult or impossible. For the lighting system this could be variations in the voltage available, the quality of the wiring and connections, and variability in the function of the switch.
- **Response** – This is the desired outcome, and in the example this would be the correct level and quality of lighting on the subject.
- **Error states** – These are possible but unwanted outcomes. In the example these could be no light, variable light, uneven light, or light that is too dull or too bright.

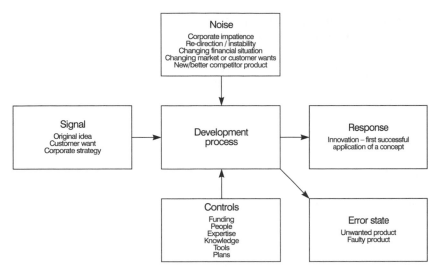

Figure 1.3 *Influences on the innovation process*

Figure 1.3 uses the 'P' diagram to look at the innovation process in order to highlight the important parameters that can have an influence.

The inputs to the innovation process are the initial idea, a customer want that can be shown to be correctly addressed by this idea, and an understanding that the development of this idea is compatible with the corporate strategy.

The controls are the resources that can be brought into play to turn the idea into an innovation. These include finances, people with the right knowledge and expertise, the right equipment, and a good and well-managed plan that brings all these aspects together. If any of these aspects is inadequate or missing, the innovation process is more likely to fail.

Noises that affect the innovation process include internally applied perturbations such as pressure from the corporation for success, failing confidence in the innovation and attendant waning support from senior people, and concern over the costs of the project.

External noises include changes to the environment into which the innovation is targeted. These changes could include competitive actions and changes to the customer wants driven, for example, by changing fashions, legal requirements or political issues.

The ideal response is that innovation should result – that the initial idea should be successfully applied.

Potential error states include a product that the customer does not want. This could be because it does not meet functional or performance expectation, because it is too costly to adopt or maintain, or because it has adverse effects upon other important customer needs. Such a condition is likely to arise when the initial understanding of the customer's needs is incorrectly or incompletely understood – an error in the input; a change in customer needs during the development; a noise in the system.

Another potential error state is when the product is faulty and fails to achieve its functional objectives. This indicates that the development process is inadequate, and possible influences here are lack of appropriate resources to support a full development of the product, or impatience that forces the product through to the customer before it is ready.

The role and importance of technology

Technical innovation as a historical shaping force

Technical innovation has been the engine at the centre of humankind's development since prehistoric times. From the first application of early hand tools to facilitate simple daily tasks, to the most complex application of many disciplines that allows humankind to live and work in space, developments in technology have provided the route to advancement.

Whichever aspect of life you choose to examine, technology is one of the major shaping forces, as a brief examination of history will illustrate. The great feats of maritime exploration were enabled by technical innovations. For example, the development of the magnetic compass, which allowed the required course to be maintained without reference to the sky; the development of the sextant, which allowed an accurate determination of latitude to be made, and the development of accurate and reliable mechanical clocks that allowed calculations to be made to determine longitude. With these three technologies mariners could establish where they were and navigate an accurate course. Charts of the world's oceans were then developed and world trade became possible. Empires were built on the basis of these trading relationships and the fortunes of many countries and millions of people were shaped by three relatively simple technical advances.

Military history is almost totally tied to advances in the technology of war. Weapons have increased in power, range and accuracy, and while it is debatable whether this is to the advantage of mankind it has certainly changed the nature of conflict. Now, wars lasting years, with relatively localized fighting have been replaced with campaigns that last only a few weeks or months, but with the potential to involve the whole world.

The other important factor in military confrontations is that the outcome is more likely to go in favour of the more technically advanced. Clearly this is not assured since there are some good examples of where this has not been so – the conflicts in Vietnam and Afghanistan, for example – but here, other very strong factors were at work which could outweigh a strong technical advantage of one of the participants.

Industrial innovation has also played a major part in the development and success of many nations. The impact of the Industrial Revolution is well known and understood, and its effects have led to higher living standards for the industrialized countries. Industrialization was made possible by a number of technical innovations which allowed industry to be organized into large productive units, and which changed the nature of the industrialized country from that of a mainly agricultural based society to one which derived its wealth from manufacturing and selling goods.

The steam engine is a very good example of a piece of technology that made all of this possible. By making large amounts of power conveniently available to factory units it became possible to organize the manufacture of goods in a far more efficient and affordable manner. The advent of technologies such as the steam engine brought about changes that had far reaching effects upon society.

In addition to these major effects, which have had a profound influence on the development of mankind, technical innovation has also been of direct benefit to society in almost all aspects of our daily lives. Three examples are chosen for illustrative purposes:

1 Advances in communication by means of phone, fax and computer links make it possible to contact people all over the world and to exchange information and ideas with them almost instantly.
2 Technology has provided for better medical care through the development of better drugs, better diagnostic instruments, and better implements for treatment and for surgical procedures.
3 Technical advances in the home have provided for more comfort in terms of heating, air conditioning, and protection from environmental extremes, and convenience in terms of domestic appliances to deal with food storage, food preparation and cleaning-related tasks. Technology has also provided entertainment with such things as television, radio, music reproduction and computer games, although critics of technology advances will argue that many of these developments bring unwanted side effects.

The Industrial Revolution triggered a demand for power that has caused atmospheric CO_2 levels to rise by 25 per cent since its start in the second half of the eighteenth century (Bridgeman, 1990) and there is concern that this will have a strong negative impact upon the global climate. The demand for, and the availability of, personal transport has led to congestion and atmospheric pollution in cities. Weapons of mass destruction threaten the world's population in a way that was never possible as little as sixty years ago.

It is true that technical innovation has created some major challenges for society to manage, but there can be no argument with the proposal that, on balance, technology has provided substantial benefits to the developed countries. For example, based on data from North America, average life expectancy has risen by 60 per cent, infant mortality has been reduced by 95 per cent and the average hours worked each week have fallen by 27 per cent, and all this since the beginning of the century (US Bureau of Census, 1975, 1996a). At the centre of all of this is technical innovation.

Innovation as a competitive tool

The DTI published these words in 1995:

> For the past twenty years the United Kingdom has experienced a severe decline in its market share of international trade, particularly within the consumer products sector. Our traditional home and export markets have been under attack from international competitors who have penetrated our markets with better products. These have frequently scored on higher specification, customer appeal, innovative features and value for money.
>
> To regain our international market share, UK companies must match or improve on the products offered by our competitors. Many company directors do not appreciate that it is the product design and development process which largely determines their ability to become competitive, affecting a company's cost base and its market performance.
>
> To create wealth and growth, a company commitment to the product is needed by manufacturing industry. (HMSO, 1995)

Innovation is the key to that product focus and to the provision of new competitive opportunities.

When designing any system, the engineer is faced with a number of compromises. The chosen solution will depend upon the target application, and the designer will seek to bias the choices in a particular direction to meet the needs of that application as fully as possible. Deciding upon the optimal compromise is one of the key tasks for the system designer, and the success of the system will be heavily affected by this. This point is illustrated in Figure 1.4 using the motor engine as an example.

The design environment can be thought of as a flexible enclosure within which the designer is constrained. In Figure 1.4, some of the key parameters for consideration in the specification of an engine are shown, such as power, fuel consumption, size and cost. The model shows those parameters that are ideally reduced (i.e. fuel consumption, weight, exhaust emissions etc.) as pushing into the enclosure, and those that should ideally be increased (i.e. safety, durability, power etc.) as pushing out. The concept of the flexible enclosure model is that each part is connected to some or all of the others and that moving one parameter will affect others, some positively, some negatively.

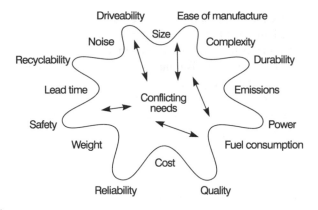

Figure 1.4

For example, low fuel consumption is an important feature of a modern engine and this can be achieved by specifying a smaller engine. This will have a positive effect on size and cost, but is likely to adversely affect power, driveability (covering issues such as the vehicle's ability to accelerate smoothly and climb hills easily), and possibly durability since it will have to work harder to meet the driver's needs.

An aluminium cylinder block could be specified for less weight and to help with fuel economy, but it would have an adverse affect on cost and radiated noise.

Each choice has positive and negative implications and the designer must consider carefully the needs of the specific application. In a large luxury car, cost and weight might not be as important as good driveability and low noise, while in a small economy car, these features might be compromised for size, cost and fuel consumption benefits.

In this context, innovation can change the relationships between the parameters involved. Links between parameters can be weakened or broken completely, and opportunities for new and better compromise may be created.

There are a number of good examples of this phenomenon at work. For instance, the introduction of inlet manifolds made from plastic provided a lighter-weight part, at a reduced cost, and with improved safety since this part would now deform during a crash (particularly important in transverse engine installations). The use of the plastic inlet manifold itself became possible only with the availability of fuel injection, since with earlier carburetted engines the surface of the manifold had to be hot (to vaporize the fuel), and the low thermal conductivity of the plastic manifold did not support this need.

Systems to provide variable inlet and exhaust valve timing have helped to break the conflict between the needs for high power, good economy and low exhaust gas emissions. Focusing on each of these needs individually would result in a camshaft design that would reduce the achievement of the other requirement, but the availability of systems that allow the timing of the cams to be changed while the engine is running allows the engine designer to come closer to meeting all these needs at one time. Such a system does of course add to weight, cost and complexity, and would carry additional reliability risks! Innovations may change the nature of the design environment, but they do not provide a means of escaping the basic issue of the interrelation between needs.

Technology as an enabler for innovation

As stated earlier, innovation can start after the generation of a new idea, and it is easy to believe that the creation of the new idea is the spark that drives the innovation process. There are many cases where this is true: the 3M 'Post-it' note is an often quoted example. The Pilkington float glass process and the 'windows' software interface are other good examples of innovations for which the invention of an initial concept was the prime trigger for the development of a commercial success.

When a new product is brought into being, or a new technical development takes place, we tend to think we are witnessing the birth of a new idea. But this is not always the case. There are numerous examples of ideas that have been around for many years but have not been developed, or have found only limited use because some factor was missing that would allow each idea to be fully realized. Very often the missing factor is a technical one. As technology progresses, new doors are opened that were previously closed and ideas that were once unfeasible may become practicable.

For example, the first helicopter flew in 1936 but Leonardo da Vinci had drawn designs of a very similar machine over 400 years before. The creativity had taken place, but the innovation had to wait for a number of technical enablers to become available.

Materials development as an 'enabler'

There is one technical enabler that has been at the heart of innovation for thousands of years and that is the development of materials. Indeed, this factor is so important to the progress of humankind that certain periods in our history are named after the new material that became available at that time.

In the Stone Age tools were developed from naturally occurring stones and flints. Knives, axes, hammers and scraping tools were produced that allowed the people of those times to be more effective at hunting, preparing food, making clothing, building shelters and defending themselves.

The Bronze Age saw the combination of copper and tin to produce a relatively hard material that could be cast and worked into a variety of tools and utensils. This material was used for knives, swords, spearheads, shields and armour, for storage and cooking vessels, and for the manufacture of sculptures and ornaments.

The Iron Age was initiated by the discovery of the means to process iron ore into iron, a material that was much harder than bronze, opening the way for the development of much more durable cutting edges, more effective weapons, and tools such as saws and farming implements.

We stopped using materials as labels for later periods in history but those labels could easily be applied. The Steel Age would have started in the mid-1800s, when the Bessemer process was invented and the bulk production of steel became possible. Steel can be produced in a number of forms and lends itself to a very wide range of applications. Its use for the structure of ships and buildings, fasteners, springs and cutting tools illustrates both the broad capability of the material and the industries that its development fostered.

Aluminium became available in usable quantities early in the twentieth century, and it rapidly found use in applications where a high strength-to-weight ratio was paramount, notably in the manufacture of aircraft frames and bodies.

The Plastic Age would have started around 1920 with the first commercial applications of early plastics. The term plastic covers such a wide variety of materials that it would be possible to assign various periods in history to the introduction of each important breakthrough. Plastic materials have found application in all walks of life. Clothing, furnishing, building, transport, domestic appliances and packaging are all areas where the application of plastic materials have had a profound effect, generally replacing a more traditional material with one that has strength, resilience, self-colour and is light in weight.

An important stage in the 'Plastic Age' is marked by the advent of plastic composites. The development of glass strands and carbon, and other fibres, for inclusion into a plastic matrix has produced materials with extremely high strength-to-weight performance, coupled with the ability to produce complex shapes.

Such a list of materials would not be complete without a mention of ceramics and metal composites. Ceramics and metal composites are providing designers with tough, wear resistant, lightweight materials that are often capable of working at very high temperatures, and for which there are no, more conventional, alternatives.

Each new material development allowed innovations to take place, and many of those innovations had been 'ideas in waiting' for a number of years. A perfect example of this is the concept of human-powered flight.

Human-powered flight had been a dream of humankind for centuries, and many attempts were made to achieve this goal, costing many lives in the process. Very limited successes started to occur from the early 1900s, but it was not until 1977 that the 'Gossamer Condor' finally succeeded in this illusive challenge, and claimed the illusive Kremer Prize. The reason it had to wait until 1977 before this could be achieved is largely a question of materials development. The success of the Gossamer Condor was reliant upon the use of very thin wall aluminium tubing for the frame, and a Mylar skin. The challenge of human-powered flight centres around power-to-weight ratio, and the entire aircraft weighed only 32 kg even though it had a wing span of almost 30 m (Reay, 1977). Without access to appropriate materials, the project would have failed, as so many had proved before.

The internal combustion engine relies for its function upon a number of different materials, with certain specific properties. Examples of these are castings of iron and aluminium, steel forgings, steel springs, high-strength steels for valves and valve seats, and aluminium alloys for the pistons. Without such materials, the concept could not have been realized.

Before leaving this subject, it is important to note that the pace of materials development has been accelerating. This characteristic of the nature of progress has been observed in many fields of technology.

Other enabling technologies

Alongside the ever-present phenomenon of materials development, other technical developments bloom and create additional opportunities for innovation of their own. A recent and very powerful example of this is the advent of microelectronics. This technology has allowed innovation to take place on an enormous scale, and it has done this in a number of ways.

By replacing known electrical concepts with smaller and more efficient designs, this technology has made known ideas much more practical. Mobile phones, for example, were available over fifty years ago (as radio telephones), so the idea is not new, but their then bulk, weight and performance were limited by the electrical technology available. The idea of being able to communicate freely without the restrictions of a physical connection is clearly a very attractive one, but fifty years ago the limitations were so severe that their use was constrained to only the most demanding applications, such as military use. The advent of microelectronics enabled this concept to become commonplace. The cost, weight, size and performance of this concept ceased to be inhibitors, the desirability of the concept of the freedom of commutation was still present (arguably more so than ever before) and thus the innovation of the mobile phone was assured.

Microelectronics have made the retention of, and ready access to, large amounts of information possible. The Internet, and similar communications networks that are now being established within many companies are obvious manifestations of this.

Perhaps the most important capability that microelectronics has provided is that of very powerful control technology, a capability that has far-reaching effects. This is well illustrated by an examination of its effects in the motor industry. Every modern car has an electronic system controlling its engine. The amount of fuel delivered, the timing of the spark to ignite that fuel, the air flow into the engine, the speed of the engine and other important parameters are monitored or controlled by electronic means. Twenty years ago this was all under mechanical control and, although the basic control processes were similar, the accuracy and speed of response were missing. Microelectronics have enabled the application of better emission control systems and modern engines are significantly cleaner and more efficient that the previous mechanically controlled systems.

Electronic controls have enabled known technology to compete for new applications. The crankcase scavenged two-stroke engine, for example, was invented in the late 1800s, at just about the same time as the four-stroke engine. This engine found successful application in many areas, particularly where power-to-weight ratio is important. But the nature of its combustion system led to the loss of unburned fuel into the exhaust. The impact of this is that the fuel economy, exhaust emission and exhaust noise of this engine are inferior to the four-stroke alternative. These characteristics meant that, in automotive applications, where these performance features are more important than the power-to-weight ratio benefits, the two-stroke engine has not been successfully used, and the four-stroke engine is the norm. In the mid-1980s that balance was changed by the development of a direct injection system for the two-stroke engine. This system removed all the negative features of the previous two-stroke design and maintained much of the beneficial power-to-weight ratio characteristic. The injection system was basically a mechanical system; its design could have been envisaged many years earlier, but there would have been little point in doing so for the system is reliant upon very accurate control that only electronics could provide. It was a concept awaiting a technical enabler, in this case a fast control system derived by use of microelectronics.

Process innovation

In a competitive marketplace, three critical parameters in the business equation are quality, cost and timing, as described below:

- Quality is the ability of a product to meet customers' expectations.
- Cost is the fully accounted cost of manufacturing the product. This cost will, in a competitive market, determine the profit the manufacturer will make, and thus is fundamental to the success of the business.

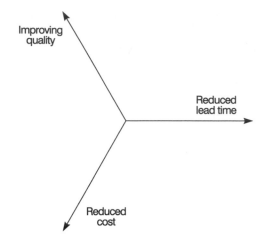

Figure 1.5

- Timing is the lead time of the product, or the amount of time taken to get the new product designed, developed, manufactured and into the market.

All are important and, on first consideration, within a given process, each potentially works against achieving the others. This is illustrated in Figure 1.5.

For example, a reduction in cost can be achieved by the specification of cheaper materials, but this might result in substandard performance and thus a loss of quality. Shorter product lead time can be achieved by reducing the scope of the design and development process, but again, product quality may suffer as a result. The quality of a product could potentially be improved by increasing the amount of time spent in the development stage but clear impacts of this would be to increase the lead time of the product and also its cost.

In a competitive market it is not acceptable to sacrifice any one of these needs, as all are important and the competitive challenge is to meet all three. The manufacturer who does this better than the competition has the edge.

The traditional engineering development process

The traditional engineering process is centred around the design, procurement of the parts, build, test and evaluation cycle. Figure 1.6 shows one cycle of this process.

The concept is designed and parts made or bought. They are assembled, tested and evaluated. The cycle is repeated a number of times as the knowledge from one cycle is used to improve the design for the next cycle.

Figure 1.6 *The traditional engineering cycle*

The process attempts to iterate to an acceptable design, which is then taken into production. There may be as many as three iterations, as shown in Figure 1.7.

Figure 1.7 *Iteration of the design process*

In the motor industry, this was the approach to engineering development right up to the 1980s, when it became apparent that this process was no longer adequate. Competition, particularly from the Far East, was delivering a better product to the marketplace, and more quickly.

On first consideration, the iterative process seems a very logical way to develop a new product. Slowly and carefully, the new product is tested and refined until the required result is obtained. However, this approach had a number of inherent problems that limited its ability to meet the three wants of quality, cost and timing. Clearly cost and timing are an issue since the process is a sequential one and each iteration extends the development time and adds to the cost. The negative effect on product quality is less obvious, since this iterative process should provide an ideal opportunity for the engineers to resolve all the design problems and to verify those resolutions.

In reality this did not always happen. Listed below are a number of reasons why:

- The knowledge that there were several iterations of the design took the pressure off the engineers to get the product right first time and encouraged experimentation.
- Early prototypes were often relatively crude representations of the intended design and thus what was learned from them was not always relevant.
- Pressure on the programme often led to the iterative cycles being overlapped so that the procurement of the next phase of parts was underway before the learning had been gleaned from the previous phase, thus negating the potential benefits of sequential testing.

- Several phases of prototype, often compounded by interim update levels, meant that maintaining an accurate understanding of what had been tested was difficult. A potential result of this is that final level parts might not be fully tested.
- Prototype parts were often not fully representative of production parts, since the manufacturing methods were often very different and, thus, testing was not fully valid. For example, a prototype aluminium engine cylinder head is likely to be sand cast, for cost and timing reasons. However, the production part will most probably be made in metal tools with sand cores, since this represents the most effective option for mass production. The resulting parts will therefore be different dimensionally, in design detail, and metallurgically. These differences, while apparently subtle, can result in problems occurring in the mass production part that did not occur in the prototype part.

The potential result of these shortfalls is that this approach to engineering development can result in a poor quality product, elevated engineering costs and extended development time: all of the negatives without any offsetting benefit. In a competitive market it is clear that such practices will not endure.

Innovations in the development process

Historically, the motor industry has used this iterative approach to its engineering programmes. However, over the last ten years, it has been forced to change its product development practices to keep abreast of fierce competition.

Process innovation has been required to effect this change, and a number of key elements have been brought together to enable this innovation to take place. The most important of these elements are:

- *The mature delivery of any new technology from the advanced engineering areas.* The effect of this is to ensure that time is not lost in the engineering process due to unforeseen problems with any new technology. Any new concept taken into a production programme should have been sufficiently well developed in the advanced areas so that the only additional work required would be to 'tailor' it to a specific application.
- *A full understanding of customers' expectation of the product.* This will require a translation from customers' perception of what the product should be capable of achieving – for example 'good performance' – to something that the engineer can design towards, in this case, measures of vehicle acceleration, vehicle gearing and weight, and the engine torque curve. The QFD process is one approach that has been established to help achieve this goal.

- *A broad approach to the engineering task.* This will enable the engineer to design each component of a system, taking into account the needs and constraints of interacting systems and components. In the past, changes have been made to parts of a system without a full appreciation of the impact on other parts and interrelated systems, with undesirable consequences.
- Systems engineering provides a disciplined approach, which enforces an integrated view of all affected parts. A cascade process passes engineering requirements down from system to subsystem and back again to ensure that all interrelationships are correctly addressed.
- *A method of retaining and reusing the knowledge and experience of previous programmes.* This prevents the repetition of known problems, and to enable the engineering programme to proceed in the most efficient way.
- Staff movement, a particular characteristic of large firms, means that the personal experience element is often lost from one project to the next. Without a means to retain the knowledge, the new engineer will have to relearn what his or her predecessor had already discovered and the company pays repeatedly for the same information.
- One part of the systems engineering discipline is to provide a means of formally documenting this knowledge such that it is naturally included in the next project. Design specifications, past problem resolution analyses, FMEAs, collated test data are all means by which the corporate knowledge can be retained and reused.
- *A rigorous approach to the acquisition of knowledge.* This is an important part of the route to product quality and process efficiency. The correct use of designed experimentation will ensure that the function of a component or system is more fully understood, and this will enable the engineer to develop more efficient and robust designs. This approach will also provide data on the component or systems performance in a way that will facilitate its capture in the corporate knowledge base, and thus make it available for future reference.
- *The people involved in the design team.* This is perhaps the most important part of the process innovation, and what is required of these people, in a nutshell, is that they work more effectively. A great deal has been written on this subject and it will not be repeated here, but the essence of this element is to develop a project team that shares a common understanding of what is to be achieved and how; one that is mutually supportive, that communicates very effectively, and is highly motivated towards success.
- *The full integration of component and subsystem suppliers into the development team and process.* This allows the focused resources of an expert group to be brought to bear on a project. It forges good commercial links between the supplier and the customer, and it is another way of making the most effective use of existing knowledge.

- *The growing availability of computers to support the engineering process.* This last issue is the most important one. Computing power is the newly available 'enabler' that allows this innovation in the engineering development process to take place.

All the items in this list except the last one have been available to the planners, managers and executors of engineering programmes for many years. Without the 'enabler' of widely available powerful computers, such a process innovation could not happen. This issue is so important that it warrants special examination.

The role of computers in engineering process innovation

There are four aspects to the use of computers in engineering that have enabled innovation in the engineering process to take place:

1 Computer-aided design (CAD).
2 Computer-aided manufacturing (CAM).
3 Computer-aided engineering (CAE).
4 Information management.

Computer-aided design

Computers are being used by designers to produce drawings of components and assemblies. This function has replaced the drawing board and has been a developing feature of the engineering process for well over a decade. It is the most mature of the computer-aided functions and is known as computer-aided design.

Computer-aided design reduces the time taken to produce a design by allowing the designer to copy often used features from a library, allowing easy changes to a design and providing automatic scaling and measurement. It also encourages the reuse of existing designs, resulting in cost and quality benefits.

A feature of CAD is that there is a significant overhead associated with establishing the system. Individuals have to be trained, component libraries established and the approach has to become accepted and understood as a normal part of the business. In fact, for a number of years, CAD was regarded as a slower means of producing a simple drawing when compared to a draughtsperson on a drawing board.

Computer-aided manufacturing

The second area of computer influence is that of computer-aided manufacturing. Again, this technology has been available for many years, having developed from earlier numerically controlled machines, and is one that has been gaining in sophistication and maturity as the power, speed and cost of computers have improved.

Computer-aided manufacturing works by directing flexible machine tools to follow specified tool paths using computer data files. It reduces the lead times and high investment costs associated with designing and building dedicated machine tools for specific actions, under hardware control, which is the traditional approach to mass production manufacturing.

Computer-aided engineering

The third way in which computers have had a major impact on the engineering process is that of computer-aided engineering. This is the most important enabler in the reduction of engineering development programmes and by far the least mature.

With CAE, computer models are used to design and provide an understanding of the performance of the product in question, and this information is used instead of physical testing.

The concept is an extremely attractive one, and it is central to the process innovation that replaces the traditional iterative approach to engineering design. Instead of refining the design physically, the iterations are done within a computer model.

The impact of this can be dramatic. One physical iteration of a design can involve a design, procure, build and test cycle of several months, depending upon the complexity of the subject component or system, whereas the computer equivalent can be completed in days. However, since this is the least mature of the computer-aided processes, many aspects of it still require a lot of development. For example, models that attempt to predict complex dynamic activities can, currently, be relied upon only to give rough, directional, indications of a system's performance. A good example here would be the modelling of the combustion process in an internal combustion engine, and the prediction of the characteristics of the resultant exhaust gases. There is, nevertheless, a great deal of activity in this area and significant improvements are being made.

The benefits of CAE are well illustrated by consideration of the case of vehicle crash testing. Legislation requires vehicle manufacturers to subject new vehicles to a number of different impact tests. The crashed vehicle is then inspected to establish if it has met various criteria for deformation that relate to the safety of vehicle occupants. If the criteria are not met, the vehicle cannot be released for sale.

The practical approach to this is to build and crash a prototype vehicle, to make any design modifications that may be indicated by the test, and then to build and crash another prototype. This process being repeated until a successful result is achieved.

The timing and costs associated with a typical crash test are as follows:

Prototype vehicle build time	three months
Prototype vehicle cost	$300,000
Crash preparation time	one to two weeks
Crash test cost	$25,000

In comparison, the timing and costs associated with a computer simulation of the same crash are as follows:

Computer model preparation time	two to three months
Computer model cost	$60,000
Crash simulation cost	$2,500

From the perspective of the time taken for the first test, there is little to choose between the practical crash and the computer-simulated alternative; it takes three months to build a vehicle and about the same to build the computer model. But that is the only area in which the two approaches are in any way similar.

In terms of cost, when a single test is considered there is a fivefold benefit in favour of the computer simulation, and when repeat tests are required to develop a design, the computer wins overwhelmingly. Each practical test costs $325,000 (the cost of the vehicle plus the cost of the test), whereas, the costs of a repeated computer simulation are only those associated with any modifications to the model (one to two days, depending on the level of design change) plus the computer costs of the crash calculation, a total of $3,000.

Thus, when repeat tests are considered, the computer-based approach beats the practical test by two orders of magnitude. In addition, several development test iterations can be conducted in just a few days.

Other benefits that the computer approach brings to this type of testing are that the crash can be examined from various viewpoints, it can be stopped at any point, it can be viewed in slow motion, and the performance of individual parts of the structure and the associated stresses can be analysed in detail. This is very valuable in the development process, since such information greatly assists the engineers when inadequacies in crash performance are revealed and design improvements are required.

The only area in which the practical test is quicker is the crash itself, which takes a few milliseconds to complete compared with several hours with current computers! This is a small price to pay for a substantial increase in overall efficiency, and even this insignificant penalty is diminishing as computer power increases.

Information management

The last area in which computers are offering the chance for change is in the storage, retrieval and dissemination of information within an organization. This is a relatively new area of opportunity, and one that is currently undergoing rapid expansion. Many large organizations are developing their own internal computer networks that allow the rapid and easy interchange of data, and this capability supports one of the stated facilitators of process innovation, that of capturing knowledge and having it available for future programmes.

Such an approach to information storage has many advantages:

* Lessons learned from one programme can be passed on to the next.
* Specifications and procedures can be centrally maintained so that all employees are working to the same up-to-date information.
* Existing designs can often be reused.
* It can operate as a conduit through which team members can pass and share data and project information; this is especially important when the team is geographically dispersed.

These four elements, CAD, CAM, CAE and integrated information management, individually provide for substantial benefits in terms of enabling efficient design, but the greatest potential is to be realized by combining the elements into one entity, as illustrated in Figure 1.8. The data used in the CAD, CAM and CAE files all set out to define the nature of the component or assembly to which they relate. They define its shape, the materials used and how it relates to its surroundings. The most efficient solution is to have one, common, data source and to use this for all the purposes of CAD, CAM and CAE.

Such an apparently obvious solution is not an easy one to achieve, largely because each methodology was derived from different roots and has different purposes.

Computer-aided design for example, in its first embodiment, simply provided an electronic form of the hand-drawn equivalent, and such drawings are often poor representations of a part, especially where complex surfaces are concerned. A good illustration of this is a complex casting. Without providing a large number of sections, much of the surface definition detail is missing and it is left to the skill and experience of the pattern-maker to fill in this missing detail.

For CAM systems to work, every movement of the machine tool must be strictly controlled, and thus the computer file must have a full description of the shape of the part. A simple CAD representation of a part does not provide this level of detail and thus cannot meet the needs of CAM.

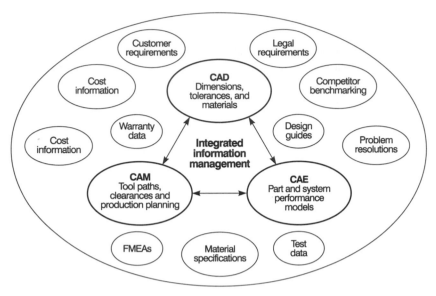

Figure 1.8

Computer-aided manufacturing information, on the other hand, would not be toleranced in the way required for a CAD drawing. Thus a representation of the part that serves the purposes of both CAD and CAM must be a more comprehensive set of data than is required for either purpose individually.

There is a further step in definition required with the move to CAE. Computer-aided engineering is intended to replace physical testing with assessments carried out using mathematical models of the part or system. Typically these models are established to predict stress levels and deflections within a system, heat flow, chemical processes, sound radiation, vibration and kinematics. To meet this need, the models must have enough physical information about the part or system to describe its nature, and they must also contain information about the external influences acting upon the part or system. This requires additional information to that needed for CAD and CAM purposes.

CAD sets out to aid the process of defining the physical nature of a part or system, CAM is in place to facilitate its manufacture and CAE attempts to provide information about the performance of that part or system.

The need for complete data, and the partially overlapping demands of the different computer-aided methodologies, explains why the fourth aspect of this approach to engineering, that of information management, is so important. A common, compatible source of information, and an ability to exchange data and predictions between the various computer-based approaches will substantially affect the efficiency of the design, development and manufacturing process.

With each step down the CAD-CAM-CAE path, more information is required and the processing requirements on that data become more demanding. CAE is the most challenging of the methodologies and, as stated earlier, the one that requires the most development.

Computer-aided engineering offers the potential to replace physical tests with predicted data, but for this to happen, a full understanding of the nature of the system under examination has to be available. Very often this is not the case. Apparently simple systems become quite complex when they are studied for the purposes of predicting their responses. Complex systems may require many years of study and experimentation before an accurate model of their performance can be developed. Even when this has happened, these models are likely to be reliable only when they are used within well-known and understood boundaries. If they are used to predict the responses of a system that is away from the usual, the accuracy of their predictions must be questioned.

If CAE can be developed to a mature level, then the traditional iterative approach to product development can be reduced to a process involving fewer prototype series. Ultimately, with fully mature CAE tools, it would in theory be possible to go directly into production without physical prototypes, since all the development would have taken place by computer simulation. It is unlikely, however, that this will ever happen since even small changes bring a potential for unknown and unpredictable responses and, therefore, some preproduction prove-out phase would be required.

A rationalized product development programme using computer-aided design techniques may well be as shown in Figure 1.9.

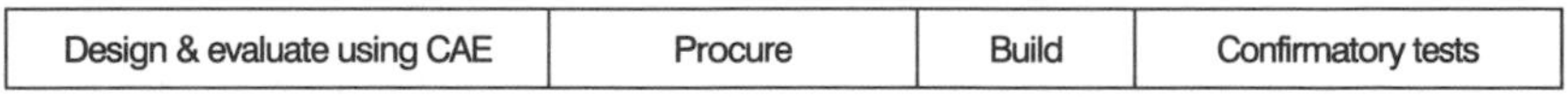

Design & evaluate using CAE	Procure	Build	Confirmatory tests

Figure 1.9 *A development approach using computer-aided engineering*

The use of computer-aided design processes brings additional benefits. Photo quality images of a part or assembly can be produced easily, thus helping the design process, and allowing subjective judgements on appearance to be made. Stereo lithography can be used to automatically generate physical replicas of parts and assemblies, which again can assist with the design and development process.

This latter process provides a major efficiency gain and is time saving, since physical models of a part can be made available directly from the computer in a matter of minutes or hours. This effectively bypasses the procurement and manufacturing processes, and all the bureaucratic delay that usually surrounds them.

Could process innovations stifle product innovation?

Process innovation can provide a route to producing better products, more quickly and at lower cost. However, it could have the undesirable side effect of stifling product innovation.

The rationale for this proposal is that shorter development lead times encourage more conservative design approaches; it is easier to deliver familiar technology than it is to develop new technology. There is a lot less learning to do, and fewer unexpected issues will appear to thwart the development process.

The issue here is how far existing knowledge and experience is to be extrapolated. Working within known boundaries of design provides for the lowest level of risk in the development of the new product. As the designer moves away from the familiar into the unfamiliar so the risk increases, and it does so rapidly.

Increasing risk implies lower product quality or extended development time and cost, both potentially incurred in order to resolve the new issues that are likely to arise.

This issue is reinforced when product is being developed using aggressive development plans such as that shown in Figure 1.9, which relies upon the use of computer simulation and modelling as a basis for the engineering.

Computer simulations rapidly become unreliable as one moves away from familiar ground and, as the process relies upon accurate predictions of part and system performance, and since the physical iteration of prototypes is not anticipated, even more conservatism is encouraged.

This trend to conservatism is reinforced by three other factors:

- the ever-increasing expectation by customers for quality and reliability
- the fact that any newly introduced product will have an initially higher cost than when it is mature
- fear of litigation, especially in North America.

Each point is expanded below.

Increasing expectations for quality and reliability

From a quality and reliability perspective, any change introduces the possibility for a new problem to get into production. The bigger the change and the further away from known technology, the bigger the attendant risk to quality and reliability.

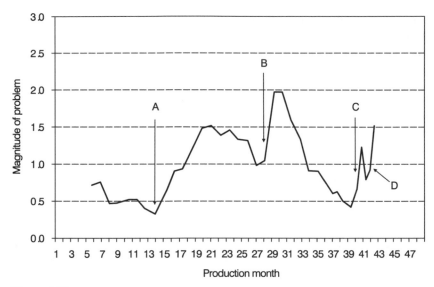

Figure 1.10

This is illustrated by Figure 1.10, which shows warranty data relating to a subsystem of a commercial product. The 'x' axis of Figure 1.10 shows the month of production. The 'y' axis shows a measure of warranty cost associated with the particular subsystem under consideration. Clearly the objective is to keep this as low as possible, as this number relates to potential customer dissatisfaction and a cost to the company in terms of warranty repairs.

A number of important issues are illustrated by Figure 1.10. Model changes with attendant design revisions tend to be introduced on an annual basis and these twelve-monthly points are emphasized by arrows 'A', 'B', and 'C' in the figure.

Figure 1.10 shows that there is a typical annual characteristic of increasing warranty costs in the first few months of the new model year, with a declining trend towards the middle and end of the twelve-month period.

Prior to point 'A', for example, the warranty cost was typically 0.50 units. Point 'A' saw the introduction of a major change to the subsystem, which was driven by changing legal requirements on the product. This change increased the subsystem complexity and introduced new components. The effects of this can be seen in the chart; warranty costs increased threefold, and were only starting to be brought back under control towards the end of the following twelve-month period when they were back to twice the starting value.

Point 'B' indicates the start of the next model year and this again shows a dramatic increase in warranty costs as a result of the associated changes to the subsystem. In the period 27 to 35 months, the warranty costs were again brought back under control, as the engineers developed a full understanding of the issues and were able to introduce product revisions progressively to resolve the problems.

Two years after the introduction of the new technology, the associated service problems were resolved and warranty costs for this subsystem had returned to the background levels that were present before. However, the net effect was a significant direct cost to the company, and the potential for a negative impact on customer satisfaction.

The beginning of the fourth year shows a sharp rise and then fall in warrant cost in the first three months and then a steep rise at point 'D'. Point 'D' can be identified as the point in which a specific design change was introduced. This design change was initiated to provide a system cost saving by the application of a more design-effective approach. It used technology for which there was previous production experience and yet in this application it was found to have unexpected problems not detected in the development programme. Although these data do not show the subsequent effects, this concern was not resolved for a further two months.

The issue illustrated here is that it is not possible to be completely certain that all problems have been discovered, addressed and eliminated from a product prior to its release into production, and any revision brings the attendant risk of problems in service. The bigger the change, and the further this change takes the design away from familiar territory, the greater the risk. This issue is well understood by industry and the natural response is to take a conservative approach to any change.

Until the 1980s, much development work was unwittingly conducted by customers; products failed in service and industry learned from these failures. This knowledge was used in the next design to improve the system performance.

The development process was far from exhaustive, as competitive pressure was not intense, and customer expectation was far below today's levels. An increase in world trade and competitiveness has led to an increase in customer awareness and expectation, making such an approach unacceptable.

The manufacturer has two choices: either to develop a much more rigorous approach to the development process, or to be more conservative in the level of product change planned. Indeed, a combination of the two may be the best approach.

Higher costs during the introductory phase

Very often the initial cost of a new technology starts high and reduces as the product matures. A number of factors are at work to produce this effect:

- The design and development process is likely to be longer since additional time will be committed to training the design engineers in new techniques and skills. New and unfamiliar issues will arise that will take more time to solve than more familiar problems.
- If new manufacturing processes are involved, an initially high, 'safe', cost will be placed on this part of the process to ensure that all contingencies are covered. As the manufacturing process becomes familiar, confidence in the ability of the manufacturing activity to make the product will increase and ways of saving cost will be found.
- On this note, it is interesting and illustrative to consider the background of the automotive camshaft. This part has lobes which are neither round nor symmetrical, and yet have to be ground to a fine surface finish and to a high degree of accuracy. It is contended that this part is only feasible for mass production today because the motor industry has 'grown up with this part'; furthermore, it is contended that if there was no such part in mass production today, it would not be possible to introduce it, since the initial cost of manufacturing it would be totally prohibitive. The knowledge, confidence and experience in the manufacture of this part were obtained in a much more benign period of industrial development.
- Cost savings will be achieved eventually through the development of more efficient designs and the integration of other functions, but these are not initially available.
- Production volumes are likely to be low initially, as the new technology is introduced progressively with growing acceptance.

The effect of these factors is to inhibit change, since the initial high cost of the new idea may be unacceptable and the forecast of future cost reductions difficult to prove.

The fear of litigation

The increasing fear of litigation, especially in North America, is leading manufacturers to be more cautious about change, especially in areas where safety is potentially involved (Sontag, 1988).

Any change to a product that is subsequently involved in a safety-related incident places the manufacturer at risk, since it can always be claimed that the new design was deficient in some way, thus leading to the incident.

The manufacturer has no history of reliability to offer by way of defence, as the change has potentially negated all the product's historical experience. The manufacturer is therefore more at risk than if there had been a policy of limited or no change.

Conclusions

In summary, innovation has been the most important shaping force in the history of humankind. This shaping force has been fuelled and driven by the creativity of the human mind and, in general, constrained by technical blocks. These technical blocks are freed when appropriate enablers are discovered, thus allowing the innovation to take place.

A constant enabler has been that of materials. Materials development is as old as mankind and is still key to our progress. However, history has seen the appearance of other, supporting, enablers of which the current example, that of microelectronics, is without doubt the most significant by far.

Innovations open new windows of opportunity and process innovations are no exception. Currently, in the manufacturing industry, process innovation is being applied to allow the potentially conflicting goals of quality, cost and timing to be achieved concurrently. Indeed, it can be argued that, with the correct approach to development, these three important goals become mutually supporting; an effective design and development process providing a good design with high confidence in a short span and hence at lower cost. An innovation (a novel approach to the design and development process) has provided a new operation environment that results in a new relationship between features that have historically been seen to be in conflict.

However, each new operational environment brings its own new constraints and this analysis contends that the new environment created by the use of the computer to improve the engineering environment, reinforced by increasing customer expectations and concerns about introduction cost and litigation, will result in a new period of conservatism. This will stifle product innovation, the very phenomenon that brought these changes into play in the first place.

References

Badawy, M. K. (1988) How to prevent creativity mismanagement. *IEEE Engineering Management Review*, **16**(2), 63.

Bridgeman, H. (1990) *Global Air Pollution*. Belhaven Press, p. 93.

HMSO (1995) *Successful Product Development – Management Case Studies*. Her Majesty's Stationery Office.

Kuhn, R. L. (1985) *Frontiers in Creative and Innovative Management*. Ballinger.

Marquis, D. G. (1969) The anatomy of successful innovations. *Innovation*, November. Reprinted in M. L. Tushman and W. L. Moore, eds (1988).

Reay, D. A. (1977) *The History of Man-Powered Flight*. Pergamon Press, p. 341.

Robertson, R. (1974) Innovation management. *Management Decision Monograph*, **12**(6), 332.

Sontag, F. B. (1988) The impact of product liability on aviation development. *The Society of Automotive Engineers*, **871330**.

Tinnesand, B. (1973) Towards a general theory of innovation. PhD thesis, University of Wisconsin, Madison, 258.

Twiss, B. (1992) *Managing Technological Innovation*. Pitman.

Udwadia, F. E. (1990) Creativity and innovation in organizations. *Technological Forecasting and Social Change*, **38**(1), 66.

Urabe, K. (1988) *Innovation and Management*. Walter de Gruyter, p. 3.

US Bureau of Census (1975) *Historical Statistics of the United States of America, Colonial Times to 1970*.

US Bureau of Census (1996a) *Statistical Abstract of the United States of America*.

US Bureau of Census (1996b) *Innovation the Best Practice – the Executive Summary*. DTI, Bicentennial edition, Part 2.

2 Market orientation for superior competitiveness

Sattam Alshammri

This chapter addresses several questions:

1 What is meant by market orientation?
2 What effect does a market orientation have on business performance?
3 What are the prerequisites for the application of market orientation?
4 What are the consequences of exhibiting a market-oriented strategy?
5 Is there any link between market orientation, quality, customer satisfaction and business profitability?

In answering the above questions, an intensive review of the literature and empirical works was undertaken. A model was developed and tested in a service context. The findings revealed significant and positive relationships between the degree of market orientation and level of customer satisfaction, relative service quality, employee organizational commitment, and profitability. Furthermore, the findings suggest that adopting a market orientation in an organization depends on senior management characteristics (emphasis, leadership, professionalism). Market orientation, in turn, leads to profitability through satisfied customers and committed employees moderated by competition intensity, market turbulence and technology turbulence. Some examples of best practice firms, derived from the application of market orientation, are included. Finally, a guide and recommendations for applying market orientation are presented.

It is rare that we enjoy virtuoso performances in any service delivery situation, yet when it occurs, it comes as a refreshing surprise. Often, such excellent customer service appears so easy and so natural, that we fail to understand why we do not receive it on a more regular basis. (David Freemantle, Chairman, Sperboss Ltd)

Managing in the new millennium

By the turn of this century and the beginning of a new millennium, management thought is shifting from an emphasis on transaction and acquisition to relationship and retention. Thus, the way of doing business has moved from an internal orientation to a balanced (external and internal) orientation (Figure 2.1). Market orientation, however, has emphasized a balanced orientation, and become a prerequisite to success and profitability for most organizations. Market orientation is the principal cultural foundation of the learning organization. Because of its external emphasis on developing information about customers and competitors, the market-driven

Figure 2.1 *Examples of emerging thinking*

business is well positioned to anticipate the developing needs of its customers and respond to them through the adoption of innovative products and services. This ability gives the market-driven business an advantage in the speed and effectiveness of its response to opportunities and threats. Thus, a market orientation is inherently a learning orientation. What is a market orientation? And what are the consequences of a market orientation? These questions should have been answered by the time this chapter has been read.

Introduction

Introduced in the early 1950s, the marketing concept (the philosophical foundation of a market orientation) represents a cornerstone of marketing thought. However, given its widely acknowledged importance, it is remarkable how little research has focused on the subject. Only a small set of conceptual articles exist which offer preliminary suggestions for engendering a market orientation (Felton, 1959; Webster, 1988). And the few empirical studies that have been conducted on the subject primarily concern the extent to which organizations have adopted the marketing concept, rather than the antecedents or consequences of a market orientation (e.g. McNamara, 1972). In recent years, however, there has been a strong resurgence of academics' and practitioners' interest in market orientation. This interest has resulted in significant conceptual and empirical researches (see, for example, Harris and Piercy, 1997; Jaworski and Kohli, 1993; Slater and Narver, 1994).

The term *market orientation* has been used to refer to the implementation of the marketing concept. Thus, a market-oriented organization is one whose actions embrace the marketing concept (Deshpande et al., 1993; Mohr-Jackson, 1991; Wong and Saunders, 1993). The study of market orientation seeks to understand the behaviour of members of the organization that is manifested by adoption of the marketing concept as a firm philosophy.

The marketing concept is a business philosophy articulated more than forty years ago. In 1954, Peter Drucker argued that marketing is not only the responsibility of people at a functional level but also a general management responsibility. The marketing concept has played a major role in business practice and management thinking since the early 1960s. According to Webster (1988) the management of many companies is rediscovering the marketing concept. This interest in the marketing concept is translated by the amount of recently published literature; books and articles that emphasized Drucker's original theme of organizing and operating business with the goal of 100 per cent customer satisfaction in mind.

Market versus other orientations

When an organization objectively co-ordinates its marketing efforts in order to fill a defined need of a set customer group for purposes of making and sustaining a profit, it is said to have a market orientation (Kohli and Jaworski, 1990; Kotler, 1997; Slater, 1997).

The concept of orientation relates to the nature of one's adaptation to a specific situation. It reflects the degree to which one accommodates the surrounding environment in order to achieve objectives. In business there have been numerous orientations that have evolved as the environment surrounding business organizations has evolved.

Historical retrospection on the topic has produced a variety of labels to describe and chronologically capture the evolution of business orientations. The first is the *product* or production orientation, which typically dominates in the periods when demand is greater than supply and few competitors exist. During such periods, whatever one produces, one can sell, and therefore it is rational to focus on the producing of goods. The second is the *sales/promotion* orientation, which flourishes when customers are perceived to need information about products before they will try them. Therefore, promoting what has been produced is considered to be the key element to success. The third is the *market* orientation, which is prevalent in times dominated by intense competition, where customers have numerous alternatives, and when information concerning customers drives product development and marketing efforts of organizations (Figure 2.2).

While each of these orientations can and does exist in modern organizations, prevailing wisdom stresses that having a market orientation is critical for superior performance and long-term success in today's highly competitive commercial environment. Market orientation is discussed in greater detail in the following section.

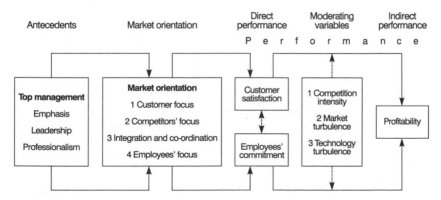

Figure 2.2 *Model of market orientation: antecedents and consequences*

Market orientation: conceptualization

In recent years, market orientation has received significant conceptual and empirical research (Jaworski and Kohli, 1993; Kohli and Jaworski, 1990; Mohr-Jackson, 1991; Narver and Slater, 1990; Ruekert, 1992; Shapiro, 1988; Slater and Narver, 1994). These recent conceptualizations are reviewed next.

According to Kohli and Jaworski (1990) existing definitions of the marketing concept are of limited practical value, and it is important to develop operational definitions of the marketing concept by identifying specific activities that translate the philosophy into practice. To delineate the market orientation construct domain, they reviewed existing literature, and interviewed several business managers in different industries. Based on this review, they define market orientation at the strategic business unit (SBU) level as: 'the organization-wide generation of the market intelligence pertaining to current and future customer needs, dissemination of market intelligence across departments, and organization-wide responsiveness to it'.

They advocate the idea that market orientation should be viewed as a continuous rather than a dichotomous either-or construct. In other words, they argue that a measure of market orientation only needs to assess the degree to which a company generates market intelligence, disseminates it and takes actions based on it. Accordingly, it is meaningless to classify a business as either or market oriented.

By their definition, market intelligence includes an analysis of current and future customer needs and preferences, and an analysis of such exogenous factors as government regulation, technology, competition and other environmental forces.

Narver and Slater (1990) define market orientation at the SBU level as: 'the organizational culture that most effectively and efficiently creates the necessary behaviours for the creation of superior value for buyers and, thus, continuous superior performance for the business'.

Further, they operationalize market orientation along five distinct components: customer orientation, competitor orientation, interfunctional co-ordination, long-term focus and profitability emphasis.

They administered a questionnaire survey to top managers of a large forest product. They reported acceptable reliability levels for the scales employed to capture customer orientation, competitor orientation and interfunctional co-ordination. However, they reported very low reliability scores for the scales used to measure long-term focus and profitability emphasis. For subsequent analysis they dropped these two components from their original operational definition.

They reported convergent validity for their conceptualization of the market orientation construct. The three retained components, customer orientation, competitor orientation and interfunctional co-ordination, were strongly correlated.

The Narver and Slater (1990) conceptualization shares some themes common with those of Kohli and Jaworski (1990). Both papers view knowledge about customers' needs and preferences, competitors' actions and interfunctional co-ordination as central to the market orientation construct; both define market orientation at the SBU level and both argue that market orientation should be conceptualized on a continuum construct.

The two approaches also differ in some aspects. Narver and Slater report that all three components, namely customer orientation, competitor orientation and interfunctional co-ordination, converged on a single dimension. They wondered if the other two proposed components, namely profitability emphasis and long-term focus, constituted a separate dimension. Kohli and Jaworski (1990) argue that it is not meaningful to include profitability as a dimension for market orientation; they assert that profitability is an outcome of a market orientation. They include long-term emphasis in their definition of market intelligence, by noting that it includes both current and future trends in the marketplace.

Shapiro (1988) argues the case for effective communication and co-ordination across department barriers as a way to become customer oriented. According to him, three factors make a company market driven (market oriented in other ways): 'Information on all important buying influences permeates every corporate function. Strategic and tactical decisions are made interfunctionally and interdivisionally, and divisions and functions make well coordinated decisions and execute them with a sense of commitment.' He argues that a company can be market oriented only if it completely understands its markets and the people who decide whether to buy its products or services.

Ruekert (1992) defines the level of market orientation in a business unit as the degree to which the business unit:

- obtains and uses information from customers
- develops a strategy which will meet needs
- implements that strategy by being responsive to customers' needs and wants.

He argues that managers at the business unit level collect and interpret information from the external environment to serve as the foundation for selecting goals and objectives, as well as allocating resources to various programmes within the business unit. While such information reflects a wide variety of domains such as the technological, human resource, legal and financial environments, the customer environment is the critical external environment in developing a market orientation.

The first dimension of Ruekert's definition is consistent with previous definitions of market orientation. Kohli and Jaworski (1990) argue that customer orientation is the degree to which customer information is both collected and used by the business unit. Similarly, Narver and Slater (1990) measure the collection and use of customer information in their scale of customer orientation. Shapiro (1988) argues that the use of customer information is one of three central aspects of being market oriented.

The second dimension of Ruekert's definition of market orientation concerns the development of a plan of action, or a customer-focused strategy. It reflects the degree to which the strategic planning process explicitly considers customers' needs and develops specific strategies for satisfying those customer demands.

The third dimension of Ruekert's definition of market orientation involves the implementation and execution of a customer-oriented strategy by being responsive to market needs and wants. Ruekert argues that these behaviours conducted by the business unit can vary in the degree to which they deliver customer satisfaction. This aspect of his definition is consistent with Narver and Slater's (1990) behavioural component of interfunctional co-ordination to deliver value and Kohli and Jaworski's (1990) responsiveness element in their definition. It is this dimension that is often described in the popular press as being central to the concept of market orientation.

The conceptual definition of market orientation presented by Ruekert (1992) is very similar to the existing definitions proposed by Kohli and Jaworski (1990), Narver and Slater (1990) and Shapiro (1988). However, the differences between these approaches to defining the construct rest more on emphasis than on substantive differences. Kohli and Jaworski, for instance, emphasize the use of market information, while Shapiro tends to focus on decision-making processes. Ruekert emphasizes the development and execution of business unit strategy as the key organizing focus of market orientation.

In contrast to the previous discussion regarding market orientation dimensions, an extended view has been found from the exploratory study by Mohr-Jackson (1991). Her study attempted to clarify the domain of the market orientation by extending the customer orientation. She argues that internal customers (employees) are the ultimate creators of products and services, and are generators of customer satisfaction. Based on her literature review, she has found that attention has been directed towards factors that facilitate or hamper the implementation of the marketing concept and overlooking the impact of human resource management factors. Consequently, little is known about the role of the internal customers within the context of the market orientation. She conducted forty-five in-depth interviews with corporate executives to assess the characteristics of the marketing concept and the employee activities that foster its implementation. She finds that a market orientation enhances performance by improving internal customer satisfaction by means such as ownership, security, job satisfaction, full participation, involvement, motivation, enthusiasm, empowerment, absenteeism, accident rate, productivity and effectiveness, all of which have a demonstrable impact on the bottom line.

Though the marketing concept is the cornerstone of the marketing discipline, businesses typically describe only limited success in implementing it. An examination of the core pillars of the marketing concept points to limitations in the first pillar, the customer's focus. This pillar is directed at the external customer, the person purchasing the firm's products and services with no attention to the internal customer – the employee. Whereas much attention has been directed to human resource practices in total quality management, marketers have overlooked its importance. The effectiveness of a market orientation depends upon how it is defined. Without an accurate definition of a market orientation, businesses typically described only limited success in implementing it. However, the employees' dimension is included in this chapter as a component of the market orientation construct.

For the purpose of this research, the author argues that the construct of market orientation is composed of interrelated, but separate dimensions. He argues that customer focus (orientation) is composed of those behaviours that seek to improve understanding of customer needs and those that seek to achieve superior levels of customer satisfaction through quality, service and value. He also argues that competitors' focus is composed of those behaviours that seek to understand competitors' weaknesses and strengths. And he argues that organizational commitment and employees' focus comprises those behaviours that seek to make the whole organization work in harmony towards common objectives. However, the market orientation has been operationalized along four components as follows:

- customer focus (orientation)
- competitors' focus (orientation)
- interfunctional integration
- employees' focus (orientation).

Many companies that say they are market oriented are often trying to do nothing more than disguise a product- or sale-based culture. According to Chvala (1991) the process of moving corporate culture toward a market orientation contains fourteen steps:

1　As chief executive officer, take an active role to champion the efforts.
2　Appoint a team or committee of cross-functional employees and managers to identify and act on necessary changes.

3 Perform a benchmark, image or customer satisfaction survey or market review.
4 Insist that the team listen to outsiders.
5 Identify the changes required.
6 Set a timetable.
7 Assemble a training and process calendar to implement the changes.
8 Communicate each step of the path to all employees.
9 Use a non-political, diplomatic facilitator to keep the effort focused.
10 Employ outsiders when the going gets tough.
11 Reward those who change.
12 Identify, lower, or remove barriers that slow the process.
13 Do not tell the customer that the company has changed until change actually occurs.
14 Communicate the message to all markets.

The four-component conceptualization of market orientation proposed in this chapter is consistent with literature (as discussed before) and encompasses, in one way or another, the fourteen steps recommended by Chvala (1991) (see Figure 2.3).

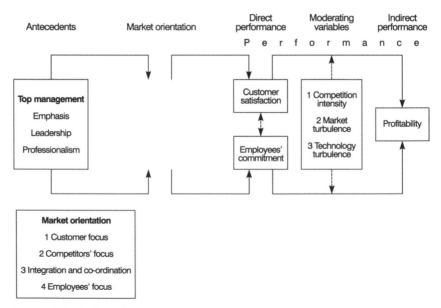

Figure 2.3 *Market orientation model: conceptualization*

Market orientation and quality

Quality is widely regarded as a driver of corporate performance measures (Anderson and Sullivan, 1993; Berry, Parasuraman and Zeithaml, 1994; Buttle, 1996; Morgan and Piercy, 1992; Woodruff, 1997; and Zairi, Letza and Oakland, 1994). Berry, Parasuraman and Zeithaml (1994) stated: 'Excellent service is a profit strategy because it results in more new customers, more business with existing customers, fewer lost customers, more insulation from price competition, and fewer mistakes requiring the performance of service.' Given the obvious importance of quality and its reflection within organizations in terms of quality functions, strategies and programmes, it appears vital that marketers are able to understand the quality issue, and thus to take an active role in the development and implementation of quality strategies and programmes.

Despite the problems of defining quality (discussed later) the concepts of quality and quality management have moved into the marketing literature in the last ten years. During this period, a number of underlying conceptual developments have emerged that have been widely accepted. It has been widely agreed that quality is not an absolute, discrete concept. Quality has come to be seen as important primarily in terms of customer perception. The concept of perceived quality has been viewed as the product of the difference between customer expectations and customer perceptions of outcomes. It has been recognized that customer quality perceptions are created via a quality evaluation process that involves not only perceptions of outcome, but also includes perceptions of the process by which that outcome has been achieved and the context in which production and exchange occur.

Increasing quality has a potentially enormous impact on profitability, both through reducing an organization's operational costs and improving its market position. The accumulating evidence concerning the relationship between quality and business performance, and the creation and continued existence of quality staff, line functions and departments in many organizations make it likely that quality is a management function that will enjoy a long life (Zairi, Letza and Oakland, 1994).

It has been mentioned earlier that customer focus is one component of the market orientation construct. And customer-oriented organizations are adept at building customers, not just building products. Building, attracting, and retaining customers can be achieved through quality, service and value. These in turn build customers' satisfaction and loyalty. Being a market-oriented organization is a customer-oriented organization simply because customer orientation is one pillar of market orientation. Thus, organizations cannot be market oriented without being customer oriented. Moreover, organizations cannot be customer oriented without providing customers with a good quality and service.

In addition to the above arguments, a study (Alshammri, 1997) has empirically investigated the link between market orientation and quality. The study has revealed that there is a significant and positive relationship between degree of market orientation and relative quality provided.

Based on the above arguments and findings, it is not surprising to argue that quality is related to market orientation. The following sections shed light on quality, service quality, distinction between quality of goods and service and the service quality model. In the next section, the link between market orientation, service quality, customer satisfaction and business performance is discussed.

Service quality

Services have always been a significant part of consumers' lives. They continue to gain in importance as world economies become more service oriented. Services contribute an average of more than 60 per cent to the gross national product (GNP) of all industrial nations. In the USA, for example, services currently generate more than 74 per cent of the US gross domestic product and account for 79 per cent of all jobs, and by the year 2000 an estimated 88 per cent of working Americans will be employed in the service sector (Henkoff, 1994). So, what is a service? Services are acts, efforts or performances that cannot be handled or examined prior to purchase and that are exchanged from producer to user without ownership rights. A service is typically an act that accomplishes some goals, whether it is providing pleasure, information, convenience, or some other form of utilities. Kotler (1997) defines service as: 'any act or performance that one party offers to another that is essentially intangible and does not result in the ownership of anything. Its production may or may not be tied to a physical product.'

Before getting into how service can differ from a physical product, it is worth discussing the concept of quality.

Definition of quality

People have different ideas of what quality is. Quality is like beauty: both are in the eye of beholder. Unfortunately, there is no universally accepted definition of quality, but those that are most widely available and accepted came from the quality gurus. These definitions include those from Crosby (1979) 'conformance to requirements', Deming (1986) 'predictable degree of conformity and dependability at low cost and suited to the market' and Oakland (1989) 'meeting the customer requirements'. They define quality in one of three ways:

1 Quality is conforming to specifications; the quality of an item depends on how well it measures up against a set of specifications; quality is achieved

when a product is produced the way it is supposed to be. According to this definition, a Mercedes-Benz may be of lower quality than a Hyundai if the Hyundai conforms better to the design and performance standards set for it. However, this definition is inadequate because it does not take into account the difference in perception between two products.

2 Quality lies in the eyes of the receiver (beholder). Different users have different needs, and to the extent that a product is designed and manufactured to meet those needs, quality is dependent on how well it fulfils them. Individual consumers are assumed to have different wants or needs, and the goods that best satisfy their preferences are the ones they regard as having the highest quality. This is a personal view of quality, and one that is highly subjective. It is a precise combination of product attributes that provide the greatest satisfaction to a specified consumer. For example, business travellers may consider the highest-quality airline is the one with the best record of on-time arrivals and departures; for holidaymakers, it may be the quickest in-flight service or the most interesting films. This definition is incomplete because quality is extremely subjective: quality is simply what the user says it is, rational or not.

3 Quality is innate excellence. This definition reflects the belief that, although styles and tastes change, there is something enduring about works of high quality. They provide a standard against which other products are judged. According to this view, excellence is both absolute and universally recognizable; whatever it consists of, it is known when it is seen.

However, from a customer-centred definition of quality, the American Society for Quality's control definition, which has been adopted worldwide, is used (Miller, 1993): 'Quality is the totality of features and characteristics of a product or service that bear on its ability to satisfy stated or implied needs.'

Differences between quality of goods and service

In general, a product may be defined as goods or a service, but most often it has both service and physical elements or 'service-goods continuum'. This dualism affects quality perception. For service-related companies, quality is a particularly elusive concept. In labour-intensive services, quality occurs during service delivery, usually in an interaction between the customer and the contact person from the service firm. The service firm may also have less managerial control over quality in services where consumer participation is intense because the customer affects the process. In these situations, the consumer's requirements become critical to the quality of service performance.

When purchasing goods, the consumer could judge quality by a tangible cue such as style, hardness, colour, label, feel etc. In contrast, when purchasing services, fewer tangible cues exist. In the absence of tangible evidence on which to evaluate quality, consumers must depend on other cues such as the service provider's physical facilities, equipment, and personnel (Parasuraman, Zeithaml and Berry, 1985).

In judging product quality, customers often use intrinsic cues such as price, advertising, or brand name. Because of service intangibility, a firm may find it more difficult to understand how consumers perceive services and service quality (Gronroos, 1990). Delivering quality service means conforming to customer expectations on a consistent basis.

The literature holds that intangibility, inseparability, heterogeneity and perishability are the most commonly cited properties of services that cause a substantial marketing difference between services and goods. These traits have been described as the fundamental distinguishing characteristics of services, from which all other differences emerge. Table 2.1 summarizes these characteristics.

Table 2.1 *Characteristics of services*

Intangibility	Inseparability	Heterogeneity	Perishability
Services are intangible. They cannot be seen, tasted, felt, heard or smelled before they are bought.	A service is inseparable from the source that provides it. Its very creation requires the source, whether person or machine, to be present. In other words, production and consumption occur simultaneously with services. This is in contrast to a product, which exists whether or not its source is present.	Heterogeneity in this context means that services are difficult to standardize. Heterogeneity concerns the potential for high variability in the performance of services. The quality and essence of a service can vary from producer to producer, from customer to customer, and from day to day. Heterogeneity in service output is a particular problem for labour intensive services.	Perishability of the service means that services are perishable in the sense that they cannot be stored for use at a later time or date. Services cannot be produced before required and then stored to meet demand. If a service is not used when available then the service capacity is wasted.

The four characteristics of services described in Table 2.1 are the most frequently defined by scholars. In general, differences between goods and service quality are:

• Service quality is more difficult for the consumer to evaluate than goods quality.
• Service quality perceptions result from a comparison of consumer expectations with actual service performance.
• Quality evaluations are not made solely on the outcome of a service; they also involve evaluations of the process of service delivery.
• Service quality is a measure of how well the service level delivered matches customer expectations.

Service quality model (SERVQUAL)

Because of the importance of service quality, marketing researchers have devoted a great deal of attention to conceptualizing and measuring 'service quality'. Parasuraman, Zeithaml and Berry (1988) have developed a conceptual model of service quality. This conceptual model of service quality views it as a construct that is similar to an attitude that results from a comparison between a consumer's service expectations and perceptions of the performance they have received on these dimensions.

Based on the expectation/performance conceptualization of service quality, Parasuraman, Zeithaml and Berry developed the SERVQUAL approach for measuring service quality in 1988. This method assesses both the consumer's service expectations and perceptions of the provider's performance. They positioned this approach as a generic method applicable to a wide range of service industries. Since then, SERVQUAL has been widely applied and frequently reported in the marketing literature.

The introduction of SERVQUAL revolutionized the discipline of services marketing. The service gap concept examined the existence of service gaps on the service provider's side: these gaps can impede the delivery of services that customers perceive to be of high quality. The five gaps proposed in the model are the difference between:

• consumer expectations and management perceptions of consumer expectations
• management perceptions of consumer expectations and service quality specifications
• service quality specifications and the service actually delivered
• service delivery and what is communicated about the service to consumers
• consumer expectations and perceived delivered service.

Table 2.2 *Service quality dimensions*

Dimension	Its meaning
1 Reliability:	consistency of service performance and dependability
2 Responsiveness:	the willingness of employees to provide service
3 Competence:	possessing the required skills to perform the service
4 Access:	approachability and ease of contact
5 Courtesy:	politeness, respect, consideration, and friendliness of employees
6 Communication:	keeping customers informed and listening to them, adjusting to their knowledge level when explaining things that the customer does not understand
7 Credibility:	trustworthiness, believability, honesty; having the customer's best interest at heart
8 Understanding/ knowing:	understanding customer's needs, providing individualized attention
9 Security:	freedom from danger, risk, or doubt
10 Tangibles:	physical evidence of the service

These gaps can be major hurdles in attempting to deliver proper service. The SERVQUAL model originally proposed ten dimensions: reliability, responsiveness, competence, access, courtesy, communication, credibility, security, understanding/knowing the customer and tangibles. These dimensions and their meaning are presented in Table 2.2.

After considerable work, the final survey used twenty-two questions and resulted in five dimensions that describe the customer experience. These dimensions are presented in Table 2.3.

Table 2.3 *Dimensions of service quality*

Dimension	Its meaning
1 Reliability:	the ability to perform the promised service dependably and accurately
2 Responsiveness:	the willingness to help customers and provide prompt service
3 Assurance:	the knowledge and courtesy of employees and their ability to convey trust and confidence
4 Empathy:	the caring, individualized attention to customers
5 Tangibles:	the appearance of physical facilities, equipment, personnel, and communication materials

Of these five dimensions of service quality, Berry, Parasuraman and Zeithaml (1994) found that reliability is the most important one. In each of their thirteen customer surveys, respondents rated reliability as the single most important feature in judging service quality. When they asked more than 1,900 customers of five large well-known US companies to allocate a total of 100 points across the five service dimensions, they found 32 per cent, 22 per cent, 19 per cent, 16 per cent and 11 per cent were placed on reliability, responsiveness, assurance, empathy and tangibles respectively.

Reliability is the core of quality service. Thus, when a service is unreliable, little else matters to customers. When a firm makes frequent mistakes in delivery or breaks its promises, customers lose confidence in the firm's ability to do what it has undertaken to do dependably and accurately. Friendliness from the staff and sincere apologies do not compensate for unreliable service. Most customers do appreciate an apology, although the apology does not erase the memory of that service from the customer's mind. If a pattern of service failure develops, customers conclude that the firm cannot be counted on whether it is friendly and apologetic or not.

Although reliability is the most important dimension, it is an outcome dimension because it is judged following the service. The dimensions of responsiveness, assurance, empathy, and tangibles, on the other hand, are judged by customers during the service delivery process.

Most service quality research explores the meaning of service quality from the customer's point of view. Parasuraman, Zeithaml and Berry (1988) argue that, to a large extent, customers determine service quality by the feeling that is produced during and after the service encounter. Customers evaluate an organization's service quality by comparing their perceptions of the service they received with their expectation for the service. The resulting feelings are primarily a function of customers' experience during the service encounter they result from customer contact with service employees.

The gap analysis model of service quality is the one that has become the most prominent in the marketing literature. In this model, Parasuraman, Zeithaml and Berry (1985) describe service quality in terms of three unique underlying themes:

1 Service quality is more difficult for the customer to evaluate than goods quality.
2 Service quality perceptions result from a comparison of customer expectations with actual service performance.
3 Quality evaluations are not made solely on the outcome of a service; they also involve evaluations of the process of service delivery.

Service quality, however, is modelled as a function of comparisons between expectations and performance perceptions. Expectations are defined as what an individual feels the service provider should offer, and performance is defined as an individual's evaluation of how well his/her expectations are fulfilled by the service (Parasuraman, Zeithaml and Berry, 1988).

Customer perceptions of service quality are largely a function of the human element of employee's beliefs, attitudes, and organizational environment on customer evaluation of service quality during actual service encounters. Perceptions of customer satisfaction and service quality significantly increased when employees treated customers who had experienced service failures with compassion, courtesy, understanding, and honesty. Bitner (1990) suggested that not only employee responses, but also employee appearance, employee competence and employee surroundings were influential in determining customers' perceptions of service quality.

Criticisms of the SERVQUAL model

Although SERVQUAL has been widely used, it has recently been criticized by several researchers. Carman (1990), for example, expressed concern over the measurement of service quality across multiple service functions, the treatment of the expectations measurement and the omission of importance in the measurement of service quality. Babakus and Boller (1992) questioned SERVQUAL's applicability across a wide variety of services, its dimensionality, the appropriateness of operationalizing service quality as a gap score and the specific measurement properties associated with SERVQUAL.

Cronin and Taylor (1992), however, argued that both the conceptualization and operationalization of SERVQUAL are inadequate. Conceptually, they point out confusion in the literature over the relationship between service quality and consumer satisfaction. They concluded that, although service quality has been conceptually described as a construct that is similar to an attitude, the operation of the SERVQUAL model is more consistent with the conceptualization and operationalization found within the consumer satisfaction/dissatisfaction paradigm. This distinction is important to both academicians and practitioners because it has a bearing on the nature of the relationships between service quality, customer satisfaction and, ultimately, purchase intentions.

Buttle (1996) argued that, notwithstanding its growing popularity and widespread application, SERVQUAL has been subjected to a number of criticisms. Two major ones have been raised. First, SERVQUAL has been inappropriately based on an expectations-disconfirmation model rather than an attitudinal model of SERVQUAL (SERVQUAL is based on the disconfirmation model widely adopted in the customer satisfaction literature). Second, it does not build on extant knowledge in economics, statistics and psychology. In the same article, Buttle stated: 'Without question, SERVQUAL has been widely applied and is highly valued. Any critique of SERVQUAL, therefore, must be seen within this broader context of strong endorsement.'

Analysis of these criticisms

It would seem these criticisms could be treated as constructive ones because they are targeted towards improving the instrument rather than blowing it up. They do not, however, detract from the merits of the conceptualization of the gap analysis model as a management tool for improving service quality.

In spite of some criticisms, the SERVQUAL model has been predominantly tested and enhanced within the USA as well as internationally, and has been widely applied and frequently reported in the marketing literature since its actual introduction in 1988.

The link between market orientation, quality, customer satisfaction and business performance

The literature provides empirical support that market orientation behaviour leads to superior performance (at least in some business environments). Kohli and Jaworski (1990) and Narver and Slater (1990) provided a theoretical basis for expecting a relationship between market orientation and performance. Narver and Slater (1990) stated that the essence of the literature on the marketing concept is that market orientation is the organization culture that most effectively and efficiently creates the necessary behaviours for the creation of superior value for buyers and, thus, continuous superior performance. Higher relative market orientation provides the firm with a competitive advantage in a similar way to other competitive advantages (Porter, 1985).

An organization achieves a competitive advantage if it is relatively high in an important dimension of market orientation and is relatively high in levels of competency in building customer value. The competitive advantage can be sustainable if competitors have difficulty copying this market orientation culture and attendant value-building competency.

The superior value created by the product/service provider could be in the form of lower price, better quality, a more differentiated product or better service. A higher level of market orientation should lead to greater sensitivity to the customers' perceptions of relative value and to striving for superior value of the firm's offering. This should lead to greater customer perceived product/service value, higher customer retention, higher sales growth, higher market share, higher margins and, consequently, higher profitability.

The study of excellent companies and the construct of performance by Chakravarthy (1986) concluded that excellent firms require the ability to transform the organization to changes in the business environment. He found that the transformations to the surrounding environment could be special and general adaptation. The former is the process of improving the goodness of fit in a given state of adaptation (exploiting the firm's current environment, while the latter is concerned with investment of the firm's net surplus of slack resources for improving its ability to adapt to an uncertain or unknown future environment. The discussion by Chakravarthy is very relevant to market orientation theory. These transformations are difficult to make if the organization is not oriented to the marketplace; market orientation in other words. But when the firm is oriented to the surrounding environment, it is in a position to make these transformations. The links between market orientation, quality, customer satisfaction, and business performance are discussed below.

Service quality and customer satisfaction

In recent years there has been a great deal of interest in the conceptualization and measurement of consumer satisfaction and perceived service quality, both by managers and academic researchers. Consumer satisfaction and service quality have each been the subject of extensive research, although many studies of consumer satisfaction have been conducted in service contexts (see for example Fornell, 1992b; Oliver, 1980). There seems to be a great deal of similarity between these two concepts, yet researchers are usually careful to state that these are different constructs. Some researchers in the service domain have maintained that these two constructs are distinct (Bitner, 1990; Carman, 1990; Parasuraman, Zeithaml and Berry, 1988; Taylor and Baker, 1994). Yet there have been repeated calls for research investigating the relationship between the two constructs (Anderson and Fornell, 1994; Patterson, 1997).

Greater understanding of the relationship between perceived service quality and satisfaction is in great demand. If they are distinct constructs, then the difference between them should be understood. Further, in spite of criticisms of the disconfirmation of expectations, researchers in the service quality area continue to state that satisfaction is the result of a comparison with predictive expectations. If satisfaction is not simply a result of meeting expectations, then managers may not be focusing on the correct things. Perceived service quality is defined by Parasuraman, Zeithaml and Berry (1988) as: 'a global judgment, or attitude, relating to the superiority of the service'.

Most researchers in the service quality literature concur with this definition. While there is not a clear consensus regarding the definition of satisfaction, most definitions would involve 'an evaluative, affective, or emotional response' (Oliver, 1989). Both satisfaction and service quality literatures have emphasized the idea that consumers make a comparison between the performance of the product or service and some standard. The service quality literature has maintained that the distinction between perceived service quality and satisfaction is that they use different standards of comparison. The standard of comparison in forming satisfaction is predictive expectations, or what the consumer believes will happen, while perceived service quality is the result of a comparison of performance and what the consumer feels a firm should provide. In a conceptual model that attempts to integrate service quality and satisfaction, Oliver (1993) similarly argues that while the antecedent of quality perceptions is the disconfirmation of ideals, the antecedents of satisfaction are disconfirmation of predictive expectations (regarding quality and non-quality dimensions) and perceived quality. Oliver suggests that the constructs are distinct, in part, because they use different standards, that is, he claims that one can be satisfied with low quality if the performance is better than one's prediction of the performance. However, Oliver (1993) states that: 'verification of the use of ideal expectations for quality and predictive expectations for satisfaction is needed'.

Oliver (1993) has proposed a model that is intended to integrate the satisfaction and the service quality literatures. He proposes that while service quality is formed by a comparison between ideals and perceptions of performance regarding quality dimensions, satisfaction is a function of the disconfirmation of predictive expectations regarding both quality dimensions and non-quality dimensions. Further, perceived service quality is proposed to be an antecedent to satisfaction.

Quality of service and customer satisfaction

Several studies have shown that perceived quality affects customer satisfaction (Anderson and Sullivan, 1993; Bearden and Teel, 1993; Fornell, 1992b). This relationship is intuitive and fundamental to all economic activities. Aggregated to the firm level, customers' current experience with a supplier's offering also should have a positive influence on their overall assessment of how satisfied they are with that supplier.

In addition to overall quality, price and expectations affect customer satisfaction. Price plays an important role in the relationship between perceived quality and satisfaction. The received value of a supplier's offering – quality relative to price – has a direct impact on how satisfied customers are with that supplier (Anderson and Sullivan, 1993).

Expectations about the quality of goods and services also have a major impact on customer satisfaction. Expectations contain information based on not only actual consumption experience but also accumulated information about quality from outside sources, such as advertising, word of mouth and general media. The role of expectations is important because the nature of an ongoing relationship between a firm and its customer base is such that expected future quality is vital to customer satisfaction and retention (Eugene, Fornell and Donald, 1994; Gronroos, 1990; Lovelock, 1996).

There is an intimate connection among product and service quality, customer satisfaction, and business profitability. Higher levels of quality result in higher levels of customer satisfaction. This in turn increases profitability. The well-known PIMS studies by Buzzell and Gale (1987) show a high correlation between relative product quality and business profitability. This is discussed in the next section.

Customer satisfaction and performance (profitability)

In the 1990s researchers have started to elaborate on the process by which delivering high-quality goods and services influences business performance – more specifically, profitability – through customer satisfaction (Anderson and Sullivan, 1993; Bearden and Teel, 1993; Fornell, 1992b; Rust and Zahorik, 1993). The literature has provided several key benefits of a high customer satisfaction for organizations. In general, high customer satisfaction is an indication of increased loyalty for current customers, reduced price elasticity, insulation of current customers from competitive efforts, reduced failure costs, lower costs of attracting new customers and enhanced reputation for the organizations. Each of these benefits is discussed in more details.

Customer satisfaction reduces price elasticity for current customers. However, satisfied customers are more willing to pay for the benefits they receive and are more likely to be tolerant of increase in price. This allows high margins. Increased loyalty of current customers means more customers will repurchase of the firm's offering in the future yielding a steady stream of future cash flow. Low customer satisfaction, on the other hand, causes greater turnover of current customers, higher replacement costs and difficulty associated with high costs of attracting customers who are satisfied with a competitor's offering. This produces low margins (Fornell, 1992b).

Devoting lots of resources for handling returns, redoing defective items and managing complaints decrease profitability (Crosby, 1979; Garvin, 1988). However, reducing these resources (failure costs) by providing goods and services that satisfy customers increase profitability.

The costs of attracting new customers should be lower for organizations that achieved a high level of customer satisfaction (Fornell, 1992b). Satisfied customers are reputedly more likely to engage in positive word of mouth, and less likely to engage in damaging negative word of mouth for the organization.

Finally, a high level of customer satisfaction also enhances the overall reputation of the organization. An enhanced reputation, in turn, can aid the introduction of new products and services by providing instant awareness and lowering the buyer's trial (Rust and Zahorik, 1993; Fornell, 1992b). Reputation also can be beneficial in establishing and maintaining relationships with key suppliers, distributors, and potential allies.

Alshammri (1997) has empirically studied the links between market orientation, customer satisfaction and profitability in service organizations. He has found that there is a significant and a positive association between the degree of market orientation and the level of customer satisfaction, the degree of market orientation and relative profitability, and the level of customer satisfaction and relative profitability. These findings are consistent with the received view in the marketing literature that a market-oriented business should perform better than those businesses that are not market oriented.

From the preceding discussions and the empirical findings, it could be concluded that increasing the degree of market orientation should enhance customer satisfaction. Customers' satisfaction in turn increases the value of a firm's customer assets and future profitability, and plays an important role in building other important assets for the firm.

Empirical evidence of the market orientation–performance link

The marketing literature reveals that a business which can track and respond to its customers' needs more effectively than its competitors should perform better than those businesses which are not as market oriented. Given the widespread acceptance of this normative idea, it is surprisingly that only in recent years have attempts been made to empirically validate it. Narver and Slater (1990, 20) stated: 'Judged by the attention paid to it by practitioners and academicians in speeches, textbooks, and scholarly papers, market orientation is the very heart of modern marketing management and strategy – yet, to date, no one has developed a valid measure of it or assessed its influence on business performance.'

Recent studies have provided an evidence of a positive relationship between market orientation and performance (Jaworski and Kohli, 1993; Kohli and Jaworski, 1990; Narver and Slater, 1990; Raju, Lonial and Gupta, 1995; Slater and Narver, 1994). All these studies have confirmed that the degree of market orientation does have a significant impact on business performance measures.

The empirical studies by Narver and Slater (1990) measured business performance as return on assets (ROA) over the past year in relation to the ROAs of all other competitors. They reported a positive linear relationship between their construct of market orientation (a simple average of measures of customer orientation, competitors' orientation and interfunctional co-ordination) and their construct of business performance. They found a substantial positive effect of a market orientation on the profitability of both types of businesses. They found those commodity businesses with the highest levels of market orientation have the highest levels of performance, while those commodity businesses with the lowest levels of market orientation have the lowest performance level.

Narver and Slater's (1990) sole reliance on one measure of profitability assumes that the relationship between market orientation is direct, rather than mediated by other dimensions of performance. Being the first of its kind, they offered a very good starting point on the subject, and recommended that future research should examine market orientation/business performance relationship in other business environments.

The empirical study by Jaworski and Kohli (1993) confirms what Narver and Slater (1990) found. Jaworski and Kohli measured business performance using both subjective and objective measures. They operationalized performance with three single measures of overall performance, market share and return on equity (ROE). They found a significant relationship between their construct of market orientation (intelligence generation, intelligence dissemination and responsiveness to market intelligence) and their measure of overall performance. However, they found no significant relationships between market orientation and market share. They also found no significant relationship between their construct of market orientation and their single measure of profitability (ROE).

The lack of significance of the parameters for these two variables may have been influenced by inaccurate measurement of the dependent variables of market share and profitability, inaccurate measurement of the construct of profitability, or possible mediating relationships of other performance variables.

Even though Jaworski and Kohli found no significant relationship between market orientation and two of their performance measures, their three measures of performance were an improvement over Narver and Slater's one measure of performance (relative ROA).

In a health-care industry setting, the empirical work by Raju, Lonial and Gupta (1995) has confirmed the findings of the previous studies. They assessed hospital performance using nineteen judgemental variables. After factor analysing the variables, they came up with three performance measures – financial performance, market/product development and internal quality. Results show that market orientation has a significant effect on each of the performance measure dimensions. Although their methodology is similar to that of Jaworski and Kohli (1993) their performance measures are better as they are non-financially based.

A review of the strategic management literature (Chakravarthy, 1986) indicates the importance of multiple measures of performance and problems with financial measures. He indicated that no single profitability measure seemed capable of distinguishing excellent companies from non-excellent ones. As he noted, financial criteria define one set of necessary and excellence, but they are not sufficient. Although profitability, growth and market share are popular indicators of performance, recently published studies have noted that customer satisfaction (Fornell, 1992) and organizational commitment (Jaworski and Kohli, 1993) should be other measures of business performance. The use of multiple measures of performance not only provides a more accurate assessment of variable relationships, but also allows the researcher to assess the possibility of other performance dimensions mediating the relationships between constructs of interest and profitability.

Alshammri (1997) has empirically tested the relationship between market orientation and business performance in a service context. Business performance was operationalized along four dimensions; that is, customer satisfaction, service quality, employee organizational commitment and profitability. He found significant and positive relationships between the degree of market orientation and all four dimensions of performance measures.

From the preceding discussions, it is possible to conclude that market orientation does have a significant and positive influence on business performance in one way or another. This conclusion leads to the supposition that market orientation could be used for superior competitiveness and, consequently, to a superior performance. Customer value delivery concept is likely to be the next major shift in managerial practice. However, there is no contradiction between market orientation and the newly evolving concept. Customer value, learning of customer value, and the skills that top management will need to create and implement superior customer value strategies will not be achieved unless the organization is market oriented. This is because market orientation is a step in the right direction towards delivering superior customer value.

Moderating variables

The environmental context of an organization is likely to influence its level of market orientation. Several scholars draw on this general argument to suggest that the importance of market orientation varies with the environmental context (Jaworski and Kohli, 1993; Houston, 1986; Kohli and Jaworski, 1990; Narver and Slater, 1990). They argue that the link between market orientation and performance depends on the environmental characteristics of an organization.

In this chapter, competitive intensity, technology turbulence and market turbulence are included and discussed (Figure 2.4). These three environmental characteristics influence the link between market orientation and performance (Kohli and Jaworski, 1990).

Kohli and Jaworski have provided a good starting point and theoretical foundation for the expected influences of the industry environment on the market orientation–performance link. They argue for the importance of competitive intensity, technological turbulence, and market turbulence as

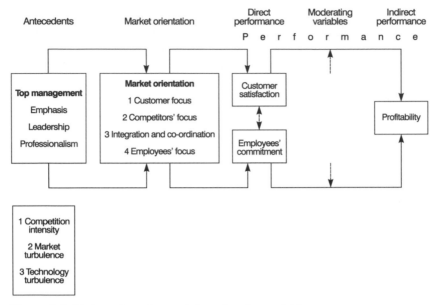

Figure 2.4 *Market orientation model: moderating variables*

moderating influences on the market orientation–performance link. The underlying theme in their discussion of the nature of these environmental moderators is that a high level of market orientation is a greater source of competitive advantage in industries characterized by high competitive intensity, low technological turbulence and high market turbulence. Each moderator is discussed in greater detail below.

Competition intensity

Kohli and Jaworski (1990) assert that the greater the competition, the stronger the relationship between market orientation and business performance. In the absence of competition an organization may perform well even if it is not market oriented, because customers do not have alternative options to satisfy their needs and wants, so they have to accept the organization's offering of products or services. On the other hand, with a high degree of competition, customers have many alternative options to satisfy their desires (Houston, 1986; Kohli and Jaworski, 1990). In a situation of strong competition an organization that is not very market oriented is most likely to lose customers to competitors. An organization that is very market oriented and focusing on its customers by understanding their needs and wants, and responding to them, is most likely to attract new customers or at least retain its current customers.

It could be argued that, in intensely competitive industries, those organizations that seek differentiation through higher relative levels of market orientation would improve their likelihood of survival, compared with organizations that continue to compete only on price. Higher levels of competitive intensity should increase the importance of developing better understanding of the relationship between the organization's offering and articulated and inarticulated customers' needs. As a result, an organization could modify its offering (product /service) based on greater understanding of customer needs.

High levels of competitive intensity should increase market orientation as a source of competitive advantage. The ability to monitor competitive activities, understand competitive strategies/capabilities, and respond quickly to competitive threats is more critical for an organization's survival in an industry environment with high levels of competitive intensity, compared to a more forgiving industry environment. This argument is consistent with the arguments of Houston (1986), Kohli and Jaworski (1990) and Jaworski and Kohli (1993) that, in the absence of competition, organizations may perform well, even if they are not very market oriented.

Technological turbulence

Kohli and Jaworski (1990) introduced technological turbulence as another moderator in the market orientation/business performance relationship. They define technology as the entire process of transforming input to output, and delivery of those outputs to the end user. Technological turbulence may be interpreted as the frequency of changes in an entire industry's technology. They argue that the greater the technological turbulence, the weaker the relationship between a market orientation and business performance.

Jaworski and Kohli (1993) have supported the argument that market orientation is a stronger determinant of performance in industries with low technological turbulence. They argue that market orientation may be a less important determinant of business performance in industries with high-changing technology compared to technologically stable industry environments. This argument is expected in a technologically turbulent environment because superior R&D capabilities offer an organization a superior competitive advantage based on a superior ability to deal with a rapidly changing technological environment and to provide customers with the demanded new technology. In contrast, organizations that operate in industries with stable technologies are not gaining any benefit by relying on technology for gaining competitive advantage. They should instead look for another dimension for obtaining competitive advantage and creating superior value for their customers and this could be market orientation.

It can be argued that, in a technologically turbulent industry, an organization's survival may depend on how it reacts to competitive change in the product/service offering. A firm's survival may also be dependent upon the right choice of positioning among competitor groups seeking to meet the needs of specific market segments.

In spite of the likelihood of a negative counter-relationship between market orientation and technology, market orientation is an important predictor of business performance, especially in the long run, whereas the benefit of technology could be in the short run. Moreover, market orientation is a better means to developing a competitive advantage than technology, because it enables an organization to understand customer needs and offer products and services that meet those needs. The benefit of market orientation is long lasting, whereas the benefit of technology is transient.

Market turbulence

Market turbulence refers to changes in the composition of customers and their preferences. According to Jaworski and Kohli (1993) the greater the market turbulence, the stronger the market orientation/business performance relationship. They assert that in a relatively stable market, with a fixed set of customers whose preferences are stable, a high level of market orientation is likely to have little effect on performance because little adjustment to marketing mix elements is needed. Organizations that operate in the more turbulent markets are most likely to modify their products and service continually in order to capture customers' changing preferences. Jaworski and Kohli (1993, 57) stated: 'Businesses operating in the more turbulent markets are likely to have a greater need to be market oriented (i.e. to track and respond to evolving customer preferences) compared to businesses in stable markets.'

Higher levels of market turbulence can be expected to help organizations to have a greater understanding of customer's changing needs and preferences. This understanding offers the organization a greater opportunity to influence positively customers' perception of the organization's product/service quality and to achieve new offering by developing new products/services geared to changing marketplace needs. Conversely, organizations that fail to modify their service/product to changing marketplace needs will have higher levels of customer turnover. High levels of customer turnover in a turbulent market environment leads to the increased importance of a customer satisfaction to maintain customer loyalty and customer retention.

Antecedents to market orientation

Antecedents to a market orientation in organizations include a set of specific senior management characteristics; emphasis, leadership and professionalism (Figure 2.5).

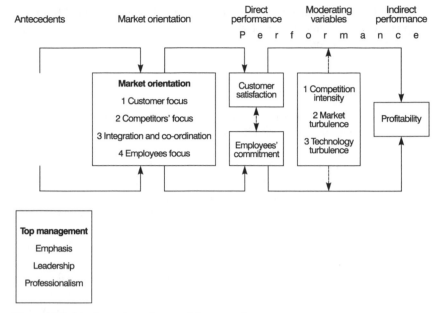

Figure 2.5 *Market orientation model: antecedents*

Like senior management characteristics, organizational characteristics and external environmental factors can be used as antecedents to market orientation (Jaworski and Kohli, 1993). With regard to the organizational characteristics, departmentalization and formalization, for example, it is not meaningful to be considered as antecedents to a market orientation because these factors, as well as human and financial resource factors, are internal factors and controlled by senior managers. Thus, senior managers can highlight and determine employee activities that translate the market orientation strategy into practice. Moreover, the organizational factors can be found in almost every organization but top management alone can implement the necessary changes in order to create a successful strategy of market orientation. Also, organizational factors were found not to be related to market orientation (Jaworski and Kohli, 1993; Slater and Narver, 1994). For the reasons mentioned above and for the purpose of this chapter, these factors should not be covered as predictors of a market orientation. They are therefore not included in this chapter.

Senior managers have no control over external factors such as government regulations, the economic situation and competition. An organization should cope with these elements rather than seek to change them. In addition, top management can do nothing (or very little) with these factors in order to exhibit a market-oriented strategy. Therefore, as it could be argued that these aspects should not be a prerequisite to market orientation, they are excluded from this chapter. Top management characteristics are discussed as the only antecedents to a market orientation.

Top management emphasis

Top management emphasis plays a very important critical role in shaping an organization's culture and orientation. The critical role of senior management in fostering an organization's orientation and value is well reflected in the literature (for example, Felton, 1959; Jaworski and Kohli, 1993; Levitt, 1960; Webster, 1988). In general, these studies view top management characteristics as influencing the value and the direction of an organization. An organization is not likely to be market oriented unless it gets clear signals from top managers to listen and respond to the needs and wants of customers and market. Webster (1988), for example, claims that customer-oriented values and beliefs are uniquely the responsibility of top management.

For an organization to be market oriented, every individual in the organization – manager or employee – must participate in satisfying customers. Also, there must be an environment where everybody is working closely with each other with a clear understanding of roles and responsibilities. Top management can develop this kind of participation, provide proper environment and excite all members of the organization with the corporate vision and the objectives that need to be achieved.

Market orientation is facilitated by the amount of emphasis placed by the top management on market orientation. Top management can dedicate a vast amount of its time to creating and then sustaining a customer focus throughout all layers and functions of an organization.

Consistent with the above discussion, empirical findings concerning the main determinants of market orientation have concluded that there is a very strong direct relationship between top management emphasis and market orientation (see for example Alshammri, 1997; Jaworski and Kohli, 1993).

Top management leadership

The term leadership means different things to different people. Researchers usually define leadership according to their individual perspective and the aspect of the phenomenon of most interest to them. There are almost as many definitions of leadership as there are persons who have attempted to define the concept. Leadership has been defined in terms of individual traits, behaviour, influence over other people, interaction patterns, role relationships, occupation of an administrative position and perception by others regarding legitimacy of influence.

For the purpose of this chapter, leadership is defined as: the process of influencing the activities of an organized group towards goal achievement in a certain time. This definition reflects the role of leaders in shaping an organization's culture.

It should be noted here that studying the leadership is not the scope and purpose of this chapter. However, the role of leaders in guiding and steering organizations is highlighted.

Leaders first recognize the need for change – for being market oriented, for example – then create a vision, set goals, and develop a strategic plan to achieve the stated goals. Creating an effective vision or strategic intent does not stop with a smart slogan or statement; it requires appropriate implementation efforts. The corporate vision must be conveyed to every employee. In this regard, leaders have the greatest potential for making the implementation process happen. They communicate their priorities, values, and concerns by their choice of things to ask about, measure, comment on, praise and criticize. Therefore, a firm's leaders can develop a customer value strategy that focuses on a unique market segment or has a distinctly differentiated value proposition. To meet the challenge, an organization must have the appropriate leadership capabilities in place to initiate and implement competitive change. However, through implementing a market-oriented strategy process, individual leaders can be schooled in the art of building management teams and networks, and they are thus more effective in dealing with the challenge of change (Slater, 1997).

A leader is responsible for providing direction, protection and orientation, for managing conflict and shaping norms. A leader provides direction by identifying the organization's adaptive challenge and framing the key questions and issues. A leader protects people by managing the rate of change and orients people to new roles and responsibilities by clarification of business realities and key values. A leader helps expose conflict, viewing it as the engine of creativity and learning and helps the organization maintain those norms that must endure and challenge those that need to change.

From the preceding discussions, it could be concluded that quality of leadership is one of the most important determinants of meeting success. And leadership is essential to the competitiveness and development of an organization. Consequently, leadership could be considered as a determinant of a market-oriented strategy. Therefore, leadership is included in this chapter as an antecedent to a market orientation.

Professionalism of top management

Professionalism of senior management has been identified to be the key factor in developing a customer orientation and consequently achieving greater success in the marketplace (Drucker, 1988; Kotler, 1997).

To ensure consistent quality service to customers, top management is increasingly making continuous efforts to enhance professionalism by attending a wide range of management sessions, seminars and conferences at well-respected institutions.

Professional improvement helps top management to better understand and service their customers and partners. Senior managers who strongly identify with their profession tend to advocate continual professional education for themselves as well as for other members of management. They make use of their professional societies and other professional development programmes. The activities of professional education are aimed at improving the knowledge and skills of organizational members so that they can ensure consistently better service to respective customers, both internally and externally. Providing better service, in turn, requires information about customers and the things that make them satisfied. Knowing these things and fulfilling them is the core philosophy of market orientation. Thus, professionalism of senior management and market orientation are related phenomena, and following on from this, professionalism of senior management could be deemed to be a prerequisite of a market orientation.

In spite of the theoretical and anecdotal support for the association between professionalism of top management and market orientation, it is surprisingly that, to date, no empirical work has been done to investigate the proclamation. However, the author has tried to examine this proclamation and to test this relationship (Alshammri, 1997). The study empirically investigated the relationship between professionalism and market orientation and found a significant relationship between the level of professional education and the degree of market orientation in the service organization sector. This finding is consistent with the view found in the literature.

Examples of best practice companies

There now follow some examples of companies who exhibit market-oriented behaviour in one way or another and their respective business results (Table 2.4). In each company, the role of top management in making the organization culture more consumer driven (including customer, employees, partners etc.) is the hallmark of the company's success. Without a clear signal from the chief executive officers (CEOs) to establish, emphasize and maintain such critical success factors, these companies would not have been successful.

For instance, Southwest Airlines' success may be due largely to Herb Kelleher, CEO, by placing an unusual focus on creating value for employees. The customer comes second at Southwest. According to him, the Southwest philosophy is to put its employees first and they will take care of the customers: taking care of company employees automatically produces better care of the customers.

Southwest has a unique recipe for personal and business success in a highly competitive industry. It all begins with the *fundamentals*, which are emphasized in every course offered at the company (Bruce, 1997). These include:

1 Hire for attitude; train for skill.
2 Do it better, faster, cheaper.
3 Deliver positively outrageous customer service (POS) to both internal and external customers.
4 Walk a mile in someone else's shoes.
5 Take accountability and ownership.
6 Celebrate and let your hair down.
7 Celebrate your mistakes as well as your triumphs.
8 Keep the corporate culture alive and well.

Linking human spirit and personal performance to training, and corporate vision to delivering customer service, emphasized by its top management, is the key to Southwest Airlines' success in the aviation industry, and this is the case with other best practice model companies.

Model of market orientation

Based on his own empirical research, and findings in the literature, the author has developed a model for improving business performance measures (Figure 2.6). This improvement could be achieved by building customer satisfaction through quality, service and value. Quality, service and value can be achieved by pursuing a value-driven customer strategy through the integration and co-ordination of all departments in an organization. Without the integration and co-ordination, company departments often act to maximize their own interests rather than those of the company and customers. This could result in a situation whereby each department erects walls that slow down the delivery of quality customer service. The proposed model (framework) comprises five variables:

1 Antecedents to market orientation (top management characteristics: emphasis, leadership, and professionalism).
2 Market orientation (customer focus, competitors' focus, integration and co-ordination, and employee focus).

Table 2.4 *Examples of model companies*

Company	Senior management emphasis on:							Results compared to rivals
	Customer	Service	Quality	Employees	Integration	Process	Cleanliness	
AT&T	✓	✓	✓	✓	✓	✓		Excellent
American Express	✓	✓	✓	✓	✓	✓		Excellent
British Airways	✓	✓	✓	✓	✓	✓	✓	Excellent
Southwest Airlines	✓	✓	✓	✓	✓	✓	✓	Excellent
McDonalds	✓	✓	✓	✓	✓	✓	✓	Excellent
Pizza Hut	✓	✓	✓	✓	✓	✓	✓	Excellent
Toyota	✓	✓	✓	✓	✓	✓		Excellent
Citibank	✓	✓	✓	✓	✓	✓		Excellent
Microsoft	✓	✓	✓	✓	✓	✓		Excellent
Hilton	✓	✓	✓	✓	✓	✓	✓	Excellent
Harvard University	✓	✓	✓	✓	✓	✓		Excellent
Mercedes Benz	✓	✓	✓	✓	✓	✓		Excellent

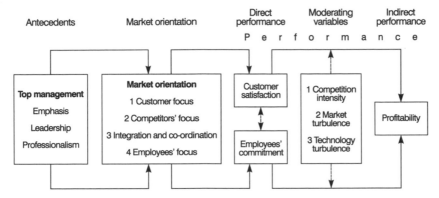

Figure 2.6 *Model of market orientation*

3 Direct consequences of market orientation (employee commitment, and customer satisfaction).
4 Moderating variables (competition intensity, market turbulence, and technological turbulence).
5 Indirect consequences of market orientation (profitability).

In very simple words, the framework suggests that adopting a market orientation in an organization relies on senior management characteristics. Market orientation, in turn, leads to profitability through satisfied customers and committed employees moderated by competition intensity, market turbulence and technological turbulence.

Is market orientation expensive?

It is quite apparent that market orientation does have an effect on customer satisfaction, employee commitment towards customers and business performance measures. However, is it expensive to implement? Harris and Piercy (1997) think not: they compare non-market-oriented and market-oriented management from a cost point of view and conclude that cost is not the critical barrier to developing a market orientation (Table 2.5).

Developing and sustaining high levels of market orientation does not place an unlimited drain on the limited resources of an organization. There are already many resource-consuming activities present in almost every organization, the cost of which could be shifted towards exhibiting a market orientation. What is really required is awareness, emphasis and commitment from the top management of an organization. Market orientation should be

Table 2.5 *Comparing non-market-orientated and market-oriented management*

Activities and resources	Non-market oriented	Market oriented	Extra cost
Training and development	Training in procedure etiquette	Training in customer service	Minimal
Information systems	Disseminating data on costs and revenues	Disseminating information about customers and market	Minimal
Formal planning	Planning around products	Planning around customers	None
Reward systems	Rewards linked to sales	Rewards linked to customer satisfaction	None
Communication systems	Data on new procedures	Communication of customer needs	None
Recruitment and induction	Select solely on formal qualifications	Select on customer service capabilities	None
Management time	Geared towards sales	Geared towards customers	None

Source: Harris and Piercy (1997, 38)

considered as an investment that would pay off not today, but tomorrow and beyond.

How can a firm be market oriented?

Market orientation has been seen to be an important determinant of a business performance (financially and non-financially). However, here are some tips for positive behaviour that could help organizations to become market driven (see also Figure 2.7):

- emphasis, commitment, and involvement of top management
- determination of customer expectations
- measurement techniques
- customer satisfaction through employees
- employee empowerment to respond to consumer needs
- innovation through customer feedback

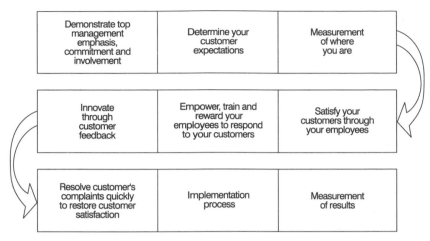

Figure 2.7 *Tips for implementing a market orientation strategy*

- complaint strategy process
- implementation
- measurement.

Conclusion

From the preceding discussions, it could be concluded that market orientation does have a significant and positive influence on business performance in one way or another. Hence, market orientation could be used for superior competitiveness and, ultimately, to achieve superior performance. Even though the customer value delivery concept is likely to be the next major shift in managerial practice, there is no contradiction between market orientation and the newly evolving concept. Customer value, learning of customer value and the skills that top management will need to create and implement superior customer value strategies cannot be achieved without creating a market-oriented organization. This is because market orientation is inherently a learning orientation and is a step in the right direction towards achieving superior delivery of customer value. This ability gives the market-driven business an advantage in the speed and effectiveness of its response to opportunities and threats. Market-driven firms are distinguished by an ability to sense events and trends in their markets ahead of their competitors. They can anticipate more accurately the responses to actions designed to retain or attract customers, improve channel relations or defeat competitors. They can act on information in a timely, coherent manner because the assumptions about the market are broadly shared.

Summary

Market orientation consists of several dimensions:

- customer focus (quality orientation, service orientation, customer value orientation)
- employee focus (empowering and caring)
- integration and co-operation (making the whole organization work in harmony)
- competitor focus (keeping eyes on rivals).

This chapter has shown the following:

- The degree of market orientation is positively related to quality, customer satisfaction, and employee organizational commitment.
- Market orientation influences the level of organizational commitment within an organization.
- Organizations that maintain a healthy employee focus and a co-operative internal work environment are more likely to have higher levels of customer treatment and caring as well as empowerment of employees.
- Top management plays a critical role in shaping a market-oriented strategy. A market-oriented strategy is more driven by top management's philosophical thinking than by the external environment.
- The critical criteria do not relate to what the organization says, but to what it does. Success comes from the consistent, on-going implementation of customer-driven principles, rather than the mere recognition of the principles.
- Cost is not the critical barrier to being a market-oriented organization. What is really required is an awareness, emphasis, and commitment from top management.
- The cost of some resource-consuming activities could be shifted towards exhibiting a market orientation.
- Market orientation should be considered as an investment, which would pay off in the future.
- There is no single complete solution to remedy all business problems. However, market orientation has been seen to be an important determinant in business performance (financially and non-financially).
- The market orientation model should be utilized as a generic model and a framework for making an empirical attempt to verify the relationship between the variables in it. Although study has shown that there are significant relationships between antecedents to market orientation, market orientation and multiple performance measures, the author hopes that the model will be further tested in different environments and industries to better understand the market orientation theory and its implications.

Acknowledgements

I wish to express my gratitude to Professor Mohamed Zairi for his encouragement, support, and inspiration. I would also like to thank my two brothers for their unbounded support. Finally, my overriding debt continues to be to my wife, who provided me with the time, support, and environment needed throughout this period of my life.

References

Alshammri, S. D. (1997) Market orientation and business performance in service organization. Unpublished thesis, University of Bradford.

Anderson, E. W. and Sullivan, M. W. (1993) The antecedents and consequences of customer satisfaction for firms. *Marketing Science*, **12**(2), 125–43.

Babakus, E. and Boller, G. W. (1992) An empirical assessment of the SERVQUAL scale. *Journal of Business Research*, **24**, 253–68.

Bearden, W. O. and Teel, J. E. (1993) Selected determinants of consumer satisfaction and complaint reports. *Journal of Marketing Research*, **20**, January, 21–8.

Berry, L., Parasuraman, A. and Zeithaml, V. (1994) Improving service quality in America: lessons learned. *Academy of Management Executive*, **8**(2), 32–52.

Bitner, M. J. (1990) Evaluating service encounters the effects of physical surroundings and employee responses. *Journal of Marketing*, **54** April, 69–82.

Bruce, A. (1997) Southwest: back to the fundamentals. *HRFOCUS*, March, 11.

Buttle, F. (1996) SERVQUAL: review, critique, research agenda. *European Journal of Marketing*, **30**(1), 8–32.

Buzzell, R. D. and Gale, B. T. (1987) *The PIMS Principles*. The Free Press.

Carman, J. M. (1990) Consumer perceptions of service quality: an assessment of SERVQUAL dimensions. *Journal of Retailing*, **66**(1), 33–53.

Chakravarthy, B. S. (1986) Measuring strategic performance. *Strategic Management Journal*, **7**, 437–58.

Chvala, R. J. (1991) How to launch a market-oriented biz-to-biz firm. *Marketing News*, **25**(5), 4 March, 8.

Cronin, J. J. and Taylor, S. A. (1992) Measuring service quality: a reexamination and extension. *Journal of Marketing*, **56**(3), 55–68.

Crosby, P. B. (1979) *Quality is Free: the Art of Making Quality Certain*.

Deshpande, R., Farley, J. U. and Webster, F. E. Jr (1993) Corporate culture, customer orientation, and innovativeness in Japanese firms: a quadrad analysis. *Journal of Marketing*, **57**, January, 23–37.

Deming, W. E. (1986) *Out of the Crisis*. MIT Press.

Drucker, P. F. (1954) *The Practice of Management*. Harper and Row.

Drucker, P. F. (1988) The management and the world's work. *Harvard Business Review*, September–October, 65–76.

Eugene, W. A., Fornell, C. and Donald, R. L. (1994) Customer satisfaction, market share, and profitability: findings from Sweden. *Journal of Marketing*, **58**, July, 53–66.

Felton, A. P. (1959) Making the marketing concept work. *Harvard Business Review*, **37**, July–August, 55–65.

Fornell, C. (1992a) A national customer satisfaction barometer: the Swedish experience. *Journal of Marketing*, **56**, January, 6–21.

Fornell, C. (1992b) A method for customer satisfaction and measuring its impact on profitability. *International Public Relations Review*, **15**(3), 6–10.

Garvin, D. A. (1988) *Managing Quality: the Strategic and Competitive Edge*. The Free Press.

Gronroos, C. (1990) *Service Management and Marketing: Managing the Moments of Truth in Service Competition*. Lexington Books.

Harris, L. C. and Piercy, N. F. (1997) Market orientation is free: the real costs of becoming market-led. *Management Decision*, **35**(1), 33–8.

Henkoff, R. (1994) Service is everybody's business. *Fortune*, **27**, 48–60.

Houston, F. S. (1986) The marketing concept: what it is and what it is not. *Journal of Marketing*, **50**(2), 81–7.

Jaworski, B. J. and Kohli, A. K. (1993) Market orientation: antecedents and consequences. *Journal of Marketing*, **57**, July, 53–70.

Kohli, A. K. and Jaworski, B. J. (1990) Market orientation: the construct, research propositions, and managerial implications. *Journal of Marketing*, **54**, April, 1–18.

Kotler, P. (1997) *Marketing Management: Analysis, Planning, Implementation and Control*. 9th edn, Prentice Hall.

Levitt, T. (1960) Marketing myopia. *Harvard Business Review*, **38**, 24–47.

Lovelock, C. H. (1996) *Service Marketing*. 3rd edn, Prentice Hall.

McNamara, C. P. (1972) The present status of the marketing concept. *Journal of Marketing*, **36**(1), 50–7.

Miller, C. (1993) US firms lag in meeting global quality standards. *Marketing News*, 15 February.

Mohr-Jackson, I. (1991) Broadening the market orientation: an added focus on internal customers. *Human Resource Management*, **30**(4), 455–67.

Morgan, N. A. and Piercy, N. F. (1992) Market-led quality. *Industrial Marketing Management*, **21**(2), 111–18.

Narver, J. C. and Slater, S. F. (1990) The effect of a market orientation on business profitability. *Journal of Marketing*, **54**, October, 20–35.

Oakland, J. S. (1989) *Total Quality Management*. Butterworth-Heinemann.

Oliver, R. L. (1980) A cognitive model of the antecedents and consequences of satisfaction decisions. *Journal of Marketing Research*, **17**, November, 460–9.

Oliver, R. L. (1989) Processing of the satisfaction response in consumption: a suggested framework and research propositions. *Journal of Consumer Satisfaction, Dissatisfaction and Complaint Behavior*, **2**, 1–16.

Oliver, R. L. (1993) A conceptual model of service quality and service satisfaction: compatible goals, different concepts, in advances in services marketing and management: research and practice. In T. A. Swartz, D. E. Bowen and S. W. Brown, eds, vol. 2, pp. 65–85.

Parasuraman, A., Zeithaml, V. A. and Berry, L. L. (1985) A conceptual model of service quality and its implications for future research. *Journal of Marketing*, **49**, Fall, 41–50.

Parasuraman, A., Zeithaml, V. A. and Berry, L. L. (1988) SERVQUAL: a multiple-item scale for measuring consumer perception of service quality. *Journal of Retailing*, **64**(1), 12–40.

Patterson, P. G., Johnson, L. W. and Spreng, R. A. (1997) Modeling the determinants of customer satisfaction for business-to-business professional services. *Journal of The Academy of Marketing Science*, **25**(1), 4–17.

Porter, M. E. (1985) *Competitive Advantage: Creating and Sustaining Superior Performance*. The Free Press.

Raju, P. S., Lonial, S. C., and Gupta, Y. P. (1995) Market orientation and performance in the hospital industry. *Journal of Health Care Marketing*, **15**(4), 34–41.

Ruekert, R. W. (1992) Developing a market orientation: an organizational strategy perspective. *International Journal of Research in Marketing*, **9**(3), 225–45.

Rust, Roland T. and Zahorik, A. J. (1993) Customer satisfaction, customer retention, and market share. *Journal of Retailing*, **69**(2), 193–215.

Shapiro, B. P. (1988) What the hell is 'market oriented'? *Harvard Business Review*, **66**, November–December, 119–25.

Slater, S. F. and Narver, J. C. (1994) Does competitive environment moderate the market orientation–performance relationship? *Journal of Marketing*, **58**, 46–55.

Slater, S. (1997) Developing a customer value-based theory of the firm. *Journal of Academy of Marketing Science*, **25**(2), 162–7.

Taylor, S. A. and Baker, T. L. (1994) An assessment of the relationship between service quality and customer satisfaction in the formation of consumer purchase intention. *Journal of Retailing*, **70**(2), 163–78.

Taylor, S. A. and Cronin, J. J. Jr (1994) Modeling patient satisfaction and service quality. *Journal of Health Care Marketing*, **14**, Spring, 34–44.

Webster, F. E. (1988) Rediscovering the marketing concept. *Business Horizons*, **31**, May–June, 29–39.

Wong, V. and Saunders, J. (1993) Business orientation and corporate success. *Journal of Strategic Marketing*, **1**, 20–40.

Woodruff, R. B. (1997) Customer value: the next source for competitive advantage. *Journal of The Academy of Marketing Science*, **25**(2), 139–53.

Zairi, M., Letza, S. and Oakland, J. (1994) Does TQM impact on bottom-line results? *The TQM Magazine*, **6**(1), 38–43.

3 Idea generation: creative problem-solving and innovation

Richard Duggan

This chapter examines tools and techniques for promoting creativity within business organizations. It begins with an extensive review of the creative process. First, the role of the individual as a creative entity is made, followed by a discussion of creativity within and between teams. The range of tools and techniques that can be used to enhance creative performance are highlighted. Coverage of creative problem techniques for the individual includes morphological analysis and problem redefinition and at the team level includes synectics, hitchhiking, creative listening and Taguchi techniques. The chapter also provides suggestions on how to run effective creative sessions, and addresses implementation. Illustrative examples and cases are widely used to enrich the discussion.

The best way to predict the future is to invent it. (Alan Kay, Apple computer scientist)

Introduction and definitions

'Creativity is thinking of novel and appropriate ideas.' 'Innovation is the successful implementation.' These were the definitions presented by Dr William Coyne at the Annual Innovation Lecture in 1996. He was representing the pragmatic viewpoint of 3M, widely regarded as one of the most innovative and successful companies of the current era. These descriptions of innovation and creativity are close to those used by the Department of Trade (DTI) Innovation Unit: for example, 'Innovation is the successful exploitation of new ideas.' However, for the definition of creativity this author prefers to be slightly more conceptual: 'Creativity is the ability to look where everyone else is looking and see what no one else can see' (Szent-Gyorgi). This definition seems to link the needs of the business person, the scientist and technologist for new ideas and novel problem solutions, with the perspectives of the artist, musician and poet and, indeed, many others in the creative arts.

Creativity spans the ability to totally break the paradigm and move one's field of enterprise into a completely new dimension, through to the ability to perceive new routes to solve day-to-day problems of all types. These can range from finding new ways of raising funds for a favourite charity, to correctly identifying the new and surprising meaning of research data. It can mean identifying new markets for skills or company capabilities by looking through the surface level to the unique competencies represented within those skills.

Components of the innovation and creative process

The European study on creativity and innovativeness in R&D (EIRMA) has found it valuable to look at the creative and innovative programme in four stages:

- the improvement of an individual's ability to use creative potential in solving problems
- the construction of a creative environment in which people can operate productively
- the ability of interdisciplinary groups to work creatively and to their full potential and, equally importantly, for them to work in partnership with each other rather than using individual groups within an organization to optimize their own capabilities at the expense of wider synergy with other teams or individuals
- successfully moving from an original idea through to successful, profitable or beneficial implementation.

This final phase is a process little studied in the UK. This missing skill contributes significantly to the belief that Britain has long been regarded as a highly creative nation but is very poor in turning its creativity into globally dominant innovation.

It is convenient in this chapter to use this four-stage structure and the first issue is to address creativity at the level of the individual. Can creativity be taught?

Helping individuals to reach their creative potential

In the 1960s, in America, work was undertaken to study the belief that scientists 'burnt out' and had lost their creativity by their mid-40s. An experimental project was set up in which tests of creativity were devised and validated by experts in the field, and a group of 45-year-old scientists were studied. The conclusion that their mean creativity was only 2 per cent seemed to support the hypothesis until parallel studies on scientists of 40, 35 and 25 years old respectively produced similar results. It was only when the age group dropped down to below 20 that one began to see a significant increase; indeed, the creativity of 6 year olds was almost 100 per cent. On returning to the definition 'to look where everyone else is looking and see what no one else can see' one can find an explanation in that formal education tends to teach children to see things exactly as others are seeing them. Hence latent creativity becomes suppressed in most individuals as they move through the educational process.

Because most educated adults operate at such a low creative level, it is relatively easy to use creative problem-solving techniques to leverage their creative potential without attempting to address the question about whether creativity is innate or can be taught. The author's experience during thirty years of using such techniques is that people can relatively easily be taught to increase the proportion of the innate creativity they exploit in everyday life. There follows a review of creative problem-solving techniques that can help with this process and encourage people to use their innate creativity more effectively (Synectics, 1971). We begin with Synectics.

Synectics

The Synectics company in Cambridge, Massachusetts, grew out of the problem-solving group of Arthur D. Little, the American management consultants. In the 1950s, this group, led by Prince and Gordon, had an excellent reputation for solving apparently intractable client problems. Following internal discussions on why they were so successful and how they could maximize and improve this effectiveness, the individual members of the Synectics company kept detailed records of the processes each individual used which led to the effective solution of problems. When they compared notes after a year, they discovered that each had a very similar although apparently idiosyncratic strategy for solving difficult problems.

The first phase was to bring together the problem owner and a carefully chosen group of people who might bring alternative perspectives to the problem; in other words, 'seeing the problem through fresh eyes'. If this process failed to produce new productive viewpoints in a relatively short time, it was observed that further attempts to identify new routes to solutions were ineffective. It was far better to break up the session for relaxation or recreation. A key observation of the consultants was that for difficult problems, after initial exposure to the 'problem as given' and the unsuccessful approaches attempted for solutions, they had a much better record of producing solutions when they were not consciously considering the problem. Solutions seemed to come when they were engrossed in an unrelated task demanding short-term concentration without the requirement of profound thought. For example, building a wall, sleeping, swimming, horse riding or playing tennis, chess or cards were productive activities. During these other activities, a sometimes completely novel solution to the problem would often come to mind.

The environment could also be changed to encourage these moments of high creativity. It was discovered that creativity could be further stimulated by considering analogous situations in completely different fields and disciplines. Searching for analogues in one's own memory, again using very different fields to the one under investigation, was an equally effective approach. Half-forgotten childhood memories, fairy stories and so on were a particularly fertile source of productive analogies. It was further observed that when people got into the habit of using the half hidden recesses of the mind not consciously close to the area of the problem, their ability to produce highly innovative viewpoints on the solution was enhanced. This is perhaps best illustrated by example. If a problem is expressed as 'how to drain a mine', most session members will immediately start thinking of engineering principles, pumps, buckets, reciprocating mechanisms and so forth. If the problem is redefined as 'how to make water fly' or 'how to make water run uphill', their viewpoints and mental images are completely different, even though both of these problem redefinitions, if solved, would achieve a solution to the original problem.

In summary to assist in difficult problem-solving:

- encourage different viewpoints from people looking at the problem through the eyes of very different disciplines
- allow the subconscious mind to operate on the problem by concentrating on some other pursuit, one which requires the full attention of the conscious mind but has no deeper implications
- find analogies to the problem in a different field of endeavour
- attempt to redefine the problem in the language of very different disciplines, using one's own knowledge of topics other than those of the problem, to look for analogies that will enable new viewpoints to be found
- look particularly for analogies among one's fund of deeply hidden knowledge.

The team who developed this problem-solving technique subsequently left the management consultancy and set up their own company teaching people to become more effective in creative problem-solving. These highly talented 'pupils', nominated by leading American corporations, worked with the Synectics company to further develop and refine the approach.

The author was trained by George Prince in the mid-1960s and has used the technique extensively.

How the creative mind works

In tackling creative challenges, it is useful to work from two simple hypotheses about the human mind. First, the mind has an enormous reservoir of stored knowledge across the range of topics to which we have been exposed in our experience. In tackling a problem, for example in engineering, one tends to fall into the trap of using only that part of the brain associated with engineering experience. But because analogies are powerful in helping problems to be solved, everything one knows is potential material for developing new viewpoints. By learning how to scan one's own knowledge base more effectively, one can very rapidly increase the power to produce novel solutions. It is important to understand one's own mental approach to tackling problems, so this is discussed below.

A process was recently developed that would enable a very wide range of materials to be produced in a structure of an infinite labyrinth. Each cell looks very much like a tiny plastic practice golf ball, with a hole in the centre and smaller holes round the periphery. All the cells are uniform and inter-connected. This labyrinth could have a central cell size of ten millimicrons (μ). The reader is invited to note down this information, then find the answers in the 3 × 3 matrix shown in Figure 3.1. The axes of this matrix are: the *x* axis = *probability that the idea will succeed,* and *y* axis = *nearness to own experience.* A 1,1 idea is near to one's own experience and likely to succeed, while a 3,3 idea represents a very unfamiliar field with an unknown (low) chance of success.

Closeness to own area of activity

		Near 1	Intermediate 2	Far 3
High	1			
Intermediate	2			
Very speculative	3			

Probability of success

Figure 3.1 *Morphological analysis*

This matrix can be used very effectively to teach people a great deal about their own creative approach. First, are all ideas in the same box in the matrix? And, if so, which box? If someone's ideas are all 1,1, that person is likely to take a simple, pragmatic view of problems. If they are all in 3,3, that person's approach is highly speculative. The real test is to force solutions in every box within the matrix. This is an excellent mental process, which very rapidly increases one's ability to tap innate personal creativity.

The matrix also introduces *morphological analysis* as a technique in creative problem-solving. This is discussed later.

The second working hypothesis which the author uses for approaches to creativity concerns three levels of consciousness in the mind. These are the *conscious*, the *subconscious* (which may be working on a completely different agenda from the conscious mind at any time) and an intermediate stage sometimes called the *preconscious*. This last could be described as 'thoughts in transit' – data moving out of the conscious mind and into 'storage' and, while in transit, unavailable for action. This could explain why a person is sometimes unable to recall something they have just said ('What did I say just then?').

This model explains why it is better to absorb into the conscious mind the pertinent information relating to a difficult problem, and then to provide a buffer period (the period spent doing something different) before attempting to produce solutions.

In summary, a person wishing to improve their latent creativity should:

- learn to use all the knowledge rather than that traditionally associated with the area under discussion
- be more aware of the workings of the mind
- provide a creative environment while tackling difficult problems.

Creative problem-solving techniques for the individual

There are a number of techniques that are of value in helping personal creativity. Of these, morphological analysis is a excellent example, again best illustrated by analogy, as follows:

Liverpool City Council was asked to lead a creative session on what to do with derelict docks. The morphological analysis table as shown in Figure 3.2 was drawn up to help with the problem. The underlying logic of this table is this: as a potential use of a derelict dock is water sports, one should select as one axis the profitable aspects of a very *successful non-water-based sport*. This should be considered as a potential development within the water-based sport under consideration. Hence, in the one axis I have chosen *golf, and all the various strategies for commercializing different aspects of golf*, and have for comparison chosen *fishing*.

Golf	Equipment manufacture	Clothing manufacture	Golf club	Teaching professional	Practice driving range	Tournament
Fishing						

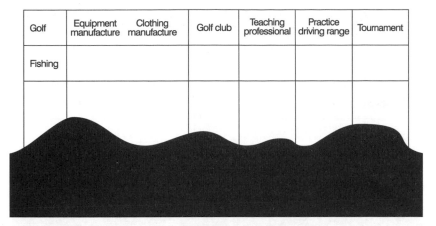

Figure 3.2 *Alternative uses of docks: morphological analysis (1)*

Each square of the table is then considered in response to the question: have all the known methodologies for making money from different aspects of golf been applied to fishing? For example, one can make money as a golf tutor in a golf club, which is where aspiring golfers naturally turn for tuition. But it is just as easy for the novice in fishing to find a fishing professional for tuition. You have therefore made an analogy between golf and fishing and solved part of the problem of what to do with the dock.

Another interesting comparison can be made with golf driving ranges. A golf driving range is a long way away conceptually from the game itself, yet in Japan, for example, driving ranges are enormously popular, despite the relative lack of golf courses. As a fishing analogy, does one need to have a remote waterway full of naturally occurring fish for there to be pleasure in the practice of fishing? Could a derelict dock be stocked with fish and developed to make it a source of pleasure for people who enjoy fishing? Do there have to be real fish? Could one scale up the equivalent of the fairground side-show where people fish with magnets for prizes? This could encourage aspiring fishermen to practise their art, and/or win a prize. This series of ideas triggered by the analysis table (Figure 3.3) for making money from fishing can then be replicated by considering other water-based sports, and indeed golf can be substituted for other non-water-based activities.

A further example of the use of morphological analysis in the social arena was our solution to the topic of doubling parish income at the local Catholic church:

On the one axis of our table we selected the different segments of the community to target, such as schoolteachers, pupils, daily mass attendants, Catholics who did not attend church, local shopkeepers, through to groups who

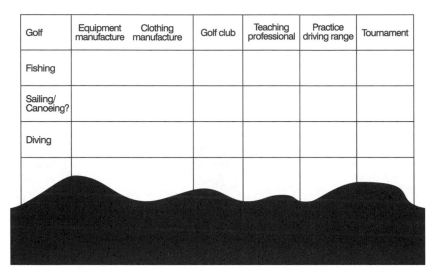

Golf	Equipment manufacture	Clothing manufacture	Golf club	Teaching professional	Practice driving range	Tournament
Fishing						
Sailing/ Canoeing?						
Diving						

Figure 3.3 *Alternative uses of docks: morphological analysis (2)*

disliked Catholics! On the other axis we chose methods used by charities for raising money, such as the church collection, the jumble sale, the Christmas fête, bingo sessions in the church hall open to parishioners, sessions open to all. We cast the net widely, including professional people using their skills on an annual basis on behalf of the church community. Finally, we assigned to each target group a sum we thought could be raised by the individual charity approach. In one sense the technique was too successful. The one idea of using professionals' skills on behalf of the church rapidly produced the required doubling of annual income on an ongoing basis without us being able to fully explore the rest of the target group analysis.

There are software tools available to aid the process. 'Seren' uses morphological analysis to enable the proprietors of small companies to identify new business opportunities for themselves. In a typical application, one axis is *the separate markets in which the company currently sells its product*, while the other axis is *the unique competencies of the company versus the competitors in achieving those sales*. The first question that arises for the small-business person is whether all the competencies of the company are being exploited in each sector in which he or she is selling products. If not, there should be obvious low-risk product opportunities. The second question is, 'What new markets could be exploited with the company's current expertise?' The final question is, 'If one new competence were added to the skill base of the company, what extra products could be sold into existing markets?'

Once the range of these questions has been explored, the software enables a business evaluation of the individual ideas. What is the potential size of the opportunity? Would new capital equipment be required to meet the demand? Would new company skills be required, such as foreign language skills? Only when the owner is unable to provide a reasonable 'guestimate' in answer to the business evaluation questions does the process stop and a colour square assigned to rank the idea's future potential. The user finally identifies two changes in circumstance that would make him or her return to the idea and exploit it further.

This system becomes an incubator for the ideas. Each time the computer is switched on the user can look at the mosaic of colour-coded incubating ideas and re-evaluate whether new circumstances make any one of the ideas more interesting and exploitable.

Problem redefinition

One can borrow from the Synectics technique to help create new personal viewpoints on an existing problem. If one defines the problem in writing as 'problem as given' and then consciously attempts to transpose the language of the problem into a diametrically different field, a range of new viewpoints rapidly emerges. These can enable the problem owner to see the issue in a new light. Problems are not often solved in a moment of inspiration, but by getting new viewpoints not previously considered, one can either make steady progress towards a solution or even occasionally see the completed solution emerge.

The scientific method

All students are taught the scientific method as the generalized approach to problem solution and some may find it incongruous to hear it discussed as a creative problem-solving technique.

There is, however, a great paradox in the scientific method: while it is often described as a logical progression from problem to solution, there are in fact two phases in which a pure divergent capability 'to look where everyone else is looking and see what no one else can see' is required. The first of these is the forming of the hypothesis. The description of great scientists as to how they have taken difficult and challenging data, data that has often been examined by other scientists, and have suddenly experienced a 'Eureka' moment in which they have seen that data in a completely new light is a good illustration of the ability 'to look where everyone else is looking and see what no one else can see'. If this phase requires pure divergent thinking, it would be appropriate for the scientist to have this extra skill.

Later in the scientific method there is a phase where the proof of the hypothesis is to predict events which, without the hypothesis, would be unpredictable. As a manager of a very large research laboratory the author found it extraordinary how few scientists understood this phase of the operation. When one has a hypothesis, there is a great tendency to undertake many experiments exploring different variables to broaden the data: to creep up on the hypothesis and perhaps make it more unlikely that it is incorrect. *This is not the scientific method.* The scientific method requires little experimentation if the highly creative question: 'If my hypothesis is correct, what can I now forecast that was previously impossible to predict?' can be resolved.

The cartoons in Figure 3.4 show Newton demonstrating his hypothesis that objects fall to earth because of an attraction between all bodies proportional to their relative mass. His proof was to predict the movement of the planets

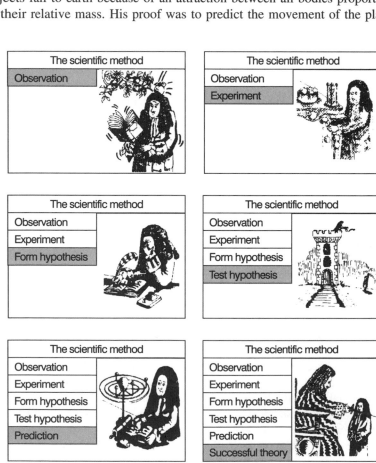

Figure 3.4 *The scientific method*

through the heavens and then have his hypothesis confirmed by known but independent observations. The author was once attempting to prove to a sceptical marketing-based company that mathematical techniques were more effective in predicting the value of advertising expenditure than the combined experience of the marketing and advertising staff and their brand advertising agencies. A brand in Italy was chosen as a test case. This was a brand which by any conventional analysis was profitable but was declining rapidly. The analysis was able to predict that, contrary to all popular experience, if investment were to be continued in the brand, it would stabilize and, if (as was expected) the competitor withdrew their advertising from the declining market sector, the brand would rebuild its volume share. This prediction was correct, and very profitable.

The proof of the mathematical approach was subsequently extended by taking a series of marketplace situations and correctly forecasting very unexpected strategies for increasing growth, price changes etc. The scientific method is a relevant approach to problem-solving for many disciplines. But for scientists in particular, paying close attention to the creative divergent skills as well as looking for the highly creative experiment that proves the hypotheses are extremely productive, both in the level of the individual and the level of the whole organization.

In summary, training in creative problem-solving techniques can rapidly assist people to increase their ability to solve problems in all aspects of their professional and personal lives. Simple mental exercises such as the morphological analysis evaluation of ideas or, indeed, the solving of cryptic crosswords while deliberately looking for new viewpoints in the interpretation in the clue, are useful exercises in enabling people to enhance their ability to be creative in the solution of everyday problems.

Creating the climate for creativity

In the 1990s, there have been a number of significant national studies in the UK on the characteristics of companies and enterprises that are outperforming the market (DTI). The culture of such companies, and the consequent capability to create a supportive climate for creativity and innovation is seen as the single most important ingredient of their successful 'mix'.

This conclusion has been regularly reinforced by leading innovators who have successively delivered the annual UK Innovation lectures. The UK Innovation Lectures, jointly sponsored by The Royal Society, The Royal Academy of Engineering, the CBI and the Design Council with the Innovation Unit of the DTI are delivered annually by an internationally reputed innovator. Inaugurated in 1992 the speakers have been Akio Morita, Sony (1992), Sir Paul Girolami, Glaxo (1993), Dr Lars Ramquist, Ericcson (1994),

Dr Peter Williams, Oxford Instruments (1995), Dr William Coyne, 3M (1996), Dr Keith Oates, Marks and Spencer (1997) and Richard Branson, Virgin (1998). The lectures are available as booklets from the Innovation Unit, DTI, 151 Buckingham Palace Road, London SW1W 9SS.

- In this organization, it is more acceptable to seek forgiveness than permission. People need to know that if they try something new and fail, they won't be punished. We expect innovation from everyone in the corporation; that means we have failures in every department, in every function. It is part of life. (3M.)
- You can create a sort of atmosphere in which odd-ball, off the wall ideas flourish and are encouraged. (Oxford Instruments.)
- Corporate culture is becoming a tool for gaining competitive edge: a tool for innovation and reaching strategic goals. (Ericsson.)

This is an improvement on the early days, when even in a very successful company committed to business excellence, a study of appraisal forms showed a very clear negative correlation between scores of judgement and creativity.

As people selected for senior roles in organizations must have excellent judgement, it would follow that those who are naturally creative should keep this talent hidden. This is clearly a self-destructive conclusion and it is very important in an organization that creativity is encouraged and revealed.

A further common theme of all the Innovation lectures is that all parts of the organization equally must be encouraged to be creative and innovative; the organization must not rely on any one part of itself to play a focal role in this initiative.

It is important to be an outwardly focused organization looking for ideas everywhere: among competitors, customers, academe, industries with a very different focus, and so on. The people of an organization represent the key strategic capability and it is crucial to ensure that everybody in the organization is fully contributing to all aspects in achieving the organizational goal. This concept of empowerment is a two-stage process. First, one must very clearly communicate the organizational desires, its mission, its goals and its culture, and then one must train the organization to recognize that every person irrespective of status can play a far more pervasive role in achieving the organizational goal than is usual in a typical hierarchical organization.

- Innovation is the constant search for a fresh approach to every aspect of running the business. (Marks and Spencer.)
- No short cuts exist to successful innovations, you must cover practically every aspect of modern industry, R&D skills and basic technologies, advanced production, totally quality management, marketing, sales and local market presence. (Ericsson.)

● The innovation mandate can only succeed in an environment which nurtures it. Declare the importance of innovation, it needs to become part of the company's image, part of its vision. (3M.)

Personnel are our most competitive asset because no other resources are capable of long-term growth and improvement. Be tolerant of initiative and the mistakes that occur because of it: people need to know that if they try something new and fail, they won't be punished. Most organizations believe in product edge; fewer believe in people edge.

The importance of a creative culture

There is a great deal of consensus on the importance of a creative culture in an organization to business success. Over a number of years, the Innovation Unit has involved itself with a number of key partners, notably the Confederation of British Industry (CBI), in identifying the character-istics of the culture within organizations that contribute to business success. The outcome of this study was described in the highly successful *Winning Report*, which has achieved the DTI Best Practice record for the publication in most demand by industry since its publication. The report concludes that:

● winning companies are led by visionary, enthusiastic champions of change
● companies know the requirements of their customers intimately, often able to anticipate future customer needs
● they welcome the challenge of demanding customers and constantly strive to learn from the customers and indeed their suppliers
● they share the business vision with their staff and empower them to use their skills to the full in achieving the business goals
● they constantly strive to introduce new and differentiated products and strive to win by delighting the customers
● above all they understand and stress the importance of harnessing the talent of the entire organization: 'a good idea does not care who has it'.

A follow-up study exploring those companies that have dramatically improved their performance by harnessing the full talents of their workforce has been published. It is called *Partnerships with People* (September 1997), using a very similar methodology for that in the *Winning Report*. The overall conclusions were that, while for a wide variety of companies with different histories and different markets and who are at different stages in their development cycle there can be no panacea for success, in general, all companies agreed on the overall importance of a series of values.

The following was also found:

- The goals and values of the company must be shared throughout the organization. This requires a shared business planning process across the total business, a supportive but competitive culture, comprehensive development of people, flexible, multiple teaming across the different functions of the company, an extensive three-way communication from top management to the workforce and the receptacle route and also across the different teams and functions of the company.
- In terms of business process, the business plan is key to aligning the whole company and it must be understood by everybody. While there is varying involvement in the planning process, there must be a feeling of participation and there must be measures and benchmarks to identify progress against long-term targets and people issues are intrinsic to the plan.
- Developing the appropriate culture is subtle. The culture must be led and managed and the required culture must be a high performing one that also enables people to develop and make mistakes. It must involve everybody. Shared values must underpin the culture and once the appropriate culture is established, it must be regarded as the most precious attribute of an organization and be continually nurtured and reinforced.
- The development of people is the single most striking characteristic of the wide range of companies studied. Team and individual training is evident and everybody gets relevant training, with Investors in People and National Vocational Qualifications (NVQs) used effectively as part of this overall training plan. The training has specific targets to shape the culture and training is also recognition and is valued highly by participants.
- Cross-functional teams are the building blocks of the organization. It has to be recognized that teamworking is difficult and has to be learnt and that management changes from control to facilitation. There is a balance to be struck between teamwork and individual inputs.
- The most powerful mode of communication is behaviour: 'Don't listen to what I say, watch what I do.' Communication is a responsibility shared by all. In many companies communication from the management to the workforce is well developed, but upward and horizontal communication has been much more neglected. Communication must be open, credible and honest, with communication of difficult and painful messages being as open as the moral boosting messages, and for this, a wide variety of tools are necessary. All the companies who have moved to this modern participative style of management have recognized that there are difficult balances to be struck at all stages. The shared values that must be worked on are:

  – mutual trust
  – honesty
  – risk taking

– openness
– mutual respect
– fairness
– a low blame culture
– learning
– commitment

• and there are paradoxes to be managed at all levels. The culture must be tough but tender, demanding but blame free, structured but fluid, proud but humble. It must learn from its competitors, customers, and suppliers and be radical but evolutionary, disciplined but innovative, confident but constantly self critical. It is recognized by most companies that the journey to a participative culture is a never-ending one and it is not possible for companies that have operated in a very hierarchical mode to change the culture easily to a receptive participative one, even if that is the management requirement. Within the report itself there is a self diagnostic table for companies to identify where they stand against the various aspects of the culture, which perhaps gives some clues to which aspect must be focused on.

3M is one of the companies to have focused most attention on the establishment of the creative culture. The company makes it clear to all employees in the organization that creativity is respected, encouraged and required at all levels. The organization consciously sets out to make 'heroes' of people who have backed their own ideas, even when they have ignored an instruction to stop working on a project about which they felt strongly. There are good examples of such flag carriers ultimately getting great reward from the business for their determination, stubbornness and Nelsonian ability to turn a blind eye.

Creative work in and between teams

It has been observed earlier that effective teamworking does not necessarily come naturally; it has to be worked for and taught. An excellent example of teamworking is that of a leader of a successful sports team such as a football manager. He or she has to make an effective team with players who are usually on opposing sides and who may even have been involved in physical confrontations with the colleagues they are supposed to be working with.

When cross-functional teams are formed within companies, departmental representatives, who by the nature of their work are often rivals, don't fit naturally into teams, so a strategy must be developed for creating effective teamworking. Two good examples of this, based on the author's experience, are described below:

There was high business tension between two organizations, Lever Brothers and Central Research. Lever Brothers had developed dishwashing liquids in America, and subsequently the UK, and had dominated the market in the 1950s with market shares of 70–80 per cent of branded goods. When Proctor and Gamble introduced Fairy Liquid, it very rapidly took a major share from the Unilever brands. The marketing staff of Lever Brothers and the R&D staff of Central Research met frequently for discussions, but these rapidly degenerated into sessions where each side blamed the other for failure of the brand. The respective directors of Lever Brothers and Central Research finally ordered a meeting of the relevant teams in a hotel halfway between London and Port Sunlight, with instructions that no one was to return until they had become a single interactive committed team with clear views as to what their strategy would be. The process of seeing each other's point of view and beginning to work to a single unifying approach across all facets of the business in this rather challenging situation took three days. But at the end of it, they had developed a much greater understanding – indeed the group of people who were involved in the process rapidly became a very strong supportive group. The relationships that developed during those three days endured for most of the team members throughout their business careers.

An experimental group of young people across all departments of an organization were given the opportunity to volunteer for an out-of-hours project. They were invited to undertake a project for nine months entirely in their own time, with the exception of one day a month for formal meetings and discussions. At the end of nine months, they were expected to have identified products to be launched by the business and, to the best of their ability, to have worked these through to full launch proposals. This seemed overly challenging as moving a new brand to the marketplace took on average five years; however, by the end of the nine-month project they had a product proposition ready for market and three other proposals at a state of near readiness. The product was subsequently launched on to the UK market and thereafter into a number of other markets throughout Europe. The most interesting aspects of the project, however, were the speed at which the group became a team and the rapid learning process about how the different facets of the business fitted. Compared with most young research scientists of the time, these young people were seen as having an extraordinarily wide understanding of the total business operation.

Every team that is created must be developed according to its own characteristics. They must play to their strengths and think through how they are going to build this strong sense of team identity, a desire to win, and willingness to 'go the extra mile' for each other. To facilitate this, there are some best practice rules which should be considered by any team.

One important consideration is the team's location. When the people in different functions are geographically separated from each other even by corridors or a few hundred yards, it is necessary to have some 'organizational glue' to pull a team together. It is useful to have some meetings offsite with some social activities in addition to the formal task confronting the team in its working role. Another important consideration is the characters of the people in the teams. Of the thirty-two companies on the EIRMA study on Best Practice in Creativity in R&D, a number use Belbin models for putting together teams for company projects. In addition, most advanced companies basing their operations on cross-functional teams are now training team leaders.

A well-designed supportive physical environment is another important aspect of team building, and is now better explored than it used to be. In a laboratory at Port Sunlight, a study on how to dramatically increase research effectiveness reached the conclusion that the key issues affecting the overall value of output was the use of space, time and resource. The key role of space design was illustrated by the concepts of the architect David Leon who specializes in designing the interior space of buildings to meet the operational needs of the participants. Since then, experiments the laboratory has performed over the last ten years have shown that, broadly speaking, one can save 20–25 per cent of the gross space of an R&D organization (or indeed many other cost centres). Thus the revenue saving and sometimes capital savings enable the rest of the operation to be purpose built to achieve communication goals and optimum teamworking goals at no net expenditure cost. A general conclusion from this work is that, in addition to the quantifiable savings of having people working more closely together, *there is a major benefit if teams can be co-located*. Furthermore, part-time members of teams, for example those involved in analytical work, statisticians and perhaps some communication support etc., should also have a team location, even if they have to share desks.

On the Science Park in Guildford, Borax originally set out to design a new research laboratory based on the teamworking concepts of David Leon (Leon, 1996). They subsequently widened this concept to include an integrated building involving both the R&D and the overall general business management. Very considerable benefits have accrued from this, with a much closer overall integration of the work between the business and research laboratories. Concepts such as a glass screen separating the board room from the major pilot plant facilities have provided a greater technological focus in the overall thinking of the organization.

Use of teams for problem-solving

Teams are usually set up to undertake projects leading to a redefined desirable outcome, but *en route* to this the team can encounter many problems. A group should, therefore, have a good grasp of creative problem-solving techniques. It has always seemed obvious that, because there are many different types of problems to be solved, it is likely that different techniques will be more or less effective. Creative problem-solving is a kind of 'toolbox' topic, where the basic strategy is to define the type of problem and then to pick the most appropriate methodology for handling it.

Simplistically speaking, if one is trying to generate a series of new ideas or approaches, the type of technique required is likely to be very different from that used for solving one single, difficult, long-term unique problem. The early findings of the EIRMA group revealed that, even among successful, leading companies, few have a sufficiently wide grasp of the range of different approaches that are most likely to solve the various types of problem. 'Let's brainstorm' is rather a generic strategy for tackling difficult problems. Most companies seem unaware that there are many different ways of brainstorming, with very different potential outcomes. Furthermore, the underlying set-up of the exercise will greatly aid or impede the potential of a technique to meet a particular problem circumstance.

Problems need to be categorized. To do this, some questions must be asked:

- Do you wish to generate lots of new approaches or tackle a single unique problem?
- Is it acceptable to the business strategy to produce a 'convergent' solution, which follows logically from a train of thought, with the likelihood that people from other competitor organizations looking at the same data are likely to get to the same answer on the same timescale?
- Are you looking for a divergent and novel solution that will inevitably enable differentiation of one's products from the competitor?
- Does the team have trained leadership for problem-solving sessions and trained individuals to take part or is it working with people who understand little of the complex group? Behavioural issues will prevent unprepared sessions working effectively.

The various well-known creative problem-solving techniques have different roles in tackling these different situations. Without attempting a comprehensive overview of the many techniques, it is worth looking at a few different approaches to give a feel of when they can work best.

Brainstorming: selecting the team and the approach

Most approaches to brainstorming require interactive group behaviour. Group leaders are not always aware that complex behavioural issues are often naïvely led. The first issue, often ignored, is: 'what skills are required for the session?' This is followed by the question, 'who should be present at the session?' *A common failing is an organizer who pulls together for a creative session a group of people who have been working on the problem in normal business mode.*

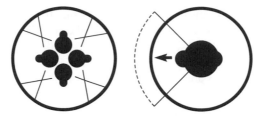

Figure 3.5

The leader should therefore consider carefully the roles of the people in a problem-solving session. The *problem owner* is a person who has a full understanding of both the problem, the attempts made to tackle it and why they have failed. One or two other members of the group should be experts in the most promising approaches which they think will lead to the problem solution. The *session facilitator* should not take an active part in the problem solution but instead should facilitate the interaction of the minds present in the room to lead them to solutions *actionable at the levels represented within the group*. The role of *other group members* is to provide alternative perspectives which enable new viewpoints on how to tackle the problem to be identified (Figure 3.5).

Getting together a group of people who have the same viewpoint on how to tackle a problem is totally counterproductive, yet this is the most widely used strategy. For example, a team for a consumer goods problem might usefully consist of a marketing manager who understood the problem and would recognize a novel solution if it emerged, and a couple of product experts who understood the product technology involved. The rest of the group might comprise a science writer, a poet, a perfumier, a creative advertising copywriter, perhaps a basic scientist from a completely different discipline and a person with deep knowledge of any topic, whether it be cactus, the life cycle of snakes, primeval tribal customs or something else entirely. And it should go without saying that the non-expert members of the team should also have some demonstrable lateral problem-solving skills.

When non-specialist, 'creative people' produce very 'off-the-wall' divergent viewpoints, the problem owners often get frustrated. Yet this of course is the whole point; one does not need a creative session to come up with conventional solutions to conventional problems. The breakthrough comes when one looks at a problem in a way that other people have looked at it and sees the solution that no one else has seen, and to do this, one needs very novel viewpoints. The sheer divergency of non-expert suggestions is not threatening – *only the problem owner can solve the problem and it is up to this person to select from the novel viewpoints offered those new ways of tackling the problem which excite him or her.*

A common phenomenon in these sessions is that the best answers do not emerge during the discussions of the group but the next day, and this fits very well, of course, with the observations of the Synectics company – that the subconscious mind is a far more powerful problem-solver than the conscious.

The brainstorming session commences with the problem owner describing briefly the problem to be tackled. A one sentence summary of the problem to be solved should be written up for all session members to see.

There are several different ways of running a brainstorming session and these tend to have different outcomes. One problem in discussing brainstorming is that, apart from a few specific techniques such as that propounded by Rawlinson, there is no clearly agreed nomenclature for the different techniques. The author has therefore used the terms with which she is familiar.

Hitchhiking

The problem owner describes the problem area succinctly and clearly identifies the problem that needs to be solved. He or she also gives a brief summary of the approaches towards the solution that have been tried and have failed. The goal of the group then is to identify a series of new viewpoints which the problem owner can select from as new ways of tackling the problem. It should be stressed that *it is usually unrealistic to expect a complete solution to a problem during such a session.* It is far better to identify new viewpoints – completely new ways of looking at the issue, with some specific route to the solution suggested for the problem owner to explore. In attempting to achieve this, a group member makes a suggestion as to a way to proceed and the theory is that other group members then 'hitchhike' on this initial suggestion, making embodiments, building in new data to help move the initial idea through to a viewpoint. If the group and its leader are not well trained, this seldom happens. What usually occurs is that one person will make a contribution, but a second will break in before the first one has finished and suggest a different approach. This causes antagonism with the first member, who may well spend the rest of the session either trying to prove that his or her idea was a better one or trying to destroy any other suggestions made by the second person. Other members can remain ignorant of the cross-currents in the discussion, merely waiting for a chance to make their own contributions.

One simple variant of hitchhiking which is very effective in achieving a more speculative discussion is the 'get fired' approach. In this variant, people are invited to start with ideas which are so outlandish that, if they were seriously suggested in their business, the inevitable response from their bosses would be 'you're fired'. It is perhaps worth giving some simple examples of how this technique can work:

The author was once part of a team trying to find out if there were any remaining fishbones in the fish mash used to produce fish fingers. It is obviously highly undesirable for small bones to be present in fish fingers, as they are eaten by small children. The 'get fired' idea to start a session was that one should regard the conveyor belt of fish fingers as a kind of ceremonial parade and as each one passed the saluting base, the bones should stand up and salute. This is a classic 'get fired' idea and quite outlandish, but if the bones could stand up and salute, then of course it would be easy to find and remove them. While trying to move this idea through to a practical viewpoint, someone observed that when one is puttying a window and finds hard bits of old putty in the new, soft putty as it is being flexed, the hard bits always come to the surface. This led to the idea of bending the fish finger pulp over a wheel. When this was tried, the bones stood out at an angle to the mix and could easily be withdrawn. Another amusing example was a solution to the problem of plucking the feathers from chickens – a very unpleasant and labour-intensive job. The 'get fired' idea in this case was to blow up the chicken. From this crazy idea came the thought 'why blow it up with TNT when compressed air might do instead?' and from this came the idea of using very hot steam. A workable process had been devised in a relatively short time, by which the flesh and feathers could be removed in a single step.

It must be stressed, however, that a well-run interactive brainstorming session requires trained leaders and that the team members must understand that key rules must always be adhered to.

Creative listening

While most people in business are taught to talk, very few are taught to listen, yet creative listening is an essential feature of group behavioural creative techniques. People must understand that when someone is making a contribution they must listen and be seen to listen. If their own thoughts are a distraction they should write a few key words on paper so that they don't forget them and then concentrate on contributing constructively.

The leader of the team must understand body language. First, he or she must assure everyone in the team that their contributions will all be heard in due course. Secondly, he or she must be aware that some team members will want to contribute to the discussion of a specific point, and not branch off into another area before they have a chance to do so. Both leader and team members require a quite sophisticated understanding of group behaviour. If these conditions are met, a successful hitchhiking approach can sometimes work instead. However, even well-trained group leaders can often have difficulty encouraging groups to raise the level of their discussion into the uninhibited creative language necessary for them to make a breakthrough into new streams of thought. They are used to having business conversations where they carefully evaluate what they are saying as they are saying it. Furthermore, as they listen to what everyone else is saying, they find it very difficult to put aside evaluation and enter a 'stream of consciousness' discussion.

Rules for running creative session

If there is no trained facilitator available, there are variants of brainstorming that avoid the group behavioural pitfalls. Rawlinson brainstorming gets round the problem of group behaviour by having the group interact individually with the leader rather than with each other.

The characteristics of Rawlinson can usually be recognized by the 'warm-up'. Typically, the group leader will hold up a pen and say to the group, 'This is not a pen. What is it?' and the group is encouraged to produce a series of answers: it's a midget space rocket, it's a back scratcher, it's earplugs. These answers seize upon some aspect of the pen – its shape, its colour, its sharpness or its ability to make marks, and so on.

In Rawlinson, once the problem is defined, all the ideas are fed directly to the chairperson, with very little interaction between the participants. While a normal session would consist of a maximum of seven people, a Rawlinson brainstorming session might have considerably more providing there are sufficient people to capture and write up all the ideas as they emerge. Rawlinson is a good technique for untrained people to generate a lot of ideas quickly.

Trigger sessions

The use of morphological analysis techniques for analysing the characteristics that ideas are based on can help codify various ideas into themes, which can often be worked up into new and useful viewpoints. However, the author's preferred approach when working with untrained participants is to use trigger sessions. Each of the seven or eight participants has two sheets of paper. The problem owner describes the problem and each member writes a solution or solutions on the first sheet. They have only two minutes to write their ideas in the form of two-word descriptors. For example, if the problem is to design a better bus ticket, potential ideas are written as, say, 'stamp forehead', 'plastic card', 'free transport', 'clip hatband', 'fluorescent tip', 'electronic scorecard' etc. The group leader then invites one of the members to describe his or her ideas. The other participants must cross out any on their own list that duplicate those being read out without making a verbal contribution.

The next person has the slightly more difficult task of reading only those answers that haven't already been thought of, and so it goes on round the group. At the end of this first pass, the group members are asked to read from the second sheet of paper the new ideas that have been triggered by what they have heard. The cycle passes backwards and forwards until everyone has had enough. This is an efficient technique because there are no long descriptions of ideas (although if a particular idea is a little obscure, the group leader might ask for a short explanation). In trigger sessions, hundreds of ideas can be developed very quickly. People have to listen very carefully and constructively; only by listening can they prevent themselves from repeating ideas or missing trigger opportunities to build from an idea they have heard. Furthermore, as the session progresses, group members produce more and more divergent ideas in order to stay in the 'game'.

The follow-up phase is very simple. All the participants hand in their sheets and the ideas that have not been crossed out are made into a list. The next day, all the team members are given a copy of the list and are invited to pick the three they think are the most interesting. The subconscious mind has had a chance to work and it is interesting to note that the same few ideas tend to emerge from the different participants.

The Taguchi method

A totally different way for a group to tackle problems is represented by the 'fish boning' or Taguchi technique. For example, a team in a factory are looking for ways to optimize the efficiency of a production process. Using the Taguchi method, the process is made into a flow chart. All the participants – often the line workers – are invited to write down their ideas for improving the process on 'Post it' notes, one idea per note. The facilitator then clusters the notes to try to build on the overall process skeleton the sets of ideas that have emerged, ideas which usually address different aspects of the process. The participants may then intervene and suggest that their idea is more generic or fits to another part of the process.

The result is a series of incremental ideas tackling different parts of the problem. Participants are then invited to test and implement the solutions. A multicoloured diagram is generated, showing in one colour all the ideas which have been generated for improving the process; in another, those which have been tried; and, in a third colour, those that have been implemented. This technique is suitable for wide participation and is an excellent communication tool.

Synectics as a brainstorming technique

For the solution of really difficult problems, the Synectics approach discussed earlier is a very powerful procedure. Synectics can only be undertaken with a trained leader and a group of people skilled in creative listening but for problems where a novel approach and a concentrated attack are needed, it has an excellent track record. To summarize:

• Difficult problems are often solved when you don't think you are thinking about them – 'I'll sleep on this one'.

- Many problems can be solved by analogy and by changing the language of the problem, say, for example, from engineer to biology or botany.
- The process of deliberately looking for solutions out of the confines of the problem's discipline seems to train the mind to search for novel solutions from one's own experience in other fields.
- Searching the memory is a good mental exercise as it becomes easier to familiarize oneself with the technique.

In the original Synectics approach, the client explains the problem, a multifunctional group proposes ideas for solutions and a leader controls the whole process. It is therefore very similar to the brainstorming approaches described earlier. It is the way Synectics moves the solution from the conscious to the subconscious mind, as well as moving the language of the problem that makes it different from other techniques.

In the variant of Synectics preferred by the author, the problem is defined and a conventional process such as Rawlinson, or trigger sessions, is used to try and achieve new viewpoints. If this does not produce enough new insights, the problem is redefined by the participants as 'problem as understood'.

This is a very powerful stage of the process as the 'problem as understood' is defined in completely different metaphors from the original problem language, for example the language of sociology instead of engineering. Then what usually happens is that the group segment the problem into different facets. This is valuable in its own right because people with a problem often cannot 'see the wood for the trees' and attempt to tackle a complex and multifaceted problem as if there were a single solution. The participants of the group, particularly those who have not been directly involved in the problem area, are able to point out that there are different facets which, if tackled individually, are much more likely to give solutions.

The next stage of Synectics is for the participants to look for analogies in such intellectually challenging fields that participants at the conscious level are no longer aware of what the original problem is. A problem in engineering may be translated into examples in social anthropology, for example, and the team are called to explore these analogies in great detail. When the group has clearly forgotten the problem, the problem owner invites them to force fit the discussions they have been having into the solution of the problem as understood. In a good session, people recall the original task, realize the ideas they have been discussing have a remarkable relevance to the original problem and produce many new viewpoints.

In Synectics, the client – the person with the problem – can make or break the session. If he or she is open minded and is willing to explore new perspectives, the session will go well. However, this also depends on a competent process leader who is both able to ensure good group dynamics and pose questions that are challenging enough to move the group from a conscious to a subconscious way of thinking. The group itself must be highly disciplined in their behaviour towards each other as well as being highly speculative. The paradox of creative sessions is that people must be very disciplined in their behaviour with each other while allowing their minds to explore new avenues freely.

The use of association in creative problem-solving

Many of the concepts of Edward De Bono are based upon the realization that when people are stuck on a problem, seeing the problem from a new viewpoint can be most helpful in achieving a solution. De Bono has many techniques for allowing random association to be made. In his 'walk through Woolworth's' he invites people with a problem to walk through a shop, look at what they regard as the most interesting item on display and ask themselves how any aspect of that item they considered might be relevant to giving a new viewpoint on the problem they are tackling. Another approach is to pick a book and, given a preset page and line number, pick the first word and try to force associations between that word and the problem. There are some similarities between these approaches and the force fit associations in Synectics. The random association approach is an extremely interesting and valuable one in enabling new viewpoints to emerge. In the author's experience, however, the 'chain' of association between the analogies in Synectics, which take the problem across a series of different languages, concepts and images, produces more effective results

Software approaches

There are now a number of software aids for problem-solving. The Seren morphological analysis software has already been mentioned. Another approach for difficult problems is the Invention Machine Laboratory (Invention Machine Ltd, South House, 3 Bond Avenue, Milton Keynes MK1 1SW. http://www.invention-machine.co.uk), which is based on the work of Genrich Altshuller who, in the late Stalin era, began to study the underlying scientific principles behind a huge number of patentable inventions. His objective was to find a scientific principle used in a novel way or for the first time in the patent literature. Something else which Altshuller took into consideration was that inventors often use a small number of 'tricks' to reconcile apparently unreconcilable requirements of a system. For example, Edison's many patents in this analysis relied on three or four inventive principles. His third observation was that the successive patents in the patent literature deriving from a new phenomenon follows a fairly predictable course. Therefore, by careful study of the literature, one can predict fairly accurately what the next phase of invention is likely to be.

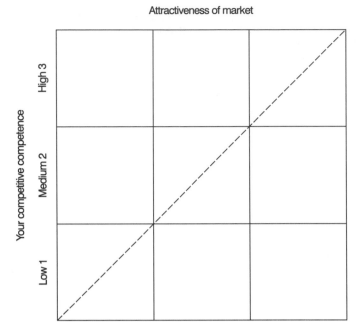

Figure 3.6 *Hax analysis*

These principles based on the study of 2 million patents are built into the Invention Machine Laboratory and there is a growing literature of successful use of this software in solving difficult technological problems. A non-software based version of this approach is known as 'triz', its name being based on the Russian acronym for the theory of inventive problem-solving. This structured methodology for bringing totally new viewpoints to bear based upon the knowledge of patent literature in different fields should be added to the list of convergent problem-solving methodologies described earlier.

There are a number of tool-kit approaches which can also help to provide new viewpoints or indeed to check that all aspects of an idea have been properly explored. Among these, the Change Maker's tool kit from Vincent Nolan and Martin Brook is a good example (Nolan and Brook). Indeed there are also good publications from the DTI, such as *Innovation Your Move* and a self-assessment guide to product development.

All practitioners wishing to master problem-solving techniques should have an understanding of enough techniques to be able to pick those suitable for the characteristics of the problem in question.

From idea to implementation

As mentioned earlier, Britain is widely perceived as a highly creative country but one which is poor in translating its inventions into innovation. As a member of the Innovation Advisory Board to the DTI and then of the Innovation Unit, the author and several colleagues have been closely involved in attempting to understand Britain's failure to innovate. Indeed, six of the key underlying reasons form the agenda of the Innovation Unit of the DTI.

When one looks at the low proportion of ideas that are turned into innovation, it is extraordinary that so little effort is put into developing an effective innovation project management system. There is no applied academic skill base that systematically looks at the process of moving from idea to implementation and evolving best practice from it, yet at a national level this could be a key to dramatically improved national competitiveness. The author believes that there is a considerable gap in the training of Innovation Project Managers in the UK and it is one which should be addressed urgently. One of the clearest early conclusions of the EIRMA group is that most companies who have looked at the idea-to-innovation process have concluded that a system is needed for determining where the highest risks of failure are in this process.

There is a broad consensus of opinion that the idea-to-implementation process described in *Innovation Project Management* and called the Bob Cooper Stagegate process is the most widely used and respected. Cooper's methodology is based on a study of attempts, both successful and unsuccessful, to innovate in over 2,000 different projects in North America and Europe. He has distilled a process using short feasibility studies and little organizational interference and expenditure but with target outcomes in time and required understanding. At the end of the study, a review group from the company looks at the outcome and agrees to either end the study or to define further resource allocation and required outputs for the next stage. This moves progressively through the life of a project with the amount of resource allocated steadily increasing and the requirements becoming increasingly stiff so that the project can continue its progress. Unilever use a similar methodology called the Innovation Funnel; this graphically describes the overall shape of the process with a large number of feasibility studies ending up in a few projects for which there is major resource and capital commitment.

The Stagegate process is well understood and documented but it appears to handle only part of the problem. In addition to this procedural approach of moving from idea to implementation, there seems to be a conceptual approach needed, which requires the project manager to apply a series of judgements at the early phases. In the UK, these judgements are normally considered much later – too late – in the project. In Britain, many companies still regard the innovation process as an exercise in technology transfer.

Issues outside the relatively narrow area of the relevant technology are not studied intensively enough – if at all – by the project managers selected to lead innovation projects. The author believes the project manager must be taught a series of what could be called master of business administration (MBA) skills so that he or she can understand far more about the market environment in which the development is being pursued. Nationally we should be building up a skill base understanding of why projects fail and how to overcome such failure.

From idea to exploitation

The information which I believe it is necessary to understand as an Innovation Project Manager is described in a lecture I gave to the Institute of Directors. It seems there is a paradox – innovation, including new product development, is central to business success in the 1990s, and: 'Innovation *is* the central issue in Competitiveness' (Michael Porter) and 'Innovation is the only unique competence in the 1990s' (Tom Peters). Yet most products fail!

To be successful, it is essential to understand and avoid the pitfalls of new product introduction while proceeding with confidence and commitment. When someone has a novel product they believe in it: but people who champion new ideas are expert in the benefits on which success may be based. However, the Innovation chain is as strong as the weakest link. Failure is most likely to occur in some minor aspect, not because the central idea is unsound.

To introduce to an external market a product which fails, particularly if just one element of it is at fault, is an enormously damaging exercise. The problems include:

- the direct cost of capital, stock and write-offs
- the loss of an opportunity
- the loss of confidence of customers and colleagues
- alerting competitors, who can often react and modify faster than your confidence-sapped group can do themselves.

The remedy is to understand and avoid barriers to success.

There are a number of ways of reducing the overall risk of failure.

Pick your market

It is easier to win in a rapidly growing market, than a mature, tightly competitive one. Table 3.1 illustrates Porter's five-force model, which is a very good diagnostic tool (Porter, 1985).

Table 3.1 *Porter's five-force model*

	Good market	*Poor market*
Barriers to entry	High	Low
Barriers to exit	Low	High
Strength of customers	Many equal size	Few dominant
Strength of supplies	Many competent	Few dominant
Availability of other technology substitutes	None as good	Many other options

Know the customer – and the competitor

Do you fully understand your unique selling proposition?

'I buy Jif because . . . .' complete in fewer than eight words.

The Hax analysis (Hax and Majluf) and a balanced scorecard of other diagnostic techniques can be very revealing (see Figure 3.6). If you are on the right-hand side of the dotted line, why waste the investment?

• Will your new product achieve a 1, 2, or 3 position in its sector within 1, 2, 3 years?
• Who is your major competitor?
• What are your unique competencies relevant to this market?
• What are theirs?
• When will they regain the advantage?

Pricing

Do you understand the unique added value of your product to your customers sufficiently to share the value with them?

Pricing should usually be based on recovering your share of value seldom on some cost plus formula. Two alternative strategies are:

1 Sensibly tight pricing. This discourages your competitors from incurring the costs of competing effectively.
2 Full-value pricing. Gain large margins initially to reinvest in widening the market scope, developing manufacturing capabilities and improving the product. Be flexible in response to real competitive threat.

- Which strategy is more suitable for your business?
- Which are you adopting?

Marketing

Who are the potential customers?
What is your route to market?

How can one ensure that the real customer experience is understood early and can be used to optimize the product?

The innovation process

There is little training currently available in the UK on Innovation Project management except in companies which themselves innovate.

At the academic/industrial interface, much current attention is focused on technology transfer – but most overall failures in innovation do not occur due to the competence of the transfer process. The author believes most new products fail for the same reasons most businesses fail – for example, failures in execution, insufficient attention to the 'weakest link in the chain', excessive optimism, inefficient feedback, poor cash flow. Training people in 'project management of innovation' can dramatically improve chances of success, helping companies avoid such problems as follows:

- Believing that the last 5 per cent of the project will take 5 per cent of the time – it may actually take as long as the first 95 per cent! This can cause major cash flow problems or crises of confidence.
- The first customer is eager to buy: there is no such thing as a first customer. Everyone wants to be the second customer with someone else acting as guinea pig.
- Not involving the manufacturer or having quality, sales and commercial input in the early stages.
- Omitting to check regulations and IPR issues.
- Not communicating regularly or too fully too often.

Conclusion

'We succeed by employing nuts with convictions' (3M). Innovation requires champions – who must be protected. In mainstream business, the good manager knows when to 'pull the plug' when things are going wrong. There are many pitfalls in the process of innovation and the author believes that the great innovator has to keep his or her nerve and be flexible in adjusting the product imperfections to achieve a winner. But in trusting one's own judgement, one must also be objective about feedback: 'If you can trust yourself when all men doubt you – but make allowance for their doubting too' (Kipling).

The daunting problems of change and innovation must not deter us from commitment to mastering the innovation process, but we must be prepared to learn and share to improve our rate of success constantly.

For a nation like Britain, which has invested very high-quality resource in its 'knowledge system', it is extraordinary that so little attention has been paid to processes which will enable the translation of the outstanding knowledge base into increased competitiveness for the country at large. Strenuous efforts are currently being made to address this balance.

References

Cooper, B. *Winning at New Products*. Addison Wesley.
Department of Trade and Industry. *Competitiveness through Partnerships with People*. DTI.
Department of Trade and Industry. *How the Best UK Companies are Winning*. DTI.
Department of Trade and Industry. *Innovation Your Move*. DTI.
Duggan, R. *Technology Foresight and Industrial Innovation*. Cartermill.
Hax, A. and Majluf, N. *The Strategy Concept and Process*.
Leon, D. (1996). *The Chemical Engineer*, 26th September.
Nolan, V. and Brook, M. *The Change Makers Toolkit*. Change Maker Publications, 9 Tideway, Mortlake High Street, London SW14 8SN.
Porter, M. (1985). *Competitive Advantage*. Free Press, New York.
Synectics (1971). *The Practice of Creativity*. Harper and Row.
Szent-Gyorgi, A. *Imagine The Synectics Company*. Synectics Europe, Hemel Hempstead.

4 Innovation by design

Dr Myfanwy Trueman

There is a growing awareness that design is an important factor in industrial competitiveness but a full implementation of this resource is often hampered by a lack of understanding about its true value and potential. This phenomenon is of growing significance in the light of intense global competition since, for many small and medium-sized companies (SMEs), design represents a tool which is at best used only in a limited way. This work provides a fresh look at the meaning and value of design. It examines a wide range of design attributes in a hierarchical framework for new product development central to company strategy. These attributes are grouped together at four levels, which represent a focus as well as control of projects in terms of their *value*, *image*, *process* and *production*. This analysis is illustrated with examples of some leading companies, which have used design as a strategic resource to facilitate and improve their competitive performance. It also applies the typology and framework in two case studies of deliberately contrasting SMEs.

Science is the attempt to make the chaotic diversity of our same experience correspond to a logically uniform system of thought. (Albert Einstein)

The role of design in industrial competition

What do we mean by design? Why do we need it and what good is it anyway? The following two quotations by Prime Minister Tony Blair (1997) illustrate the problem. (The salient points are in my italic.)

Britain was once the workshop of the world. It led the Industrial Revolution. It was defined by ship-building, mining and heavy industry. Even today, if MPs pushed for a debate on ship-building they would probably get one. *But if they pushed for a debate on the design industry, they would probably be dismissed as concentrating on trivia.*

Yet more people now work in film and TV than the car industry – let alone ship-building. Britain's architects lead the world in the range and quality of their work. *Innovative new products are winning new markets for us.* Nine out of ten Formula One cars are designed and built in Britain. Psion personal organizers, Bullfrog electronic games, the Duracell torch, James Dyson's bagless vacuum cleaner, the artificial limbs designed by Blatchfords – *they all demonstrate the breadth of British product design.* (Rt Hon Tony Blair, Prime Minister, 1997)

On the one hand, there is an observation which suggests that design is trivial, while on the other, design is clearly understood to be related to innovation and the development of new products and therefore could be deemed as central to competitiveness. This clearly illustrates a dilemma which arises not because design is unimportant or trivial, but mainly because the majority of people do not know what design is! In fact, Lorenz (1995) suggests that many companies have overlooked design as a competitive tool or strategy through a lack of understanding about its meaning and value. He considers that this is chiefly because consultants and researchers have failed to develop a clear design typology, equivalent to the four Ps of marketing.

This does not mean that there have been no champions of design. In fact, Wasserman (1990) argues that design is the only remaining tool in industrial competition because it offers the facility of product differentiation. At the same time, Clark and Fujimoto (1990) advocate the power of design in developing 'product integrity' – a blend of the 'usability', 'producibility' and 'appropriateness' of new products that is vital for successful innovation. The impact of design in relation to quality is examined by Clausing and Simpson (1990) and Walsh et al. (1992) who describe and illustrate ways in which good design can add 'perceived value' to products since customers are often prepared to pay more for something which is well designed and is produced to a high standard of finish. In this way companies are able to increase profit margins and improve their performance as well as instil customer confidence.

Another perspective is provided by Olins (1986) and, more recently, Schmitt, Simonson and Marcus (1995) who examine design in terms of corporate image and identity. Here, design aesthetics and advertising are fundamental to creating and sustaining the image and identity projected by a company, from logo, stationery, livery and packaging to showrooms, office decor and architecture. At product level this perspective is closely linked with 'branding', since the same creative design 'integrity' is needed in launching and maintaining a brand (Southgate, 1994). Furthermore, at product level, design can be seen to offer a practical facility in terms of reducing time to market and speeding up production (Trueman and Jobber, 1995), since the redesign of products can reduce the number of parts for manufacture as well as producing savings in materials and costs. Finally, designers can be used to generate, interpret, integrate and communicate new ideas. This is an important enabling factor for multidisciplinary teamwork as well speeding up the product development process (Fujimoto, 1990).

All these interpretations provide different insights into the potential of design but each has a unique perspective and application. This further illustrates the *breadth* of design described by Blair, but also highlights the potential confusion of hard-pressed company managers if they wish to integrate this resource into the competitive armoury of their company. What then do we mean by design and how can it be used to competitive advantage? The definition adopted by this work is based on previous research at the London Business School and the Boston Design Institute. It is also related to the definitions of 'technological innovation' and 'marketing' (see Figure 4.1).

Definitions

Design process

'Planning, decision making and the management of activities which determine the function and characteristics of a finished product or process'

(Trueman, 1992; Gorb, 1988; Lawrence,1988)

Technological innovation

'The transformation of an idea into a new or improved saleable product or operational process in industry or commerce'

(OECD, 1981)

Marketing

'The management process which identifies, anticipates, and supplies customer requirements efficiently and profitability'

(Chartered Institute of Marketing)

Figure 4.1 *Relationships between the definitions of design, technological innovation and marketing*

The close relationship between these definitions is significant since it indicates the similarities as well as differences between these concepts. It also introduces the notion of design which is seen and better understood as a 'process' rather than a finished product, or merely the outcome of that development process (Archer, 1985). However, it is one thing to stress the importance and context of design but quite another to examine the constituent parts or attributes of this process. If companies are to take advantage of the design phenomenon they will need a clear understanding of precisely what is on offer and how this may be applicable to their particular circumstances and products. Furthermore, accepted wisdom would suggest that design should be an integral part of new projects from the outset if real benefits are to be gained (e.g. Cooper and Chew, 1996; Hollins and Pugh, 1990; Lawrence, 1989). Consequently, timing, level of involvement and 'design aware' personnel are as important as a clear understanding and support for a design 'culture' by senior managers if new products are to be successful and early in the marketplace (Ittner and Larcker, 1997).

Design dimensions and attributes

In order to shed some light on the issue of design and competitiveness, this research has made wide reference to previous work in this field taken from a number of different perspectives. It has built on this work by carrying out a large-scale survey of 108 British industrial companies, which compares attitudes towards design with company performance (Trueman and Jobber, 1995), and has subsequently developed a new typology of design attributes as well as a new dimensional model of the product development process (Trueman, 1997). In other words, it breaks down the concept of design into a range of constituent facets or interpretations (attributes) such as 'design and product quality' and 'design and product differentiation', and groups these together at four different levels of implementation.

Here, the focus at level one is customer-perceived product *value* which can be strongly influenced by attributes such as 'quality' and 'aesthetics', followed by level two which considers the relationship between product *image* achieved through design attributes such as 'differentiation', 'communication' and 'advertising'. Level three reflects upon how design can facilitate the *process* of developing new products in terms of 'interpretation' and 'integration' of ideas, whereas level four examines *production* where issues such as 'speed', 'reduced complexity' and 'economic use of materials' can be controlled or modified by design. At each level attitudes towards design in the company can be compared with performance (Figure 4.2).

Product value

Although this research would argue that the sequence is hierarchical and that product value represents the preferred starting point for new projects, the iterative nature of the development process is recognized so that throughout the course of product evolution, each level may be revisited many times. But value also represents a benchmark for assessment and measurement which is vital for 'accept/reject' or 'go/kill' decisions about the form and nature of products throughout their life span. In order to be successful, managers must ensure that the customer-perceived value of products is met by the value

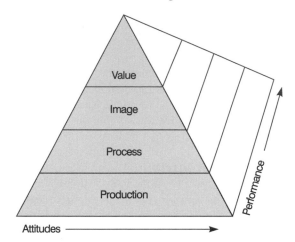

Figure 4.2 *VIPP design dimensions* Source: © *Trueman (1996)*

attached to those products by the company (Bowman and Faulkner, 1994). Here, the descriptor **value** rather than QUALITY has been adopted; since this appears to represent more accurately what both customers and company desire, whereas quality is only one part of the 'perceived added value', that may be influenced by design. (See Table 4.1.)

An example of perceived product value is the Dyson Dual Cyclone vacuum cleaner, with no bag and a lot of suction (Figure 4.3), quoted by Blair (1997). Its designer, James Dyson, had difficulty in getting existing major vacuum cleaner manufacturers to back his idea, so he sold licences to Japanese and American companies to make the Dual Cyclone vacuum cleaners. In Japan, the G-force vacuum retailed at £1,200, far higher than the perceived value of European customers (Roy, 1993). With money generated from the licences, Dyson established his own company in 1993 to manufacture and distribute Dyson Dual Cyclone vacuum cleaners in the UK and Europe. Retailing at around £200, the Dyson is the market leader in the UK floor care industry, and shows that consumers are prepared to pay for a product which is of high quality and which works more efficiently than conventional vacuum cleaners with bags. They can also see how much dust they have collected and if some small object has been 'hoovered up' by mistake! The company now has an annual turnover of more than £100 million (Walters, 1997).

Value is also closely related to Fujimoto's (1990) notion of 'integrity' discussed earlier, since product 'usability', 'producibility' and 'appropriateness' are bound up in identifying and establishing the correct perceived value. However, as Cooper and Chew (1996) explain, it is not easy to determine an appropriate product value even though this can be controlled by using design

Table 4.1 *Attributes grouped according to VIPP typology*

Design attributes	Focus at product level	Focus at corporate level
VALUE (starting point)		
Product styling	Product styling	1 Corporate culture and identity
Aesthetics	Aesthetics	(Total design commitment at all levels)
Quality	Quality	Develop a culture of design standards and
Standards	Standards	quality that pervades the company
		(cf. Dumas and Mintzberg, 1989, 'Infuse
		Level')
Added value	Added value	
	Adds perceived **Value** to products and	
	customer confidence in company (**Image**)	
IMAGE (reinforces value)		
Product differentiation		Product differentiation
Product diversification		Product diversification
		2 Strategic activity
		(Top level design commitment)
Product identity	Product identity	Build design attributes into corporate
Brand creation	Brand creation	strategy
		Examine where and how design can
Corporate identity	(Corporate identity)	enhance current and future company
Corporate culture	(Corporate culture)	**Image** and strategy
		(cf. Lorenz, 1995, 'Strategic design')

Table 4.1 *Continued*

Design attributes	*Focus at product level*	*Focus at corporate level*
Update products Generate new ideas Communicate ideas Interpret ideas Integrate ideas Interface (between managers, project team, production, customers) (cf. Lorenz, 1995, 'Design policy') Promote, advertise products	**PROCESS** Generate new ideas Idea communication Interpret ideas Integrate ideas Promote products	3 Fulcrum for new projects (Full design focus at project level) Use design as a fulcrum for new product development. Design not only shapes and directs new products but also interprets, integrates and communicates new ideas at each stage of the development Process
PRODUCTION Reduce complexity Reduce production costs Design as a tool in new product development Reduce production time Use new technology Use new materials Recycle products and materials	4. Strategic tool Reduce complexity Reduce production time	(Some commitment at product level) Use new technology and materials Where and how design attributes can be used to improve the **Process** and **Production** of new products, may facilitate teamwork (cf. Lorenz, 1995, 'Design policy')

5 Limited use
(small commitment at product level)
Design attributes used in very limited way in **Process** and/or **Production** of new products
(cf. Lorenz, 1995, 'Shallow design')

Figure 4.3 *Dyson Dual Cyclone DC01 vacuum cleaner.* Source: *Sarah Breckenridge, Dyson Communications, 1997*

as an integral part of the project. Managers will constantly need to reassess product value as market and company perceptions change and there is also a problem in the interpretation of results for the project team. For example, Srinivasan, Lovejoy and Beach (1997) warn that 'There is no reliable and generally recognized and accepted measure that can order the set of possible products that industrial designers may create by aesthetic content.' They explain that industrial designers are often trained to see a product and its environment as an integral whole, a 'gestalt' so that different product attributes, price, aesthetics, usability and quality of manufacture are 'aligned similarly' and reinforce each other. 'Consequently, designers and market researchers differ fundamentally in the level of trust that they place in rationalist, decompositional techniques and statistical survey instruments for product development, leading to tensions between the disciplines.' By contrast, Craig and Hart (1992) point out that it is much safer to adopt a range of measures, including those which are perceptual and operational, so that company, customers and other external factors are included, rather than rely solely upon one or two financial performance packages. In practice, research at Bradford found a relationship between a strong focus upon product 'reliability' and an increase in profit margins as well as return on capital investment (ROC). This reinforces the importance of customer confidence, repeat business and perceived product value. Here, design has a facility for adding value to products achieved through attributes such as 'aesthetics', 'styling' and a 'high quality standard of finish' associated with well-designed new products.

Product image

Product image reinforces the perceived value established at the outset of projects. However, although image and identity may be the most visible or tangible aspect of new products, they may be more difficult to quantify. For example, Schmitt, Simonson and Marcus (1995) state that: 'Corporate aesthetics deliver tangible benefits by reducing communication costs, increasing sales, and elevating the image of a company and its products. Over time, corporate aesthetics provide a sustainable competitive advantage', but go on to quote Nakanishi of the Japanese corporate identity firm PAOS who states: 'Many corporations are more comfortable dealing with quantitative data than with aesthetic considerations. Beauty is unfamiliar, uncomfortable, subjective, transitory, even personal. And it can't be measured.'

In other words, image may present the ultimate design dilemma described by Tony Blair since it represents what many people perceive as the 'design' or 'aesthetic' aspect of new products. Companies and products with a 'good image' leading to increased sales demonstrate the significance of visual impact, but simultaneously introduce the problem of how to assess or quantify what we see. This notion of image is taken further if one considers the concept of brand creation, development and management. The true value of brands can be gauged by the acute interest in brand equity and acquisition, which has mushroomed over the past decade, having a direct effect on stock market performance (Southgate, 1994). Here, design can not only create new images and brands, but also directly affect the performance or repositioning of established products and companies. A recent example of this is the competition between British Airways and Virgin Atlantic. As part of its new and caring strategy, British Airways approached artists from different communities around the world to create a series of 'World Images'. The collection of calligraphy, paintings, ceramics, carvings and textiles celebrate the cultural diversity of the many countries the airline serves and are now used

Figure 4.4 *Virgin Atlantic Airways new livery includes the British flag.* Source: *Ginnie Leatham, Virgin Atlantic Airways, 1997*

throughout the company's corporate identity. This stimulated a major debate on the nature of 'Britishness' and the importance of corporate identity, since some parties believe that British Airways has vacated its traditional image niche, which included the British flag. Almost immediately, Richard Branson adopted a new version of the discarded flag for Britannia's cloak on Virgin's aircraft and livery, thereby securing a new perceived niche as *the* 'British' airline company, which British Airways appear to have vacated in the bid for a global status and identity (Figures 4.4 and 4.5). This highlights the design attributes associated with image such as 'product identity' (how to give products a unique identity), 'product differentiation' (how to differentiate products from a competitor's), 'product diversification' (how to diversify into a range of products but keep the same image or brand), and also how to create and manage the brand itself. For example, the Virgin brand has diversified, even 'stretched' to include soft drinks (Virgin Cola) and finance (Virgin Direct), from its origins in the music industry.

But it is no use promoting a new image if value is not put into place, something which the new British Utility companies have learnt to their cost when poor service and delivery has seriously undermined customer confidence. For example, Yorkshire Water badly miscalculated the promotion of its new environmentally responsible image in the light of water shortages, leading to restricted supply during the 1995 drought. This shortage was coupled with excessive profits for shareholders and disproportionately high

Figure 4.5 *British Airways' new livery featuring 'Global Images' to match global business.* Source: *Chris Holt, British Airways, 1997*

salaries for senior managers, leading to an 'evaporation' of confidence (Mitchell, 1996)! This state of affairs has been cumulative, since a number of similarly placed companies have made serious miscalculations in the transfer of ownership from public to private sector, leading to a poor perceived value on the part of the customer, even though they may be received well on the stock market (Hutton, 1996).

In this case, advertising and promotion alone will not suffice to restore customer confidence, since the company must seriously consider all levels of operation and customer relationships. This phenomenon might encourage a further, deeper interpretation where image may lead to the notion of 'identity' and a 'corporate design culture'. Here, customer confidence is inspired since everything about a company operates to the same high-quality design, consistency and standards. Perhaps a good long-term example of this is Marks and Spencer (M&S), which has a long-established brand name built upon design, quality and standards, so that customers have a perceived high value attached to M&S goods, which consistently command a higher price.

But once a company's image has been devalued or lost, it is much harder to regain. For instance, British Steel has had to fight hard to restore its 'tarnished' image after near collapse with the demise of British shipbuilding and coal over three decades (Blair, 1997). However, after a protracted period of change and restructuring, the company has become re-established and is now the largest steel producer in Europe with an annual turnover of over £8 billion. In part, this new image has evolved not only by re-examining corporate culture, but also by association with a number of international projects which are an embodiment of prestigious design, such as the new Hong Kong Stadium, Japan's Kansai Airport and Kuala Lumpur's Petronas Towers (Figure 4.6). At the same time, it has actively involved consumers on in-depth consultations about environmental issues and recycling so that public perception about the company and how it operates has changed (Dwek, 1997).

Figure 4.6 *British Steel's Petronas Towers, Kuala Lumpur, Malaysia.* Source: *Brian Richards, British Steel, photograph by PPL Ltd*

In fact, it appears that companies that have a strong design culture are generally more competitive. To this end, a number of firms that attach a high value to design have been tracked on the US stock exchange where their performance rose by 350 per cent over a period of five years. This compares to the Standard and Poor's 500 Index, which rose by less than 90 per cent, and indicates that market leaders tend to be the 'best able', or 'most likely' to use design (Aldersley-Williams, 1996). However, it is one thing to aspire to develop an appropriate company image, but quite another to manage the process of developing new products so that they are successful in the marketplace.

The Bradford research found that image is closely related to company turnover. In other words, if companies work to improve their image (by using design), this would in turn improve new product sales. Image in this context includes variables such as advertising, design awards, green design and design in the built environment as well as in the development of a corporate identity. At product level, attributes such as 'product identity', 'product differentiation' and 'brand creation' also feature.

Product process

According to Cooper and Kleinschmidt (1996) the new product development process can be reduced to two performance measures of 'profitability' and 'impact'. But how does this relate to design? The notion of 'impact' has been addressed to some extent by the concepts of value and image discussed earlier, since they are a manifestation of impact in the marketplace. But design can also have a direct bearing on profitability – primarily as an enabling factor. At one end of the spectrum design can be used to generate new ideas as well as to interpret, integrate and communicate those ideas both within the company and to the customer or supplier. At the other end, design can become the fulcrum or central driver for new projects which might otherwise fail through lack of commitment, flair or coherency (Pugh, 1986). In this respect, the level of design involvement can be set against profitability since the resulting efficiencies and productivity gained will not only save valuable time but also reduce development costs. Few companies today can afford unnecessary delays resulting from misunderstandings and poor communications or, even worse, a poorly conceived product which takes longer than its competitors to reach the marketplace (Brown and Lattin, 1994). In fact, research at Bradford has shown that strong commitment to design, often using external consultants, is associated with a reduced time to market (Trueman and Jobber, 1993). This reinforces work carried out by an Open University/UMIST research team who found that external design consultants could not only reduce time to market but also improve profits with an average payback period – where investment costs had been recouped, being fifteen months from product launch (DTI, 1991).

Cooper and Kleinschmidt (1996) also found that investment in R&D was a critical success factor. Traditionally western countries including Britain have had a poor track record of inward investment into new research, averaging only 1 or 2 per cent of company turnover. By contrast, the Asia-Pacific region, notably countries such as Korea and Japan, have made a serious commitment to R&D, with the Japanese government recently investing ¥17,000 billion (£100 billion) on science and technology over the next five years 'in an attempt to quash the view that the country is good at developing existing ideas but weak at dreaming up new ones' (Dawkins, 1996). China, too, is emerging strongly as a country prepared to make huge investments in order to become more established in world markets, now with its own Industrial Design Council playing an increasingly important role (founded in 1987 after nine years of preparation) (Wu, 1997).

But however much is spent on investment, innovative new products will not be successful unless the development process is properly orchestrated, with a focus upon best use of time. The successful approach towards innovation taken by Japanese companies in the 1980s was to extend the creative 'front-end' of new projects as much as possible in order to widen product scope and possibilities as well as providing time for in-depth evaluation of realistic alternative solutions. This extended analysis was compensated for by an increasingly truncated development and production schedule, afforded by simultaneous (concurrent) engineering on the one hand, and continual investment in new technology on the other (Takeuchi and Nonaka, 1986). This trend has created a precedent for many companies in the 1990s, where design, in collaboration with communications and information technology (CIT) to support the 'what if' analysis, can be combined to manage and control if not direct the new product process (Freeman, 1997). In fact, there has been an intense focus in the literature on the best way to innovate, fuelled by the successes of Japanese and Pacific Rim companies in the 1970s and 1980s. Many of these have concntrated on issues such as the need to examine customer needs and reduce time to market, with particular emphasis on quality of process and production (Topfer, 1995), although few have acknowledged the contribution made by design (Rassam, 1995). However, Cooper and Kleinschmidt (1996) explain that it is not so much the process that counts but the attitudes and approach of company personnel and commitment from senior managers.

Another dimension is whether the project in hand is a radical new development or an incremental improvement of an existing product. Not surprisingly, radical new proposals carry a much greater risk than modifications to something with which the company, suppliers and customers are familiar; therefore, most successful new products fall into the latter category

(Freeman, 1997). In fact, problems faced in launching the Dyson vacuum cleaner are typical of those faced by radical innovations even though this was well researched and designed. In this case, the process of development was centred around the inventor, his experience, personal contacts and commitment, but the launch situation was made more acute by a lack of resources and infrastructure that would be present in a large company with an established market.

In companies such as these, products derived from related technologies with incremental changes can help sustain a firm's position, the costs of investment can be offset and risks minimized (Nobeoka and Cusumano, 1997). For example, Psion's 'pocket sized' personal organizers referred to by Blair have been incrementally advanced so that the new Series 5 includes a communications system linked to mobile telephones. These developments have kept the company abreast, and often ahead of competitors (Price and Taylor, 1997). This continual product review is bound up with (a) the need for companies to consider and review products in the long term so that life cycles can be extended and (b) a corresponding review of the development process and project teams. In order to maintain this leading-edge technology, Psion has enlisted the help of ARM, the Cambridge-based technology group which has developed an appropriate advanced microprocessor. At the same time, to allay customer fears of lack of standardization in new technology, it has ensured that data can be exchanged easily with desktop personal computers (PCs). However, this focus on the new has led to some problems with distributors in maintaining supply and the infrastructure of previous products with some loss of confidence in customer perception in the company.

This highlights the difficulties associated with technological upgrades and customer confidence during the transition from one series to another. It also demonstrates some of problems associated with the process of developing, launching and monitoring new products where timing, communications, confidence and resources form the cornerstones of success (Nobeoka and Cusumana, 1997). Here, the VIPP attributes of 'communication', 'interpretation' and 'integration' take on a more urgent connotation since design can play the all important role as an interface between project team members and other company personnel as well as stakeholders who may be suppliers, distributors, customers or shareholders. Furthermore, this role is made supremely visible in the process of 'advertising' and 'promotion' of new products where appropriate standards of ideas, aesthetics, presentation and style all contribute to customer perception of the product and confidence in the company.

None the less, there is a strong relationship between a review of the product development process and a reduced time to market. To this end, 'process' includes issues such as an incremental product review, use of multi-disciplinary design teams, market feedback, corporate design management, research and development, senior management commitment to design and qualified skilled designers. Design in this context plays a key role in ensuring that new products are developed in an integrated, cohesive manner, and reducing the likelihood of wasted time through misunderstandings and poor communications.

Production

The final level of this VIPP model is production, which will be directly affected by design decisions at the front end of new projects. As Walsh et al. (1992) point out, 80 or 90 per cent of production costs are committed at this stage. Consequently, tangible savings can be made, often in collaboration with new technology, since design can 'reduce product complexity', often by cutting down the number of parts and removing unnecessary clutter. It can also take advantage of the scope and potential offered by the introduction of new materials. For example, the classic Fisher Price toy – the children's 'chatterbox telephone' – has undergone many changes over a period of twenty years, mostly indiscernible to the consumer, but all aimed at improving quality on the one hand and reducing production time on the other. A wooden base and riveted cover for the sound box has been replaced by one moulded plastic unit and the 'telephone' lead, which previously got caught up in the wheels, is now a retractable coil. Even the lead attachment is built into the moulded base rather than using a separate and potentially dangerous wire staple. Yet the original invention in terms of colour scheme, decor, shape and propulsion mechanism has remained virtually unchanged so that it is instantly recognizable to existing and new customers.

Similarly, the McBean foul weather clothing company, which took part in the Bradford survey, reduced production time of a pocket from half an hour to three minutes by redesigning a garment. The savings made in terms of manufacturing time, wages and materials are considerable and have also precipitated a reduction in overhead costs, altogether making a significant contribution towards the company's competitive position. At the same time, this company has made a sizeable capital investment in 'state of the art' technology with the latest cutting equipment, computer-aided design and production techniques, supported by a facility for examining fabrics electronically. This reinforces the blend of technology with qualitative, reliable designs that have provided company strengths for growth and expansion overseas (Trueman and Jobber, 1995).

However, this expansion has led to further demands on design. It transpires that workmen in some European countries are more 'fashion conscious' than their British counterparts, so that adjustments have had to be made accordingly. Similarly, the newly acquired Japanese market has a different taste in style and fitting requirements. In each case, the precise demands and production implications have to be carefully and thoroughly researched. This reinforces the close link between design and technology transfer, particularly where different cultures are involved and highlights the need for flexibility in response to these differing demands. It also underlines the valuable role that design can play in interpreting ideas where language and cultural differences may otherwise prove a barrier to communication and progress. This phenomenon is of increasing importance since in addition to trading overseas it is now common practice to manufacture goods more cheaply in countries which have favourable terms such as relatively cheap, skilled labour and low overhead costs, reducing production costs to a minimum (Lasserre, 1995).

A further lesson to be learnt from this globalization of production and markets is the need for a flexible manufacturing system to support changes in demand as well as product range and choice. In fact, Porter (1990) in his seminal work 'The Competitive Advantage of Nations', points out that automation means that a large, low-cost labour force is less important in many processes than a small but highly trained one, which is more likely to be flexible and responsive to changing customer needs. Here, continual 'training' and upgrading are increasingly important for companies in order to keep abreast of the latest technological developments on the one hand and sophisticated customer requirements as well as competitors on the other. It also emphasizes the need for multidisciplinary teams who can address the complexity of markets, design, production and financial implications at the outset of new projects, since the value, image and process benchmarks will have a profound effect upon production and subsequently the logistics of a successful product launch.

In terms of performance measures at production level, there is an association between raising the corporate design profile and speedier productions, precipitating a reduced time to market. In this case, the use of external design consultants is considered to have a strong influence. Production time can also be reduced by using new technology at the front end of new projects as well as within the process itself. Naturally, efficiency in production depends a great deal on ironing out problems beforehand and design has a facility for reducing complexity which can enhance a smooth production as well as saving time, materials and overhead costs.

Strategy at the front end

Most researchers appear to agree that, all things being equal, it is the front end of the process where real difference between success and failure can be made. However, recent work has shown that surprisingly few of even the top performing companies have a clear integrated strategy at the outset of new products (Khurana and Rosenthal, 1997). Furthermore, many hard-pressed companies do not have a long-term vision of the life span for a product range, since intense competition in the marketplace encourages a focus on launch and payback periods (Booz, Allen and Hamilton, 1982; Cooper and Kleinschmidt, 1996). This research would argue that front end decisions can be greatly enhanced by adopting a VIPP strategy to maximize the competitive advantage afforded by design. But often UK companies tend to tack design on to the end of the development process, making little use of the country's design talents. In contrast, many successful Japanese industrial firms have adopted the USA approach of integrating design at the outset of new projects with a strong emphasis on styling and marketing (Ohtani, 1995).

While it is recognized that a balance must be achieved between identifying changing customer needs through market research (Kotler and Armstrong, 1996), keeping abreast of new technological developments, and identifying company distinctive competencies and limitations (Hayes and Allinson 1994), the usability, producibility and appropriateness of new products advocated by Fujimoto (1990) become more apparent. In fact, the notion of perceived product value supported by company and product image provide a clear focus or goal for project teams – a distinct advantage in the face of pressures from uncertainty, risk, a myriad of requirements and a plethora of information in an increasingly complex business environment. Furthermore, design attributes can be used as a strategic tool to enhance, control and direct perceived product value as well as product and company image (Walsh et al., 1992), providing the fulcrum around which process and production can be orchestrated.

For example, the development of a new hoverplane by the Florida-based Wingship company has been driven by customer-perceived value influenced by a need for 'speed', 'safety' and 'environmentally friendly travel' (Figure 4.7). This is matched by the company need for 'fuel efficiency' in terms of operation, 'lightweight, strong construction', and a need to 'circumvent restrictive legislation' of the Civil Aviation Authority by developing a prototype which falls within laws governing ferry transport by the International Maritime Organization. The resulting hoverplane can travel at speeds of up to 200 mph (322 kph), which is five times faster than current craft, yet efficiencies are gained since it uses only one fifth of the fuel because of reduced drag and increased lift! Furthermore, the technology allows a safer passage since, by riding on a cushion of air above the water, it is much less likely to be affected by inclement weather, floating debris or hidden rocks. This project represents a combination of perceived customer needs, sophisticated design and the latest technology built upon 'Wise' (wing in surface effect) research carried out by the Soviet Union during the Cold War (Windle, 1997). The image of the hoverplane is sleek, aerodynamic, modern and sophisticated, so that in aesthetic design terms it could be described as elegant, of new technological age and uncluttered. In other words, it combines leading-

Figure 4.7 *Florida Wingship Company 30 Seat Hoverplane.* Source: *David Windle. Sunday Times, Innovation, 24 August 1997*

edge technology with the practical considerations of safety and fuel efficiency, representing a good example of 'interpretation' and 'integration' of ideas in the development process of, as well as a reduction in, complexity.

By contrast, the image presented by Laura Ashley today does not reinforce the customer-perceived product value as it did in the 1970s and 1980s. Although products produced under this 'brand' are still considered to be well made and qualitative, and there remains a small market sector of loyal customers, for many the world of fashion has changed leaving the company behind in a virtual 'time warp'. Consequently, share prices have reached an all-time low and the organization is experiencing perhaps the most serious crisis since its foundation in 1953. Here, new designs could make a direct impact on rebuilding customer-perceived value and realigning its image to attract new interest and confidence as well as maintaining current supporters (Reid, 1997). This scenario illustrates the importance of building a regular product value and image review into the process strategy adopted by companies. It also indicates that not even large established companies can afford complacency, particularly those operating in leading-edge technology. To this end, a giant corporation such as Microsoft has continually expanded, invested in research and updated its products, as well as reviewing processes and production in line with constant changes in technology and customer needs. On the other hand, small companies are still able to compete by using the same strategy but focusing on niche markets.

A further example of a VIPP integrated approach towards product development can be seen in new car design in collaboration with an international consortium of thirty-five steelmakers. In this case, there is a need to meet a customer-perceived need for lighter, safer cars to improve performance and reduce fuel consumption, thus representing an increase in the perceived value of cars as a means of transport. There is also a need to counteract a perception that steel must always be heavy and therefore costly on fuel, although it has the benefit of strength over its rivals in the aluminium industry. The new image of steel discussed earlier in this chapter has been coupled with leading-edge technology that can produce high strength steel

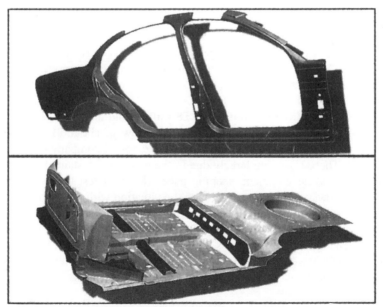

Light and strong: the body side outer and the one-piece floorplan

Figure 4.8 *Ultra Light Steel Auto Body (Uslab), Massachusetts Institute of Technology and Ibis Associates (USA).* Source: *John Griffiths,* Financial Times, *29 April 1997*

bodies which are 35 per cent lighter and cheaper to produce than existing models. This new process has been developed by the Ultra Light Steel Auto Body (Uslab) at the Massachusetts Institute of Technology and includes a similar design approach to the Fisher Price Chatterbox telephone discussed above since the car floor has a 'one piece' floor plan (Figure 4.8). However, in this case, the savings in production may be on a considerably greater scale (Griffiths, 1997).

Examples of applications

In order to explore the VIPP model in more detail and examine ways in which it can be integrated into company strategy, the following account of two deliberately contrasting SMEs is presented. This shows how the model and typology can not only provide a focus for developing new products, but also highlight the relative strengths and weakness of each organization. At one end of the spectrum is Company A, which has developed new multimedia information and communications systems and is at the forefront of leading-edge technology (sunrise). By contrast, Company B is an old, long-established firm which produces contract wooden framed seating for the health-care industry (sunset). The latter has considered innovations such as a new 'recliner' or 'recovery chair' for use in day-care centres and a new line of chrome metal frame office furniture aimed at the executive market. Both of these SMEs have about 200 employees. Company B's turnover has been steady over the past five years at about £7–8 million per annum with profits between £500,000 and £1 million. Company A, on the other hand, has fluctuated widely from £19 million to £8 million and has made a loss rather than profit, with a debt which appeared to grow at about £1 million per annum, slowing down in 1996 with a rationalization of company strategy and personnel. These losses are largely due to the enormous sustained investment in research and development, keeping pace with the latest technology, even though there was an attempt to stabilize the situation with the flotation of the company on the UK stock market in 1993. Both companies have city centre locations, and particular problems in developing new products because of dramatic changes in their business and marketing environments. In each case, senior managers were able to relate to the VIPP typology in terms of overall company strategy, as well as in relation to specific projects.

Company A

In some respects the element of risk is greater for Company A since it is a *new* company developing custom-built *new* technological innovations in

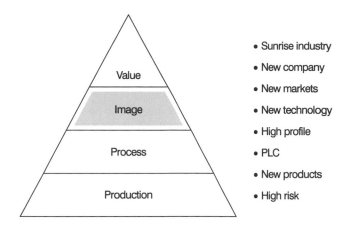

Figure 4.9 *Main VIPP focus of Company A*

new markets. At the same time, it is becoming increasingly difficult to recoup the enormous cost of investment since the relatively expensive, tailor-made products offered by this company have been seriously challenged by some competitors' 'off the shelf' products, which are now relatively cheap. As a result, this could be considered a 'high risk' venture, with a strategy described by Iansiti (1995) as 'shooting the rapids'.

If the VIPP typology is applied to Company A (Figure 4.9), it would appear that there is a strong 'external' focus on promoting the image of the company and its new products, possibly influenced by the fact that it has been developed by an organization whose roots are in advertising. However, this organization has not clearly identified the product value attributes before moving on to the next innovation. In other words, a preoccupation of keeping pace with the speed of technological change has led to a lack of attention to market research as well as a temptation to address perhaps too many markets simultaneously. Consequently, as the nature of products has changed, the main benefits have not been communicated to clearly identified market sectors, nor does it appear that sufficient attention has been paid to the current needs of those sectors. In this respect, the notion of Fujimoto's (1990) product 'appropriateness' has not been met. But strong links in the form of joint ventures with suppliers with well-known brand names have gone some way to reduce uncertainty, to some extent increasing customer confidence as well as perceived product value. For example, long-established brand names such as BT (British Telecom) supply the ISDN lines for these products and Hewlett Packard is now involved in a joint research venture.

Process and production in Company A

This company has now reached a stage where process and production need urgent attention in order to make efficiency gains. Both require standardization across the range of products to bring down very large 'overhead' costs and improve profit margins within which the company must operate. These measures would also allow a reduction in time to market, since a number of contracts have been lost through extended deadlines, as well as an increasingly uncompetitive-competitive product price. Such factors show a weakness which positions the company at an imbalance, on the wrong side of Abernathy's (1985) productivity/technology dilemma – the development process has become inefficient and does not meet Fujimoto's criteria for product 'producibility'. Consequently, the company is currently undergoing a period of consolidation and may be able to build upon its experience gained from nearly a decade of working in multimedia. To this end, they may examine the way in which their customers' needs, perceived values and work patterns have changed and match this with company perceived values and procedures.

For example, the first CD-ROM based system launched in 1989 was deliberately set up with a 'user friendly interface' and promoted for those working in the construction industry so that they could 'work in a traditional way'. It was priced realistically for technology at that time (£2,765) so as to be affordable by small practices. The cost of this might be set against the estimated time per week (say fifteen hours) and per year that architects or other construction workers might spend in getting hold of information. To this may be added the cost of journals, floor space and the management of 'hard copy' magazines and promotional literature. However, to abandon the traditional reference sources requires a considerable 'act of faith', as well as a certain element of new practice. Potential users have to be certain that the new information source is reliable, comprehensive and up to date (Higgins, 1985). Nevertheless these first systems received quite a bit of attention and may well have formed a sound customer base if the product launch into the construction industry had not coincided with the UK recession which affected this industrial sector more than most!

New strategy and technology

As a result of the above, this company has had to change its new product strategy and review target markets. At the same time, the explosion of online systems prompted the company to re-examine the limitations of a CD-ROM technology, even though new advances meant that more information could be compressed on to two discs rather than the twelve required for the first model. The disadvantage is that, however compact these discs were, they still needed monthly or quarterly updating. Information is only as recent as the latest discs and may be up to three months out of date! As a result, the decision was made to develop an online system which could link up to a host computer. The promotional material describes this as 'the digital version of all the colour images and video programs which would have traditionally been on paper or tape'. Now information can be updated on a daily if not hourly basis. It has also led to a joint venture with BT since the new system would use BT ISDN lines. This had two advantages: (1) BT now promotes the new multimedia online system as a user of ISDN, and (2) the company gains further credibility from its association with BT.

As far as perceived value is concerned, the new 'Advantage' multimedia system has been developed and promoted in a very different manner. Rather than working in a 'traditional way', people are actively encouraged to grasp the opportunities for change and competitive advantage afforded by new technology. A measure of the initial success of this new system was seen by a flotation of the company on the Stock Exchange in 1993, using a new company name and image to reflect the nature of the business. The new 'online' system more accurately embraces the concept of 'multimedia' since it includes a video facility as well as sound and an integrated telephone link. In fact, at the time of the flotation of the company the consultants Padiachy and Norris (1994) considered that 'the company's core asset is the vision to see new applications for ISDN technology'. But their investment recommendations, which compares eight companies in this field, warn that 'As new entrants appear, the technology will become universally available. The importance of technology is largely in the first mover advantage of establishing a strong customer base', but in terms of management and culture the 'Ability to move fast in new markets will be a key differentiating issue and a potential hurdle for larger companies.' In their view Company A was in a strong position to take advantage of the technology having the flexibility of a smaller company. But since the launch, the need to establish a strong customer base has become a major stumbling block (Trueman and Jobber, 1995)

Outpacing competitors and the need for technological change

Although new markets are constantly being explored, the company is beginning to lose out through the speed of technological change on the one hand and a large reduction in 'off the shelf' products on the other. In short, this company has demonstrated the characteristic of a company which, according to Kanter (1984), thrives on change and has the 'vision' to see new applications for ISDN technology but is now in danger of losing out to competitors who may have concentrated on niche market applications. It has been in a fortunate position to be able to afford a large-scale R & D effort and has worked hard to develop a new image and get established in new markets,

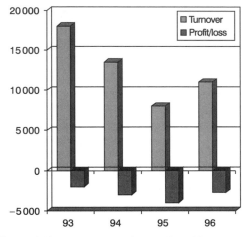

1988 Introduce *new* CD-ROM product to construction industry but hit by UK recession.

1992 Strategic alliances with BT, BSI and Hewlett Packard.

1993 Stock market floatation (sp.60p), *new* online product (high risk innovation and environment).

1994 Share price 210p.

1996 Strategic review with *new* intranet management product.

1997 Restructure company and shed some staff (sp.17p).

Figure 4.10 *Company A's financial profile*

but now urgently needs to consolidate its position and financial performance (Figure 4.10). More recently there has been a focus upon process and production with a rationalization in the range of bespoke systems and a new approach towards the production of standard parts. However, the analysis of product perceived value on the part of the customer has been slow to get established. Company A has also been reviewing its mode of operation in the light of poor performance on the stock market where confidence in shares has reached an all time low of 17p from a launch price of 60p and a record high of 120p during the first six months. However, this fresh look at company strategy has taken the form of a consultant's report and shedding of staff, rather than a participative review in collaboration with employees.

Company B

By way of contrast, Company B may be described as having a predominantly internal focus on process and production, reinforced with the current preoccupation of installing a new comprehensive information technology and communications (ITC) system to handle all the requirements of the organization. This does not mean that image has not been considered; in fact, a new corporate identity was adopted in the 1980s and another is planned to meet the millennium. But this company policy is to consolidate process and production before moving on to image. Both companies have neglected value, a situation which has been exacerbated by a weakness in market research in each case.

   However, Company B has increased the risk factor with its tentative move into a new market (office furniture), using new technology (chrome-framed furniture). Although it does have a clearly defined customer base for its main business in health care it has yet to get established in the executive office furniture market. But in contrast to Company A, the new business is still within the furniture industry and its realm of competence. In terms of similarity both companies have had rather autocratic styles of leadership and in each case the 'trigger' for innovation was 'top down' rather than 'bottom up' and not reinforced by rigorous market research. The furniture company has recently altered its approach towards employees with the arrival of a new director, who has generated a more participative style of leadership and is instigating something of a cultural change.

Since the established market in domestic furniture had become increasingly competitive, the company became more dependent on contracts to supply furniture to the National Health Service (NHS). However, with deregulation of health-care supplies in the 1990s, it has entered a new, volatile market environment where intense competition from British and overseas competitors has placed the company in a more vulnerable and uncertain position. A small market had developed in the hotel and leisure industry but this was also affected by the UK recession so that the core business still relies on the supply of wooden-framed seating to established contacts in health care. Developing new products is important if not vital to the future stability of the company but presents high risk in terms of limited investment capabilities. Furthermore, any new departures may be difficult for a company which is steeped in traditional practice rather than adjusting to the management of change. This is illustrated by a cautious investigation of the feasibility of diversification into 'recliner chairs' for the now deregulated health-care industry and a new departure into chrome-framed executive office seating (Figure 4.11).

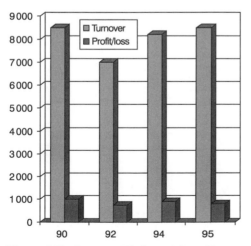

1989 Core business to supply contract furniture to NHS but *new* company name and launches into *new* market (hotel and leisure).

1990 BS5750 award, but NHS deregulates health care.

1993 Feasibility study of new recliner chair for health care.

1994 Cease domestic furniture. Research chrome-frame executive office furniture.

1996 Launch *new* chrome furniture in *new* exec market. (Increase risk.)

1997 Install *new* IT system and maintain NHS customer base with wooden-frame furniture.

Figure 4.11 *Company B's financial profile*

Process and production in Company B

Most new products are incremental extensions to existing ranges and take between two and six months to develop. The current product range consists of over 600 items but there is concern that there are now too many, precipitating a need to reduce the range and focus on best-selling lines. In other words, the company may need to systematically remove less profitable items as well as developing new innovations.

To address these needs, a 'Product review committee' has recently been set up with a brief to focus on issues such as price and design sensitivity. However, an efficient means for control, analysis and evaluation is only just being put into place with the installation of the new ITC system, since it will be able to handle all company needs from inventory, accounts and wages to production and design. The efficiency requirements from the new system are to reduce bottlenecks in production, make better use of personnel across the company particularly in terms of new projects and decrease the need for expensive storage space. This will enhance the general efficiency and productivity of the company so that it can more quickly respond to customer needs, replacing previous systems which were incompatible, inefficient and time consuming (Figure 4.12). As the finance director explained, 'we have lost the advantage of the new technology installed ten years ago when we were the only company with advanced technology in this market – now all our competitors have caught up'. Until this new system is fully installed the company cannot easily carry out a comparative analysis of successful products or determine the feasibility of proposed innovations.

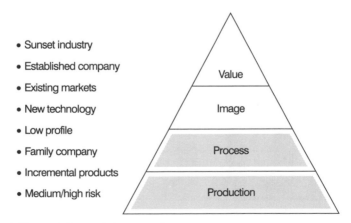

Figure 4.12 *VIPP focus of Company B*

Problems associated with innovation in health care

But developing new products for health care is particularly difficult because
there are many levels of interest to be considered. Each has its own agenda
and perceived value as to what constitutes an appropriate product. This is
because of the complex process of procurement and supplies, which although
deregulated, still needs to address a host of variables including standards,
regulatory control, safety, clinical, ergonomic, financial and aesthetic
requirements. Companies have to deal not only with the NHS and Regional
Supplies Departments, but also the supplies representative from each hospital
or health centre. Beyond these main players are hospital managers, surgeons
and physicians, nurses and other medical staff, cleaners and, of course, the
patients. Each has a different perception about the requirements and value of
furniture for health care. For example, the supplies departments may consider
balancing budgets and ensuring that official safety regulations are met, while
the hospital manager may view not only finance but patient throughput, since
four patient 'chairs' can occupy the space taken by one hospital bed. The
surgeon may examine a chair in terms of safety if patients are recovering from
an anaesthetic, while an occupational therapist views a chair as an instrument
for healing, 'something which patients get well from' (Trueman, 1995).

On the other hand, nurses may consider patients' comfort and issues such
as the weight of the chair if it has to be moved, the seat height in relation to
an adjoining table, and whether or not it matches the overall colour scheme of
a new or refurbished room. Finally, the cleaners may be faced with hygiene
and the need for 'wipe clean' surfaces, while the patients themselves consider
not only comfort but chair position (Is it in a good, secure vantage point?) and
self-esteem (Does it look respectable, attractive?). No one is likely to feel
happy using a chair that is dowdy or damaged in some way. At the same time,
there is a move towards the development of hospital furniture with a domestic,
friendly appearance, away from the clinical 'functional' products of the 1950s
and 1960s. In this respect it could be argued that the patient's perceived value
of a chair could supersede that of all other parties.

Meanwhile deregulation has opened up the market to competitors so that
the company needs to review all its procedures to ensure that the productivity
and efficiency measures gained from the new IPC system are equal if not
better than its new rivals. At the same time, the company will need to
reposition and reassess its image to ensure that it matches the aspirations of all
those concerned in the new health-care industry.

Consequently, the company is now in a more vulnerable position since
rapid changes in the health-care market threaten to destabilize the customer
base. These changes have been brought about by technological developments
in medicine, restructuring of practices and demographic trends, as well as new
competition. At the same time, the company is anxious to maintain its

workforce and 'in-house expertise'. The need to innovate is considered to be a priority so that the need to diversify has become more acute, and has inspired the tentative move towards high-quality chrome-framed office furniture. This does represent a higher risk in terms of product innovation (metal rather than wood technology), and a new market for the company, but is being developed along existing lines in the factory so that the operating overhead costs are at present under control. If this new departure proves successful, then the appropriate production processes will be upgraded to run on separate, more efficient lines.

Market research, information technology and perceived value

The company has also recruited some new employees who may influence innovation on the one hand and efficiency on the other, even though the size of the company presents some problems since they cannot afford to offer 'top range' salaries to attract 'high flier' graduates. A new market research post has been created for a young graduate who is being trained to assume responsibility in this area. In this way, innovations are more likely to be driven by market needs rather than being sales dominated, as was the case in the past. At the same time, an IT specialist is now in post who has been appointed on a slightly higher grade than most employees. This specialist has the responsibility of supervising the installation and running of the new, expensive ITC system

These recent developments are an indication of a major cultural change for Company B as well as a small change of attitude towards innovation. Once the process and production reviews are completed, the focus will shift back towards image, since a new corporate identity is planned for the year 2000. At the same time, a new approach towards new products and their perceived value is likely to arise from the new appointment in marketing.

Summary and conclusions

Sony's Akio Morita (1992) stresses that the innovation process begins with a mandate that must be set at the highest level of the corporation by identifying goals and priorities; and once identified, these must be communicated all the way down the line. Certainly these companies do not lack motivation and their directors do not lack vision. However, they are typical of most SMEs today, which are faced with an increasingly complex, constantly changing business environment and intense competition. If they do not manage to address the process of innovation at a number of different levels they are unlikely to be successful in the long term. Although they may be concerned with the development of very different products, many of the problems they face are surprisingly similar. For example, both were faced with the need to re-examine their use of new technology since they had lost the competitive edge gained from investments made about ten years ago. Similarly, both companies recognized a need to rationalize the product range in order to meet requirements for efficiency in production and a reduced time to market, even though the approach taken was different in each case. Furthermore, senior managers in both companies were able to relate to the VIPP model at strategic as well as project level. In other words, they consider issues such as the value and image of the company as well as the individual product.

But if all four dimensions of the model have to be addressed in equal measure for successful innovation, Company A's radical innovation appears all the more 'risky', with an undue focus upon 'image' to the neglect of 'value', 'process' and 'production'. It is now seeking to address problems relating to 'process' and 'production' in a bid to redress poor performance on the stock market. By contrast, Company B is able to shift focus across three dimensions of 'image', 'process' and 'production' on a more regular basis, within a cycle of about ten years. Both companies had neglected product value, in terms of customer perception, partly through a weakness in the area of market research. In the case of Company B, this has been addressed by the creation of a new marketing post, although in terms of quality and standards, this company has considered these attributes with its accreditation of BS 5750 and ISO 9000. However, in Company A, the notion of perceived product value and market research has become blurred with a preoccupation in advertising and image. But although neither company appears to have fully addressed the notion of perceived product value, both now show signs of moving in this direction (Figure 4.13).

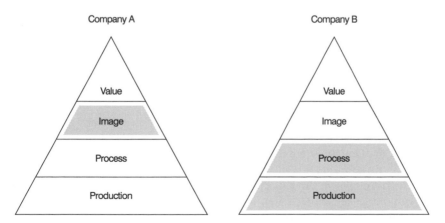

Figure 4.13 *VIPP focus of Company A and Company B*

These case studies are illuminating and may suggest that a change of attitude towards the use of design at different levels of the innovation process is likely to facilitate the control and development of successful new products, thereby making some reduction to risk and uncertainty. However, it is not clear how much design attributes contribute to the development of new products or at which level they could or should make the greatest contribution, since this exploratory research has focused upon the examination of current and past practice rather than testing a prescriptive model. At the same time, it is recognized that dimensions such as perceived value may alter over time as variables change. For example, the relatively cheap price and increased sophistication of technology today compared with that on offer ten or even five years ago will have altered customer perception of value even if this change has not been reviewed by the company. This research would argue that such a phenomenon heightens the need for a strong design input to new technological developments since evidence of quality, standards and reliability in new products will allow companies to command a higher sale price than inferior competing products at any one time.

Concluding statements

1 Two SMEs working in very different industries have surprisingly similar problems in keeping up to date with the latest technology and managing their innovation strategies in the face of intense competition and complex, rapidly changing business and market environments. These problems manifest themselves in different ways.

2 If the VIPP design typology is applied to these companies it is apparent that both have not properly addressed value, and that Company A has become preoccupied with its image and may be described as 'externally focused'. Conversely Company B has had a major upheaval in order to address process and production and has a tendency towards an 'internal focus', although there are plans to re-examine image in the near future.

3 A focus upon perceived product value is a key starting point for new projects, where customer perceptions can be enhanced by design attributes. This is especially important for radical new products, which may be at the leading edge of technology.

4 Product 'value' can be reinforced with an appropriate company and product image, but advertising and promoting this image will not be successful if 'value' calculations are inaccurate. To this end, both value and image need to be reviewed on a regular basis.

5 The development process should be extended beyond product launch and may be enhanced by design to interpret, integrate and communicate new ideas. In this way new products will be produced speedily and in a cohesive manner.

6 Costly overheads and production time can be reduced by using design to simplify complex products, save materials and take advantage of new technological developments.
7 The VIPP typology is a step towards demystifying the process of design and may go some way to facilitating hard pressed companies in the development of 'radical' as well as 'incremental' new products in an increasingly competitive business environment. By examining the current and potential use of design attributes at each level of the development process, it may be possible to reduce risk and uncertainty, thereby increasing the likelihood of launching more successful new products such as those discussed by Prime Minister Blair.

Acknowledgements

We would like to acknowledge the support and advice from Sarah Breckenridge, Marketing Manager at Dyson Dual Cyclone Technology, Ginnie Leatham, Marketing Manager at Virgin Atlantic Airways, Brian Richards, Manager of Publicity and Company Image at British Steel and Paul Wylde in Design Management at British Airways. We would also like to thank Barry Pickthall at PPL for efficient technical advice, Susan Kew at the *Financial Times* Picture Desk and David Windle at the *Sunday Times* Innovation Unit.

References

Abernathy, W. (1985) The productivity dilemma. In *The Uneasy Alliance* (K. B. Clark, R. H. Hayes and C. Lorenz, eds), Harvard Business School Press.

Aldersley-Willams, H. (1996) Measurement turns a profit. *Financial Times,* 3 March.

Archer, L. B. (1985) The designerly ways of knowing. Seminar series at the Royal College of Art Department of Design Research, London.

Blair, T. (1997) Britain can remake it. *Guardian,* 22 July.

Booz, Allen and Hamilton Consultants (1982) *New Product Management for the 1980s.* Booz, Allen and Hamilton Consultants, New York.

Bowman, C. and Faulkner, D. (1994) Measuring product advantage using competitive benchmarking and customer perceptions. *Long Range Planning,* **27**(1), 119–32.

Brown, C. L. and Lattin, J. M. (1994) Investigating the relationship between time in market and pioneering advantage. *Management Science,* **40**(10), October.

Clark, K. and Fujimoto, T. (1990) The power of product integrity. *Harvard Business Review*, November–December.

Clausing, D. and Simpson, B. H. (1990) Quality by design. *Quality Progress*, **23**(1).

Cooper, R. and Chew, W. B. (1996) Control tomorrow's costs through today's designs. *Harvard Business Review*, January–February.

Cooper, R. G. and Kleinschmidt, E. J. (1996) Winning businesses in product development: the critical success factors. *Research-Technology Management*, **39**(4) July–August, 18–29.

Craig, A. and Hart, S. (1992) Dimensions of success in new product development. Conference proceedings, *Marketing for Europe – Marketing for the Future*, 21st, Annual Conference of European Marketing Academy, (K. G. Grunert and D. Fuglede, eds), Aarhus, Denmark, 26–29 May.

Dawkins, W. (1996) Japan to inject billions into 'ideas research'. *Financial Times*, 3 July.

DTI (1991) *Profits by Design. A summary of the findings of an investigation into the commercial returns of investing in design by the Open University/ UMIST research team.* HMSO.

Dumas, A. and Mintzberg, H. (1989) Managing design, designing management. *Design Management Journal*, Fall.

Dwek, R. (1997) Proving its metal. *Marketing Business*, April, 26–30.

Freeman, C. (1997) The greening of technology and models of innovation. *Technology Forecasting and Social Change*, **53**, 27–39.

Fujimoto, T. (1990) Growth of international competition and the importance of effective product development management and the role of design. Conference proceedings: Product strategies for the 1990s, *Financial Times*.

Gorb, P. (1988) The business of design management. *Design Studies*, **7**(2).

Griffiths, J. (1997) Steel car design races for the finishing line. Manufacturers hope to fight off aluminium. *Financial Times*, 29 April, p. 16.

Hayes, J. and Allinson, C. W. (1994) Cognitive style and its relevance for management practice. *British Journal of Management*, **5**, 53–71.

Higgins, J. M. (1985) Innovate or evaporate: creative techniques for strategies. *Long Range Planning*, **29**, June.

Hollins, B. and Pugh, S. (1990) *Successful Product Design*. Butterworth.

Hutton, W. (1996) *The State We're In*. Vintage.

Iansiti, M. (1995) Shooting the rapids: managing product development in turbulent environments. *Californian Management Review*, **38**(1), Fall.

Ittner, C. D. and Larker, D. F. (1997) Product development cycle time and organizational performance. *Journal of Marketing Research*, February.

Kanter, R. M. (1984) *The Change Masters, Corporate Entrepreneurs at Work*. Allen and Unwin.

Khurana, A. and Rosenthal, S. R. (1997) Integrating the fuzzy front end of new product development. *Sloan Management Review*, Winter.

Kotler, P. and Armstrong, G. (1996) *The Principles of Marketing*. 7th edn, Prentice Hall.

Lasserre, P. (1995) Corporate strategies for the Asia Pacific region. *Long Range Planning*, **28**(1), 13–30.

Lawrence, P. (1989) The design asset. *The Corporate Board*, July–August.

Lorenz, C. (1995) Harnessing design as a strategic resource. *Long Range Planning*, **27**(5), 73–84.

Mitchell, A. (1996) Limited companies: service industries are having a hard time dealing with the stakeholder concept, *Marketing Business*, May.

Morita, A. (1992) The First United Kingdom Innovation Lecture: 'S' does not equal 'T' and 'T' does not equal 'I'. The Royal Society, London, 6 February.

Nobeoka, K. and Cusumano, M. A. (1997) Multiple strategy and sales growth: the benefits of rapid design transfer in new product development. *Strategic Management Journal*, **18**(3), 169–86.

OECD (1981) The measurement of scientific and technical activities. *Frascati Manual*, Organization for Economic Co-operation and Development.

Ohtani, N. (1995) Exploiting the potential. *World Class Design to Manufacture*, **2**(1), 13–16.

Olins, W. (1986) The strategy of design. *Management Today*, May.

Padiachy, V. and Norris, P. (1994) *Interactive Media: a Survey of Pioneer Products in Media*, Barclays de Zoette Wedd Research Ltd, June.

Porter, M. E. (1990) The comparative advantage of nations. *Harvard Business Review*, **90**(2).

Price, C. and Taylor, P. (1997) Psion hit by slowing sales: computer group's shares tumble 19 per cent ahead of Series 5 launch, *Financial Times*, 17 June, p. 21.

Pugh, S. (1986) Design activity models: worldwide emergence and convergence. *Design Studies*, **7**(3).

Rassam, C. (1995) *Design and Corporate Success – The Design Council*. Gower.

Reid, S. (1997) Tell Laura I love her. The dresses might be dated and the company in trouble but Laura Ashley still has its flowery fans. *Sunday Times* Style, 31 August.

Roy, R. (1993) Case studies of creativity in innovative product development. *Design Studies*, **14**(4), 423–44.

Schmitt, B. H., Simonson, A. and Marcus, J. (1995) Managing corporate image and identity. *Long Range Planning*, **28**, October.

Southgate, P. (1994) *Total Branding by Design*. Kogan Page.

Srinivasan, V., Lovejoy, W. S. and Beach, D. (1997) Integrated product design for marketability and manufacturing. *Journal of Marketing Research*, **34**, February, 154–63.

Takeuchi, H. and Nonaka, I. (1986) The new product development game. *Harvard Business Review*, January–February.

Topfer, A. (1995) New products – cutting the time to market. *Long Range Planning*, **28**(2), 61–78.

Trueman, M. (1992) Company Orientation Towards New Product Design. PhD Thesis, Bradford University Management Centre.

Trueman, M. (1995) It all depends where you're sitting: changing supplier/customer relationships in the healthcare industry and how they affect attitudes towards the development of innovative new products in the contract furniture industry. Proceedings of 1995 Annual MEG Conference, *Making Marketing Work*, June.

Trueman, M. (1996) *Your Global Perspective of Design*. Survey carried out at Elmwood Design Innovation Conference, Leeds, 18 September.

Trueman, M. (1997) *Demystifying Innovation by Design: How a new design typology may facilitate the product development process in industrial companies and provide competitive advantage*. Seventh International Forum on Technology Management. Conference Proceedings, Kyoto, Japan, 3–7 November, pp. 278–87.

Trueman, M. and Jobber, D. (1993) *New Product Design and Corporate Success. How Corporate Attitudes towards New Product Design Relate to Company Profitability*. Bradford Management Centre report.

Trueman, M. and Jobber, D. (1995) Designing the front end: how attitudes are related to company performance. *World Class Design to Manufacture*, **1**(3), January–February.

Walsh, V., Roy, R., Bruce, M. and Potter, S. (1992) *Winning by Design: Technology, Product Design and International Competitiveness*. Blackwell.

Walters, G. (1997) Amway action over Dyson book. *The Times*, 16 May.

Wasserman, A. (1990) Learning by experience: an approach to design strategies for product success. *Product Strategies for the 90s*, Conference proceedings, *Financial Times*.

Windle, D. (1997) Ferry bridges gap between hovercraft and planes. *Sunday Times* Innovation, 24 August, pp. 2, 18.

Wu, D. (1997) Chinese contemporary design problems and achievements. MA thesis, Staffordshire University.

5 Bringing in and focusing on customer true needs

D. M. Ginn

This chapter focuses on how a very successful quality function deployment (QFD) team within Ford of Europe has adapted to the new Ford 2000 culture to become an example of best practice in ascertaining customer true needs. Within seven years, the Emissions QFD team matured into an Emissions Quality Forum co-ordinating all the emissions-related quality, robustness and systems engineering sub-system team activities within the globalized Ford Automotive Operations. The Emissions QFD and Quality Forum have produced excellent results in terms of improved quality, timing and cost criteria, by focusing in on true customer needs.

This team has developed its own proforma for integrating a comprehensive toolbox of customer-driven quality techniques within the company-wide product development process. It has also shown flexibility in customizing existing tools, especially QFD and robustness engineering. In doing so, the team has assisted the continuous improvement of the company-wide quality process.

The chapter is divided into eight sections starting with a brief introduction to three of the fundamental themes of the chapter: the needs of the customer; the needs of the automotive industry and the need for QFD. This is followed by a detailed look at the four key components of bringing in and focusing on customer true needs by looking at a definition of the customer within the Ford 2000 perspective. To reinforce all these arguments, the sixth section identifies a best practice case study from within Ford that demonstrates how a QFD team became a worldwide quality forum. The criteria of success within the case study is then correlated with the results of an internal Ford benchmarking survey corroborated by a Massachusetts Institute of Technology (MIT) survey to assess effective QFD. The chapter concludes by bringing together all the arguments discussed into a coherent strategy for bringing in and focusing on customer true needs, with an emphasis on deployment.

The World will not evolve beyond its present state of crisis by using the same thinking that created the situation. (Albert Einstein)

Customers, motor vehicles and quality function deployment

There are three main 'characters' in this chapter: the customer, the motor industry and the quality technique of QFD. From these three elements we will learn to view the customer in more complex terms than merely as an end user and to consider how to focus on customer needs with an integrated approach to quality tools, teamwork and processes. Examples are given throughout from the perspective of the motor industry in general, Ford Motor Company in particular and the Emissions QFD and Quality Forum specifically. A summary proposes a best practice scenario to ensure how customer true needs can be effectively brought in and focused on, with an emphasis on deployment through the product delivery cycle.

The needs of the customer

The current highly competitive nature of the commercial world has brought high customer satisfaction and product loyalty to the forefront of corporate strategies. It can be argued that these two factors depend on the quality of a product, which in turn depends on the product function performing to, or exceeding, customer expectation. It can also be reasonably assumed that the customer expects the product to provide excitement and perform for the duration of its useful life, all at a cost that represents value for money (Kano et al., 1994).

It would also be unrealistic for a producer to assume critical customer requirements without first asking the customer. Equally, it would be unrealistic for the customer to assume that the qualities of the product are there by chance. Furthermore, the perception of product quality is dependent on the performance, robustness and reliability of the product, including after-sales service. The customer is also demanding the product to be available in the marketplace more quickly than ever before, a point emphasized by Ponticel (1996) with reference to the motor industry in particular. Ponticel adds that the ultimate goal for Ford Motor Company, in response to customer need, is to enable consumers to custom order a vehicle and drive it home within fifteen days. He observes that this is typically a sixty-five day process at present. Achievement of this target, says Ponticel, depends not only on the new leanness of Ford 2000, but through the company's new commitment to making sure that responsibility within the organization is closer to where the action takes place. This effectively brings the employees closer to the customer needs than ever before.

After-sales customer needs is another key area. Ehinlanwo and Zairi (1996) emphasize the importance of this, especially as motor product design, technology and process are becoming increasingly difficult to differentiate. Ehinlanwo and Zairi use Ford, Toyota, Nissan and Fiat as examples, adding that this potential for after-sales competitive advantage can be achieved only if producers can persuade customers to place an equally subjective value on product. The importance of customer satisfaction to producers is seen as a powerful strategic tool for corporations and nations alike. This is demonstrated by such nationally sponsored satisfaction polls and tools as the American Customer Satisfaction Index (conducted by the University of Michigan and American Society for Quality Control), Sweden's annual Customer Satisfaction Barometer and Germany's national measure of customer satisfaction (Fornell, 1994). According to Fornell, results of the Swedish 'barometer' have led to research studies on higher financial returns on increased customer satisfaction, public policy implications, corporate strategies, industrial organization and customer behaviour. Oakland and Beardmore (1995) also emphasize that the use of customer satisfaction surveys, whether in-house or externally produced, is widespread and believed to be a key technique for listening to customer needs and expectations.

When Kramer and Mina (1996) interviewed John Golding, a senior executive at the Swedish motor manufacturer Volvo, they learnt that the company had engineered a change in culture (based on customer perspective) in order to adapt to changing market forces. The authors identified three categories for redesigning, including customer facing, dealer facing and core, but emphasized the importance of the customer-facing process. Zairi and Sinclair (1997) also concluded that organizations in general are attempting to move towards a proactive customer-focused performance improvement, with respect to management and a re-engineering of their product delivery processes. Brown (1996) suggests that recent national recessions, emerging worldwide markets, boundless choice, customers demanding faster product-to-market time and shareholders demanding leaner and fitter business structures are forcing producers to reshape their process structures and redefine old market boundaries. He adds that these factors are acting as change drivers and triggers for investment commitment. And Kimberley (1997) quotes Ian Strachan of the Rover Group, who says, 'technology is moving so fast that it's a question of keeping everyone up to date with the latest developments, especially in electronics and vehicle dynamics'. Kimberley states that this need to train engineers internally within the company is coupled with the need to recruit or subcontract from the supplier chains. This in turn places increasing pressure on suppliers to maintain the right calibre of personnel while meeting high customer expectations. This makes more complex the attempt to define where customer true needs begin and end. In practice, it is possible to trace a cascade of impacting customer needs from the end user to the supplier, to the producer and back to the end user, both in external and internal organizational levels and also from a time perspective.

It is perhaps already becoming clear that both the definition of the customer and the identification of customer true needs is a more complex task than merely assuming end user needs and expectations. It is also clear that, with all the changes occurring within the global marketplace driven mainly by the changing needs and expectations of the customer, customers and producers must talk to each other at some point before the inception of a new or revised product. For this to make sense it must also be assumed that there is a technique for ensuring that what the customer requires is built into the product at every level. This can be summarized as follows.

A producer identifies the key customer requirements for product quality and translates them into measurable product functions, which can then be incorporated into the development process. This is called quality function deployment. One might assume that QFD is common practice among most, if not all, producers. In reality, many producers do not even know of QFD's existence, and those that do either ignore it, or practise it badly because they do not understand it. There are, in fact, fewer success stories than failures in the use of QFD, and perhaps not surprisingly, most of those successes are in Japan, where the technique was invented. This chapter focuses on QFD best practice, while acknowledging its shortcomings. It will be seen that, for QFD to be successful, a multidisciplinary, cross-functional, high-performance team is required in order to integrate other quality techniques. This ensures that the deployment part of QFD is successfully transferred to the quality function part.

To further understand the complex term 'customer true needs', we now consider the needs of the motor industry in order to paint a complete picture, since, as we have seen, the two are inextricably linked.

The needs of the motor industry and its suppliers

The motor manufacturers' market is one of the best examples of the fierce battle for customer loyalty and market placement of product. Robinson (1995) stated that motor vehicle numbers worldwide were around 622 million at the end of 1993, and calculates that by the year 2010, there will be 1 billion vehicles. Car population is expected to rise with new emerging market needs, with Ford Motor Company predicting a doubling of current output by the early 21st century. Benko, Pochiluk and Sorge (1997) predict that by 2000, the 240 car makers will have built 20 million more vehicles than the world needs. Brooke (1997) quotes Alex Trotman (former President of Ford) as stating that there will have been 52 million passenger cars and trucks sold worldwide in 1997, with an annual growth rate of 0.5 per cent to the year 2002. Brooke further quotes Trotman as saying that emerging markets will double their sales by 2005, to over 35 per cent of worldwide production. Conversely, he also says that the combined North American and European market share will shrink to 50 per cent of worldwide sales, and he continues to warn of an enormous over-capacity problem, creating fallout among the competing motor companies (Brooke, 1997). This reinforces a statement made earlier regarding the changes affecting all industries, and the motor industry in particular. As a result of this, Trotman emphasizes the rationale behind why Ford has become the first motor company to reorganize into a globalized structure, in the form of Ford 2000, to improve efficiency and save US$11 billion by 2002. Brooke adds that Ford saved US$2 billion in supplies alone in 1996, again adding to the importance of integrating corporate needs with supplier needs to give added value to shareholders and, of course, the end user. Ed Hagenlocker (1997), Chairman of Ford Motor Company, stated that there will be 100 global motor suppliers by 1998, compared with none in 1987. This again emphasizes the change to a global market that is forcing the motor industry to focus more on global customer need. There are still lessons waiting to be learnt by suppliers and Original Equipment Manufacturer (OEM) motor producers alike, as Keller (1996), Parolini (1997) and Sorge (1996) point out. These three authors from the motor industry state that there is still a problem with the motor supply chain and communicating customer-to-supplier-to-OEM needs. Sorge says this is compounded by the process of customer wants entering the OEMs first, then systematically filtering down through Tier 1, 2, 3 and 4 suppliers and back to the OEM and the end user. Keller and Parolini state that the new globalized Ford 2000 matrix management process is still suffering growing pains, with both Ford in general and Ford of Europe trying to refocus their attention on products and customer needs rather than on the process.

To add to Trotman's warnings, Brooke (1997), Ginn (1996) and Robinson (1995) note that long-established car manufacturers in traditionally strong markets have suffered diminished market share, buy-outs and amalgamations. Ford Motor Company are a typical example. In 1988, they held a 33 per cent share of the UK market for vehicle sales; in 1995, this had dropped to 17 per cent. Aston Martin and Jaguar were bought out by Ford, while Mazda sold a controlling 51 per cent of its share to them. General Motors (GM) have controlling ownership over Vauxhall in Britain and Opel in Germany, while in Italy, Fiat own most of the Italian car industry. In France, Peugeot and Talbot have joined forces and Renault is struggling to retain its autonomy. In Germany, Volkswagen and Audi have joined forces, with control over such exotic companies as Porsche. A few companies such as Mercedes hold autonomy over their future, although there are links with Rolls-Royce. BMW have recently bought out Rover. The list goes on. A key reason for this rationalization of the motor manufacturing industry in the West is not just the need to meet changing market forces, but to meet and beat competition from the East. Japanese companies such as Toyota and Honda have made such fierce penetration into the US and European markets that companies are now fighting just to maintain their reduced market shares. In the USA, Japanese competition has forced the 'big three', Ford, GM and Chrysler, to form a collective technical pool of knowledge to develop leading-edge technology just to beat Japanese competition. Even in Japan, some vehicle manufacturing names such as Datsun no longer exist. Three issues, six words, are behind the changing motor manufacturing market: higher quality, more choice, customer satisfaction.

There has never been a more critical time for the motor industry to respond more quickly, effectively and responsibly to customer demands. The customer has also become a more complex animal, with demands made on motor manufacturers such as higher quality, more durability, long reliability, good ride, low maintenance, better performance, better fuel economy, comfortable ergonomics, better styling and brand image and higher safety standards, and all with better value for money. These customers include governments and industrial lobbies, who impose safety and emission legislation, often led by strong environmental lobbies. The companies themselves impose internal requirements for departments to meet along the product development cycle, often called technical targets, and gateways. All these external and internal requirements have to be met before the vehicle is shipped out of the factory or driven out of the dealership door.

It is not difficult to understand the many ramifications the 'customer true needs' has. Customer demand ranges from the end user through the producer to the supplier and back to the end user, with other customers' demands including government legislation, environmental lobbies and shareholder concerns, with threatening competitor buy-outs coming in as 'noise' to the system. Despite this, there is a process of at least documenting and prioritizing these complex customer needs by turning them from subjective and often emotive statements into objective and rational data-driven measurables. This process is quality function deployment.

The need for quality function deployment

The three areas of higher quality, more choice and customer satisfaction that are driving the motor industry in particular, and all industries and services in general, need two components to begin the process of delivery. The first is the initial customer requirements, i.e. what the customer wants. The second is the technical translation of these 'whats' into 'hows' – that is to say how to convert qualitative whats into technical measurables that can allow the benchmarking, testing and targets to be set for the product being developed, or offered as a service. Depending on the size of the product, it may be necessary to convert 'whats' to 'hows' through several iterations, from the total product design level to a system level to a component level, down to a production process level. Examples of such large and complex products may include a ship, an aircraft, a car or a building. Due to the size of this conversion process within product development, it may be necessary to prioritize the 'hows' at each step to contain the complexity and rationalize the necessary resources. It may then become necessary to rank the 'hows' against the 'wants' to ensure that the most important customer requirements are being satisfied. This is described here as a customer-driven product (or service) development process.

The logic and process described above is what quality function deployment or QFD aims to achieve. The mechanics of the process are described briefly in the 'Ford 2000' section but, as is argued throughout this chapter, there is the need to integrate all the quality techniques through high-performance teamwork to effectively deploy the customer true needs throughout the product delivery process.

Although the concept of QFD makes sense, and the basic methodology is simple, the practice, especially within the motor industry and at Ford Motor Company in particular, is far from simple. To the engineer, QFD does not always make sense. In fact, within Ford Motor Company's North American Motor Operations, the phrase 'QFD is not a job but a career' emphasizes the frustration of using the technique, which in many cases has become a millstone rather than a simple, common-sense method for customer-driven engineering. This chapter focuses on how one Ford team in particular has overcome the problems typically associated with QFD. This team, the Emissions QFD and Quality Forum, has not only brought in all the complexities of the customer true needs, but has managed to maintain a focus on its customer-driven engineering process. This team is a pocket of excellence and best practice in the field of both emissions-related techno-logical development and total quality management (TQM). It has combined task, teamwork and individual criteria of success into what it calls its Emissions Quality Plan.

The need for QFD within Ford Motor Company

Peters and Waterman (1982), Pegels (1994) and Freeman (1996a; 1996b) describe how Ford are now flattening management structure in line with that of Toyota. In doing so, a greater emphasis is being placed on empowerment within the company, and teamwork (Peters and Waterman, 1982). Freeman (1996a) describes the current globalization within Ford 2000 as taking the initiative in optimizing its operation to meet worldwide market demands. Ginn (1996) also describes this as being consistent with other manufacturers such as BMW, Mercedes-Benz, Honda, Toyota and Nissan, who are also setting up production capacities away from home markets. Ford plan to produce 6 million cars a year alone by the year 2000, compared to 4.6 million in 1996. As a result of this, Ford will need to continue using QFD as a technique to bring in and focus on the critical customer needs in this context of the globalized customer requirements (Ginn, 1996). Pegels (1994) brings TQM into the picture by observing that Ford Motor Company uses a variety of tactics to improve performance, the most important of which is the employee suggestion scheme. Pegels adds that between 1983 and 1993 Ford had made improvements of $795 per vehicle advantage over GM, and between 1980 and 1983, reduced vehicle production time from 15 to 7.2 hours. Although employee suggestions have helped as a type of internal customer requirement scheme, QFD, which Ford have used since 1987, has added greater rigour to the internal company requirements (Ginn, 1996).

In summary, it is clear that QFD has been, or will continue to be a strategic tool for Ford's culture, aims and fortunes. The key question is not so much whether QFD has or has not been used, but whether Ford and the motor industry in general offer the best environment for QFD to flourish. Cristiano, Liker and White III (1995) consider the motor industry to be one of the biggest users of QFD in the USA (and the West). Its success and failure rest with the motor company culture, which has to support global customer satisfaction, not just local market segmented satisfaction. If QFD were stretched to the limits of flexibility and effectiveness within home markets, then the support of the global marketplace will be a critical challenge for future QFD teams.

QFD adoption within Ford Motor Company

This section summarizes what the Ford (1992a) *QFD Reference Manual* states as being the basis for QFD adoption within Ford, supplemented by observations by Ginn (1996) and records from the Powertrain QFD Library compiled by Ginn (1997).

The original driving forces that led to the use of QFD within Ford began in the late 1970s and early 1980s when the company faced loss in market shares, record profit losses and increased competition from Japan. In line with the whole motor industry, Ford had to acknowledge problems such as increased competition, increasing labour and investment costs, poor productivity, shorter product life cycles, more legislation and rising customer expectations. This forced Ford to consider reducing headcount while improving quality and customer satisfaction. However, the contemporary manufacturing and design product improvement methods demanded a labour- and time-intensive 'find and fix' approach, which patently was not going to improve the situation. Ford was, however, committed to investing its future in its people and processes to support its new Taurus/Sable programme in an effort to change its 'find and fix' culture. At this time, Ford and many other leading US companies became interested in the tools and techniques being used by many successful Japanese companies, as well as some of its own domestic high-performance companies. The tools included statistical process control, quality circles, just-in-time, total preventative maintenance and Taguchi methods, to name a few. This prompted an in-depth investigation of Ford's best competitors, as part of a benchmarking exercise, which unfortunately led to as much confusion as enlightenment, as tools and techniques were often studied out of context to the environment in which they were being used. To make sense of all these, Ford laid out these quality methods in the form of an Ishakawa diagram that helped identify the causes for 'competitive products at or below cost objectives, on time and good quality'. From this it was discovered that each of the successful competitors was improving one or more aspects of the product development process. The conclusion was that, to achieve improvements in line with the competition, Ford had to deliver competitive products on time, at or below cost objectives and with good quality as defined by the customer.

This search for a quality improvement set of tools and processes was an expense in addition to the billions of dollars being spent on the new Taurus/Sable DE-class passenger car for the US market. It was within this context that Ford began its path from a quality by inspection company to a company committed to total quality excellence. It was during 1997 that the company prompted the formal use of QFD within its North American Operations for its then new Taurus/Sable DE-Class vehicle at a total vehicle level (Ginn, 1997). This was followed by Ford's European Motor Operations' first formal use of QFD in 1989 with the Powertrain-based Ease of Starting QFD team (Ginn, 1997), which proved to be one of few successful teams within Ford to complete all four phases of QFD to production level. Ginn (1996) also describes how this team customized QFD to suit its needs and integrated many other quality techniques to fully deploy the customer needs to production level. This culminated in the team winning both the Powertrain and Corporate Customer Driven Quality Award in September 1996. Full details of the Start QFD team efforts and other Ford QFD team efforts are described in detail by Ginn (1996). However, this chapter focuses on the Emissions QFD and Quality Forum team who have not only pushed the boundaries of QFD within Ford to greater limits, but have matured into a current best practice Quality Forum within Ford 2000.

Ford 2000 customer-driven strategy: understanding customer true needs

Before considering Ford Motor Company's understanding of customer true needs, it is important to consider how Ford is now structured and how some of its senior managers interpret the meaning of Ford 2000 in terms of customer needs through meeting customer satisfaction, brand loyalty and shareholder expectation, and its impact on marketing, research, engineering and production.

Ford 2000 is more than just a company restructuring process. It is a new cultural change that Ford is still undergoing, up to the year 2000 and beyond. Ford 2000 is also about its people and the way it conducts its business with a focus on the customer. Birch (1996) quotes Richard Parry-Jones (the then Vice-President of Ford of Europe) as stating that Ford 2000 was a culmination of many studies aimed at reducing international duplication of work within the company and to cut down on wasted money and effort. Historically, Parry-Jones (1995a, 1995b, 1997) acknowledged that Ford was not good at cross-fertilization, and that when Alex Trotman became Chairman, he decided to globalize the company. Trotman stated that a Ford 2000 goal was to use economy of scale and best practices from around the world to give customers higher quality with lower cost at a faster pace. Jacques Nasser, current Chairman of Ford, now regularly issues an open intranet note to the employees of Ford Automotive Operations (FAO) worldwide discussing business initiatives and FAO's events around the world. This emphasizes the new approach of senior management, and Nasser continues to endorse the Ford 2000 theme of a 'focus on quality, cost, speed (of product delivery), and a passion for customer satisfaction and shareholder value' (Nasser, 1997). Based on such statements and sentiment, this chapter rests comfortably with the theme of effectively bringing in and focusing on customer true needs through the effective use of QFD-driven teamwork integrated with all quality techniques within a quality operating system. The needs of the end user of Ford products have to be balanced with Ford's internal and external needs to ensure that all the success criteria associated with quality, cost, speed and value are all by-products of the complete product delivery process. The integration and reliance of suppliers is also a key part of Ford 2000, but as Hagenlocker says, as quoted by Hunston (1996), the quality standards and requirements Ford expects of its own people will be rigorously audited with its Q1 (Quality first) listed suppliers. The need to meet shareholder expectation on stock value is also an often-repeated need within the company, as stated by Jacques Nasser (1997). This adds further complexity to the equation of customer true needs, and is a big cost driver within Ford 2000.

The mechanics of Ford 2000 and its impact on the globalized customer

At a macro level, Ford 2000 began on 1 January 1995 as a five-year plan, changing its North American Motor Operations and European Motor Operations into Vehicle Centres, with its Australian and International Motor Operations developing similar affiliated Vehicles Centres. This new Ford structure has been renamed Ford Automotive Operations (FAO). The physical restructuring of Vehicle Centres was further rationalized from five to three between North America and Europe by late 1996. This left the Small (and Medium) Vehicle Centres (SVC), which used to produce vehicles for Europe, now developing products for the worldwide market. Jaguar, Aston Martin, Mazda and Nissan badged vehicles would also be built in Europe.

The restructuring of Ford's workforce aimed to form a matrix of management as opposed to the chimneys of organizations within the company, such as Body, Chassis, Electrical, Powertrain and Motor Components division, with other departments more or less operating within their own remits. The new matrix is based more on a systems engineering concept where product centres form the so-called vertical lines of the organization within the Vehicle Centres. Strategic aspects of the business such Programming, Marketing, Research and Finance activities, coupled with what is now referred to as Advanced Vehicle Technologies (the largest arm within FAO) form the horizontal lines of the management matrix. This at least ensures a higher level of cross-functional and multidisciplinary management. It also helps to spread resources more evenly during their rationalization. There is now a leaner look to Ford, which has also been accompanied by a systematic flattening of the management structure. The supplier base is also being cut to a quarter of its original size, with platforms, the complexity of its product line-ups being reduced to half, with some products being deleted altogether, while others such as the Maverick and Probe, co-produced by Nissan and Auto Alliance, represent new market niches within Europe. Cars such as the Ka and Puma represent a new class of Ford vehicles being introduced to the Ford line-up in Europe. Other successful US market (Vehicle Centre) vehicles such as the Explorer and Cougar are being offered in Europe for the first time, in 1997 and 1998. All these new changes, coupled with the continuing face-lifts and redevelopment of the existing product line-ups, reflect the growing global-ization of customer needs within Europe and worldwide.

The customer satisfaction triangle and brand loyalty within Ford 2000

This section reviews the senior management standpoint on the direction of Ford 2000, its understanding of who its customers are and how the company intends to ensure the highest levels of customer satisfaction and promote brand loyalty.

Ed Hagenlocker (1996), President of Ford Motor Operations, states in his 1995 Christmas statement to all employees that the pay-off to the globalization process through Ford 2000 will be Ford's world leadership in the motor industry. To achieve this, Hagenlocker added that over the next five years (up to the year 2000) Ford will introduce 50 per cent more new models worldwide, which will be the most comprehensive new product programme in Ford history. He concludes that 'our goal of world motor leadership is a bold one', but 'by unleashing the power of our people, we achieve our vision'. By this, he is referring to the Ford 2000 principle of empowerment for individuals and teams. Anderson (1995) reports on Richard Parry-Jones, the Vice-President to VC1 (Vehicle Centre 1, now Small and Medium Vehicle Centre, SVC) who speaks of the 'breakthrough in quality' to help fulfil the company's vision of becoming the world's leading motor company by 2000. To do this, says Anderson, Richard Parry-Jones wishes to encourage the training of all staff using the Engineering Quality Improvement Program (EQUIP) training schedule that incorporates both technical and people skills. Parry-Jones (1995a) states that to achieve this breakthrough in quality, five key initiatives are required to meet the goal of Customer Satisfaction and Owner Loyalty, as listed below:

1 Implement quality operating systems in every vehicle team.
2 Implement plant vehicle teams at all lead plants.
3 Achieve a 3Q quality improvement strategy (of find, fix and prevent).
4 Use systems engineering in all programmes.
5 Provide quality training to employees.

These five initiatives support the Hagenlocker (1996) message that places an emphasis on people and corroborates the broad focus of this chapter on teams, training and quality process support for mainstream engineering. Anderson (1996a, 1996b, 1996c) describes the 3Q strategy (find, fix and prevent) as a 'three-fold reduction in quality defects'. This is effectively a reactive solution to quality. The part that deals with prevention is an opportunity for QFD to support the 3Q strategy by developing Real World Usage Profiles of customers within the various segments. These profiles would help to enhance customer-driven quality initiatives such as Key Life Testing within systems engineering to validate the targets set by such tools as QFD, failure mode effects analysis (FMEA) and Taguchi, discussed later. Already Powertrain QFD teams (described by Ginn, 1996) and including Emissions and Fuel Economy in particular are actively pursuing such customer-derived real-life usage profiles.

In support of this 3Q strategy, Alex Trotman, former Chairman of Ford, is quoted by Bemowski (1994) as stating his support of TOPS 8D process (Team Oriented Problem Solving-Eight Discipline process). Despite Trotman's strong support of a reactive downstream fire-fighting tool such as TOPS 8D, it is clear that he equally supports upstream quality improvement through his implementation of a new continuous improvement recognition system (CIRS) which replaces the former employee suggestion programme. CIRS, however, is not an organized or formal quality tool such as QFD. Bemowski (1994) does quote Trotman's commitment to quality of products, service and customer satisfaction, and his support for best quality training practices to assist the achievement of these goals. Trotman also adds that standardized training will assist in the greater mobility of the Ford workforce, making them more flexible when working in cross-located teams (Bemowski, 1994). In support of greater customer satisfaction, John Williamson, Manager of the VC1 (now SVC) MRO, was quoted by Freeman (1996b) as saying 'one of the key marketing and sales objectives is to maximize owner-loyalty by providing an outstanding sales and service experience for our customers'. The MRO also produce a regular monthly newsletter called *Voice of the Customer* to keep employees informed of worldwide customer trends (Freeman, 1996). Freeman adds that the MRO has ambitious plans to ensure its internal customers get the most accurate and timely knowledge possible of the world's automotive markets. A key part of MRO's commitment to a greater definition of its worldwide *Voice of the Customer* is its commitment to support the engineering QFD community with dedicated management and supplier support. Vaughan Freeman (1995a, 1995b) has also quoted the VC1 (SVC) Quality Office 'Best Practices' supervisor Trevor Sparrow, who states his support of the QFD process, describing it as the team tool for translating customer wants into technical specifications.

In summation of the above statements, made by some of the most senior management within Ford, it is clear there are both direct and indirect opportunities for QFD practice within the new globalized strategy of Ford Motor Company. As described later, the use of QFD assists greatly in adding innovation, excitement and high-performance quality functions to any aspect of a new vehicle. By doing so QFD will, and can support higher customer satisfaction, which in turn will gain the higher levels of customer loyalty that the company aims to achieve.

It is also clear by the statements above and emphasized throughout this chapter, that QFD would also have to be an integral part of a systems engineering process. This would also require the continued support and facilitation of a quality techniques training programme that includes QFD, such as EQUIP and the newly developed FTEP (Ford technical engineering programme), which is aiming to expand on a standardized globalized scale. The EQUIP style of training has been shown to be an important process to ensure that all the technical tools and people skills including team-building are taught together. This combination of people and technical skills is essential if expert multidisciplinary and cross-functional feature teams are to exist at all. As described later in this chapter, the most effective deployment of QFD practice is through just such expert multidisciplinary teams. These teams do not rely on QFD alone, but use the technique as an integral core tool that supports and is supported by all the other quality techniques. Once these teams are in place, the next step is to ensure the continued effective use of QFD and customer-driven quality techniques, as described in the Emissions QFD and Quality Forum case study later in the chapter.

The voice of the customer within Ford 2000

Customer satisfaction, with a focus on how Ford Motor Company as a whole approaches this key goal through the use of various marketing initiatives, will now be looked at. Most of the review below is drawn from the Powertrain QFD Library by Ginn (1990–7), as well more specific internal Ford Motor Company references that are available without confidentiality constraints. During the globalization process of Ford Motor Company and its migration into the worldwide market there have been a series of marketing and MRO initiatives to broadcast the message of customer satisfaction and the voice of the customer. There are perhaps three key areas that are regularly broadcast to all employees within the company, which are now discussed in turn.

The first was the monthly newsletter, a colour A4 flysheet sent internally to all employees worldwide by the MRO, called *The Voice of the Customer*. There were twenty-two issues of this, with the last one issued in March 1996. The *Voice of the Customer* typically covered themes from different markets or market segments from around the world.

The second initiative, which still exists, takes the form of biannual customer information days (CIDs), also organized by the MRO. These go to up to 1,000 employees at Ford sites such as Dearborn (USA), Basildon (UK) or Cologne (Germany). They typically have guest presentations from customer satisfaction or industry experts, including personalities such as Richard Branson of Virgin Airways, as well as live open discussion with real customers.

A third of these initiatives is a monthly internal Ford newspaper feature on customer satisfaction and quality (including references to QFD). Examples of this can be found in *The Ford News* Industry Insight supplements, such as that edited by Vaughan Freeman (1995a, 1995b) or one-off articles in the main body of the newspaper by Mike Bowyer (1995). Customer satisfaction is a key theme within Ford and it is appropriate to consider some of the articles on this subject.

Within *Ford News*, Freeman (1995a, 1995b) points to numerous initiatives on customer satisfaction, including the now famous 'customer satisfaction triangle', which is also illustrated in the *Ford Communications Network* newspaper (based in Dearborn, USA) (1995). With reference to this customer satisfaction strategy Freeman (1995a, 1995b) quotes Geoff Hicks (manager of Customer Satisfaction and Loyalty Division, Europe) as describing the company strategy as triangular, with Ford wanting to develop exciting and innovative vehicles, produce vehicles of the highest possible quality and deliver a superior service experience. Bowyer (1995) also quotes Don Cook (European Sales and Marketing Vice President) who reinforces the Ford aim to achieve owner loyalty as part of this strategy, and emphasizes the need for QFD to support it. Even when QFD is not mentioned directly in these articles, such in Freeman (1995a, 1995b), the process described by the managers being interviewed is to all intents and purposes QFD.

With regard to the better dissemination of QFD information within Ford, there was a Ford QFD newsletter co-edited by Helle-Lorentzen and Ginn (1995). Richard Parry-Jones (1995a, 1995b) goes into the details of this 'customer satisfaction triangle' and the 'breakthrough in quality' process as described above. It is this process that combines all the critical details such as employee involvement and co-operation with quality improvement programmes at all levels, both individually and within teams. Parry-Jones continues to say that it also requires using systematic data-driven methods and metrics for guidance and recommends that customer-focused engineering (an EQUIP term for QFD linked to all quality tools) is applied within a quality operating system (known as QOS). Such a quality operating system is being piloted by the new generation Escort programme (Ginn, 1990–7). Parry-Jones (1995a, 1995b) also emphasized the importance of robustness engineering (also part of the EQUIP and FTEP training schedule) as an integral part of the design verification plans and sign-off reports. Finally, he reiterates the need for a committed training programme to make it all happen. What is clear from the Vehicle Centre 1 (SVC) 'Breakthrough in Quality' initiative is that it represented the first real attempt by Ford (within Europe) to adopt a TQM or company-wide quality control (CWQC) process, with QFD as an integral part of this plan.

Marketing research and QFD interface within Ford 2000

As part of this discussion and review on Ford's approach to quality, and customer satisfaction, it is appropriate to consider some of the details of changes that are occurring to support the 'Breakthrough in Quality'. Emmert (1995) reported on the MRO within Ford developing a revised format for collecting customer satisfaction data as well as improving the QFD/MRO interface. This has been in response to concerns in the globalization of, and problems encountered with, the application of QFD in emerging markets (Brazil, for instance) where no differentiation was encountered, with all the customer wants previously established. Although the details are proprietary, the response was to commonize customer satisfaction data collection through a series of round-tables between USA and Europe within the company. The end product, the Global Quality Research System was piloted at Ford in 1996 and rolled out during 1997 (Ginn, 1990–7). Also, a QFD/MRO conference was set up in March 1996 sponsored by Williamson and documented by Ginn (1996), which had all areas of Ford's QFD community discussing issues with the MRO community and the MRO Tier 1 suppliers worldwide. The MRO has incorporated many of the key resolutions that resulted from this QFD/MRO interface, as described by Collins (1996) with the relevant internal stakeholders of the QFD process within Ford Motor Company. The net result of all these round-tables and conference discussions resulted in cross-functional steering teams that corroborate the customer-supplier chain extended-team concept, as described by Kern (1995).

Quality function deployment: bring in and focus on customer true needs

This section describes the definition, mechanics and benefits of QFD. QFD is a conundrum, because it is a simple concept and a complex device at the same time. It has also become many things to many people. Because QFD is a key theme to this chapter and is widely accepted as a key technique for bringing in and focusing on customer true needs, it is important to understand, with references to the literature, benchmarking and case studies, why QFD has had an equal amount of failure as well as success. This is certainly true from a Ford perspective.

Defining the QFD technique

Quality function deployment is often referred to as a *tool* in broad terms (Reynolds, 1992). More specifically, it is called a *competitive tool* (Kathawala and Motwani, 1994); a *communication tool* (Fowler, 1991); a *marketing tool* (Potter, 1994) and a *design tool* (Slinger, 1992). It is frequently described as a *planning tool* (McElroy, 1989; Sullivan, 1988; and in various Ford Motor Company QFD training manuals) and also as a *quality tool* (ASI Quality Systems QFD, 1992; Barlow, 1995; Ealey, 1987). The description of QFD as a quality tool is perhaps the best of all these terms, although it needs a definition in order to understand better the roots of QFD.

Straker (1995) describes quality tools as 'structured activities that contribute towards increasing or maintaining business quality'. By 'structured activities', Straker means using a defined set of rules; by 'contribute' he means adding value; by 'increasing or maintaining' he means it can be used in all areas of quality improvement, and by 'business quality' he means that the company benefits from the quality tool use. In simple terms, Straker suggests that quality tools can be used as a serious and valuable way of doing business at an organizational or individual level.

This definition of quality tools helps outline the fundamental basis of any quality tool, including QFD. However, according to Straker (1995) who lists some thirty-three individual tools in a relationship diagram with their information uses, it is apparent that not all tools are suitable for all areas of use, or are of equal use. Asaka and Ozeki (1990) list fifteen individual quality tool types, while Nickols (1996) lists just three suites of tool types. It is clear, then, that the interpretation of what constitutes a tool, a tool type, or a suite of tools is largely dependent on the perspective of the various authors and the application of the tool(s) in question. Nickols (1996) considers the question of tools in terms of their problem-solving capability, and proposes his three tool types, as follows: *repair tools* for technical troubleshooting, *improvement tools* such as kaizen, continuous improvement, TQM and re-engineering, and *engineering tools* for design or solution engineering from scratch.

Nickols's approach is based on the premise that tasks are best performed using the proper tool. Although he goes into more detail as to what tools fit into the above groups, it is clearly based on the findings of Ginn (1996) that QFD could fit into either of the second two groups and a tool such as FMEA or TOPS 8D would fit into the first of these groups.

From observations made by Ginn (1996) it can be assumed that either QFD is not a quality tool in the singular sense but a complex and flexible tool of many facets and uses. It will be seen from the case study that through the use of teamwork, and the integration of all quality tools, QFD is not *just* a tool, but a process, a methodology and even a philosophy to effect culture change. The most important role of QFD, however, is to instil quality function into the product as a route to customer satisfaction (Ginn, 1996).

Ford's (Ford Motor Company, 1987) *Quality Function Deployment: Executive Briefing* stated that there was no single definition for QFD, but described it as: 'a system for translating customer requirements into appropriate company requirements at each stage (of the product development cycle) from research and product development to engineering and manu-facturing to marketing/sales and distribution'.

More recent QFD definitions within the company have added breadth by including key words such as quality, value, target-setting process, planning tool, customer-driven product development process, customer-focused engi-neering and customer satisfaction. But its essence remains the same. Drawing upon references of over ten years of Ford QFD-related manuals, including the Ford Quality Operating Process manuals (Ford Motor Company 1987, 1989, 1992, 1993, 1994, 1995, 1997) and based on Ginn's (1996) work on Effective QFD Application, a composite Ford Motor Company definition of QFD might be something like this:

Quality function deployment is the mechanism for identifying and prioritizing subjective customer needs from both external end user and legislative and internal corporate requirements.

These needs must meet expectation throughout the product design life at a cost that represents value to all customers. This is done by translating and designing these needs into objective, prioritized and integrated engineering measurables and targets sequentially through vehicle, system, subsystem and component levels on a timely basis into the finished product.

No single Ford definition describes QFD in such a comprehensive way. Some stop well short of this, such as the Ford Quick-QFD (Ford Motor Company, 1994a) definition, while others over-reach themselves. Suffice it to say that over the extended use of QFD within Ford, all the elements have been recognized as a composite wish list of QFD deliverables. The term 'Quick-QFD' is a Ford North American Motor Operation term for a single phase 1 QFD house of quality (HOQ) that precedes the rest of the product development process, in favour of a typical four phase or multiphase cascade of houses of quality, as is traditionally taught. The idea of this approach is to quickly instil the high priority customer wants, needs, expectations and targets into the high level vehicle (or system level) programme (or project), and then allow mainstream engineering activities to ensure that key customer needs become design intent.

From the above review of how QFD has developed within Ford over the past ten years, it can be seen how valuable QFD is perceived within the company. To continue the definition and interpretation of QFD worldwide, this section now reviews a cross-section of authors.

Kathawala and Motwani (1994) simply state 'QFD can reduce the risk of misinterpreting customer requirements'. They later quote (1995) from the work of Maddux, Amos and Wyskidcy (1991) that 'QFD's objectives are to: identify the customer, determine what the customer wants, and provide a way to meet the customer's desires'. Asaka and Ozeki (1990) place great emphasis on the word 'planning' in their descriptions of QFD as do Sullivan (1988), McElroy (1989), and Ford Motor Company (1987–97). Asaka and Ozeki (1990), however, prefer to shorten the term 'quality function deployment' to just 'quality deployment', and state that quality deployment (or QFD) 'defines the functions of planning, development, design and manufacturing of a product to satisfy the quality requirements of customers'. This shortening of QFD is consistent with Akao (1990). Quality deployment refers to the charts, tables and descriptive matrices used to design in the quality (or goodness) required by the customer in the product. Akao (1990) has two definitions for QFD, one narrow, and one broad:

1 Narrow QFD definition: 'The business or task functions responsible for quality (design, manufacturing, production).'
2 Broad QFD definition: 'A combination of these business or task functions responsible for quality (design, manufacturing, production etc.) and the quality deployment charts.'

Akao (1990) adds that 'function deployment is often a later step in QFD where the basic functions of the product or service are identified by experienced people at the production company.' Akao (1990) likens function deployment to the 'voice of the engineer' who has the task of identifying the 'must be' attributes of the product. Akao gives an example of 'must be' as an unspoken customer requirement, an attribute that must be there (such as a bed and bathroom in a hotel, that the customer must have). However, he asserts that these 'must be' attributes, or functions, do not guarantee customer satisfaction, they ensure only a lack of strong dissatisfaction. Akao summarizes this argument by stating that when a customer's spoken quality demand opposes these 'must be' attributes or functions, the producer of the product or service must balance the spoken demands with practical functional requirements of the product or service. He ties in the purpose of the quality charts or quality tables (which have already been referred to as houses of quality or QFD matrices by other authors) as a 'means to' not 'an end in themselves'; that is to say they are there to provide an insight into the nature of the product or service and what is necessary to improve it in relation to the spoken quality demands of the customer.

Asaka and Ozeki (1990) further develop what they mean by quality requirements of the customer by stating that the product or service must meet or fulfil customer standards, needs, expectations and future unanticipated needs and aspirations, 100 per cent of the time. This total product development cycle definition of QFD driven by an extreme level of customer expectation, proposes a very stringent test for QFD success.

Slinger (1992) neatly proposes that 'Quality function deployment is a design tool which is a powerful support to "encouraging" engineering design teams to take a structured, thorough approach to product design.' Slinger (1992) and Metherell (1991) further describe a four-stage (phase) QFD process as part of an integrated engineering process, which they illustrate as linked into simultaneous engineering using teamwork, training and planning. Metherell adds to this in association with integrated engineering by emphasizing the focus for team effort. He also intimates that QFD is consistent with the highest 'opportunity for change' at the concept levels and offers traceability throughout the product cycle.

Consistent with the previous two authors, Hauser and Clausing (1988a) propose a definition of QFD through reference to its classic house of quality matrix. This reads: 'the house of quality is a kind of conceptual map that provides the means for inter-functional planning and communications'. They further suggest that people with different problems and responsibilities can thrash out design priorities by referring to patterns of evidence from the house of quality. This interpretation adds to the argument that QFD is more than just a planning tool, but is also as a tool for interdisciplinary communications within any company. Hauser and Clausing's (1988a) definition proposes that QFD is both a planning and communications tool that helps focus and co-ordinate skills within an organization, from design to manufacture, into a product that customers want and will continue to buy. This definition is concurred by McElroy (1989) who refers to QFD as a 'powerful planning tool', and quotes Dana Cound (a Vice President within GenCorp Motor) as saying it is 'a typical Japanese take-nothing-for-granted procedure that makes you write everything down' (as opposed to the traditional approach that leaves too much to chance). McElroy also quotes Bill Eureka (ASI president) who states that 'QFD is a process that will bring out the "hidden knowledge" in your organization'. Bob Porter (Texas Instruments) also suggests that the QFD process is an 'exercise in culture change' and that whenever a group of people sit in a room discussing the customer there will be conflict, but from this conflict comes creativity. Fowler (1991) states that the QFD 'matrix is a communication tool for members of a broad-based, cross-functional design team that serves three key functions: (1) it develops within the team and the organization a better understanding of how customer needs relate to design requirements; (2) it focuses design effort on areas where effort is justified; and (3) it identifies problems during the design phase to minimize later redesign effort. 'From the quotes above, it is clear that QFD is more than a customer satisfaction delivery tool but also an improver of communications, a prompter for creativity, a discoverer of latent knowledge, a documentation of process, an identifier of problems, and perhaps most importantly a change of culture.

Sullivan (1988) corroborates the view that QFD is both a planning tool and an aid to communication and observes that several US companies (notably Ford) have prepared case studies that show QFD matrix charts having been successfully applied. This in turn has helped integrate the various diverse activities within that company. Sullivan (1988) develops this argument, however, by suggesting that QFD can be used as the 'hardware' through which policy management, which he refers to as the 'software', can be integrated. The difference between policy management and the more usual objective management is that the latter is based on measuring performance by results, while the former develops the means of achieving results through methods, systems, or resources. In summary, Sullivan (1988) proposes that 'soft technologies' such as policy management are important to achieve the business plan, and that this must be integrated through congruent objectives with the use of 'hard technologies' such as QFD, Taguchi methods and SPC, to deploy product requirements. All these elements combined deliver the key goal of meeting customer expectations. This argument for QFD being an integral part of business planning is corroborated by Barlow (1995) and Greenall (1995) who describe policy deployment as process focused, rather than management by objectives. Barlow's description of policy deployment mirrors the key elements of a QFD in that both ensure a clear understanding of the company objectives, goals and direction, both are diagnostic tools that set targets through focusing on the 'vital few objectives', both place emphasis on team-building and good communications, and both focus on the interaction of all tools (including QFD) to achieve an integrated business plan. Greenall

(1995) adds to this by suggesting that the policy deployment process is formalized and measurable, with goals and targets negotiated and set by the employees which tend to be stiffer than if they had been set by management. A benefit of policy deployment is that improvements are continuous and everyone ends up pulling in the same direction. These three arguments by Sullivan (1988), Greenall (1995) and Barlow (1995) strongly suggest that a suite of quality tools including QFD must be used as part of a process-oriented business plan and that the full benefits of any one tool cannot be realized without such an approach. Ealey (1987) adds to this by suggesting that QFD can be used to identify where a company could usefully use such tools as Taguchi, an example of a sometimes forgotten benefit of QFD – it can be used to tell manufacturers where *not* to invest time and money.

The benefits of using QFD as an aid to business planning are now discussed. Zairi (1993) summarizes four key benefits: higher quality, lower cost, shorter timing and marketing advantage. He also quotes Akao's survey of QFD benefits within Japanese industry with its five key process benefits: decreased start-up problems, competitive analysis, control points clarified, effective communications between divisions and design intent carried through to manufacturing. Aoki, Kawasaki and Taniguchi (1990) summarize two broad benefits of QFD:

- the timely development of new products that meets the customers' demands and wins their trust
- the improvement of interdepartmental communication on product development, by identifying problems from early pre-design stage to speed up development and production.

Finally, Aoki, Kawasaki and Taniguchi add that from planning to preproduction, QFD enables the relationships between systems to be clearly understood, thus benefiting the development of more diversified projects. This argument implies that QFD, although complicated in itself, can help clarify complex intersystem relationships. This line of thought is captured by Sullivan (1986) who describes the overall QFD system as based on four key documents that trace a continuous flow of information from customer requirements to plant operating instructions. This, says Sullivan, is in line with what W. Edwards Deming calls a 'clear operational definition'.

The argument from Aoki, Kawasaki and Taniguchi (1990) regarding the ability of QFD to assist more diversified projects from planning to pre-production is seen by Takamura and Ohoka (1990) as a key aim of QFD. They state that the goal of QFD is to 'achieve mass production of a product with assured quality, with ease of manufacturing, and at minimum cost'. They then advocate production participation at the development stage for greatest efficiency. A key process within QFD, particularly in today's competitive market, is, they say, more focused prioritization. Methods to assist with prioritization are reviewed by Takezawa and Takahashi (1990) who suggest using 'fault tree analysis (analysing the system)' to deploy high priority quality items accurately, as relationships alone cannot do this. They also suggest using a 'concept deployment chart' in tandem with QFD to determine key feature values and to identify engineering bottlenecks. Concept selection is also seen as a valuable part of QFD by De Vera et al. (1988) for four reasons: as a much-needed focus on satisfying customer needs as a quality issue, as a reasonable technique to consider alternatives, as representing a paradigm shift by defining quality by design concept rather than quality control and as a simple process that invites more interaction from management. This last point perhaps suggests that concept selection charts may act as an intermediary between the QFD team and management. These authors also propose that when QFD is integrated with concept selection, the team's learning curve increases and its level of efficiency climbs with the increased range of experience bought to the forum when conducting such an exercise. This in turn benefits new product development and start-up times.

It would appear, however, that QFD is only one of many techniques available to companies wishing to improve product development times. Reinertsen (1991) reviews how companies can overcome fifteen common barriers to timing product-development cycles, and refers to QFD and concurrent engineering (CE) as valuable. But from the fifteen common barriers, QFD is completely successful in only two areas, while CE is successful in only four areas. These are: 'hitting moving targets' (QFD), 'lack of concurrence' (CE), 'moving locus of control' (CE), 'phased development systems' (CE), 'focus on communication' (QFD/CE). The Reinertsen (1991) list of remaining barriers, largely self-explanatory, that QFD specifically does not adequately address include: 'taking giant steps', 'ignoring market clocks', 'overloading capacity', 'ignoring queue time', 'burn rate management', 'lack of concurrence', 'inattention to architecture', 'moving locus of control', 'phased development systems', 'inappropriate testing strategies', 'failure to quantify the problem' and 'make/buy decisions'. Reinertsen (1991) does, however, acknowledge the crucial role of QFD in assisting customer-driven communications in developing products rapidly.

Having considered the definition of QFD in detail, it is clear it is a complex technique for the simple process of translating customer needs into the product. This has prompted as many definitions and interpretations of its use and usefulness as there are practitioners. One common theme remains, however, and that is the fact that QFD is a fundamental technique for bringing in and focusing on customer true needs. It is now appropriate to consider the mechanics of QFD in a systematic review of the 'house of quality' and the so-called 'rooms' that are contained within its walls and 'roof'.

The QFD matrix diagram

Asaka and Ozeki (1990) describe matrix diagrams as a method to 'show the relationships between results and causes, or between objectives and methods, when each of these consists of two or more elements or factors'. They continue by stating that 'various symbols are used to indicate the presence and degree of strength of a relationship between two sets of essential items' and propose four key benefits of using matrix diagrams with symbols, as follows:

1 The use of symbols makes it visually clear whether or not a problem is localized (symbols appear isolated) or more broad ranging (symbols in rows or columns).
2 It possible to show the problem as a whole, and view all the various relationships between the various problems at once.
3 By testing and evaluating each relationship intersection of the essential factors it becomes easier to discuss the problem at finer levels of detail.
4 A matrix makes it possible to look at specific combinations, determine essential factors and develop an effective strategy for solving the problem.

Asaka and Ozeki (1990) refer to four different types of matrix:

- the 'L-type', a two-dimensional pairing of rows and columns
- the 'T-type', a three-dimensional matrix comprising two 'L-type' matrices
- the 'Y-type', a combination of three 'L-type' matrices
- the 'X-type', a combination of four 'L-type' matrices.

In the context of QFD, as typically used by most companies worldwide, including Ford, it is assumed that the 'L-type' matrix is used. The mechanics of producing such a QFD 'house of quality' matrix is now discussed, based largely on the Ford Motor Company (1987 to 1997) QFD references.

The house of quality mechanics within QFD

It may benefit the reader to begin with an explanation of the way a QFD matrix chart or 'house of quality' is constructed. It is also essential to explain the way in which the 'customer whats' and 'technical hows' that make up the basis of any QFD project are incorporated into the matrix and analysed. The baseline assumptions for the mechanics of QFD will be taken from Ford Motor Company QFD manuals, from 1987 to 1997, but other references will be stated where applicable.

Kim and Ooi (1991) remind the reader that 'QFD is a set of planning and scheduling routines that has proven effective in producing high quality as well as low cost products'. Burton (1995) proposes that the QFD chart, often referred to as a 'house of quality' due to its so-called construction of 'rooms' and a 'roof', is essentially a chart comprising nothing more complicated than a series of 'lists' and 'relationship matrices'. Clausing (1994) agrees with the term 'rooms', but says they can also be referred to as 'cells' and adds that the basic QFD matrix diagram comprises eight such rooms (or cells) which, in turn, contain twenty steps. The American Suppliers Institute (ASI Quality Systems QFD, 1992) also refer to ten 'analytical steps' for studying the completed house of quality at the product planning level. They suggest the same principles apply to all the QFD matrix charts used at each phase of the process, and that these steps can take anywhere from a few minutes to several days to complete.

Burton's (1995) description of lists and matrices also include any of the QFD phases. However, Clausing's (1994) description of eight rooms and twenty steps for the basic QFD refers specifically to the first phase. He proposes, however, that to complete an 'Enhanced QFD' matrix, a total of forty-three steps (another twenty-three steps beyond the first twenty) are required for a successful concept phase. The key difference between what Clausing describes as basic and enhanced QFD (discussed more fully later) is that the initial twenty steps are divided among the eight rooms of the QFD planning matrix, while steps 21 to 43 are product-planning enhancements. These enhancements include selecting a 'winning concept' via a Pugh concept selection chart, which in turn leads to a subsystem level. This subsystem QFD route from design concept to component level is practised by Ford (detailed in the 'Ford Customer Satisfaction Process Within WCP (World Class Process)' brochure). Clausing also gives an example of this subsystem QFD approach by referring to the Ford Motor Company NVH (Noise Vibration and Harshness) QFD, reinforced by Ginn (1996). Knoot, Horner and Patterson (1992) also endorse the use of subsystem QFD phases when applying process improvements for low noise amplifiers.

The eight rooms Clausing describes are effectively the same rooms that Ford use for their house of quality charts at planning level. However, the *Ford Customer Satisfaction Process* (Ford Motor Company, 1994c) and *Quick QFD* (Ford Motor Company, 1994a) go further by adding a ninth 'quality plan' room (excluding the relationship matrix), which is a key strategic aspect of the QFD process within the company. Both the Ford 'Quick-QFD' Phase 1 Matrix and the Ford QFDNET matrix exhibit a nine-room format, with a relationships matrix, plus a further four rooms and two relationships matrices to include, among other things, safety and regulatory requirements.

According to Burton (1995), the lists and relationships matrices in the house of quality chart are aligned along two axes, where the x axis is the customer axis, and the y axis is the technical axis. This twin axis description is supported by Asaka and Ozeki (1990) who suggest that QFD is generally charted using a 'two-dimensional diagram', with customer quality requirements on the vertical axis and the elements needed to satisfy these requirements on the horizontal axis. These two axes, say Asaka and Ozeki, provide quality information incorporating the problems and desires of the market and workplace. Sullivan (1988) emphasizes that the use of matrix charts is key to this process as the correspondence or interaction between heterogeneous elements cannot be viewed in a one-dimensional space. He also says that this process requires a two- or three-dimensional space to evaluate interactive relationships effectively, and confirms what most authors suggest, that symbols are the ideal way to identify the relationships between the vertical and horizontal axes.

The symbols are also usually assigned numeric values, often weighted in favour of the strongest relationships: 9 = strong, 3 = medium, and 1 = weak, as used by Ford Motor Company QFD literature (1987 to 1997), the ASI (ASI Quality Systems QFD, 1992) and ITI (International Technology Incorporated), and Burton (1995). They can also be expressed in a linear fashion: 3 = strong, 2 = medium and 1 = weak as described by Asaka and Ozeki (1990). In most cases, however, the symbols can be customized as required, depending on whether the process is carried out on paper as traditionally done by Japanese companies (Akao, 1990), or with specifically designed in-house QFD software. In all cases, however, if no relationship (or correlation) is apparent, the 'cell' or 'value' in the relationships matrix remains blank (or zero). Akao (1990) refers to these symbols as indicators of correlation between the customers' 'demanded qualities' and the technical 'quality elements', and also refers to the symbols depicting strong, medium and weak as a double circle, circle and triangle respectively. This is corroborated by Asaka and Ozeki (1990).

Akao (1990) also differentiates between two types of quality charts within QFD. The first is the 'demanded quality deployment chart' and the second the 'quality elements deployment chart'. The demanded quality chart includes information provided by the customers on the qualities they want from the product. These demands can be further divided into first-, second- and third-level order. Akao gives the examples of the use of these levels thus: the first level is 'easy to manoeuvre'; the second level is 'easy to hold' and the third level is 'easy to hold because it is light'. This subdivides customer wants so that the company can focus on their requirements and is consistent with most practitioners. However, it must be noted that what Akao refers to as a demanded quality chart is what Clausing (1994), Burton (1995), the ASI (ASI Quality Systems QFD, 1992) and Ford (Ford Motor Company, 1987–97) have collectively referred to as customer requirements, customer wants, customer attributes and whats, and to a room, list, cell, field or list, and not a chart. This mismatch between the Japanese 'chart', and the western 'room' is perpetuated

(a) Has two elements = Lists + Matrices

(b) Has two axes = Customer + Technical

(c) Has two tasks = Benchmarking + Targets

(d) Has two roles = Planning + Prioritizing

Figure 5.1 *Key components of QFD mechanics*

with Akao's quality elements deployment chart, which is a technical translation of the customers' demanded qualities.

An example of a quality element for the demand 'easy to hold because it is light' would be 'weight'. These quality elements have been referred to over time by the various western QFD practitioners (Clausing, Burton, the ASI and Ford) as engineering characteristics, substitute quality characteristics, product expectations, design characteristics, hows and technical system expectations. It is clear, however, that the first building blocks to any QFD chart are these two components of the initial customer requirements, regardless of terminology, and their subsequent incorporation into the product or service. Figure 5.1 summarizes the key components of QFD mechanics.

The cascading phase-to-phase mechanics of QFD

Sullivan (1986, 1988) defines four levels of QFD matrices that reflect four stages of application in the product development cycle. The first of these is the planning matrix that culminates with selected control characteristics (based on customer importance, selling points and competitive evaluations). The second is the component deployment matrix which defines the finished component characteristics (based on the planning matrix targets). The third stage is the process plan chart, culminating in the production process monitoring plan required by the operators and the fourth stage is the control plan which culminates in defining quality controls such as control points, control methods, sampling size frequency and checking methods. In each case, the previous charts' key outputs feed into the next chart as key inputs, and represent the transition from the development phase to the execution of the production phase within the product development cycle. This four-phase process is consistent with most authors, and is used by Ford in its European Motor Operations division. This approach is also typically taught by the ASI as described by Verduyn and Wu (1995) even though flexibility, customization and overlap with other quality tools is becoming common.

Although the argument for deploying only the first phase of the four is strong within Ford and reiterated by others, there is an equally strong argument for supporting a four-phase approach. A strong supporting argument for continuing the QFD phases through the product delivering process is the provision of 'design traceability' to the voice of the customer.

Phase 1 prioritization mechanics of QFD and its implications within Ford

A unanimous benefit of QFD is its identification of customer requirement priorities to assist in focusing resources. We now discuss four key areas of this prioritization process, all crucial components of the Phase 1 'house of quality' (HOQ). The first is benchmarking. The second is, in Ford Motor Company language, the 'customer desirability index' (or CDI). The CDI has also been referred to as customer importance rating (Ford Motor Company, 1987–97). The third prioritization process is an end product of the first two, and relates to the technical importance rating of the technical systems expectations (TSEs), which represent the company measurables. These measurables usually take the form of a test or metric that can be assigned a target with technical data to support an actionable follow-up by the system or component engineer, who is the next internal customer of this data. The fourth and least used form of prioritization within the QFD house of quality is the 'roof correlation matrix' (Ford Motor Company, 1987–97), which is where conflicting technical system expectations (or company measurables) can be identified. It is least used partly because of the extra time it takes to complete, and partly because it is often difficult to resolve the technical conflicts that ensue from setting optimized targets for all the key technical measurables. As a result, the roof is rarely completed or is viewed with fear and suspicion. (The term 'roof', incidentally, derives from the triangular nature of this matrix, which sits on top of the main matrix.)

There are two Ford Motor Company approaches to QFD, as described in *Quick QFD* (Ford Motor Company, 1994a) and the *Ford Customer Satisfaction Process* (Ford Motor Company, 1994c). How a QFD is carried out within the company has been a matter of resource availability or strategic intention.

The direct deployment of technical system level targets into mainstream engineering after Phase 1 is known as 'Quick QFD'. The deployment of technical system level targets into a subsystem level or directly into a component level phase followed by a production process phase and finally into a production control phase is known as CFE (customer focused engineering) QFD. One area of commonality between Quick QFD and CFE QFD within Ford is the use of a preplanning QFD house of quality. This is called 'Phase 0'. The use of a phase 0 or preplanning matrix was originally proposed by Akashi Fukuhara who was an early developer of QFD in Japan (Czupniski and Kerska, 1992). The preplanning matrix assists with the prioritization of complex products such as cars and resolves what 'attributes' at a 'total vehicle' level (such as fuel economy or performance feel) require the full rigour of QFD at a design or system level. Czupinski and Kerska (1992) cite a cascade of preplanning to design level to system level to parts level within the Chrysler Corporation. This high level of prioritization is critical in an industry such as the motor business, where any allocation of resources to support QFD involves millions of dollars or pounds. A review of these four key prioritization methods follows.

The mechanics of the benchmarking process within prioritization

Benchmarking within the Phase 1 HOQ comes in two forms. The first is the customer competitive assessment (or evaluation) (CCA or CCE). As the title suggests, this is the qualitative benchmarking that the customer participates in within the horizontal customer axis. Customers evaluate the products by comparing the relative perceived performance according to the key customer requirements (using customer language) as identified by prior market research with the support of the QFD team. This exercise has the company product (or service) among its key competitive products (or services).

The second benchmarking activity is the quantitative engineering competitive assessment (or evaluation) (ECA or ECE). This technical benchmarking exercise will compare the same products (or services) by conducting tests that are 'global and measurable' (Ford QFD manuals, 1993–7) and have been correlated objectively or subjectively to best represent the technical function of the subjective customer wants. These tests have been typically referred to by Akao (1990) as substitute quality characteristics (1988), or design requirements (Ford Motor Company, QFD manuals, 1987, 1989), Technical System Expectations, Ford Quick QFD (Ford Motor Company, 1994a) and Ford Customer Satisfaction Process (Ford Motor Company, 1994c), or 'hows' by ASI Quality Systems (1996). These are the technical company measures as described by Verduyn and Wu (1995) and comprise the key element of the technical axis, described in Ford Quick QFD (Ford Motor Company, 1994a).

The benefit of conducting both benchmarking exercises within the same HOQ matrix is that it is possible to compare subjective customer ratings to objective engineering ratings. The first benefit is to show the company where improvements are required the most, and where there is already high satisfaction relative to competition. The second key benefit is that it is possible to compare discrepancies between customer perception and technical reality. Where discrepancy occurs, it is either because the wrong technical measure is in place, there are hidden customer wants that require further research, or quite simply – as occurred with a Ford Driveability QFD benchmarking exercise in Germany and Britain in July and September 1990 – a complexity of brand image as well as other complex secondary factors, which play a part in customer perception. The specific example involved the performance feel of two vehicles, the first, a BMW, the second, a Citroen. The customer perception was that the BMW was faster, although in fact, the Citroen was faster. The basic element of vehicle acceleration, peak power and velocity over time were in the Citroen's favour on paper. This proved to be a powerful lesson to the driveability QFD, prompting later performance-feel QFD research with outside suppliers. Lotus, Braunschweig University in Germany and Loughborough University studied these secondary factors, which were outside the time resources of the Powertrain engineering community supporting the QFD exercise. These lessons learnt are both a feature and an indication of the power of benchmarking within QFD.

Competitive benchmarking to set goals is a powerful tool and is supported by Vaziri (1992) who adds that it helps companies to anticipate customer needs. This ability to anticipate is a critical measure of success within any QFD exercise, and in the absence of any other form of futuring provides the engineer with a key tool in setting so-called 'stretch' targets (Ginn, 1990–7). Vaziri also states that it is important to obtain this benchmarking data in a timely fashion to be effective. He argues that QFD-derived customer requirements are a precursor to benchmarking, but not a prerequisite, although he does reinforce the argument that the combination of QFD and benchmarking results in feeding information to quality improvement teams. Ohinata (1994) supports the idea that benchmarking was originally a Japanese invention (rather than an American one, usually attributed to Xerox) used by small companies for modelling best practice from other larger Japanese and American companies. Ohinata (1994) cites five areas for benchmarking, namely product, function, process, management and strategy. He adds to this the five steps for successful benchmarking: clarifying goals, organizing a team, selecting target organizations (products or services), collecting and analysing information and devising an action plan.

These five areas and steps are arguably a mirror image of the basic key areas and steps required to set up and run a QFD exercise. The compatibility of QFD and benchmarking can be recognized by the fact that the two key axes of QFD include a benchmarking exercise to support the target setting and prioritization of both axes. Finally, De Toro (1995) warns of ten pitfalls that confront the benchmarking team and which he refers to as 'miscues', thus supporting the argument that QFD and benchmarking are from the same mould.

The mechanics of the quality strategy plan within prioritization

The quality strategy or plan is the area or room within the QFD HOQ where consideration of the customer importance rating (CIR) or customer desirability index (CDI) for the key customer wants is effectively weighted using a combination of techniques. First it is important to emphasize the subtle difference between CIR and CDI. CIRs were usually individually rated by the customer during drive surveys within Ford (Ginn, 1990–7). Although this practice still exists, a more recent practice initiated by the Ford Quick QFD process (Ford Motor Company, 1994a) is based on the Thurstone methodology as described by Guildford (1954) and more recently Bergeon (1996), which uses triplicate comparisons. The CDI method as based on Thurstone is one of many methods that can be used to compare customer wants, although it is current Ford practice, established by the Strategic Standards Office within the company in Dearborn, Michigan, USA. In simple terms, the CDI is a customer-assigned rating of desirability for each customer want relative to every other want. From this process, a Pareto list of customer wants is developed, where typically only the top 25 per cent of wants are taken and put into the QFD house of quality matrix within Ford Quick QFD. Effectively, this is a form of prioritization before the QFD HOQ is constructed in an effort to keep the total matrix size containable. The more traditional form of QFD, still practised at Ford, will take all the identified customer wants and rely on the prioritization of resources and the end of Phase 1 by taking only the top 25 per cent of the technical importance ratings into Phase 2, the component design level, as described in the Ford Customer Satisfaction Process. With either route, the basic mechanics for the Quality Plan (or Strategy) remain the same. The CIR or CDI will then be weighted by a combination of strategic pointers such as sales points, product attribute leadership strategy (PALS), customer satisfaction data, marketing brand strategies and benchmarking. Sales points are directly influenced by benchmarking results and support weightings to customer wants CIRs or CDIs by assigning preagreed weighting factors. PALS is programme related (within Ford Motor Company) and provides weightings to the customer requirements CIR or CDI by assigning a best in class (BIC) weighting. Customer satisfaction data is also a source of potential weighting, as is brand marketing strategy. The expert support of team members knowledgeable in the relevant areas of the Quality Plan is essential to form a balanced final weighting to all the customer wants, as this will have a direct impact on the software that calculates the final technical importance ratings (TIRs) for the technical system expectations (TSEs). This third area of prioritization is discussed in the following section.

The mechanics of technical importance ratings within prioritization

Although the software algorithms and strategies for determining weightings of customer wants CIRs and CDIs are often a closely guarded secret with most companies, including Ford, the basic QFD HOQ calculations for determining the final technical axis TIRs remains universal. Each TIR is the sum of the final weighted CIR multiplied with each respective relationship value (typically 9, 3 or 1) across the horizontal axis, and then summed down the vertical axis. Typically, the CIRs are also normalized between 1 and 5, although the strategic CDI (which as the weighted CDI is a result of the quality strategy maths and algorithms to produce a futuring effect) may vary, and even include decimal points. The maths is an automatic feature of any QFD software, including the proprietary 'QFDnet' and 'Quick QFD' software at Ford Motor Company.

The mechanics of the roof correlation matrix within prioritization

This last section of the mechanics of QFD is perhaps the least utilized by many QFD teams within Ford Motor Company (Ginn, 1996, 1990–7). The first reason for this is that since 1992 the US Quick-QFD process within Ford, accounting for some 150 QFD Phase 1 projects, have advocated the deletion of this 'room' (Ford Motor Company, 1994a). The second is that, even with experienced practitioner teams at Ford, past and present, the completion of the Phase 1 'roof' correlation has either been a simple tick box item or completed with only the strong negative trade-offs and little follow-up to deploy recommendations to avoid conflicting TSEs. The full function of the roof correlation is to assign weak and strong positive and negative relationship symbols between the technical measurables of the QFD HOQ. Thus it has become the practice to assign only the strong negatives that highlight the critical conflicts between optimized technical measurables. For example, the Emissions QFD's aim to reduce hydrocarbons will tend to increase nitrogen oxide, and vice versa. However, there is now much interest at Ford in the systems engineering approach, which in turn must consider system interactions. As a result, the conflicts typically found with key systems are becoming more crucial when developing a complex product such as a motor vehicle. A common set of attribute level conflicts within a car are: quality (or noise vibration and harshness), vehicle weight, safety packaging, emissions packaging, perform- ance and fuel economy. The list could also include sublevel conflicts such as idle quality, air conditioning, smoothness and styling. The key issue here is that to resolve these conflicts in a rational approach, a structured data-driven process is required. Such a process already exists with QFD, with the support of other quality tools. The QFD 'roof' correlation matrix has already been customized at Ford to consider key TSEs (measurables) from all the same level attributes of systems as appropriate. There is also a formula for weighting the key TSEs from different QFD attributes or systems. This customized 'extended' version of the QFD HOQ 'roof' is also referred to as the 'Super-Roof' within the Ford Customer Satisfaction Process (Ford Motor Company, 1995). Companies suffer the most – particularly when developing a complex product – when conflicting targets set early in the process become increasingly more difficult to rectify by the time the final product leaves the factory floor. It is these conflicts that can be identified and resolved early in the product development process through the use of QFD, particularly within the least used 'room', the roof correlation matrix.

Some key benefits of QFD philosophy and process

Many of the inherent benefits of QFD have been alluded to in the previous sections. The following discussion reviews the types of benefits already mentioned and establish other key benefits so that the effectiveness of QFD can be better understood.

Kim and Ooi (1991) neatly summarize some of the benefits of quality function deployment as a useful tool for 'integrating the human expertise of marketing, design, production, and service personnel to address all relevant issues and to achieve the single goal of customer satisfaction'. They place this benefit in the context of an organization's need to be effective by making full use of its disposable knowledge, and suggest using QFD to focus and co-ordinate the skills of the organization from the design stage through to manufacturing. In agreement, De Melo Cavalcanti (1993) in his summary of key QFD features specifically quotes the benefit of computer files of company generic information as a source of knowledge. He also points out that QFD gave the process of benchmarking to ICL, another great source of knowledge. In further agreement with Kim and Ooi (1991), De Melo Cavalcanti quotes several QFD case study benefits from ICL, Elida Gibbs and Milliken (with whom he benchmarked) and observed the reiterated benefit of teamwork, which helped ICL in particular to develop improved customer/supplier chains within the organization that developed into partnerships rather than barriers.

Hauser and Clausing (1988) reiterate the emphasis on co-ordination and focus suggested by Kim and Ooi (1991) but place the word 'focus' in relation to the customer by citing a Toyota example as follows: 'Toyota improved its rust prevention record from one of the worst in the world to one of the best by co-ordinating design and production decisions to focus on this customer concern'. They also quote three other benefits:

1 Reduced preproduction and start-up costs by using QFD.
2 The emphasis QFD places on moving the design changes upstream to avoid more costly and time-consuming downstream changes.

3 The help QFD brings, through using the house of quality technique, in breaking down functional barriers and encouraging teamwork.

Cristiano, Liker and White III (1995) reinforce the second benefit of QFD, which is to shorten the overall product development cycle (with time and cost savings) reducing both the product design stage and the product redesign stage, despite the fact that the product definition stage has been extended. The third benefit, that of breaking down barriers, has already been noted by De Melo Cavalcanti (1993) within ICL. It is also noted as a fundamental benefit by Hunter and Van Landingham (1994), and it is one that even the detractors of QFD concede. It has been suggested that one of the key barriers QFD helps to break down is that between marketers and engineers, who often feel that QFD does not provide anything they would not have guessed with a little more effort (Hunter and Van Landingham, 1994). Potter (1994) also emphasizes the importance of 'breaking down organizational barriers', illustrated by truly cross-functional teams, such as those in the Digital Equipment Corporation example he cites from Van Treeck and Thackeray (1991): 'the product development QFD team gets closer to the customer than to the marketers, destroying the traditional barriers between marketing and engineering'.

These arguments would suggest that it is precisely because QFD breaks down barriers that it succeeds, where perhaps isolated and more entrenched processes would not. The benefit that QFD offers in terms of teamwork in breaking down organizational barriers and QFD's ability to solve quality problems in key market segments as a marketing tool is a key argument for Potter (1994). However, it is the potential QFD offers as a marketing tool for finding new customers, and not just satisfying or exceeding the expectations of current customers that Potter explores more deeply. He describes this as 'finding customers to implement the strategy of obtaining broader horizontal market position', and supports this claim by proposing two frameworks: 'cross fertilization across market segments' and 'co-suppliers as match-makers'. In the first framework, Potter suggests that compiling the customer requirements from several QFD charts selected for their fit with the company's skills would add a valuable tool for the sales force when prospecting for new business. In the second framework, he suggests that by selectively finding contacts with needs that would fit the company's skills, a broader customer base could be established. A key benefit of QFD, he says, is that QFD helps to 'visualize the information on organizational fit' (to the customer's application process). This reference to the visual benefits of QFD is strongly reiterated by Clausing (1994), and is discussed later.

Brown (1991) refers to QFD as a 'system of highly traceable engineering procedures in a cross-functional team framework that uses graphical displays to drive all phases of product deployment without stifling the voice of the customer'. His argument for an integrated process that includes traceability, cross-functional teamwork, concurrent engineering, concise graphical displays and an emphasis on the voice of the customer, precipitates three key benefits of greater customer satisfaction, shorter time to market and improved product performance. As a result of using a 'QFD-based product realization' process in favour of more traditional processes, Brown further suggests that clear competitive advantages can be gained. He concludes that as customer satisfaction, timeliness, and correctness become more crucial in the international marketplace, more companies will apply QFD. With regard to timeliness and competitive gain, De Melo Cavalcanti (1993) quotes an example from a 1992 paper by Nickols, 'Getting it Right First Time', that gives clear benefits gained by some 100 QFD studies carried out at Digital Equipment. Compared with previous results with their VT1000 computer terminal product, Digital claimed a 75 per cent reduction in concept time, a 40 per cent reduction in total engineering changes to get the product to market, and a 25 per cent reduction in product features offered by designing exactly what the customer wanted, rather than including costly extra features the customer might want.

One of Brown's observations that QFD builds 'credibility with customers' and a 'rich accessible product-definition' is echoed by Hunter and Van Landingham (1994), who describe how QFD can help identify product segmentation. They give as an example Siemens International Automation, who used QFD to solve the problem of what product features to include without adding unnecessary cost or reducing performance. Through making trade-offs within the QFD house of quality it was possible to identify product features unique to various market segments. It was then possible to carry out fast and narrowly focused customer surveys to test the hypothesized segmentation. This, say Hunter and Van Landingham (1994), makes it possible to add cost over function an integral part of the QFD process. If an organization includes a 'cost-adding function' to their process, Hunter and Van Landingham go on to say it is often possible to give customers what they want using a low-tech, low-cost solution. This way, customer satisfaction is assured, the products gain credibility with customers and the products are well defined, both within the company and with customer segments being targeted (Brown, 1991).

Hunter and Van Landingham (1994) also point out that the mechanics of QFD are so easily understood that it is often dismissed as obvious and low-tech. But, they say, it is the simple philosophy of QFD that gives it its strength. This is reiterated throughout the literature.

Another often repeated benefit of QFD is the link it offers between the upstream design process and the downstream manufacturing process. There are many arguments for and against using QFD, but where the argument for its use downstream appears, it is either in the form of a reported success as a case study, or a retrospective wish from new users of QFD. Digital's case study reporting their success with using QFD downstream appears earlier in this section. An example of a retrospective wish is reported by Liner (1992), who says, 'In retrospect, the team felt that several initial manufacturing problems could have been avoided through continuing the use of QFD in process development', going on to say that the earlier QFD work on technical requirements and parts features helped to ease the process development by creating a better understanding of the part tolerances required. She concludes by saying that the development of detailed process control plans in partnership with vendors remains a future goal (for their Telecom Division). Liner also describes how Raychem share their QFD charts with customers who are familiar with QFD, to increase communication. This suggests that it is not just the process, but the charts themselves that are used as a visual aid to assist the customer/supplier dialogue. Stewart (1994) supports this argument by pointing out that the combination of the customer and technical axes in the house of quality can uncover 'inconsistencies' or 'hidden/missing information or patterns of data that would go undetected with a checklist approach'. He points out how QFD tries to strike a balance between customer orientation and technology (product orientation). To further emphasize the visual impact of QFD charts, Clausing (1994) identifies several advantages. The large visual formats, he says, make it easier to find relevant information, understand logical connections and focus team discussions.

In summary, it is important to emphasize that the flexibility of QFD is one of its greatest assets. The root cause for many of the failures of QFD is inextricably linked to its success; it is precisely because it is so flexible and covers such a broad base of business categories. Below are some examples of the flexibility of QFD.

Hochman and O'Connell (1993) state that the basic four-phase model of QFD is in itself a cyclical process with tremendous flexibility. Mailer (1995) describes four levels of use for QFD with the second level being a modified version, and the third and fourth being linked to satisfaction models using a revised interaction matrix, thus reinforcing the argument that QFD is a flexible tool. He first describes the use of QFD to support an electrical engineering level attribute such as digital data receiving, then to support a new QFD matrix format used to cascade the electrical attribute targets through the company. The third and fourth levels, says Mailer, use a customer satisfaction model with either qualitative or quantitative data, and through the use of interaction matrices, shows how this data can be deployed. He concludes that QFD is an exceptionally powerful tool that need not be considered for quality personnel or qualitative evaluation, but can be developed into a central repository for quantitative engineering design data linked into a corporate TQM process. This flexible and holistic approach to QFD is corroborated by Crow (1992), Liner (1992) and Mallon and Mulligan (1993) who discuss QFD in terms of concurrent engineering practice linked to TQM. Mallon and Mulligan also reinforce the arguments made by Ginn (1996) and Baggs (1995) regarding eastern versus western cultural applications of QFD and the need for QFD to be integrated within a company-wide quality control process.

The breadth of QFD use has been alluded to, but there are wide-ranging examples of very successful QFD use in business categories other than motor, aerospace and electronics. These include: education; food packaging; machine castings; construction; chemicals; environmental design; software and system architecture.

It is also worth noting that QFD has also been used to support and enhance many strategic processes such as those described by Potter (1994), Sullivan (1988), Greenall (1995) and Barlow (1995). Casey et al. (1993) describe the data quality objective (DQO) process used by the US Environmental Protection Agency (EPA). The data quality objective process combined with QFD helped the EPA to co-ordinate and prioritize resources to clean up very hazardous chemical wastelands. Casey et al. say that QFD helped with decision-making, reduced the costs of collecting data while increasing its quality and improved communications and teamwork.

In conclusion, the wide-ranging benefits and examples of successful QFD applications emphasize both the depth and flexibility of this quality technique. Ginn (1996) argues, however, it is these same strength and ease of flexible usage that cause the misunderstanding, misuse, frustration and failure of QFD projects. These frustrations and failures led Goldense (1993) to formulate the 80:20 rule, which effectively states that 80 per cent of the benefit of QFD can

(a) Application: Single phase to multi-phase

(b) Perception:	+ve	−ve
	'Task'	'Career'
	'Essential'	'Never again'
	'Milestone'	'Millstone'
	'Simple'	'Complex'
	'Easy'	'Difficult'
	'Quick'	'Slow'
	'Structured'	'Bureaucratic'
	'Innovative'	'Frustrating'
	'Flexible'	'Inflexible'
	'Customer'	'Engineer'

Figure 5.2 *Benefits and problems of QFD*

be gained during the first 20 per cent of the product development cycle. This is clearly why Ford tended towards the use of Quick QFD early on in the programme cycle as prescribed by Termaat et al. (1995). To summarize typical benefits and problems experienced with applying QFD, see Figure 5.2.

The next section examines how QFD requires the integration with other quality tools, techniques and processes to 'deploy' customer requirements effectively down through the product (or service) delivery process.

Customer-focused process: a toolbox for deploying customer true needs

Customer-focused process is a generic term given in this chapter for the term customer-focused engineering, described by Ford EQUIP Customer-Focused Engineering, Levels 1 and 2 QFD (Ford Motor Company, 1993c), and others. The term covers the use of QFD as a focal quality tool and it is the aim of this section to identify the importance of QFD as a key link with all the quality tools and techniques that focus on customer needs and expectations. Within Ford, the term customer-focused engineering assumes that all the quality tools and techniques used in the product development process will have an impact on customer needs or expectations, if Kano's theory of expanded quality is accepted. Kano's (1993) theory states that all customer needs and expectations can be segmented into basic, performance and excitement qualities that change over time as technology and market forces change. With this in mind, Ford EQUIP training has attempted to instil a customer-focused engineering ethic within the company, integrating all the key engineering quality tools of QFD, FMEA, TOPS 8D, process management, experimentation, quality engineering and reliability engineering. The EQUIP training takes this a step further by proposing that, as the key driver is the customer, the key tool to drive, or at least link the integration of all these techniques, is QFD. QFD is seen as one of the basic starting blocks to ensure that customer true needs are brought in and focused on when designing the product.

This section now considers the reasons why QFD has been problematic in its application by itself and how, by integrating it with other quality tools, it has become an integral part of the Ford Quality Operating System toolbox.

Although QFD is a simple idea with excellent potential, its effective use can be realized only within organizations who have a quality culture that permeates the whole organizational structure from top to bottom (Ginn, 1996). Many Japanese companies have had this strategic quality culture in place for a long time, typically seen in the form of company-wide quality control (CWQC) or total quality control (TQC). Where companies operate a culture of CWQC or TQC the use of tactical quality tools such as QFD is integral, automatic and transparent. Western companies, particularly within the USA, have developed a similar quality culture (TQM) which, although similar to the Japanese systems, tends to adopt sequential and specific use of these tactical quality tools, including QFD. In this western approach, the use of tactical quality tools such as QFD are neither transparent nor automatic. This has forced many western companies to abandon or customize QFD to the point that in some cases it is either not fully deployed, or not fully supported. As a result (as has happened at Ford), QFD not only has a poor image, but it has reached a point where it is sometimes used only when resources permit, and often too late. It becomes an 'after the event' technique used to support other quality processes that are not coherently managed on a company-wide basis. The technique's poor image can also result in it being used more in some areas of an organization than in others, so that attempts to expand its use within the company – either to other departments or as part of a broader engineering process – are met with resistance.

This problem has been further compounded at Ford by their recent 'globalization'. The early days of Ford 2000 saw many process initiatives both globally and Vehicle Centre specific intended to make the globalization run more smoothly. However, many well-meaning and well-thought-out process initiatives competed for attention with less well-conceived processes, making it very difficult for management to untangle this process overload. It is not surprising then, that long-established quality tools such as QFD became tangled up with both successful and unsuccessful attempts at process improvement. In many cases, it was forgotten altogether or was renamed and changed for the sake of it without a balanced look at what the process is capable of achieving.

The overlap and integration of QFD with other quality tools

One of the key elements of the Ford's EQUIP within Europe, now largely adopted by the new 'globalized' Ford Technical Education Programme (FTEP), was the linking of seven quality tool techniques with QFD at the core. This process is described in detail by Henshall (1995) and Herrick (1995). Another key element of EQUIP is to train people in the teamwork skills required to bond the use of and communication between the technical tools. Ed Henshall (1995) states, however, that this process is not so much training, but a process for quality engineering to promote an environment for change within Ford. He adds that EQUIP wants to engineer in what the customer wants by focusing on positive quality (using QFD) and maximizing the ideal function (using Taguchi methodology), moving away from engineering out what the customer did not want. The seven technical tools within EQUIP are taught within a systems engineering framework and are also integrated into the 'Ford Customer Satisfaction Process' (Ford Motor Company, 1994c). The seven EQUIP tools are: TOPS 8D (team-oriented problem-solving, eight disciplines), process management, FMEA (failure mode effects analysis), experimentation, Taguchi, reliability engineering and QFD (referred to as customer-focused engineering). A full descriptive list of EQUIP people skills and technical skills can be found in the Ford Customer Satisfaction Process (Ford Motor Company, 1994c).

In support of Henshall's (1995) statement that QFD and Taguchi are the key to the EQUIP philosophy, Clausing (1994) also strongly recommends the integration of QFD with Taguchi's quality engineering tool and prescribes their integration into the systems engineering process; to apply either in isolation would be ineffective. Clausing considers that, to develop complex and dynamic products such as cars, two key enhancements of QFD must include the Pugh concept selection and subsystem development between design requirements and component development. He also recommends other quality tools such as fault tree analysis (FTA), FMEA, functional analysis system techniques (FAST), value analysis/value engineering (VA/VE), and quality engineering (QE). This EQFD (enhanced QFD), says Clausing, is an important corporate capability integrating the corporation holistically with a concentrated focus on customer satisfaction. He therefore proposes three major elements in total quality development:

- basic improvements in clarity and unity (basic quality engineering)
- enhanced quality function deployment (EQFD)
- quality engineering using robust design.

Clausing subdivides the first element, basic quality engineering, further, as follows:

- concurrent process
- focus on quality
- cost and delivery
- emphasis on customer satisfaction
- competitive benchmarking
- better teamwork (including multifunctional teams, employee involvement and strategic supplier relations).

The point Clausing makes is that to attain a truly world-class concurrent engineering process, all the above criteria need to be met, otherwise results will be disappointing.

Within Ford 2000, many of these ideas are included within its Ford Reliability Guide (Ford Motor Company, 1997c), which in turn is fully integrated into the Ford Product Delivery System (FPDS), formally introduced in 1996. Kilpin (1997) identifies all the objectives and benefits of the Ford Product Delivery System and identifies the voice of the customer as key input, with the use of the Ford Reliability Guide to integrate all the quality techniques to implement to voice of the customer.

The suppliers role, from meeting the end user through to legislative and corporate customer requirements, is also critical for completing the customer-focused engineering loop (Ansari and Modarress, 1994). Within the motor industry, this integration of end user needs, supplier needs and motor OEM needs from the 'big three' (Ford, General Motors and Chrysler) are well documented in a process called Advanced Product Quality Planning (APQP) (Chrysler Corporation, 1995; Ford Motor Company, 1996c). Supplier base globalization used by the big three has prompted this common communication method for supplier-customer product development and the delivery process. Ford 2000 has been a key driver of this APQP communication tool, which effectively integrates and identifies twenty-three APQP elements that span areas of customer needs, engineering target setting, programme and supplier need dates, cost agreements, responsibility, recovery plans, as well as all the quality tools and techniques needed to meet these requirements. Of these twenty-three elements there are eight focus elements that Ford in particular use as a means to determine the so-called critical path of the programme, and which are the focal needs of Ford as the customer; these include both basic and expanded expectations, previously agreed between the customer (Ford) and the supplier. Again, this emphasizes the importance of the APQP document as a communication tool to ensure that all customer requirements are met. APQP is also an integrator of all quality tools. In summary, the APQP process improves communications, with the by-product of customer satisfaction, where the term 'customer' includes end users, suppliers and producers.

As stated earlier, the Ford 2000 quality operating system, which is integral to FPDS, is the Ford Reliability Guide (Ford Motor Company, 1997c) which uses a so-called systems engineering 'V' process as a framework. This process is key to both how Ford operates its engineering and quality processes, and has provided the linchpin to the Emissions QFD and Quality Forum process. The basic concept of systems engineering, with its basic input of customer requirements (wants and needs) and its basic output of customer satisfaction (from product function, performance and quality) from both a general industry and Ford 2000 perspective is now reviewed.

A successful strategy to bring in and focus on customer true needs

This chapter began by reviewing in detail what constitutes a customer and how this affects the definition of true needs. It also put customer satisfaction, customer brand loyalty and customer supplier chains in context. We then looked at the rationale, mechanics and deployment of bringing in and focusing on these customer true needs. In doing so, QFD was examined in detail, including its definition, mechanics, philosophy, benefits and integration with TQM and other quality tools. In discussing QFD, other quality tools and TQM it became clear how important teamwork is as a critical enabler in the process of bringing in and focusing on the customer true needs. The three key success criteria and one key binding force are listed below:

- the key dynamic 'enabler' for QFD is *teamwork*
- the key process integrator of other quality tools is *QFD*
- a key process 'enabler' for TQM/CWQC is *QFD*
- the key binding force is *common goals*.

Bearing in mind that the glue that holds together this co-ordinated customer-driven product development best practice is 'common goals', it is important to recognize two driving forces. The first is the voice of the customer (including external and internal customer desires, expectations, satisfaction and loyalty). The second is quality product or service (including innovation, functional performance, robustness of design and value).

There are three broad steps, then, that need to be identified when any company wishes to implement with any success an effective QFD-based team or customer-focused process (CFP) to bring in and focus on customer true needs, as follows:

1 Clearly define both the customer and all the requirements, including both external and internal customers to the company as well as taking great care in establishing the full customer/supplier chain of requirements. In doing so ensure that responsibilities and goals are aimed at customer satisfaction, product or service quality and that action plans for the QFD (customer-focused process) project is consistent with the timings and objectives of a single quality process adopted company-wide at all levels.
2 Integrate or overlap QFD with other quality tools and the product (or service) development cycles as applicable to the task within a single quality company-wide quality process (TQM/CWQC) whenever possible.
3 Co-ordinate all the key customer requirements, supplier responsibilities and quality tool applications together with a cross-functional, multidisciplinary teamwork ethic. The teams must be flexible and dedicated to the achievement of customer satisfaction in its use of QFD and other quality tools and processes. The team must also be trained in all the quality tools to ensure their appropriate and effective use. It is also important that the team individuals are skilled in communication skills and team dynamics to ensure a high performance of their teams.

References

Akao, Y. (1990) *Quality Function Deployment: Integrating Customer Requirements into Product Design.* Productivity Press. (Originally published in 1988 as, *Hinshitutenkai katsuyo no jissai.* Japan Standards Association.)

Anderson, A. (1995) Vital to achieve 'breakthrough in quality' to fulfil Ford 2000 vision. *Ford News (Industry Insight Supplement)*, **34**(12), December, 4.

Anderson, A. (1996a) 3Q – all out drive for a 3 fold reduction in quality defects. Industry Insight Supplement, *Ford News*, **35**(1), 19 January, 3.

Anderson, A. (1996b) A Quality operating system that gives customers the best – and a bonus. Industry Insight, *Ford News*, March, 2.

Anderson, A. (1996c) Systems engineering will get it right first time for the customer. Industry Insight, *Ford News*, **35**(4), 12 April, 3.

Aoki, H., Kawasaki, Y. and Taniguchi, T. (1990) Using quality deployment charts: subsystems, parts deployment, quality assurance charts. In *Quality Function Deployment, Integrating Customer Requirements into Product Design*, Y. Akao, ed., Productivity Press, pp. 83–111.

Ansari, A. and Modarress, B. (1994) *Quality Function Deployment: the Role of Suppliers.* National Association of Purchasing Management, Inc., October, pp. 28–35.

Asaka, T. and Ozeki, K. (1990) *Handbook of Quality Tools: the Japanese Approach.* Productivity Press. (Originally published in 1988 as, *Genbacho no tameno QC Hikkei.* Japanese Standards Association, Tokyo.)

ASI Quality Systems QFD (1992) *Phase 1 – Product Planning, Analysing and Diagnosing the Product Planning Matrix.* American Suppliers Institute, pp. 51–4.

ASI Quality Systems (1996) *Improving Quality and Reducing Costs.* Catalogue of Services, American Suppliers Institute.

Baggs, J. (1995) Thinking and culture. Part 2 of the Ford Motor Company EQUIP *Reliability Engineering* module 8, draft 1.0, Boreham Airfield, UK, 24 January.

Barlow, K. (1995) Policy deployment in action at Kawneer. ASI Quality Systems 6th European Symposium for Taguchi Methods and QFD, Kenilworth, Warwickshire, 16–18 May.

Bemowski, K. (1994) Ford chairman was, and continues to be a progress chaser. *Quality Progress*, October, 29–32.

Benko, J., Pochiluk, W. and Sorge, M. (1997) Global overcapacity looms. *Motor Industries*, **177**(1), January, 45–8.

Bergeon, S. (1996) Strategic CDI and parent process with Quick QFD. A presentation by Strategic Standards Office, QFD/Market Research Office Conference, FAO, Fairline Training and Development Centres, Dearborn, Michigan, 11–15 March.

Birch, S. (1996) Driving Ford 2000. *Motor Engineering, SAE International*, **104**(12), December, 76–80.

Bowyer, M. (1995) Rewards are great if we can only swing the customer loyalty needle in our favour. *Ford News*, **34**(11), 10 November, 13.

Brooke, L. (1997) Ford's outlook: shrimp, bacon and eggs. *Motor Industries*, **177**(1), January, 29.

Brown, K. (ed.) (1996) Change drivers. *Investor in People*, (3), 29.

Brown, P. G. (1991) QFD: echoing the voice of the customer. *AT&T Technical Journal*, March–April, 18–32.

Burton, D. (1995) The ideal lunch, building the heart of quality, the complete 'how to', QFD. QFD Workshop Conference, Bradford Management Centre, University of Bradford, 27 June.

Casey, C., Esparza, V., Graden, C. J. and Reep, P. J. (1993) Systematic planning for data collection. *Quality Progress*, December, 55–9.

Chrysler Corporation/Ford Motor Company/General Motors Corporation (1995) *Advanced Product Quality Planning and Control Plan Reference Manual*. Joint publication from Chrysler Corporation, Ford Motor Company and General Motors Corporation, February.

Clausing, D. (1994) *Total Quality Development: a Step-by-Step Guide to World-Class Concurrent Engineering*. ASME Press.

Collins, L. (1996) Proposals for a revised marketing research office interface with QFD. Presentation Ford Motor Company, Fairlane Training and Development Centre, Dearborn, Michigan, 11–15 March.

Cristiano, J. J., Liker, J. K., and White III, C. C. (1995) An investigation into quality function deployment (QFD) usage in the US. The Seventh Symposium on Quality Function Deployment, American Suppliers Institute, NOVI, Michigan, pp. 531–3.

Crow, K. (1992) Implementing concurred engineering: lessons learned. *Autofactor Conference Proceedings*, SME Publisher Manufacturing, Detroit, Michigan, pp. II.I–II.

Czupnski, G. W. and Kerska, D. H. (1992) The utilization of QFD in the LH Powertrain program. The Fourth Symposium on Quality Function Deployment, Detroit, Michigan, pp. 545–53.

De Melo Cavalcanti, L. M. (1993) An investigation into the use of QFD in ICL, the establishment of best practice. MBA thesis, Management Centre, Bradford University.

De Toro, II. (1995) The 10 pitfalls of benchmarking. *Quality Progress*, **28**(7), January, 61–3.

De Vera, D. et al. (1988) A motor case study. *Quality Progress*, June, 35–8.

Ealey, L. (1987) QFD – bad name for a great system. *Motor Industries*, **167**, July, 21.

Ehinlanwo, O. O. and Zairi, M. (1996) Best practice in the after-sales service:

an empirical study of Ford, Toyota, Nissan and Fiat in Germany, Part II. *Business Process Re-Engineering and Management Journal*, **2**(3), pp. 39–53.

Emmert, R. (1995) Global quality research round table discussions, USA/UK. MRO, *The Voice of the Customer*, 31 October, Doc. GL/QA-95038.

Ford Motor Company (1984) Continuous improvement through participation. *Ford Education and Personnel Research Development*, Ford Motor Company, September.

Ford Motor Company (1987) *Quality Function Deployment, Executive Briefing*, American Suppliers Institute Incorporated, Dearborn, Michigan, ASI Press, QFD00250.

Ford Motor Company (1988) Team, we are a team. *Ford Education and Personnel Research Development*, Ford Motor Company, 17.

Ford Motor Company (1989) *QFD Awareness Seminar*, QETC (Quality Education and Training Centre), Ford Motor Company, Dearborn, Michigan, (1) January, (2) May.

Ford Motor Company (1992a) *QFD Reference Manual*. Car Product Development, Technical Training and Educational Planning, Ford Motor Company, Dearborn, Michigan, (confidential) May.

Ford Motor Company (1992b) *Customer-Focused Engineering through QFD*. Ford European Motor Operations EQUIP Foundations Module, June, 7.1–14.

Ford Motor Company (1992c) *Concept To Customer*. European Motor Operations, Ford Motor Company, Product Development Process and Timing Guidelines, v1, (confidential, deleted) July.

Ford Motor Company (1993a) *System Design Handbook*. Ford Motor Company, Revision: 0/4–19–93, (confidential) 19 April.

Ford Motor Company (1993b) *Module 7, Customer-Focused Engineering, Level 1, QFD Manual*. EQUIP (Engineering Quality Improvement Programme), Ford Motor Company Ltd, Published by Education and Training, EQUIP Centre, 26/500, Boreham Airfield, Essex.

Ford Motor Company (1993c) *Module 7, Customer-Focused Engineering, Level 2, QFD Manual*, EQUIP (Engineering Quality Improvement Programme), Ford Motor Company Ltd, Published by Education and Training, EQUIP Centre, GB-26/500, Boreham Airfield, Essex.

Ford Motor Company (1993d) *Team Roles: Summary*. Ford Motor Company, Extract from EQUIP 'Foundation Module' (1), July.

Ford Motor Company (1994a) *Quick QFD, The Marketing-Engineering Interface*. Motor Safety and Engineering Standards Office, Ford Motor Company Ltd, Fairlane Plaza, Dearborn, v3.0, (confidential).

Ford Motor Company (1994b) *QFD/SDS Relationships*. Document: QFDSDS3–3VSD, Revision 1, (confidential) 18 October.

Ford Motor Company (1994c) *Ford Customer Satisfaction Process*. European

Motor Operations Powertrain QFD Steering Team, issued by the Customer-Focused Engineering Group, Ford Motor Company, VC1, Dunton Research and Engineering Centre, Essex, v1, (confidential) December.

Ford Motor Company (1995a) *Quality Criteria Process Guide.* Ford Motor Company, Quality Office, VC1, Dunton Research and Engineering Centre, Laindon, Essex, Revision 1.00, (confidential) 31 July.

Ford Motor Company (1995b) *Reliability Engineering – Systems Engineering.* EQUIP (Engineering Quality Improvement Programme), Ford Motor Company, Boreham Airfield, 26/500, Essex, draft August, pp. 7.2; 7.18–25.

Ford Motor Company (1995c) *Useful Life Reliability Engineering Process.* New Generation Escort Program Office, VC1, Dunton Research and Engineering Centre, (confidential) October, 27.

Ford Design Institute (1995d) *The Robustness Imperative.* Guidebook, Ford Design Institute, Ford Motor Company, Dearborn, Michigan, (confidential).

Ford Motor Company (1996a) *Advanced Product Quality Planning Status Guideline.* Ford Motor Operations Quality, National Reproductions Corporation, 29400 Stephenson Highway, Madison Heights, MI 48071, January.

Ford Motor Company (1996b) *Ford Product Development System: Defining Pre SI Process Reduces Time-to-Market.* FPDS Digest, (confidential) December.

Ford Motor Company (1996c) *Advanced Product Quality Planning: Status Reporting Process and Guideline.* Ford Education and Development Publication, 3060 PG APQP (Rev. 1/96), January.

Ford Motor Company (1997a) Ford Product Development System. *Ford Intranet Netscape*, (confidential).

Ford Motor Company (1997b) Hagenlocker to suppliers: 'Globalisation a key to future success and a huge challenge'. The Grapevine, *Ford 2000 Communications*, (119), 25 April, 1.

Ford Motor Company (1997c) Ford reliability guide. *Ford Intranet Netscape*, (confidential) September.

Ford Motor Company (1997d) Worldwide customer requirements. *Ford Intranet Netscape*, (confidential) September.

Ford Motor Company MRO (last issued April 1996) *The Voice of the Customer.* Monthly internal mail on worldwide customer survey findings, MRO (1–22).

Ford Motor Company MRO (1997) Customer Information Day. Bi-annual presentations, *Ford Intranet Netscape*, (confidential).

Fornell, C. (1994) Perspective: American Customer Satisfaction Index. *The Total Quality Review*, (Payback on Quality), Alister Rainsford, November–December, 4–6.

Fowler, C. T. (1991) QFD-easy as 1-2-3. *SAVE (Society of American Engineers) Proceedings*, Kansas City, Missouri, SAVE National Business Office, **26**, 177–82.

Freeman, V. (1995a) Customer satisfaction: prime goal to foster loyalty of our buyers. *Ford News*, **24**(9), 8 September, 4–5.

Freeman, V. (1995b) Quality is our keyword. *Ford News*, **28**(7), July.

Freeman, V. (1996a) Marketing Research Office has a major role in keeping track of customer needs. *Ford News*, **35**(2), February, 3

Freeman, V. (1996b) Pace setters. *Ford News*, **36**(3) March, 1.

Ginn, D. M. (1990–7) *Powertrain QFD Minutes 1990–1997 Library*. Customer-Focused Engineering Department, Ford Motor Operations, SVC, AUT-CAPE-AIGDE, Dunton, Research and Engineering Centre, Laindon, Essex.

Ginn, D. M. (1996) Effective application of quality function deployment: a flexible proposal for best practice within a changing quality improvement environment to ensure highest customer satisfaction. MSc thesis, Bradford University, July.

Goldense, B. L. (1993) QFD: applying the '80–20 rule'. *Design News*, 20 December, 150.

Greenall, R. (1995) Policy Deployment. ASI Quality Systems 6th European Symposium for Taguchi Methods and QFD, Kenilworth, Warwickshire, 6–18 May.

Guildford, J. P. (1954) *Psychometric Methods* (2nd edn). McGraw-Hill, pp. 153–75.

Hagenlocker, E. (1996) Now Ford 2000 must press on to greater things: message to all employees from Ed Hagenlocker. Editorial in, *Ford News*, **35**(1), 19 January, 1.

Hagenlocker, E. (1997) Hagenlocker to suppliers: 'Globalisation a key to future success and a huge challenge'. The Grapevine, *Ford 2000 Communications*, (119), 25 April, 1.

Hauser, J. R. and Clausing, D. (1988a) Design is a team effort but how do marketing and engineering talk to each other? The house of quality. *Harvard Business Review*, May–June, 63–73.

Hauser, J. R. and Clausing, D. (1988b) The house of quality. *Harvard Business Review*, May–June, 63–73.

Helle-Lorentzen, R. and Ginn, D. (1995) *QFD Newsletter*. Ford Motor Company, Dunton Research and Engineering Centre, (1), July.

Henshall, E. (1995) EQUIP (Engineering Quality Improvement Programme) at Ford Motor Company. ASI Quality System 6th European Symposium for Taguchi Methods and QFD, Kenilworth, Warwickshire, 16–18 May.

Herrick, R. (1995) Quality methodology application – the application of technical and behavioural methodologies by companies involved in industrial design, development and manufacturing processes. MSc thesis, Bradford University.

Hochman, S. D. and O'Connell, P. A. (1993) Quality function deployment: using the customer to outperform the competition on environmental design. IEE International Symposium on Electronics and Environment, Arlington, pp. 165–72.

Hunston, H. (1996) Ford to keep up purge on supplier quality. *Motor International*, (31), September, 3.

Hunter, M. R. and Van Landingham, R. D. (1994) Listening to the customer (using QFD). *Quality Progress*, April, pp. 55–9.

ITI (International Technegroup Incorporated) (1995) 'QFD Capture' software, ITI, 5303 DuPont Circle, Mitford, Ohio.

Kano, N. (1993) A perspective on quality activities in American firms. *Quarterly California Management Review*, Spring, 12–31.

Kano, N., Takashi, F. and Tsuji, S. (1994) Attractive quality and must-be quality. *Journal of Japanese Society for Quality Control*, **14**(2), 39–48.

Kathawala, Y. and Motwani, J. (1994) Implementing quality function deployment, a systems approach. *The TQM Magazine*, **6**(6), 31–7.

Keller, M. (1996) Ford Europe: what went wrong? *Motor Industries*, **176**(12), December, 35.

Kern, J. P. (1995) The chicken is involved, but the pig is committed. *Quality Progress*, October, 37–42.

Kilpin, M. (1997) How the Ford Product Development System is radically changing ways of doing things'. *Ford News*, February, 3.

Kim, S. H. and Ooi, J. A. (1991) Product performance as a unifying theme in Concurrent Design-II. Software. *Robotics and Computer-Integrated Manufacturing*, **8**(2), 127–34.

Kimberley, W. (1997) Thin on the ground. *Motor Engineer*, **22**(2), March, 27.

Knoot, P. A., Horner, R. J. and Patterson, W. C. (1992) Process Improvements For Low Noise Amplifiers. 6th International SAMPE Electronics Conference, Baltimore, 22–25 June, pp. 406–16.

Kramer, R. P. and Mina, P. (1996) Organisational change at Volvo – from the customer perspective. *Managing Service Quality*, **6**(6), pp. 12–16.

Liner, M. (1992) First experiences using QFD in product development. *Design for Manufacture*, **51**, 8–13 November, 57–63.

Mailer, M. W. (1995) Quantitative engineering analysis with QFD. *Quality Engineering*, **7**(4), 733–46.

Maddux, G. A., Amos, R. W. and Wyskidcy, A. R. (1991) Organizations can apply quality function deployment as a strategic planning tool. *Industrial Engineering*, **23**, September, 33–7.

Mallon, J. G. and Mulligan, D. E. (1993) Quality function deployment – a system for meeting customers' needs. *Journal of Construction Engineering and Management*, **119**(3), September, 516–31.

McElroy, J. (1989) QFD, building the house of quality. *Motor Industries*, January, 30–2.

Metherell, S. M. (1991) Quality function deployment: less firefighting and more forward planning. Proceedings of the Fourth International Conference on Total Quality Management, June.

Nasser, J. (1997) Let's chat about business. Ford Motor Company, PROFS-Office Vision e-mail, Newsletter, September.

Nickols, F. W. (1996) Yes, it makes a difference. *Quality Progress*, January, 83–7.

Oakland, J. S. and Beardmore, D. (1995) Best practice customer service. *Total Management, Journal*, **6**(2), 135–48.

Ohinata, Y. (1994) Benchmarking: the Japanese experience. *International Journal of Strategic Management and Long Range Planning*, **27**(4), August, 48–53.

Parolini, D. (1997) Matrix management doesn't work. *Motor Industries*, **177**(8), August, 79.

Parry-Jones, R. (1995a) You don't just throw a switch and things all change overnight. *Ford News,* 21 October, 7–8.

Parry-Jones, R. (1995b) Breakthrough in quality. Open letter by the Vice President, Ford Motor Company, FAO VC1, November.

Parry-Jones, R. (1997) State of the nation address. Presentation to SVC employees, Dunton, UK and Merkenich (Germany), Research and Engineering Centres, Ford of Europe, April.

Pegels, C. C. (1994) Total quality management defined in terms of reported practice. *International Journal of Quality and Reliability Management*, **11**(5), pp. 6–18.

Peters, T. J. and Waterman, R. H. Jr (1982) *In Search of Excellence: Lessons From America's Best Run Companies.* Harper and Row.

Ponticel, P. (1996) Ford getting lean. *Motor Engineering*, SAE International, **104**(11), November, 92.

Potter, M. (1994) *QFD as a Marketing Tool.* MBA thesis, Management Centre, University of Bradford, December.

Reinertsen, D. (1991) Outrunning the pack in faster product development. *Electronic Design*, 10 January, 111–124.

Reynolds, M. (1992) Quality assertive companies to benefit from recovery. *Elastometrics*, February, 19.

Robinson, P. (1995) Wheels within wheels. *Autocar*, 1 February.

Slinger, M. (1992) To practise QFD with success requires a new approach to product design. *Kontinuert Forbedring*, Copenhagen, 20–21 February.

Sorge, M. (1996) Dialing for supplier dollars. *Motor Industries*, **176**(8), August, 5.

Stewart, D. (1994) Improve engineering's dialogue with marketing. *Electronic Design*, **42**, 18 April, 85–92.

Straker, D. (1995) The tools of the trade. *Quality World*, **21**(1), January, 28–9.

Sullivan, L. P. (1986) Quality function deployment: a system to assure that customer needs drive the product design and production process. *Quality Progress*, June, 39–50.

Sullivan, L. P. (1988) Policy management through quality function deployment. *Quality Progress*, June, 18–20.

Takamura, H. and Ohoka, T. (1990) Using quality control process charts: quality function deployment at the pre-production stage. In *Quality Function Deployment, Integrating Customer Requirements into Product Design*, Y. Aqua, ed., Productivity Press, pp. 112–46.

Takezawa, N. and Takahashi, M. (1990) Quality deployment and reliability deployment. In *Quality Function Deployment, Integrating Customer Requirements into Product Design*, Akao, Y., ed., Productivity Press, pp. 180–210.

Termaat, K., Sroka, K., Schmidt, J. and Finkelstein, S. (1995) *Customer to Product Quality Process*. Strategic Standards Office, Ford Motor Company, Dearborn, Michigan, 31 January.

Van Treeck, G. and Thackeray, R. (1991) Matching customer requirements with function and design. *QFD at Digital, Product and Process Innovation*, **1**(5), 68.

Vaziri, K. (1992) Using competitive benchmarking to set goals. *Quality Progress*, **25**, October, 81–3.

Verduyn, D. M. and Wu, A. (1995) Integration of QFD, TRIZ and robust design overview and 'mountain bike' case study. ASI Total Product Development Symposium, Novi, Michigan, 1–3 November.

Zairi, M. (1993) *Quality Function Deployment: a Modern Competitive Tool*. TQM Practitioner Series, European Foundation for Quality Management in association with Technical Communications (Publishing) Ltd.

Zairi, M. and Sinclair, D. (1997) *Integrated Management through BPR and TQM: a Survey of Best Practice and Future Trends*. European Centre for TQM, Bradford University Management Centre, Report No. R97/2.

6 Project management and modern tools of innovation

Mohamed Zairi and Pervaiz Ahmed

The chapter looks at project management in the modern innovation context, highlighting the characteristics of successful project management and project leadership. It goes on to elaborate how cultures of effective project management can be built and sustained by examining examples of best practice. Case studies of Rover, IBM, 3M, Ford and Kodak are used to illustrate and develop theory. A review of tools for effective project management is also presented.

Nothing is particularly hard if you divide it into small jobs. (Henry Ford)

Introduction

Successful innovation management is very much dependent on effective project management. Expressions such as, 'Teams are the heroes of the 1990s', 'Innovate or you are dead' are used by leading organizations to emphasize the importance of innovation for modern competitiveness and the role of teams and project management.

Effective project management can help create corporate focus and successful implementation of strategy. Many organizations, including the ones that are successful, suffer from what has been termed 'initiativitis'. They allow an explosion of activities and initiatives, without any clear prioritization, analysis of resource consumption, lack of role clarity and responsibility for delivering projects etc.

In fact, project management can be described as a total discipline for running business operations and effectively implementing strategies for competitive results. Joshi (1996) describes project management thus: 'Formalized project management enables development of strategic and business priority, easier monitoring of progress, improved management of business risks and better communication.'

The complete deployment of project management may include some of the following.

Taking stock of strategic initiatives

Organizations often tend to launch too many initiatives and embark on too many projects. A corporate audit may reveal the following questions:

- What is the stock of corporate activity?
- What backlog is there?
- How many conflicting initiatives are there?
- What is the resource situation?
- Which 20 per cent would lead to 80 per cent of the strategic value?
- Where should leverage be applied?
- How many teams are involved?
- What are the various roles and responsibilities?

Prioritization and development of a corporate aggregate project plan

Cost-benefit analysis needs to be carried out and activities classified according to their impact on profit generation and profit improvement. All activities tend to compete for the same resource level and unless this stage takes place, trivial activities will compete for the same resource levels as important ones.

It may be that by going through a prioritization exercise, senior managers will decide to halve some trivial projects and redirect the remaining resources towards the areas which badly need them.

Innovation processes

Effective project management requires a proper finalized structure and a disciplined approach, such as stage/gate systems with decision points for tracking progress and making decisions. Further, the stage/gate system can be supported by documentation to provide effective control of each project and build the history of each initiative.

Project teams

Different team formats can be used to deliver projects. Most projects need a broad skills base and a multidisciplinary approach. This calls for a lot of delegation, the development of decision-making processes, empowerment and bottom-up strategic input. Some of the skills that team members and project leaders need to have include problem-solving, report writing etc.

Project planning tools

The micro aspects of project management include planning, which determines the necessary activities, roles and responsibilities, costs and timescale, and so on. One of the tasks of the project leader is to produce a 'network' with a critical path for key activities to be delivered in the correct order, at least cost, on time and with minimum risk. The project network is then distributed among all the team members with individually allocated tasks for completion and clear roles and responsibilities. The overall responsibility for the project network belongs to the project leader.

Project networks have milestones in them, in the form of activities and tasks which get completed on the way. They are a very good means for reporting to senior managers and for effective communication between the project team members.

Review and monitoring

Using project plans and an aggregate view of all projects, senior managers can have an overall view of activity and bottlenecks and can be updated on overall performance.

Why is project management still an issue?

The problem with project management is understanding its full scope and, as such, determining the key criteria of success. Baker et al. (1983), for instance, define a quality project as follows:

> If the project meets the technical performance specifications and/or mission to be performed, and if there is a high level of satisfaction concerning the project outcome among key people in the parent organization, key people on the project team, and key users or clientele of the project effort, the project is considered an overall success.

It seems that success depends on certain criteria:

- strategic ones such as the parent organization's commitment to instil an innovative spirit by developing internal capabililty, communication of clear direction and intent, where appropriate, and the involvement of internal and external customers
- administrative ones such as quality documentation and briefings, with the minimum of bureaucracy
- high morale within teams (positive attitudes, enthusiasm and so on)

- the quality of project leaders and their desire to succeed
- effective planning tools.

The factors that tend to inhibit successful project outcomes are exactly the opposite: poor vision, lack of goal clarity, failure to harness the energies of project teams positively, or create a climate for effective project management, not training people and lack of incentives, career paths, customer focus and so on.

Such project management problems are not uncommon; they can be found in some of the most successful and highly innovative organizations. Indeed, they have been observed in organizations the author knows extremely well and has had several dealings with. The following problems have been reported in the fast-moving consumer goods sector:

- Imposing end dates on projects and embarking on activity without proper planning, briefing and wider ownership.
- Passive role project sponsors who adopt a 'sign off/hands off' kind of perspective. They distance themselves from the project so they cannot be blamed if things go wrong.
- Stakeholders are not properly identified or involved and their specific requirements are not met.
- The vision for the project is not shared, resulting in conflicting expectations and team members not knowing what the real critical factors of success are.
- The management of meetings is not treated seriously enough. Decisions and outcomes from meetings are easily overturned by senior managers.
- There is a lack of empowerment and restrictive measures are imposed on project team members, so the decision-making process becomes slow, cumbersome and ineffective.
- The training and preparation of teams, team leaders for their roles is a big issue. Most individuals spend time communicating and updating senior managers rather than investigating the true problem. There is a lack of activity management and liaison with other stakeholders that would lend real added value to the projects.
- Project leaders have no real influence over team members' activities.
- There is a poor reward structure, which focuses more on individual performance than on team performance.
- There is a reluctance to 'kill' projects that are failing. 'Good money gets thrown after bad and the heroes are those who keep trying (and usually failing in the end) rather than those who 'pull the plug' when failure is inescapable.
- Motivation and commitment are lacking. Very often, individuals feel insecure and uneasy about working on projects, so they try to do what is

obvious and safe rather then take risks and do what is right. They adopt an 'I told you so' attitude rather than striving for success.

- Project management is not given its true value but is taken for granted as a natural capability.
- Ownership and accountability have not been instilled in team members. Functional bosses have difficulty accepting individual's commitments to 'non-functional' activities.
- There is a lack of understanding of what a project is and how it differs from everyday processes.

The role of project leaders

> A leader is not an administrator who loves to run others, but someone who carries water for his people so they can get on with their jobs. (Robert Townsend)

The best way to understand project leaders is to establish what they are expected to do, what roles they are supposed to assume and what personal attributes they are expected to possess.

Managers versus leaders

- There must be a distinction between the role of a project leader and project manager. At the moment there is still some debate about whether individuals have to be both technically and commercially conversant in the industry before they are allowed to lead projects and be in charge of teams. In reality, however, project leaders are often chosen for their interpersonal skills and their strength in managing team work. An in-depth knowledge of technical aspects and commercial pressures is highly desirable but not necessarily detrimental to the project's success if it is not very strong. As long as there is enough knowledge among team members, the project is not threatened.
- Another point to remember is that each project is different. The choice for project leaders therefore has to be based on a process of leading teams time and time again rather than on their specific interest/knowledge of a particular project.
- Project leaders are individuals who understand how all business processes function. They have the ability to grasp the whole picture and are quick at establishing what is required in terms of achieving overall objectives.
- Good project leaders can rally support and influence people to perform, provide information and resources and give support to their project.

- Competent project leaders can, through their good knowledge of the organization, avoid pitfalls, learn from previous mistakes, and check before they act.
- A good leader is a person with high negotiation skills who is looking for quality in conducting the project and completeness of all the tasks, using continuous learning, good ideas, and best practice from other organizations.
- A good leader is a person who subscribes to the slogan 'hard on the problem – soft on people' and continuously wants to defeat the problem and protect the team effort.

What are the key tasks of project leader?

- *Proper briefing* on the project and its outcomes. This is perhaps the most critical factor to impinge on the success of the project. There has to be overall agreement on the goal of the project. This can only happen through proper briefing of the team leader in the first place. Without a good understanding of what is expected, the project can only fail.
- *Communicating requirements to various individuals/sections needed to contribute towards the project as early as possible.* This is essential if support is to be obtained and the project is allowed to proceed on time.
- *Securing adequate resources for the project.* The project leader must use a helicopter view approach to the project and its requirements. This is an essential skill and could perhaps be developed with experience.
- *Getting the team together.* Communication between various members should be encouraged as early as possible to ensure that there is togetherness and a commitment to move forward with the agreed plan of work.
- *Role definition and clarification of team members.* It is very important for team members to understand how they are going to contribute, where they will be contributing and when they will contribute. Roles have to be made visible from the outset.
- *Ability to move the project forward.* The project leader should take the necessary actions, and sometimes calculated risks, particularly during unforeseen circumstances, so that momentum continues and timeliness is still feasible.
- *Communicating to the various sponsors.* This should be done on a regular basis and very effectively so that there is continuous awareness on progress and so that support is gained for difficult decisions to be made.
- *Capture the learning from every project.* Things that slow down progress, are cumbersome and have cost/resource implications should be changed.
- *Managing beyond the project brief.* There should be a thorough understanding of process implications (the project fit in the context of the five-stage innovation process, for instance).

What are the key personal attributes of project leaders?

- Ideally, project leaders are individuals who are, among other things, *analytical, patient, persuasive, open and honest, decisive, highly motivated, committed, open-minded, flexible, outgoing and friendly, good facilitators* and *creative*.
- *Good communication skills* are a prerequisite.
- *Good negotiating power* is needed for the acquisition of resources.

Typical pitfalls in project leadership

- Project leaders tend to focus on the task/technical aspects rather than human aspects.
- Project leaders are chosen for their flair and dynamic nature rather than their interpersonal skills.
- Project leaders are unwilling and reluctant to consult a senior manager when the project is still ambiguous or in a hostile environment.
- Overt consultation is not seen as part of the role – the sponsor may be unwilling or unable to support broader interaction.
- Project leaders may have a desire to avoid confrontation, fearing that consultation may divert the project from where they want it to go.
- Long-standing differences between people in different departments may get in the way of progressing the project.

The role of project teams

Projects are managed through teams whose members bring in several perspectives, a multitude of skills and areas of expertise and who, together, can channel their individual efforts and energies for successful project outcomes. Teams come in various shapes and forms. The following points explain the merits of the team-based approach:

- Project leaders are an integral part of the *core* team concept.
- The core team leader accepts responsibilities for managing budgets, resources and schedules.
- The leader leaves it up to the core team members to co-ordinate their own functional activities.

The core team concept, which is used widely by organizations, is a very powerful approach to project management. In order for teams to meet required goals and objectives, they should be given the authority and power to make decisions on the project implementation and thus be more accountable for its success or failure.

This concept enables senior managers to focus on *critical strategic decisions* and the core project team can then be allowed to make decisions on *implementation* and *tactical aspects*. This empowerment will lead to two distinctive benefits:

- Executive time can be spent providing strategic direction and control instead of dealing with what is referred to as *micro-managing* lower-level decisions.
- Project-related decisions can be made by the core team closest to the project. These are the people who live and breathe the project every day as it progresses and are therefore the only ones with the right information and knowledge to act.

When leadership and teamwork are inadequate

There are several reasons for ineffective project leadership: inexperienced project leaders, a poorly defined role for project leadership within the company, inadequate training, and a flawed definition of the project team organization. Teams are ineffective when there is confusion over what the members are supposed to do, for example, when its members think they are functional reviewers rather than contributors. The following list provides some reasons for the poor performance of teams:

- Team members are not empowered to accomplish the objectives. In some cases, they are given the responsibility but not the authority or resources.
- Concurrent engineering is lacking because some functions and skills are not properly integrated into the team's activities.
- Results are not achieved because the team lacks the staff and skills to do it. Resources are frequently moved from team to team without any clear decision.
- Conflict and confusion arise between the project team and the functional organization because the way they work together is not clearly defined. Usually the emphasis continues to be the function rather than the project.

Table 6.1 illustrates several problems faced by project leaders.

Developing a culture of project management

It is perhaps about time that organizations started to realize that project management is not tools- and documentation-oriented and is much influenced by collective behaviour within an organization.

Table 6.1 *Problems and issues of project management*

Type of innovation	Problems and issues
Continuous	Delays because decisions are not made quickly enough.
	Projects miss opportunity because of too many revisions and changes.
	Timing is wrong.
	Practical/technical problems.
	Changes in strategic focus.
	Indecisiveness and inability to accept risk-taking.
	Enormous number of stakeholders in the new brand.
	Power breakers can stifle the process if they so wish.
	Vast bureaucracy (backbiting, backcovering).
	Spending time justifying things rather than making them happen.
	The company has a 'careful culture'.
	Valuable minds diverted to do mechanical work.
	People feeling the need to do something to appear active and busy.
	Revisiting previous projects tends to be perceived as a weakness, so that the company encourages a progressive approach without taking stock of previous experiences.
	Competition among groups of people – usually among those with fewer resources, who could hold things up or slow them down.
	There is no culture of commitment based on making things happen. The culture is one of keeping things ongoing.
	Total dependency on market research – a laborious process – rather than on judgement and intuition.
	Do not develop best practice, but repeat the learning curve again and again.
	Do not generate innovation as an on-going activity; rather than work in parallel, there is no rhythm of activity. One thing is developed at a time.
	Resources are unbalanced (the feast or famine approach). There are different desire intensities for making things happen.
Discontinuous	Company naïve in not assessing the risks of having a radical discontinuity, which is meant to change consumer perceptions and behaviour.
	The company misjudge the likely impact on market trends and consumer demands. Company is inexperienced in handling big discontinuities.
	The internal focused approach is unable to cope with the necessary changes in methods, capacity requirements, process flexibility and dealing with various demands.
	There is an incompatible culture with major discontinuity. This is proved when the board feels it necessary to rely on market research and ample information before making a decision. Discontinuities normally rely on instinct and judgement rather than hard facts.

There are hard and soft factors that can relate directly to the success or failure of projects and whether good projects can be sustained. The issues are how to be consistent, how to be predictable with regard to outcomes, how the value added factor can be optimized, how the mould can be broken and how to speed up the process.

Table 6.2 is an analysis of various cultures of project management. The critical factors of success include hard and soft elements and the role of senior managers in shaping up individual project management cultures. The lack of disruptive processes, tools and techniques shows a 'blind' approach to project management, as does the lack of planning and strategic analysis. From a 'hit and miss', 'wishful thinking' kind of perspective, the table demonstrates that, with the presence of all the key factors, there is an embellishment and the development of a positive culture of project management. For a world-class, consistent and disciplined culture, for instance, performance is based on good vision, empowerment, experienced core teams and the fact that the object scheduling is taken well beyond the success of the project by focusing on improvement areas in the process. It has already been argued that, even in the case of experienced organizations, project management does still present a challenge. It is not necessarily whether the projects themselves are complex; in fact, many projects can still falter even if they represent simple improvements and relaunches.

On the other hand, complex and pioneering innovation projects can still be successful if some of the ingredients covered in Table 6.2 and discussed in earlier sections are present. Even in areas such as R&D, the effective application of project management can lead to big breakthroughs. The following extract is from an article discussing the merits of project management (Ford, 1995):

> Science is traditionally a sequential process. We like to see the results of one set of theories before setting out on another. Now the timescales and planning disciplines which we have learned, combined with decision papers, mean that we can offer our stakeholders the possibility of speeding up the process of development by carrying out different parts of the project alongside each other.

An analysis of various organizations in the fast moving consumer goods sector by the author has revealed that problems associated with project management could spread from simple 'continuous innovations' to 'breakthrough and discontinuous ones'. On the other hand, a position culture of project management can lead to full success and major breakthroughs. The following have been reported as critical factors of success in the context of fast moving consumer goods:

Table 6.2 *Managing projects for excellence: an evolutionary cultural approach*

	Stage 0 Troubled	Stage 1 Functional	Stage 2 Integrated	Stage 3 World class
Product development process	• Informal • Formal process not practised or atrophied	• A process for each function with disparate steps etc. Varying definitions abound	• One integrated process known to all and followed consistently	• Process among the best in the world and continuously improving • High rate of successful innovation or new product introduction
Project organization	• 'Missiles and grenades over walls' • 'Free for all'	• Strong functional walls/boundaries • Internal 'politics' are strong	• Dedicated cross-functional core teams • Good functional integration • Strong project management	• Experienced core teams • Capable of multilocation development
Management review process	• Focus is on release problems	• Monthly project reviews	• Event-based throughout the process	• Internalized as part of the culture
Strategic role	• Process failures threaten survival	• Process is detrimental to competitiveness	• Process permits parity with industry leaders	• Process as a source of competitive superiority • Strategies exploit process
Project management	• No project planning or schedules done once then shelved	• Schedules exist in abundance, but are not integrated	• Teams use schedules and tools as keys for project success	• Scheduling linked to process improvement
Design tools	• None	• Some, but not integrated	• Integrated tools	• Completed EDA linked to factory vendors
Design standard and techniques	• 'We never do the same thing twice'	• Partial unrelated standards exist within areas of specialization	• In place and training available	• Continuously updated • Used as performance indicators

Product cost	• Not predictable	• Different estimate	• Product cost highly predictable	• Uses life-cycle cost models
Target setting	• Wishful thinking or none at all	• By edict ('you will complete this by . . .')	• Based on process norms (e.g. cycle-time guidelines)	• Based on world-class benchmarks
Product planning	• Not done or done opportunistically	• Done periodically • Often disconnected • Usually only 1–2 yrs out	• A cross-functional responsibility • Focuses on product line strategy	• Highly integrated • Common vision
Technology planning	• None	• R&D responsibility • Tendency to ivory tower • Distinction between technology and product development not well maintained	• Long range • Distinction between technology and product development	• Long range and integrated • Product strategy • Strategic options identified
People management	• Random	• Functional kingdoms • Headcount important	• Teaming skills highly valued	• Everyone wants to work here
Customer involvement (QFD)	• None	• Marketing seen as surrogate for customer	• QFD and related techniques in some use	• Customer effectively integrated into process
Strategic vendor alliances	• None. Hostile relationship	• Critical components only, one-way street	• Seen as strengthening the process	• Integrated into process
Performance measurement	• None quantified. Information disguised	• Functional only • No process metrics	• Metrics used as management tool	• Consistent metrics • Regular external benchmarking
Time-to-market performance	• May be infinite	• Inconsistent and unpredictable	• 40–60% of Stage 1	• Best in industry and declining

- the ability to work closely with as many stakeholders as possible
- the encouragement of secondments and exchanges of information to enable each party to appreciate the nature of the work and the major constraints
- having good mentors to facilitate the learning process of the seconded person
- recognizing that method and culture are key things to successful innovations – that having a good process is not enough to lead to successful innovations and that there has to be a strong focus on people
- an enormous amount of individual decision-making, process ownership and commitment to make things happen
- making sure every meeting resulted in an agreed plan of action supported by all concerned and a clear vision about where and how to proceed.

Some critical factors reported to have led to three major discontinuities are:

- simple formal reviews
- lots of contacts at all levels
- efficiency of contacts and meetings
- very efficient communications.

Best practice project management

An analysis of best practice in project management was reported in Wheelwright and Clark (1992), through examining four world-class organizations, Kodak, General Electric, Motorola and Lockheed Skunkworks. It revealed that effective project management comes from:

- making sure project management is driven by teams of various types
- teams having control of resources and the process and being supported in all aspects
- a project leader who is fully in charge, with full budget authority and the responsibility and choice for hand-picking team members
- the full use of innovation processes with phases, stages and a gate system
- an emphasis on measurement, using performance drives such as resource utilization, technical advancement, risk management, system solution, speed and technical performance
- periodic reviews involving senior management
- managing projects through total flexibility, using problem-solving to keep the project on track and trying out creative means in order to ensure total success.

Table 6.3 *Examples of best practice in project management*

	Kodak	General Electric	Motorola	Lockheed Skunkworks
A. Overview				
Company's characterization of the process	Phases and gates (Manufacturability Assurance process – MAP)	Tollgate process	Contract-driven Cross-functional teams	Tiger team
Dominant characteristics	Strong functional orientation with discipline and focus in the process	Functional orientation, but cross-functional phases and a project team to achieve integration	Team focus with functional support and clear links to senior management	Fully dedicated team with control over resources and process
Key mechanisms	Phases, gates; customer mission statement; gatekeepers	Tollgates; project manager; senior management review at milestones; cross-functional phases	Dedicated core team; general manager as project leader; the contract; senior management sponsor	Dedicated support resources; co-location; full budget authority; leader as CEO; small, hand-picked team
Major phases in a development project	*6 phases* I. Customer mission/vision II. Technical demonstration III. Technical/operational feasibility IV. Capability demonstration V. Product/process design VI. Acceptance and production	*10 phases* (defined by reviews) I. Customer needs II. Concept III. Feasibility IV. Preliminary design V. Final design VI. Critical producibility VII. Market/field test VIII. Manufacturing feasibility IX. Market readiness X. Market introduction follow-up	*4+ phases* I. Product definition II. Contract development III. Development through manufacturing start-up (team defines subphases) IV. Program wrap-up (learning)	Non-standard (team specifies major milestones and review procedures for those)

Table 6.3 Continued

	Kodak	General Electric	Motorola	Lockheed Skunkworks
Dominant type of project	Manufacturing process; projects where technical advancement is paramount	Evolutions, enhancements, and incremental improvements; technical solutions important but balance across functions crucial; some emphasis on speed	Platform/next generation; system solution crucial; environment turbulent; speed critical	Breakthrough projects; high risk; experimental efforts
Typical project duration	24–40 months	24–48 months	18–30 months	24–60 months
Primary performance drivers	a. Resource utilization b. Technical advancement	a. Risk management b. Resource utilization	a. System solution b. Speed	a. Technical performance b. Speed
B. Basic framework elements				
1. Project definition	Ideas initiated from many sources; Initial funding can come from any function; 'Definition' reflects funding source	Initial phase is market need definition; Ideas initiated from many sources; Marketing must approve need/opportunity	Phase I – 'Blitz' product definition (7-day limit); Cross-functional; Co-located during definition	Concept champion emerges (usually a technically trained general manager); Senior management agrees in principle on strategic opportunity; Team details the concept definition
2. Project organization and staffing	Functions control their phase(s) of project; Functions assign people as needed; Work is done by a functional subgroup; Some overlap of R&D/engineering in Phase IV	Representatives from each function assigned to the team at outset; Team members serve as functional liaisons; Detailed work done in the functions by staff assigned by the functional manager	Job postings for cross-functional, dedicated/co-located core team; Part-time support groups; Core team responsible for development procedures (within broad corporate guidelines)	Project champion hand picks the team; Team relatively small, people have broad assignments; Most important support people also dedicated and co-located; Other support work subcontracted; Team develops own procedures without constraints

3. Project management and leadership	Shifts from marketing (Phase I) to R&D (Phases II–IV) to engineering (Phases IV–V) to marketing (Phase VI); At phase transitions, a gatekeeper (upstream) releases project, and a stakeholder (downstream) accepts the project	Programme manager maintains schedule, follows up between reviews, facilitates transitions between functions; Functional managers direct the project work done by their people	Full-time, general manager project head; Core team reports to project head; Project head is concept champion and allocates resources within the project	Project leader is in charge – CEO of the effort; Does own hiring, training, and evaluation; Manages all aspects; Often creates an entire business unit
4. Problem-solving, testing and prototyping	Problem-solving and prototyping done largely within the functions; Many specialized test and prototype groups used as subcontractors; Quality assurance does primary testing in Phases V–VI	Problem-solving done largely within single functions; Cross-functional issues raised in reviews and later prototypes; Testing and prototyping done by specialized support groups	Cross-functional is dominant; Prototypes are project tests, not functional tests; Substantial testing to verify 10X progress	Cross-functional, but early phases dominated by technical concerns; Emphasis on technical performance on critical dimensions; Engineers work directly with key customer(s) and do own prototypes
5. Senior management review and control	Senior functional manager does most reviews (their resources and funds); Senior, cross-functional advisory groups used on special issues (e.g. environmental) or to achieve special co-ordination (e.g. international)	Occurs at key reviews; Strict criteria defined to move to next phase; Emphasis on identifying and managing risks; Management 'signs' approval at each tollgate	Senior management as sponsor and coach; Reviews tied to key project events; Manage to team 'contract'; Sponsor is focal point for others on executive staff	Periodic one-to-one between project leader and corporate top manager; Limited formal reviews, but may hold 'communication' exchanges; Senior management sets aggregate resource limits; Team is largely on its own
6. Real time/ midcourse corrections	Done primarily within single functions; Send projects back to an earlier phase if major problem identified later; Major transition from R&D to engineering (technical feasibility to commercialization)	Senior management involvement in conflict resolution; In concept, vary resources and time line in response to problems; Can halt project at any review if a serious problem	Low-level problem solving by competent, core team members; Continual, extensive communication; Revise detailed plans periodically; Team changes tasks, their sequences, and groupings	Do what is required for success; Creative, always trying new ways; Extensive discussions of options and next steps within the team

Source: Wheetwright and Clark (1992)

Table 6.3 illustrates a comparative analysis of best practices found to be inherent in the four organizations mentioned above.

The following are mini cases of best practice compiled by the author during his studies in the field of innovation management.

Case study 1: Rover Cars

Rover Cars recognizes that time-based measures are critical to the business (Table 6.4). This has meant a significant change from an old, financially oriented culture of measurement to one which recognizes that time-to-market is critical to the company's competitiveness. Through time-focused competitiveness, the following have been achieved:

- a three- to four-year product cycle achieved with computerization and automation
- cost and time reductions in various aspects
- parallel working and activity integration
- pulling suppliers into the company's network
- reaching out to dealers and eliminating waste
- a 90 per cent achievement of a two-week maximum order-to-delivery time to ensure adequate customer responses

Table 6.4 *Moving towards time-based measures at Rover*

Financial	Time-based
Direct labour costs	Delivery time/demand time ratio
Machine utilization	Schedule adherence
Direct/Indirect ratio	Changeover time distribution
Overhead absorption	Empty floor space
Sales booked	Forecast accuracy
value	volume
	mix
Product standard cost	Demand stability
new products	
current products	
Performance to budget	Common/unique parts ratio
	Delivery time
	Product variety
	number of products
	number of parts
	number of processes

- a three-year product cycle, to permit a fast response to customer needs and desires.

The above achievements came through Rover's recognition that customer targeting is the strategy for the 1990s and as a result of this, make to order and building customer loyalty became of paramount importance.

Time-to-market is achieved through an integrated system activity, with time the interlinking element affecting every sphere of automotive activity, thus:

- reducing the size of production runs and maximizing the percentage of value-adding time within the production cycle
- centrally controlled scheduling processes linked to protracted procurement cycles, giving way to local scheduling and greater immediacy
- improving productivity by some 200 per cent
- making response times eight to ten times faster.

Rover has adopted great evolutionary thinking based on the fact that the *customer* is not market research. Customer loyalty can only be established through building brand loyalty, with the realization that the latter is heavily dependent on quality and service. The business drivers for the 1990s are customer satisfaction, time-to-market and brand loyalty. The differentiator is quality and service, achieved through a flexible factory system capable of fast responsiveness.

There is a determination to understand customer types and needs through the use of *product planning matrices*, *market research*, *customer targeting*, *customer mapping* and *product image*, and the use of *QFD*.

Project management policy (PMP) – route map

The innovation process within Rover Group is based on three major phases:

- decision and planning
- delivery
- post-launch.

The implementation of the innovation process is through the project management policy, a comprehensive system covering stages, activities, deliverables, reviews and measures.

Product template – product selection

This phase of the process generates and reviews several product opportunities that meet the requirements of the product template and establishes the 'prime route', product selection. Successful completion of this phase leads to the issue of the product development letter and commitment of engineering resource to achieve a robust D-Zero event.

The following key activities take place during this phase of feasibility:

- vehicle aesthetics
- product 'market' description
- product 'process and manufacturing' description
- product investment – including vendor tooling
- product variable cost
- programme costs
- volumes and prices
- profit programme resources
- programme timing
- event.

Product 'process and manufacturing': some deliverables

- Establish logistics strategy.
- Agree supplier nominations.
- Agree costs for piece price.
- Establish any capacity/facility constraints.
- Establish manufacturing strategy with regard to TPM standards.
- Establish the volume/option implications to cost and capacity.
- Establish batching and just-in-time (JIT).
- Advise possible packaging and palletization concerns through the vendors.
- Evaluate the potential manufacturing routes.
- Agree facilities investment and lead times.
- Outline manufacturing feasibility studies undertaken.
- Outline significant vendors' timing plans.
- Outline the volume/option implication to cost and capacity.
- Agree manufacturing process to be used in product.
- Evaluate 'time to return to normal quality and production' after new model introduction: does it equal company targets?
- Outline of 'prime route' development plans and costs.
- Develop plans with suppliers and manufacturing to achieve reliability target.
- Develop plans with suppliers and logistics partner to meet logistic objectives.
- Establish process capability plans.

Case study 2: IBM

IBM have introduced what they call their integrated produce development process. This is described as follows.

Overall process

The design/development process, as with other operations, fits into the overall process overview:

> develop and implement strategy ==> market products
> ==> design/develop products and services ==> manufacture/test products

Included in the system are also processes for:

- drive for continuous improvement
- support services, human resources (HR), marketing etc.

The product development process

Customer requirements are translated into a detailed product and service specification. Analysis of the specification leads to the design of the process:

- capability analysis
- establish additional requirements
- costing
- set performance targets
- product quality plan.

Note: This includes extensive discussions between customer and the cross-functional team, including early involvement in manufacturing.

Product management

A project plan is completed for all activities so as to maintain a project schedule. A checklist guide (comprising the following factors: relevance, stage completed and by whom). This is then used to trace the project through the phases of the project from initial funding to general availability.
   The objective is to:

- establish firm product definition early
- ensure agreement
- define activities.

Two Gantt charts are used: a phase Gantt chart, which shows at what stage the project is currently and who is involved (e.g. manufacturing) and a review/ inspection chart (completed by product assurance), which is used to track how well the project is keeping to schedule. Assessment is judged on the completion and review of:

- specification and requirement
- schedules
- dependencies
- testing
- review
- documentation
- problem log
- resource
- outlook.

Initial design checklist

This is the list of deliverables to be completed prior to proceeding with detail design:

1 Concept
  – define at checkpoint O
  – outstanding items closed?

2 Design
  Electrical:
  – design definition document
  – schematics – tolerances
  – power/thermal study
  – test specification and strategy outline
  – impedance/cross-talk analysis

  Mechanical:
  – 3D modelling/tolerance study – profile
  – bill structure established
  – tooling: testers, specs, dependencies etc.
  – profile/panel layout
  – REC controlled drawings
  – stress analysis
  – component release status check

Physical design:
- worksheets (1 to 3) started
- components, connectors etc. defined
- libraries complete
- initial ground rules checked

Processes:
- proposed process documented
- development requirement documented
- proposed test strategy documented

Project file:
- master hardcopy folder created
- contents list up to date

3 Manufacture
- PPE/MEI meeting held
- panelization

4 Evaluation
- quality-strategy proposal documented

5 Business
- contract proposal
- schedule/costs
- first pass cost request
- first pass schedule
- risk assessment (any CP deficiencies)
- bid review appropriate
- acceptable to proceed?

Case study 3: 3M

An emphasis on cross-functional teams led to the sales in 1990 of 60,000 from a base of 110 technologies. New products are based on ideas coming from 3M laboratories around the world: idea acquisitions, licensing, joint ventures and factoring. A key source, however, is internal venturing or *intrapreneuring*.

3M's new product strategies need a point of balance between learning and efficiency to be maintained. This gives an overall have-a-go approach rather than a blast-off approach, where technologies look for applications and applications are studied to develop new technologies.

The climate for effective cross-functional teamwork is achieved through top management's commitment to initiating successful programmes for developing new products based on a clear set of goals and plans, resulting in clear action.

Cross-functional teams are triggered off through a process whereby an individual (an 'intrapreneur') is needed who can gain support for his/her idea from colleagues around the organization.

An entrepreneur is a person capable of turning an idea into a profitable reality within the existing organization. It can be the inventor, but fundamentally he or she is the person with the commitment to push an idea through the system.

3M has a range of programmes to foster an environment where individuals and cross-functional teams can flourish, as follows:

1 The 15 per cent rule
2 The dual ladder
3 Technical forums, fairs, councils
4 Programmes: The Genesis Fund
                  Pathfinder
                  The Alpha Fund
                  Circle Of Technical Excellence
                  The Carlton Society
                  The Golden Step.

Planning teams

In order to ensure a sustainable climate for cross-functional teams to develop new products, 3M has put in place an Innovation Steering Committee to stress the following guidelines for line managers:

- Allow people freedom to do their jobs their own way.
- Challenge people to use part of their time to explore innovative projects of their own choosing.
- Strive to get more than 25 per cent sales from new products in the last five years.
- Let people learn from their own mistakes.
- Remember that 'making a little, selling a little', and learning with the market is a way to start important new business.
- Honour the heroes of innovation who courageously do what is right.
- Stay visible, accessible, and open to new ideas, while managing.
- Find more ways to reward innovators.
- Stay committed to the best ideas, despite obstacles.
- Use cross-functional teams to bridge organizational boundaries.
- Sponsor others in their efforts to innovate.

The culture of innovation within 3M stresses the need to stay close to the customer through leading-edge technologies, understanding and anticipating their needs, pursuing relevant R&D and being committed to solving customer problems.

Ingredients for successful innovation therefore include:

- a stated corporate dependence on innovation
- management commitment and genuine interest in innovation
- a clear understanding by the technical community of the business direction
- an environment that encourages people to take risks without being punished for failure and allows them the freedom to pursue their ideas
- good interaction and communication across business and functional boundaries
- a culture where sponsorship is a specified responsibility of management
- meaningful, high-visibility programmes and awards that recognize innovation
- human resource principles that preserve and respect the rights of the individual.

Case study 3: Ford

Engineering skills

Simultaneous engineering has been implemented in an effective and unique way by using a blend of technical and soft skills. Ford launched their engineering quality improvement programme (EQUIP) to provide engineers with the necessary skills to innovate and improve products in a climate of simultaneous engineering processes. EQUIP was developed from the need for design and manufacturing engineers to support a simultaneous engineering process by:

- updating their existing technical skills in the area of product quality improvement
- learning new technical and people skills
- changing their approach to engineering.

EQUIP is seen as a vehicle for introducing innovation and change within Ford Europe. The programme covers engineering skills for carrying out tasks effectively and behavioural skills to enable engineers to work in a team format in the context of simultaneous engineering.

Technical skills

There are various programmes and tools used within the company to help develop technical skills:

- *Tops (8D)*: problem-solving using an eight-step discipline approach.
- *Process management*: understanding, controlling and improving processes with emphasis on the manufacturing process.
- *FMEA*: the identification of potential problems during the design of the product or process in order to take action to prevent problems occurring.
- *Experimentation*: gaining knowledge of the manner in which a product or system functions in order to optimize performance through efficient experimentation.
- *Quality engineering*: engineering what the customer wants by maximizing the primary or ideal function of a component, system or product and thereby minimizing error states.
- *Customer focused engineering*: planning an engineering process that will deliver to the customer a product that will meet and exceed his or her expectations. This is based on quality function deployment (QFD).

People skills

People skills include the following:

- *Team-building*: the development of a cohesive and synergistic team. Almost all applications of the EQUIP quality improvement skills in Ford Europe will be applied in cross-functional teams, with many of these teams being cross national.
- *Communication*: the maximization of overlap between intention and reception in the exchange of information between people.
- *Implementation*: the effective use of tools and techniques to ensure that the EQUIP quality improvement skills are implemented to their full advantage in the workplace.
- *Innovation*: the expansion of the engineering mind beyond the numeric and analytical skills within which it may have been constrained in the past in order to seek new ideas and fresh approaches.

The quality operating system

The quality operating system (QOS) was introduced in 1992. It is defined as a systematic, disciplined approach that uses standardized tools and practices to manage business and achieve ever-increasing levels of customer satisfaction.

Ford felt it needed an operating system guide for the following reasons:

- The company trained thousands of employees in the use of quality engineering tools and developed Q-1 facilities, only to find they needed more. QOS was the management 'glue' that improved their success with customers.
- QOS is a generic process which can be applied in manufacturing and non-manufacturing operations. It is based on eight steps driven by a continuous involvement of all employees and the principle of Plan-Do-Check and Act.

The benefits of a formalized QOS include:

- providing management with a tool to determine the correlation between customer expectations and company results
- enhancement of empowerment
- the ability to combine the power of team dynamics and management authority.

Through QOS, Ford measures two aspects:

- Process (production focus).
- Result (customer focus).

Case study 4: Cadillac

Simultaneous engineering

Cadillac uses simultaneous engineering (SE) as a multidisciplinary approach relying on cross-functional teams to conceive, approve, develop, and continuously improve all Cadillac products. Figure 6.1 illustrates the approach used by Cadillac for SE. The executive management team is responsible for sanctioning the SE process, setting policy and direction and providing an environment in which SE teams can succeed.

The SE steering committee (SESC) is responsible for allocating the resources necessary to execute product programmes. It liaises with the organization as a whole, and monitors and manages the process.

Each product line is assigned a Vehicle Team to manage the development of new models and ensure continuous improvement of existing models. These Vehicle Teams work closely with the Vehicle Systems Management Teams (VSMTs) to establish product programmes. VSMTs are responsible for developing plans to achieve world-class attributes in all the major vehicle systems for each of Cadillac's products.

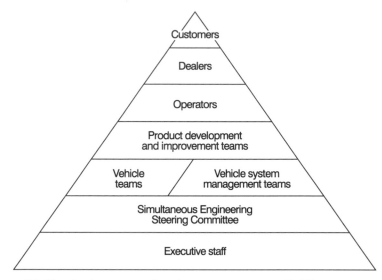

Figure 6.1 *The simultaneous engineering team structure at Cadillac*

Product Development and Improvement Teams (PDITs) are responsible for the design and continuous quality improvement of each component of all the major systems. PDIT membership includes assembly operators from the plants – referred to collectively as the Voice of the Assembler – and supplier representatives.

At the top of the pyramid, the role of the SE team is to support the operator at the assembly plant in building high-quality products to satisfy Cadillac dealers and customers.

The product programme management process (PPMP)

PPMP co-ordinates all aspects of a specific car programme, which is known as 'Four Phase' (Figure 6.2).

Concepts for vehicles that integrate customer needs and expectations, business plan objectives and future product and process technology plans are continuously generated in an activity known as *bubble up*. During the 'technology and concept development' phase, the Vehicle Team converts these concepts into a Produce Plan that includes:

- a marketing strategy
- vehicle content and performance criteria
- manufacturing objectives, and other details.

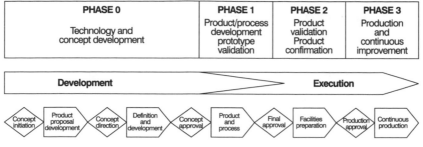

Figure 6.2 *The four-phase process model at Cadillac*

Once the exterior and interior designs have been verified in customer clinics, and the process and product technology have been proven, the concept is approved and moves to the next stage of development, the 'product/process development and prototype validation' phase, when part characteristics and process requirements are formalized. Vehicle prototypes are demonstrated and validated, and the manufacturing and assembly design is completed.

In the 'process validation and product confirmation' phase, pilot vehicles are built from actual production tools that meet quality requirements. Then, once the assembly facilities are ready for production, and sales and service programmes have been completed, approval is given for the final phase, 'production and continuous improvement'.

Throughout the PPMP, *critical path charts* are developed to highlight programme timing and process bottlenecks. These charts are reviewed on a regular basis to ensure that timing and project objectives are properly set and achieved.

In process, quality is assessed at every stage. Also, during assembly, in-process audits verify quality during the build process and when the car is finished, quality levels of the entire vehicle are verified. Continuous improvement is facilitated by post-production audits.

Ford's 'quality network five-step problem-solving' is used to identify root causes of process upsets (Figure 6.3), while suppliers are integrated into the process of quality through the 'targets for excellence' programme. This programme sets out the requirements in five key business areas: quality, cost, delivery, technology and management. The programme includes quality procedures, and the problem-reporting and resolution process, and a supplier assessment process is used to verify the supplier's capability to meet expectations. This process has four basic steps:

1 Supplier self-assessment against the targets for excellence criteria.
2 On-site assessment by a three-person team.
3 Development planning and implementation.
4 Reassessment.

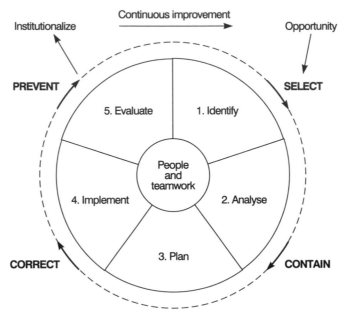

Figure 6.3 *The five-step problem-solving process at Cadillac*

Case study 5: Kodak

Multifunction teams form the foundation of the Kodak innovation process. For each project, there must be at least one sponsor, and there may be up to three. The project teams must include members with skills in all the following areas:

- customer knowledge
- marketing
- business
- systems engineering
- various technical areas, and experimentation
- various aspects of manufacturing
- highly developed problem-solving capabilities
- good interpersonal communication abilities for working in a team structure.

Kodak outlines the need for effective project leaders, who should be able to:

- keep purpose and goals meaningful
- build team commitment and confidence

- apply disciplined project management
- guide the team in managing breakdowns
- manage team interfaces, leading the integration of various project teams
- strengthen the skill mix and level
- provide opportunities for personal growth and development for team members
- be competent working members of the project team
- lead the team in measuring their progress.

There must be a disciplined approach to project management, with particular reference to the following:

- the development of specific project performance goals
- the ability to link the above to the project plan
- project scheduling
- task-specific activities and deliverables
- responsibilities.

Integrated project planning means that the project team needs to maintain effective communications with manufacturing (i.e. site selection, cost and waste targets, process requirements) and marketing (product positioning, pricing strategies, optimum launch opportunities, post-launch support services). Linkages are best maintained through functional representations.

The tools for effective project management

A variety of tools can be used for the effective management of innovation.

Technology assessment and market assessment tools

These tools are used to develop innovation goals and objectives, often using matrix analysis, as shown in Figure 6.4.

A new product development strategy can be developed from this, which will enable the organization concerned to decide how to achieve its innovation target, what project types are going to be sponsored, what is the most desirable mix, resource requirement issues and so on.

An aggregate project plan

The aggregate project plan is intended to help the organization decide the right number and mix of projects, the best scenarios for delivering strategic goals, the best approach for using existing resources and the optimum involvement of people with expertise in managing the various projects.

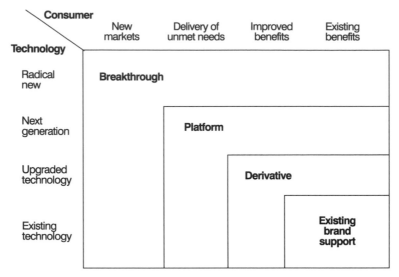

Figure 6.4 *An example of market/technology assessment tools*

Stage-gate innovation process

The stage-gate innovation process manages innovation and delivers projects. Most innovation organizations should have an innovation process with phases ranging from 2 to 7 and a number of appropriate gates. Tasks are progressed in parallel through the phases by the teams concerned and the gates are key points where 'gatekeepers' review progress and decide whether a project should proceed or be terminated.

The innovation process usually includes:

- an idea phase
- a feasibility phase
- a capability phase
- a launch phase
- a post-launch review phase.

The purpose of each phase

- *The idea phase.* This generates ideas consistent with strategic objectives and in response to competitive requirements. They should be capable of delivering customer needs and must be technically feasible.
- *The feasibility phase.* This further develops the idea by allocating clear roles and responsibilities for delivering the project, checking technical feasibility and ensuring design for manufacturability (DFM). In addition,

performance in terms of quality, cost and delivery are put together, customer satisfaction targets are determined and the business case completed. Involvement of the various stakeholders continues thoughout.

- *The capability phase*. During this phase, design for production aspects are finalized with full product functionality and features worked out. Design is optimized using all the necessary indicators, including those related to quality, cost and delivery. This phase also includes a demonstration of product design, stability and DFM through an iterative pilot, in order to check the readiness of the manufacturing process.
- *The launch phase*. This is when manufacturing scale-up takes place to full production capability. During this phase, product acceptability is also verified using formal acceptance testing. Field readiness for national, regional and global product introduction and market engagement is also confirmed.
- *The post launch review phase*. This is the stage when product performance is verified through quality, cost and delivery commitments, field and market performance is assessed and customer acceptance is confirmed in support of asset management and end-of-life strategic objectives. Production build-up continues to meet worldwide customer demands and product review and profit performance are optimized through product improvement and/or maintenance activities.

Activity planning

Activity planning is a micro level, detailed tool to be used so that projects are managed effectively. Figure 6.5 shows a pro forma for developing an activity schedule. Essentially, the following are the stages involved in activity planning:

- identifying key activities required at each stage of the project and milestones to be reached
- identifying all the key people to be involved for each activity
- clearly identify roles and responsibilities for each task/activity
- producing an estimate of resources required for each activity
- producing a schedule for all the key activities.

Activity planning within Rank Xerox Corporation

Rank Xerox uses a variety of tools to spur its innovation activity. For driving project management, the company uses a product delivery process (PDP) defined as: 'a common process for product delivery, which enables the consistent delivery of leadership products and systems to worldwide market-products which meet all internal Quality, Cost of Delivery commitments while fully satisfying end user customer requirements'. The produce delivery process is supported by the leadership through a quality programme, which

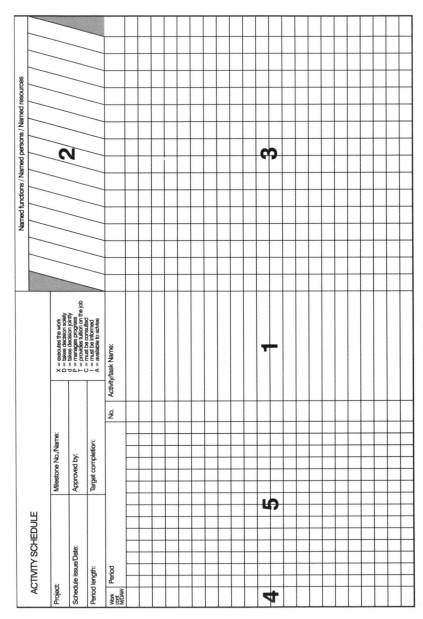

Figure 6.5 *A pro forma of activity planning and scheduling*

CE – Chief engineering/PDT managment
ENG/SVC – Eng/service managment
ENG/TPM – Eng/technical program management
LOG – Logistics and asset management
MFG/MRT – Mfg/Mfg resource team management
MKTG – Worldwide product marketing
OP UNIT – Operating unit
PP – Product planning
PPM – Process and planning manager
PQL – Program quality launch management
SUP – Supplies

Address	Phase Activity	MKTG	PP	CE	ENG/TPM	ENG/SVC	MFG/MRT	PPM	PQL	LOG	OP UNIT	SUP
C1	Assign interim program quality launch responsibility			A								
C2	Complete Q launch internal product comparison	IR	IR						A			
C3	Define launch window/setback schedule	IR	IR		IR		IR		A			
C4	Identify unique program support requirements	IR	IR		IR				A			
C5	Develop initial program quality launch strategy	IR							A			
C6	Finalize marketing and customer support strategy	A							IR			
C7	Develop preliminary international product marketing plan	A							IR			
C8	Develop market forecast	A									IR	
C9	Define customer satisfaction targets	A	IR	CR					IR			
C10	Complete business case	A		CR	IR	IR	IR			IR		IO
C11	Consolidate operative unit inputs	A									IR	
C12	Complete PAT/PDT transition			A								
C13	Implement concept phase plan	IR	IR	A	IR	IR	IR	IR	IR	IR		IR
C14	Finalize product goals	CR	A	CR								
C15	Complete program strategy	IR		CR	IR	IR	IR	A	IR	IR		IR
C16	Develop initial integrated program plan	IR	IR	CR	IR	IR	IR	A	IR	IR		IR
C17	Update program A level schedule							A				
C18	Establish program exception criteria	CR	IR	A	IR	IR	IR	IR	IR	IR		IR
C19	Develop design phase plan	IR		CR	IR	IR	IR	A	IR	IR		IR
C20	Complete program self-assessment	IR	IR	A	IR	IR	IR	IR	IR	IR		IR
C21	Complete PAAT assessment	IR		A				IR				
C22	Complete product initiation review	IR		A								
C23	Develop subsystem best of breed model		IR		A		IR					IR
C24	Issue initial product specifications	IR	CR	CR	A	IR	IR			IR		IR
C25	Develop engineering plan				A	IR	IR					IR
C26	Select mainline supplies		IR	CR	CR							A
C27	Develop integrated test plan	IR		CR	A	IR	IR			IR	IR	IR
C28	Develop software development project plan		IR		A	IR	IR					

Responsibility code

A (Accountable) – identifies the accountable/responsible function or organization; the decision-maker.

CR (Concurrence required) – identifies the function/organization required to provide written response to a proposed decision, action or approach; response is mandatory.

IR (Input required) – identifies the function/organization required to provide input to a proposed decision, action or approach; input is mandatory.

IO (Input optional) – identifies the function/organization requested to provide input to a proposed decision, action or approach; input is optional.

Figure 6.6 *Activity/responsibility matrix at Rank Xerox Corporation*

extends the emphasis on meeting customer requirements.

Activity planning at Rank Xerox is described in the form of a matrix referred to as the *phase activity/responsibility matrix* (Figure 6.6). This integrates all the key activities and identifies roles and responsibilities.

These roles and responsibilities are described as A, CR, IR and IO respectively and are listed below:

- *A (accountable)*. This identifies the accountable/responsible function or organization – the decision-maker.
- *CR (concurrence required)*. This identifies the function/organization required to provide a written response to a proposed decision, action or approach. This response is mandatory.
- *IR (input required)*. This identifies the function/organization required to provide input to a proposed decision, action or approach and is mandatory.
- *IO (input optional)*. This identifies the function/organization requested to provide input to a proposed decision, action or approach. Input is optional.

Other tools and techniques

There are countless numbers of tools and techniques that can be used for project management. For instance, Kodak has implemented what they call the Kodak integrated innovation process, which has the following four stages:

- defining and refining value proposition
- product and market launch design
- marketing and manufacturing implementation
- production and sales.

The programme uses a multitude of tools, including the following:

- quality function deployment (QFD)
- customer oriented product conceptualization (COPC)
- Pugh's concept generation and selection process
- voice of the customer (VOC)
- decision and risk analysis
- seven old tools (problem-solving tools)
- seven new tools (planning tools)
- target costing
- value analysis
- value engineering
- benchmarking
- process flowchart developed and modified

- checklists
- design of experiments statistical design
- Taguchi techniques (5)
- Design for 'X'
- manufacturing process capabilities assessment
- traditional engineering analysis tools
- functional flow diagrams
- failure modes and effects analysis
- fault tree analysis
- project management course
- performance management
- project leadership development tool.

Summary

Project management will perhaps always remain a key challenge for successful innovation since its pervasiveness is through all aspects of organizational activity and performance. The challenge for senior managers is going to be to:

- continue exploiting technological avenues and opportunities
- update methodologies, systems and 'hard aspects' of managing projects
- ensure that people are well trained, well briefed and well conversant with new approaches
- continue to tackle issues of importance to customers, such as quality, cost and speed
- respond to external environmental issues
- rely on synergy levels coming from external partnerships and strategic alliances
- build streamlined processes, process-focused methods and value-driven approaches
- develop a culture that is flexible, adaptable and responsive to change.

References

Baker et al. (1983) Factors affecting product success. In *Project Management Handbook* (D. I. Clepand and W. R. King (eds). Van Nostrand Reinhold, New York.

Ford, C. (1995) Teaming with talent. *Unilever Magazine*, **3**(97), 36–9.

Joshi, M. (1996) Project management – a practical approach to deliver strategies. *Strategy*, **3**, March, 12–13.

Wheelwright, S. C. and Clark, D. (1992) *Revolutionising Product Development – Quantum Leaps in Speed, Efficiency and Quality*. Free Press.

Appendix 6.I: Innovation process documentation and key deliverables

1 Idea phase

1 Purpose

To generate ideas which are consistent with strategic objectives and in response to competitive requirements, capable of delivering consumer needs and which are technically feasible.

2 Activities

- Examination and refinement of potential business opportunities and technical capabilities.
- Identification of business needs and opportunities to market and deliver consumer requirements.
- Categorization of type of launch and its degree of imapct in the market-place.
- Mid-idea phase assessment to ensure that work can continue and investment can go ahead.
- Formation of Band Management Team and appointment of Team Leader.
- Initial planning in terms of resources, facilities, tooling, skills etc.
- Check initial manufacturability requirements and suitability of existing technologies.
- Preliminary communications to all stakeholders concerned.

3 Deliverables

A Marketing

- Idea Charter Document issued.
- Market/Consumer requirements clearly defined, based on input from internal functions and through market research.
- Brand technical/competitive details worked out, linkages determined and initial customer satisfaction goals highlighted.
- Preliminary market testing carried out to ensure that work can continue on the idea.
- A scoped business case put together to ensure that the proposed launch and the size of the market opportunity is commensurate with business needs.

B Technical development

- Technical assessments completed.
- Technical options evaluated and defined from best of breed perspective.
- Technical strategy clearly defined.
- Design for production initiated and Technical Readined Plan prepared.
- Assessment on materials and supplies completed.

C Supply chain

- Brand goals developed and completed.
- Product performance determined.
- Initial manufacturing strategy defined.

2 Feasibility phase

1 Purpose

To further develop the idea by allocating clear roles and responsibilities for delivering the project, check technical feasibility, ensure DFM is possible. In addition, performance in terms of quality, cost and delivery are put together, customer satisfaction targets determined and the business case completed. Involvement of the various stakeholders continues.

2 Activities

- Technical specifications finalized prior to start of prototyping.
- Technical team represented with all various skills.
- Use of various tools such as competitive benchmarking, Continuous Supplier Involvement (CSI), Taguchi, Computer-Aided Design etc.
- DFM and Detailed Plan for Production Intent reviewed and integrated.
- Tooling and process technology readiness is checked together with sources of supply.
- Planning for production Intent Baseline is estabished.
- Business case is completed.

3 Deliverables

A Marketing

- Contract book developed for the launch.
- Market requirements for the brand determined and confirmed, pricing/ forecast demands, launch configurations, target markets and marketing chanels, all determined.

B Technical development

- Product formulation developed based on best in breed practices.
- Technical specifications and procedures checked and prepared.
- Technology optimization studies completed for tooling and process lines.
- DFM initiated taking into account performance targets on quality, cost, delivery and profitability projections.
- Supplies Delivery Process assessment completed.

C Supply chain

- Initial Manufacturing Plan Completed.
- Manufacturing assessment (using manufacturing operations for customer requirements).

3 Capability phase

1 Purpose

During this phase, design for production aspects are finalized with full product functionality and features worked out. Design is optimized using all necessary indicators including those related to Quality, Cost, Delivery. This phase also includes demonstration of product design stability and DFM through an iterative pilot to check the readiness of the manufacturing process.

2 Activities

- Design team manages and controls the design process.
- Supplier commitments are generated for Production Intent.
- Check that Design reflects customer needs and that features and functionality are validated against performance indicators of quality, cost and delivery and against customer satisfaction targets by means of iterative development and score testing processes (sequential recycling).
- Launch Proposal developed consistent with global marketing plan.
- Supplier capability and commitment verified and implemented in all areas concerned.
- Product design stability is confirmed before actual spending of funds/ resources for production scale-up is authorized.
- Pilot production to confirm production conformance to specifications requirements and also for the validation of support documentation.
- Launch plans are developed.

3 Deliverables

A Marketing

- Global Brand Marketing Plan completed – Business Case updated.
- Comments on Launch Proposal received from various stakeholders and Global Brand Marketing Plan consolidated.

B Technical development

- All project specifications completed and management procedures put in place.
- Design process completed.
- DFM in terms of test results and established performance standards – Quality, Cost, Delivery analysis completed.
- Integrated Test Plan updated.
- Supplies delivery assessment completed.
- Follow on Design For Production completed, with emphasis on design quality and problem management.

C Supply chain

- Production Intent Baseline plan ready and manufacturing assessment using customer criteria.
- Production Commitment Baseline plan ready.
- Manufacturing assessment and manufacturing production process completed.
- Supplier readiness assessments completed – (Quality and delivery commitments established).
- Inventory standards set and Manufacturing Cost Variance Plan defined.
- Supply/Demand process implemented – Production plan developed.

4 Launch phase

1 Purpose

This is when manufacturing scale-up takes place, to full production capability. During this phase product acceptability is also verified using formal acceptance testing. Field readiness for national, regional and global product introduction and market engagement is also confirmed.

The launch stage is when the product is introduced to the end consumer through the various launch implementation plans.

2 Activities

- Production processes are planned and personnel are given appropriate training to handle new brand.
- Supplier quality validations are complete in all areas.
- Product quality objectives are focused on performance and customer satisfaction requirements.
- Product conformance to specific market and customer requirements is assessed through end user testing and customer focus group interviews.
- Sales, logistics, administration and support systems are validated and launch readiness assessed.
- Manufacturing sustained build and continued production quality is verified.
- Product Quality Launch objectives are focused on meeting customer satisfaction targets through early warning/launch performance measurement procedures.

3 Deliverables

A Marketing

- Focus Group Interviews conducted.

B Technical development

- Launch baseline completed, tested and verified.
- Supplies delivery process assessment completed.

C Supply chain

- Production build versus Required Production Plan/Launch requirement statused.
- Manufacturing assessment completed.
- Maintain Supply/Demand Process.

5 Post-launch review phase

1 Purpose

Product performance is then verified through Quality, Cost, Delivery commitments, field and market performance is assessed, and customer acceptance is confirmed in support of asset management and end of life strategic objectives. Production build-up continues to meet worldwide customer demands, product revenue and profit performance are optimized through product improvement and/or maintenance activities.

2 Activities

- Project 'lessons learnt' are developed and assessed through audit process.
- Product improvements and enhancements are implemented.
- New business opportunities are evaluated and product variants/extensions are proposed.
- End-of-life Plan for product withdrawal is implemented.

2 Deliverables

A Marketing

- Product/Product family end-of-life Plan developed and implemented.
- Customer satisfaction audit completed.
- Marketing and field audits completed.
- Product/Product Family End of Life Strategy developed and confirmed.
- Product/Product Family enhancement, improvement and upgrade requirements developed and agreed.

B Technical development

- Design changes and corresponding justification criteria implemented.
- Launch baseline maintained per project change management process.
- Supplies delivery process assessment completed.

C Supply chain

- Maintain manufacturing/support.
- Production build maintained.
- Financial variance analysis completed – manufacturing assessment completed.
- Manufacturing line balance achieved – Manufacturing Sustained Production Review Conducted.

Appendix 6.II: A model of gatekeepers' logbook

GATEKEEPER LOGBOOK
Gate 1: Is idea worth pursuing?

Critical factors	Bad									Good
	1	2	3	4	5	6	7	8	9	10
Strategic fit										
Impact on market share										
Likely costs/benefits measurement										
Technical feasibility										
Environmental issues										
Impact on customer satisfaction										
Competitive advantage										
Others:										

Score: Scale 0–100%

Anecdotal – Systemized	
Submission format	Relevance to business strategy
Data support and facts	Cost/benefit analysis

Reasons for support		Reasons against	

Final decision					
Go		Abort		Revise/review	
				Timescale	

GATEKEEPER LOGBOOK

Gate 2: What is the size of the opportunity?
Cost/benefit analysis?

Critical factors	Bad									Good
	1	2	3	4	5	6	7	8	9	10
Market mix										
Identification of clear benefits to customer										
Identification of sources of supply										
Preliminary financial evaluation										
Appraisal of technical aspects										
Level of customer early interest										
Others:										

Score: Scale 0–100%

Anecdotal – Systemized	
Fullness of marketing plan	R&D plan (feasibility of technical route)
Supply chain plan	Sales operations plan

Reasons for support		Reasons against	

Final decision							
Go		Abort		Revise/review		Timescale	

GATEKEEPER LOGBOOK

Gate 3: Technical assessment, marketing assessment, customer early assessment

Critical factors	Bad									Good
	1	2	3	4	5	6	7	8	9	10
Competitor intelligence analysis										
Early market research results										
Submission of preliminary business plan										
Clearance of safety/environmental issues										
DFMA route determined										
HR issues clarified										
Supplier sourcing finalized										
Process capability established										
Preliminary financial										
Considerations determined										
Others:										

Score: Scale 0–100%

Anecdotal – Systemized	
Preliminary business plan (advertising, market size)	R&D (DFMA development plan)
Supply chain (HR resources, raw materials, process design)	Sales operations (forecasts, customer development, distribution plans)

Reasons for support		Reasons against	

Final decision						
Go		Abort		Revise/review		Timescale	

GATEKEEPER LOGBOOK
Gate 4: Developing the commitment to launch

Critical factors	Bad								Good	
	1	2	3	4	5	6	7	8	9	10
Customer sampling/testing										
Full market research										
Full analysis of competitor's capability for same idea										
Process capability/capacity										
Systematic business plan										
Environmental/safety plan										
Product description sheets										
Financial estimates revised										
Prototypes developed/tested										
Process trails/sampling										
Technical route finalized										
Personnel plans completed										
Raw materials sourcing finalized										
Packaging/warehousing plans in place										
Others:										

Score: Scale 0–100%

Anecdotal – Systemized	
Business plan, communications Readiness for launch	Prototype development process trials Technical specifications
Supply chain readiness	Sales operations readiness

Reasons for support		Reasons against	

Final decision							
Go		Abort		Revise/review		Timescale	

GATEKEEPER LOGBOOK

Gate 5: Launching and reviewing product, fine tuning, optimizing product performance

Critical factors	Bad									Good
	1	2	3	4	5	6	7	8	9	10
Effectiveness of marketing plan										
Impact on market share										
Response of competitors										
Effectiveness of advertising campaign										
Feedback on technical specifications										
Technical improvements for process optimization										
Supplier performance										
Quality, reliability of supply										
Process capability/capacity issues										
People productivity										
Speed, responsiveness for packaging and distribution										
Financial reports accuracy										

Score: Scale 0–100%

Anecdotal – Systemized	
Marketing launch success (market share, customer delight)	R&D design optimization right first time
Supply chain (capability/capacity optimization, efficiency and effectiveness)	Sales operations (achievement sales plan, managing customer accounts)

Reasons for support		Reasons against	

Final decision						
Go		Abort		Revise/review		Timescale	

7 Total supply chain for innovation

Mohamed Zairi

This chapter discusses the role of the supply chain within innovation. The chapter highlights the necessity of having an integrated approach to the supply chain if the process is to be effective in producing successful innovation outcomes. The chapter uses case study evidence to highlight key issues of supply chain management. Many cases are discussed in detail, including Nissan, Kodak, Rank Xerox, ICL(D2D), the National Roads and Motorists Organization (NRMA), Cadillac Motors, Zytec and Texas Instruments. The chapter ends by proposing a model of best practice on the basis of evidence collected from a benchmarking exercise.

Every moment spent planning saves three or four in execution. (Crawford Greenwalt, President, DuPont)

Introduction

It is very difficult to talk about innovation management without addressing the area of supply chain. Many of the problems associated with failed new product launches are due to:

- disruption in production
- tooling
- process limitations
- supplier issues.

Effective innovation management comes through the interface of the creative part and the productive part (supply chain), and this relates to logistics, production and physical distribution.

Having an integrated approach to supply chain can assist in the battle for a close and smooth interface with brand development. It is now quite common to define supply chain through the following key activities:

- production engineering
- process development
- production planning
- buying
- sales forecasting
- distribution.

Through research involving the author, some of the most commonly cited issues of ineffective innovation management are due to the following:

1 No equitable approach to the sharing of responsibility in project management.
2 Failure to address issues of:
   - supply chain (deliver quality, on time and at least cost)
   - brand development (the prime objective is new product development (NPD) rather than continuity of what is being done). The key question to ask here is, can we do this?
3 The traditional supply chain is concerned with simplicity rather than discontinuity.
4 The planning function does not represent the total supply chain. The role of the planner should be a subtle one and not that of a police officer.
5 Failure to manage suppliers effectively.

What is supply chain management?

Supply chain management is not merely the elevation and glorification of the purchasing function at the strategic level. As Macbeth et al. (1989) argue: 'While a procurement function may still have final responsibility for purchased materials, operationally, vendor engineering and quality, materials logistics and sometimes line operator to line operator communication and contact place.'

The concept of supply chain management is new only in so far as linkages and integration are concerned. Integrated logistics of upstream and down-stream activities over the years. The supply chain management process itself is one which starts and finishes with the customer.

As quoted in Gattorna and Walters (1996), a logistics director at DuPont argues that:

> [Supply chain] requires looking at your business as one continuous process. This process absorbs such traditionally distinct functions as forecasting, purchasing, manufacturing, distribution and sale and marketing in a continuous flow of business interaction. Gone are the functional 'stove pipes' of corporate activity, instead departments are structured as a pipeline that stretches between a company's suppliers and its customers.

Supply chain management is demand led rather than supply led; in fact, it is often called demand chain management. This is because it has changed from being a focus on purchasing, converting, storing and distributing, to a focus on demands made by the customer, made possible by the advent of new technology.

Supply chain management now consists of value adding, optimizing the use of all resources, materials, people and technology and information for the benefit of the end customer. Christopher (1990) describes the concept of value added and customer services as:

> Customer service is concerned with making the product available to the customer . . . there is no value in a product or service until it is in the hands of the customer . . . 'Availability' in itself is a complex concept, impacted by many factors which might include delivery frequency and reliability, stock levels and order cycle time. Ultimately customer service is determined by the interaction of all those factors that affect the process of making products and services available to the buyer.

Lamey (1996) discusses the integrated supply chain process through an interdependency of function (Figure 7.1), where there has to be overall total control to optimize the value chain. Gattorna and Walters (1996) on the other hand argue that the development of an integrated supply chain needs its dynamics to be considered at three levels:

1 *The strategic level*: to develop objectives and policies for the supply chain, determine its physical components having a statement of customer service; an organization structure which would be capable of bridging the gap between various functions.

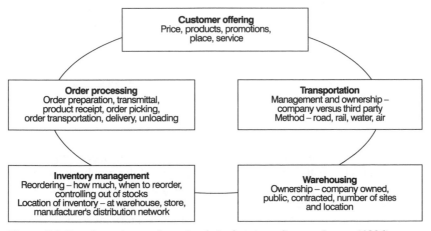

Figure 7.1 *Interdependency of supply chain functions.* Source: *Lamey (1996)*

2 *The tactical perspective*: to focus on the means by which the strategic objectives may be realized.
3 *Operational perspectives*: to focus on the efficient operation of the supply chain.

Gattorna and Walters (1996) state that the whole purpose of a value-based supply chain is to produce a balanced perspective that is not determined by customer service. They describe a model proposed by Stevens (1989), which presents supply chain through functional trade-offs (Figure 7.2).

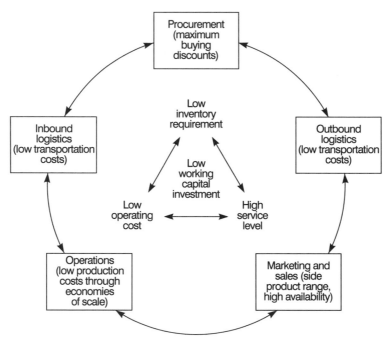

Figure 7.2 *A balanced supply chain requires workable functional trade-offs within the value chain.* Source: *Stevens (1989)*

In relation to a balanced approach to supply chain management, Gattorna and Walters (1996) also argue that: 'The objective of the supply chain concept is to synchronize the service requirements of the customer with the flow of materials from suppliers such that the apparent contradictory situation of conflicting goals of high customer service, low inventory investment and low operating costs may be balanced (or optimized).'

From supply to demand chain management

It is impossible to predict the future with accuracy but the recent developments in technology exploitation indicate that the customer is king, and that we are likely to be talking more about demand-led rather than supply-led value chains.

Recent surveys of supply chains in Europe have provided a very useful insight into how these issues are going to be dealt with in the future. For instance, some of the key issues highlighted by a P.E. Consulting report (1996) include:

- Changes in customer service needs will be by far the most important influence on logistics management during the next decade.
- Developments in information technology is the next most important factor. It is reported to be one of the key factors enabling development in European logistics to take place.

Supply chain: win-win or win-lose?

Two reported surveys have attempted to address the factors which can lead to effective partnerships and those which make it difficult for partnerships to evolve and move forward. A report by European Logistics Consultants (1995) concluded:

- There is a move towards customer domination and the expectation that the product flows will be mainly demand driven.
- There will be wider use of electronic data interchange (EDI).
- The receipt of information from customers will increase extensively because customers started to see the benefits to be gained from reduced inventories and the lowering of operating costs.

The real barriers to effective supply chain collaboration are found to be:

- the inadequacy and incompatibility of computer systems and the need for investment in this area
- the attitudes of senior managers towards close supply chain collaborations and their lack of support.

Another report by P.E. Consulting (P.E. International, 1994) lists the following views on supplier customer relationships:

1 A joint approach will enable 'waste' to be driven from the supply chain rather than pushed up or down the chain.

2 A deep-rooted suspicion of the motives of suppliers and an excessively sensitive attitude towards any fraternization with suppliers is the main barrier to any co-ordinated efforts to reduce mutual costs.

3 A major issue is to convince suppliers of the benefits of investing for long-term gains in the purchase of information technology.

4 By increasing the amount of accurate data on production build and forecasts given to suppliers, organizations have experienced an improvement in the timely receipt of suppliers. There are fewer line stoppages and lower extraordinary costs for transport and setting-up charges.

5 Organizations continue to be actively involved in supply chain integration developments, since it locks customers in-house.

6 Logistics will become key to company success. Supplier differentiation will be less on quality of product, which will be assured, and more on swiftness of response, the ability to be flexible and the provision of high levels of customer service.

7 The emerging picture is that major customers are moving in different directions in their supply chain developments. There is no common approach. This means that organizations have to adjust their physical distribution in more than one direction.

Supplier partnerships – the key trigger

Suppliers in all industry sectors are the key trigger for driving our costs down, optimizing value and speeding up work processes. Supplier partnerships, however, cannot be developed overnight; they take many years of gradual education, change, experimentation and a willingness to tolerate deficiencies, share know-how and information. Several successful models can for instance be found in the car industry, the aerospace industry and largely in the electronics and computer industry.

Supplier partnerships require a complete metamorphosis, as a report produced by the DTI (1994) argues:

> The real challenge is finding a way to influence suppliers to make extraordinary contributions to what you are trying to achieve, time after time. The answer is to abandon the traditional, adversarial approach towards suppliers and build relationships which encourage co-operation and collaboration. These types of relationships are characterized by material confidence in each other's abilities and the expectation that any benefits of success will be shared.

The Japanese model of supplier partnerships

The West has learnt many lessons from the Japanese about the establishment of effective supplier partnerships. In the car industry, for instance, it was

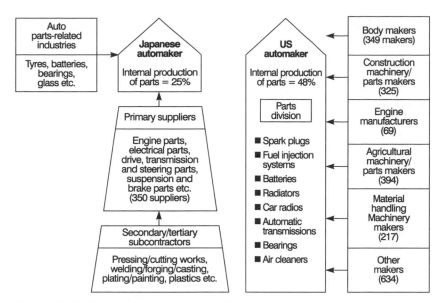

Figure 7.3 *Differences in Japanese and US auto industry (value chain) structures.*
Source: *Ministry of International Trade and Industry (1987: 36)*

found that the total cost of components for Japanese cars was more than 30 per cent below that for comparable US models (Dyer and Ouchi, 1993).

The difference between the two approaches is best explained in Figure 7.3. The US model tended to rely on a traditional system where suppliers were regarded with suspicion, producing under short-term contracts and excluded from manufacturers' core activities such as design and engineering. In the Japanese model, suppliers are involved in the early stages of NPD, they have critical roles to play and communication is very often found to be significant at all levels. Contracts are awarded on performance and on a long-term basis.

The following statement from the Japanese Ministry of International Trade and Industry (1987) acknowledges the importance and power of supplier partnerships: 'The Japanese manufacturing industry owes its competitive advantage and strength to its subcontracting structure.'

Essentially the nature of supplier-purchaser relationships in Japan is based on the fact that the common drive is on maximizing the efficiency of the entire business process (value chain). The nature of relationships stretches from total exclusive, semi-exclusive or independent.

The Japanese refer to these as:

- kankei-gaisha (affiliated companies)
- dokuritsu-gaisha (independent companies).

Dyer and Ouchi (1993) report the following key characteristics of Japanese style partnerships (JSPs) in the motor industry:

- long-term relationships
- mutual assistance and a focus on total cost and quality
- willingness to make significant customized investments in plant, equipment and personnel as well as share valuable technical information
- intensive and regular sharing of technical and cost information
- trust building practices (e.g. owning stock transfer of employees, flexible legal contracts etc.).

The Japanese experience has been very inspirational to the West, both in Europe and the USA. In fact, Europe and the USA are developing supplier capability on a global scale, something that was found to be lacking in the Japanese experience.

An article in the *International Herald Tribune* (Pollock, 1995) reported on the collapse of Japanese structure. In the last decade, it is reported that more that 2,000 factories have vanished from Ota (an area of southern Tokyo) because of high land prices, recession, difficulties in recruiting workers and the rise of the yen. These factories represent second or third tier suppliers to the likes of Honda and Hitachi. These small companies are expected to cut prices of their parts in order to help the big companies maintain their profits otherwise they risk losing business when the bigger companies relocate factories off-shore. There is already some evidence indicating that US parts suppliers in China, South Korea and many other countries are benefiting.

The article concludes that: 'these factories have been instrumental in making Japan Inc. what it is – an efficient producer of high quality goods. As their numbers keep dropping, there is growing fear that Japan is losing some of its fundamental manufacturing know-how and possibly its ability to come out with new products.'

The approach used in developing effective supplier-producer relationships varies from industry to industry. The following two case studies from the electronics and car manufacturing sector demonstrate two contrasting models of supplier appraisal and supplier development for long-term partnerships.

Case study 1: Nissan

Philosophy

The advent of Japanese companies such as Nissan into the European motor industry caused a radical shift in customer-supplier relationships and the traditional adversarial relationship has given way to closer co-operation. This is because manufacturers now realize the importance of the suppliers' contribution to competitiveness. Competitiveness cannot be achieved in the 1990s by the OEM manufacturer alone; more success will be achieved if its suppliers are aligned to its strategic vision. The effectiveness of this depends on the supplier's:

• insight into the market, customer and competitive needs
• flexibility and responsiveness to competitive thrusts
• efficiency in the use of combined assets
• elimination of any non-value added activities in the chain
• adoption of a vigorous culture of 'continuous improvement'.

The increasing trend is to source a greater proportion of components from outside, thus reducing vertical integration. There is also a trend for the manufacturer to design and assemble products. Unlike traditional European mass producers, which do not retain a high proportion of the value chain in-house and are not involved in the detailed design, the supplier has a very high profile at Nissan.

Nissan tend to source subassemblies from fewer suppliers rather than sourcing components comprising the lower levels of the bills of materials. Nissan can thus pay more attention to fewer suppliers. The costs associated with dealing with a larger number of suppliers are eliminated and more attention can be paid to the remaining suppliers in terms of helping them and monitoring their performance. Suppliers who used to cater to the lower levels of bills of materials are eliminated. They now comprise the second tier suppliers and are managed by their customer, who supplies the subsystem to the final assembler.

This facilitates a close relationship between the customer and supplier. This close relationship also allows more security for suppliers but makes their operations more visible and exposed to customer demand for continuous improvement in terms of cost, quality and delivery.

The main reason for this stems from the need to be cost competitive. The increased proportion of sourced components offers an opportunity to reduce costs in several ways. The responsibility of the cost for holding stock is transferred to the supplier. This statement might imply that the supplier now holds the inventory but this only occurs if the supplier's manufacturing system is inefficient and no assistance is given to rectify this. There is also a demand for the supplier to be cost competitive and to pass on any productivity savings to the customer; since the proportion of components sourced externally is increasing, the supply chain is the largest area to improve upon. This is achieved by allowing the customer to examine the costing structure of the supplier and working with them to reduce costs. The supplier is integrated into the production schedule in order to reduce the cost of stock-holding.

Another aspect of cost saving is that of specialization. The supplier no longer produces to a given design. Instead, the supplier is given the required performance and cost parameters and has a free rein to develop the product. The trend is for the supplier to build subassemblies, thus reducing research and development costs and in-house engineering staff levels. Another benefit is that the supplier's technical expertise can be made use of.

The supplier development process

Nissan represents the present benchmark in the UK for customer-supplier relationships in the European motor industry. It has only 160 suppliers compared to Rover, who has 350. Nissan has introduced to the UK its supplier quality assurance system, which is similar to the one it implements in Japan.

The supplier development process comprises three stages:

1 **The proactive stage** – this is when the company agrees and commits to a standard in terms of price, quality and delivery. The emphasis is on proper and thorough project management and planning. This stage is where a new supplier is initiated or a new component/new model is introduced.
2 **The interactive stage** – this is the dynamic, in-production period. The competence and integrity of the supplier is monitored and efforts are made to help resolve any problems. Problems are regarded as an opportunity to improve and not a cause for recrimination.
3 **The reactive stage** – the process of continuous improvement. Kaizen teams undertake improvement projects with an emphasis on people involvement. These teams are not management driven, problem-solving task forces. In a similar vein, Nissan embarks on a programme of supplier development by giving direct assistance towards quality and productivity improvement. Targets are set and the benefits are shared by both parties. Sometimes, Nissan finances capital equipment required for substantial improvements on very easy terms.

In conclusion, Nissan has been very successful with their suppliers by working with them to systematically plan, do and improve. Suppliers may not make large profits but their profits are stable and certain. Nissan distinguishes its supply quality system from that of other manufacturers by the use of good planning and project management.

Supplier performance assessment

Nissan's evaluation questionnaire (shown in Appendix 7.I) addresses the following areas:

- Management.
- Quality manual.
- Drawing/document and specification control.
- Control of purchased material.
- Control of process/finished parts.
- Calibration of gauge and test equipment.
- Control of non-conforming products.
- Machine control.

Questions are asked on various aspects. The auditor makes comments and scores these aspects accordingly. Provision is made on the form for the supplier to reply and, where necessary, to record what pertinent action is to be taken and time scales for this to be implemented.

Case study 2: Kodak

Philosophy

Kodak states its philosophy thus:

> Kodak Ltd has a well earned reputation for the high quality of its products and services. The company is committed to continuous quality improvement in all of its products and services and all company units have quality goals consistent with this commitment. This requires teamwork on the part of those who share an interest in the company's success. Kodak believes that all of its suppliers play a key role in maintaining and enhancing this reputation for high quality.
>
> Continuous improvement in today's competitive marketplace is essential. We, therefore, intend to establish long-term relationships with our most qualified, preferred suppliers in order to enhance the competitive position of both our company and our suppliers. Continuous improvement in both total cost and conformance to all specifications for products and services in an atmosphere of total teamwork and mutual trust is the basis upon which our supplier relationships will be built. (Mike J. Hahn, Manager, Company Purchasing and Material Supply)

Kodak's dedication to TQM in the manufacture and supply of all its products and services extends from the marketplace, through manufacturing to its suppliers. Kodak recognizes that its quality objectives cannot be cost effectively achieved without ensuring consistent quality in their incoming materials and services. To achieve this, they have found it mutually beneficial to enter into a quality partnership with key suppliers to achieve continuous improvement in the quality of their supplies to Kodak. This forms the basis of the Kodak 'quality first supplier programme' (Q1).

The Q1 programme is co-ordinated by the Purchasing department. Key suppliers are invited to work closely with the relevant Kodak users and buyers in improving the quality and value for money of the materials and services they supply.

The programme identifies and tackles individual areas of opportunity for improvement on a project priority basis. This is accomplished through small dynamic teams, involving the skills and resources of supplier personnel in conjunction with the Kodak Purchasing and User departments. Working together, these team efforts are directed towards total quality improvement in all aspects of Kodak's business relationship.

The sharing of information, co-operation, trust and mutual understanding are fundamental to the programme and create a climate in which the supplier is encouraged to employ innovative methods of problem-solving and quality control which will enhance the quality of the product/service supplied.

Supplier development

The characteristics of an ideal Kodak supplier are defined as follows.

- Products are 100 per cent correct and reliable.
- Deliveries are always on time.
- Quantities delivered are always correct.
- Deliveries occur frequently to minimize stock carried by user.
- The supplier provides appropriate response to urgent requirements.
- If something goes wrong, there is total commitment to rectifying it as soon as possible.
- Competitive product pricing.
- Invoices and documentation free from errors.
- The supplier is totally open and honest about processes, costs and pricing methods.
- Suppliers work with us to continuously improve their performance.

Supplier development is conducted in a series of progressive stages. The supplier is accorded a particular status during each stage. These are defined as follows:

1 Potential.
2 Accredited/Approved.
3 Level 1 (Preferred).
4 Level 2.
5 Level 3.

- **Potential** This stage is where quotations and samples are provided for various specifications and trials are conducted.

- **Accredited/approved** Visits are made to suppliers and specifications are agreed and set. Limited business is conducted and the supplied products are subjected to inward inspection.

    After this stage, a formal system of awards is implemented. This comprises three different levels of achievement. To qualify for these awards, a supplier would be expected to participate in a quality management programme that entails regular buyer/client/supplier quality team meetings. These are: identification of opportunities for improvement, establishment of appropriate improvement projects and goals, and measurement, monitoring and review of progress.

- **Level 1 (Preferred) – Quality First Preferred Supplier certificate** This is the basic-level award and demands that high levels of conformance to specifications and supply are consistently maintained and no significant failures occur over a defined period, normally six months or a year. Performance should be monitored by means of a checklist or a performance matrix. Separate criteria are used for materials and services.

- **Level 2 (Product Control) – Silver Award/ Service award** To qualify for awards at this level, a quality team (QT) should be appointed. In addition to the criteria for Level 1, there must be confidence in a supplier's ability to consistently meet requirements such that Kodak's incoming inspection and testing of goods is dispensed with. This state is referred to as 'product control' and responsibility for conformance rests solely with the supplier. Quality of design enhancements and other quality improvement should be realized by meeting the quality team's continuous improvement objectives. Nominations for a Silver Award must be accompanied by a performance matrix (Appendix 7.II), as well as a 'self-audit checklist' completed by the QT unless the supplier has a recognized third party accredited quality system (i.e. BS 5750).

    Services providers will have proved their ability to provide a significantly high level of service over a sustained period, and a fault-free service. The supplier will have reached goals and objectives set and monitored by the quality team. The quality team shall also have completed the 'self-audit checklist', unless third party accredited.

- **Level 3 (Process Control) – Gold Award/Service Excellence award** In addition to the criteria for Level 2, the supplier uses statistical quality monitoring and data analysis techniques to control all the key process parameters and has a minimum process capability (Cpk) of 1.3 for these parameters. This state is referred to as being in 'process control'. Nomination to this level also requires a satisfactory formal assessment of the supplier's quality systems by Kodak quality control specialists, unless third party accredited. In addition, a high level of proactivity and dedication to continuous improvement should be evident (i.e. exceeding the criteria).

Service providers are expected to provide outstanding contributions in all areas of the business relationship, being proactive in proposing improvements to goods, services, methods and design. Again, all continuous improvement objectives and goals should be exceeded and there must be a satisfactory assessment of the supplier's quality systems.

Supplier performance measurement

The key areas that Kodak address when assessing suppliers are:

- quality of conformance to specifications
- quality of design
- quality of service
- statistical process control.

The tool used to measure these dimensions is the performance matrix enclosed in Appendix 7.II. This is the primary means of tracking progress in a Kodak Quality First Supplier programme. The matrix is used for:

- benchmarking current performance
- establishing the quality team objectives and goals
- monitoring ongoing progress
- communicating progress within the team and to Kodak/vendor management
- summarizing the programme for award nomination purposes.

Various performance dimensions are assessed on a scale of 1–10. These dimensions should satisfy certain criteria to ensure that they are fair. Further details about the criteria and the workings of the matrix are contained in Appendix 7.II.

Expectations

Suppliers can expect from Kodak:

- early involvement in the design and establishment of its requirements
- early involvement in the optimization of the production process
- realistic and understandable specifications
- accurate forecasts of Kodak's needs and early sharing of pertinent information
- timely payment

- open, timely and accurate communications of any change in plans and requirements and any less than satisfactory condition in any phase of the customer/supplier interface
- involvement in and support for joint customer/supplier improvement activities
- recognition for meeting or exceeding Kodak quality objectives.

Kodak expects from its suppliers:

- commitment to continuous improvement
- conformance to contract agreements: on time delivery, delivery to proper location, proper quantities, proper labelling, packaging etc.
- high quality, invariant products and services which meet their specifications and require no receiving inspection and extra cost
- co-operative management
- mutual sharing of the benefits achieved as a result of supplier/customer team improvements
- open, timely and accurate communication of any process change and any less than satisfactory condition in any phase of the customer/supplier interface
- supplier management that is committed to exploring state-of-the-art technologies in their field of endeavour.

Achievements

Both Kodak and its suppliers have gained by following these guidelines. These are outlined in Table 7.1.

Table 7.1 *Achievements gained by Kodak and its suppliers*

Suppliers	Kodak
Increased effectiveness	Optimum product design
Lower total cost	Increased effectiveness
Increased business opportunities	Strengthened long-term relationships with suppliers
Formal recognition by Kodak with suppliers	Receipts conform to specifications
	Lower total cost

Measuring supplier performance: example of best practice

There has been a significant shift in the way producers monitor the performance of their suppliers. Measurement of performance has been extended to focus on the entire value chain on processes and systems as an outcome and to signal an integrated approach to innovation management throughout.

The following is an extensive catalogue of best practices, compiled from winners of prestigious quality awards, such as the European Quality Award (EQA), the Malcolm Baldrige National Quality Awards (MBNQA) and the Australian Quality Award.

Case study 3: Rank Xerox Ltd (winner of EQA Award 1992)

At Rank Xerox Ltd, over 80 per cent of production costs are made up of purchased materials, which makes them heavily dependent on their suppliers for the quality of product output.

In 1981, Rank Xerox started a programme aimed at a significant reduction of failures in the manufacturing process, through ensuring consistent quality of raw materials and components supply. In 1984, they introduced a new initiative called the continuous supplier involvement process (CSI) with the following key factors showing Xerox's commitment:

1 We work in full partnership with all our manufacturing suppliers to pursue continuous improvement in product design, manufacturing and services.
2 We provide training and support in quality enablers including our experience of Leadership Through Quality, to help suppliers to develop their own Total Quality Strategies (Table 7.2).
3 Our suppliers take part in product design and manufacturing activity at every stage from the first product concept onwards; they share and contribute knowledge and expertise as full members of the team.
4 Recognition through our Certified Supplier Award so that suppliers can meet our exacting quality requirements, including consistent quality, cost, and delivery performance over two years, the approach of supplier management to total quality, continuous improvement, and commitment to partnership with us through CSI.

Managing supplier partnerships through the building of a prevention-based process has meant that there are regular reviews taking place to increase the effectiveness of the manufacturing process within Rank Xerox and also the quality of products delivered to the end customer (Table 7.3).

The reduction of Xerox's worldwide manufacturing supplier base from around 5,000 to 414 at present, since the mid-1980s years has further

Table 7.2 *Rank Xerox quality support to suppliers*

Continuing programmes

1981	Centralized Commodity Management
1982	Process Certification
1983	Model Supplier Strategy
1984	Commodity Teams
1984	Continuous Supplier Involvement
1986	Model Customer Process
1987	Total Quality Strategy
1989	Supplier Certification

On demand programmes

1981	Statistical Process Control
1985	Failsafing
1986	Taguchi training
1986	JIT training

Table 7.3 *The impact of continuous supplier involvement programmes at Rank Xerox Ltd*

% parts certified (suppliers)	89	90	91	92		GOAL
	89	91	94	95	95	PLAN
Line fall out (parts per million)	220	160	131	125	125	

Note: As we move closer to full partnership with our production suppliers the improvement in the quality of their input (parts certified) has had a beneficial effect on our manufacturing performance (Line Fall Out).

improved the quality of the manufacturing sold to customers. The company receives feedback from its suppliers on a regular basis to enable it to improve the standard of its operations.

In addition to a general survey involving all its suppliers every year, Rank Xerox encourages its senior managers to visit various supplier sites to obtain face-to-face feedback/assessment of Xerox's performance against a list of nineteen factors. Emerging issues of concern are further discussed with the suppliers concerned and action takes place. For example, feedback in 1989 showed that only 24 per cent of manufacturing suppliers reported that they were paid their invoices in reasonable time. After taking action, the 1991 survey showed that 74 per cent of suppliers were satisfied with the time it takes Rank Xerox to settle invoices.

Case study 4: ICL – Design to distribution (winner of the EQA in 1994)

Supplier recognition

Suppliers are recognized through Vendor Accreditation. Vendor performance measurement focuses objectively on their performance against clearly defined and documented quality cost and service criteria. Performance is reviewed by a meeting with vendors every three months.

At the annual vendor conference, vendors are thanked for their efforts by the Chairman of ICL. Those vendors who have performed exceptionally well are singled out for annual vendor awards presented by the Chairman. They are given plaques to display in their company premises.

Table 7.4 illustrates the development of vendor partnerships at ICL.

Table 7.4 *Development of vendor partnerships at ICL*

Date	Processes
1981	Zero defect process with Texas Instruments
1982	Vendor Awards start
1984	All major integrated circuit vendors on zero defects process
1985	Ship to stock process starts
1986	Just-in-time process starts
1988	All major vendors on zero defect/ship to stock process (120 vendors)
1990	Vendor Accreditation starts
1991	Electronic Data Interchange starts with vendors

Senior management actively encourage employees to establish and be part of joint improvement teams with major suppliers in order to improve quality and cost of ownership. There are 75 well-established joint improvement teams within the manufacturing division.

Under the Vendor Accreditation scheme, managers are appointed as Vendor managers. They meet vendors on a quarterly basis and agree a score against the vendor's performance. This score is based on cost, quality and service criteria. The accreditation status of the vendor is also reviewed, but on an annual basis. Manufacturing division managers monitor the performance of all vendors in terms of cost, quality and service, and will meet suppliers as necessary to address any performance which has a negative impact on ICL's business. ICL actively supports the Vendor Accreditation programme, and uses this to forge long-term partnerships. They offer quality training to all the major suppliers.

ICL calculates the cost of ownership of products by calculating the extra costs incurred for supporting the product, replacing failing units etc. The highest quality equipment has the lowest cost of ownership.

In terms of feedback, ICL personnel regularly meet with vendors at various levels to review past performance and agree on future strategy.

Senior purchasing management are required to input vendor and business environment status feedback into the annual strategic review. For example, ICL's Accredited Vendors identified a need for support on ISO 9000 implementation. Consequently, ICL's procurement teams have a strategic goal to support and train the concerned suppliers in successful ISO 9000 registration.

The supply and management of raw materials

Manufacturing's mission on the management of material source is as follows: 'To ensure that the total supply chain management system, with minimal inventory and costs, provides customers with agreed levels of service and flexibility.'

The materials strategy is updated yearly, from which cascaded objectives for all purchasing and materials staff are derived. These objectives are designed to:

- reduce the time taken by various processes
- reduce the inventory and other asset investments required to support the agreed level of customer flexibility and service
- continually improve the reliability of the process.

In 1992, material resource management objectives included:

- five and a half weeks of stock
- automatic output flexibility of +50 per cent within a 10 week window
- vendor delivery performance up to 98 per cent
- 100 per cent key vendor quality accredited
- ship-to-stock targets by commodity to be achieved
- Up to 85 per cent of orders transmitted to vendors by EDI.

The ICL vendor accreditation scheme was launched at the ICL Vendor conference in spring 1990. Targets led to:

- two pilot vendors being accredited in 1990
- fifty-one vendors added in 1991
- twelve vendors added in 1992.

(All strategic vendors are now accredited.) The vendor must satisfy key entry criteria in:

- total quality management
- electronic trading
- financial stability
- leading edge processes and technology
- logistics
- commitment to Europe
- commitment to training.

(The manufacturing division currently has sixty-five accredited vendors.)

The basic principles of Vendor Accreditation means that ICL must be spending at least £500,000 sterling with the vendor or that the vendor is supplying ICL with a strategic product or service, vital to ICL's competitiveness.

Case study 5: The National Roads and Motorists' Association – winner of the Australian Quality Award in 1992

The NRMA devised their supplier code of performance (SCOP) with the view to improve their customer service and satisfaction levels, and to help its suppliers introduce TQM. The need for SCOP arose because of delays in the delivery cycle – the length of time between order and delivery.

SCOP involves the following initiatives.

Supplier assessment questionnaires

These invite suppliers to respond, in writing, to questions regarding NRMA's performance in dealing with them. It includes questions such as:

- Does NRMA pay them on time?
- Do suppliers understand/agree with NRMA's requirements?
- Are communication lines clear?
- Do suppliers have a good relationship with the buyer concerned from NRMA?

Face-to-face interviews

These take place between suppliers and the NRMA's key buying departments, and address issues such as:

- quality of goods supplied (no defects, returns/rejects)
- agreed realistic delivery times
- supplier capability to store goods (just-in-time delivery)

- agreed price review periods
- ease/accuracy of communication with supplier representative
- supplier performance history – response to complaints, administration of accounts.

Direct supplier/customer contact

This involves the following:

- providing feedback to suppliers
- joint quality teams
- regular quality meetings.

On-site visits to supplier plants

Major buyers visit supplier plants to update their knowledge of production processes, capabilities and future technologies. These visits raise the opportunity to discuss and agree on the best practice of supply.

A future strategy is the development of long-term 'client/supplier partnering'. NRMA aims to build stronger relationships with fewer (referred) suppliers to realize enhanced quality, customer service and cost-saving benefits. Supplier selection will be critical and will depend on the ability of the supplier to grow with NRMA and fill the role of a strategic partner, rather than simply a source of supply.

NRMA's motto is: 'We want to TASTE successful partnering':

T = 100 per cent **T**rust.
A = 100 per cent **A**ccountability.
S = 100 per cent **S**upport.
T = 100 per cent **T**ruth.
E = 100 per cent **E**ffort.

Case study 6: Cadillac Motors (winner of MBNQA in 1990)

A supplier assessment process is used to verify the supplier's capability to meet GM's expectations. This process has four basic steps:

1 Supplier self-assessment against the 'targets for excellence' criteria.
2 On-site assessment by a three-person team.
3 Development planning.
4 Implementation and reassessment.

Also included in the target for excellence programme is an approval process through which suppliers qualify parts for production use. This process is called General Procedure No. 3, and is conducted by the supplier during the Process Validation and Product Confirmation stage. It is confirmed with an approval notice issued by the Materials Management staff.

Case study 7: Zytex (winner of MBNQA in 1991)

The quality improvement programme at Zytec extends beyond its internal operations and includes all its suppliers. For their suppliers, the principal quality requirements are:

- six sigma levels of quality
- 96 per cent on-time delivery to the day
- twenty-five day lead time.

(All the above three targets are underscored in all communications with suppliers and supported by technical assistance and training.)

Zytec uses three procedures to make sure its suppliers are meeting the company quality requirements:

'Upstream' supplier selection and communication procedures

Zytec is committed to open communication and the development of true partnerships with its suppliers, and it often involves suppliers in the early stages of a development programme to benefit from their knowledge.

Receiving inspection and dock-to-stock

Critical parameters have been defined for each commodity so that Zytec can complete capability studies at incoming inspection. The capability study dictates the number of lots to be inspected before going dock-to-stock.

Supplier certification

This programme defines Zytec's quality requirements for its suppliers. At present, the programme defines a PPM level for each commodity and a delivery percentage which is generic for all commodities.

Case study 8: Texas Instruments (TI) – Defence Systems and Electronics Group (DSEG), winner of the MBNQA in 1992

TI DSEG monitors supplier quality through its industry-leading integrated information system. The company obtains an objective assessment of supplier quality by measuring incoming defective parts per million opportunities. It has revealed that suppliers have improved their on-time delivery by 46 per cent since 1988.

The supplier alliances TI is establishing require that they reduce the number of suppliers they deal with. They limit their major supplier management efforts to suppliers that provide substantial and/or critical items. TI's supplier reduction goals have been aggressive; suppliers have been cut by more than 30 per cent in the last ten years.

Supplier partnerships for effective innovation: a proposed model of best practice

The model described in this section is based on a benchmarking exercise which looked at partnerships. The questions asked are: How are they defined? How are they set up? How are they managed? How are their successes and failures measured?

The project team included a group of senior managers and the author as a facilitator for the project. The companies visited included:

- J R Compton Ltd – specialist paper manufacturers
- DGR Ltd – packaging material converters
- Elida Faberge Ltd – personal products manufacturers
- Monsanto – chemical manufacturers
- Nissan – car manufacturers
- Tetra Pak UK – packaging system manufacturers
- Tesco – supermarket retailers.

The team involved came up with the following definition of a supplier partnership: 'A continuous programme which secures for both parties measurable benefits beyond those that can be secured through independent action and which provides for sustainable growth.'

It was agreed during the benchmarking project that any supplier partnership which completely meets this definition may be considered as a full partnership agreement.

The model is described through the following five elements: strategy, setting up, management, assessment and action programme.

Strategy

Both suppliers and customers now recognize that there are benefits to be gained by working together as partners, benefits that cannot be obtained by operating separately in the traditional manner. Supplier partnerships are the mechanism for obtaining these benefits.

A successful partnership is a win/win relationship, which may have a variety of forms according to the area of business and the wishes and needs of the parties. However, essential characteristics common to all partnerships are:

- recognition of the opportunity to achieve benefits from working together
- commitment to a long-term working relationship
- agreement upon specific objectives for the partnership
- measurable benefits for both parties
- benefits in line with the strategic aim of long-term growth.

The process of constantly seeking improvement, in this case material benefits not hitherto obtained, is central to the total quality (TQ) philosophy, and thus supplier partnerships will be a common consequence of TQ. However, partnership sourcing has also been successfully exploited by businesses that have no formal TQ programme.

Partnerships are demanding of resource from both parties. They are also relatively slow to bear fruit; the first benefits may not be seen for six months, while the most fruitful period may be eighteen months to two years into the partnership. Therefore, boardroom commitment and support of both the philosophy and specific projects are essential.

The areas selected for partnership should be consistent with company strategic planning and vision, and commitments to partnership must be supported by sufficient resource. Because these projects are demanding, it is wise to select at most two or three areas to develop initially.

The areas with most potential for such benefit should be addressed first. Usually, one or two known problem areas will become apparent, and it is advantageous to select initially a high profile problem where success can be expected. However, experience has shown that potential benefits of great significance are often hidden, and it is necessary to 'dig around' to find them.

Potential benefits for either party may fall into three categories:

1 Product related
- Increased value for customer, e.g. reduced customer production cost, increased customer product quality, increased customer production capacity
- Reduced cost for supplier, e.g. cheaper raw materials for supplier, reduced supplier production time and/or cost, increased supplier production capacity
- Value analysis: joint development of new products/processes, choice of bespoke or standard product, optimized specification

2 Logistic related
   - Inventory reduction (total supply chain inventory)
   - Reduced stock outs
   - Just-in-time supply
   - Reduced cost/time of transport
   - Better forecasting
   - Exchange of availability/demand information
   - Security of supply and demand
3 Price related
   - Price may be expected by both parties to reflect: (1) and (2) above, long-term commitment and confidence, single sourcing
   - Price arrangements may be: fixed, linked to costs, linked to the market or competition, linked to other agreed factors or published indices, by periodic renegotiation.

Partnerships demand openness and in many cases the issue of confidentiality will need to be addressed.

Setting up

In establishing a supplier partnership programme, key stages are

- the definition of selection parameters
- the review/audit of candidates' performance
- the identification of suitable candidates, both current and potential
- the sale of the idea to the potential partner.

Any company with a supplier assessment/vendor rating programme may already be in a strong position, since it will have an indication of potential candidates for a partnership. The selection parameters encompass:

- *Product/process quality*: the capability of the supplier's process to meet consistently the quality requirements of the customer.
- *Supply chain logistics*: the ability of the supplier to deliver consistently the quantities of product required by the customer.
- *Price/cost*: the factors that affect the cost to both businesses and, ultimately, the competitiveness of the customer's final product.
- *Innovation/design*: the ability of the supplier to adapt to change, either on a reactive or proactive basis.
- *Management*: the capability, training, experience and philosophy to survive and continuously improve both business, e.g. TQ companies.

These 'five pillars' need to be measured, but the weightings attached to them will depend on circumstances. Each represents a two-way channel through which the key partnership processes operate.

Management

In managing one or more partnerships, a variety of methods is possible, from the 'hands-off, let it happen' approach to a more structured, resourced and managed style. The latter appears to be most prevalent and is where true success has been achieved.

Issues which require close consideration are as follows:

- The factors and processes critical to the success of the joint venture should be clearly identified and weighted, using the 'five pillars' itemized above. The processes, identified jointly in this way, should be fully mapped as a means of clarifying the relationship between customer and supplier, identifying the nature of communications links, person to person contacts etc.
- Partnership activity is best put into the hands of a joint steering group using, if necessary, third party assistance to help in overcoming initial fears and concerns. It is the role of the steering group to decide the operating protocol or charter for the joint working teams, and to direct the selection and resourcing of the teams. A means of review of objectives, team progress, and partnership strategy is essential.
- From the work of the steering group should come the target activity areas of the joint working group, with tangible objectives, backed up with meaningful measures of the existing situation, and of the target outcome. This clarity of objective(s) appears crucial to success.
- The most successful partnerships are based on the recognition that resource is necessary to achieve meaningful results. Training should be considered for team members, particularly in problem-solving activity and teamwork.
- In some circumstances it may be necessary to address aspects of confidentiality, no-go areas or contractual issues. Although opinions on the value of this approach vary, incorporation of such concerns can form part of the operating protocol rather than any legally binding approach. New technology may require more formal protection.
- Partnerships should develop into an integral part of the company's business strategy.

There are also some clear signs of failure worth identifying:

- A lack of understanding and commitment from the 'top' in each business will lead to rapid degradation of efforts. Achieving and sustaining the top-down support is an essential foundation to a partnership programme.
- Inadequate resource will produce inadequate results and eventual 'cosmeti-cizing' of the programme.

- Constraining the teams in terms of empowerment will slow and even still the rate of achievement.
- Team performance will be severely hindered if team members are frequently changed.
- Poor communications.

It is clear from the above that successful partnerships are positively managed towards clear objectives. The success or otherwise of such ventures is determined by a variety of assessment and measurement approaches of this 'soft area' of activity.

Assessment

The operation of a supplier partnership needs to be assessed in terms of how well it fulfils the requirements specified in the definition. Bearing in mind that 'partnership' is a two-way relationship, the steering group should:

1 Define partnership objectives.
2 Categorize these under the five pillars.
3 Agree the weighting for each pillar.
4 Choose the parameters for measurement.
5 Agree the start points.
6 Set targets for improvement.
7 Set up working groups to achieve targets.

The overall performance of the partnership can be assessed in terms of the rate of improvement achieved in the agreed areas, subject to the agreed weightings.

The parameters that can be measured are illustrated in Table 7.5. Some may need to be set up to start and others may emerge as the partnership progresses, particularly 'soft' conversation to 'hard'.

Action programme

To help those embarking on supplier partnerships, the following action programme addresses the key issues.

1 A board policy statement endorsing the establishment of supplier partnerships should be created.

   Success factors:
   - empowerment/encouragement of those advocating supplier partnerships

Table 7.5 *A model of supplier-manufacturer partnerships in FMCG*

Pillar	Hard	Unit	Soft
Product/ process quality	Reject materials	ppm	Technical expertise
	Process efficiency related to materials	%	Professionalism
	Response to problems	Time	
	External measure	ISO 9000	
	Internal measures – faulty product related to materials	%	
Supply chain logistics	Delivery		Professionalism
	Time/quality	%	Flexibility
	Document accuracy	ISO 9000	
	Response to problems	Time	
Price/cost	Productivity improvement	%	Trust/honesty
			Professionalism
	Facility efficiency	%	
	Stock levels	%	
	O/H reduction	%	
	Lead times reduction	%	
	Energy savings	%	
	Raw material cost reduction	%	
	Transport cost reduction	%	
Innovation/ design	Lead time to new products	Time	Trust/honesty
			Technical expertise
			Professionalism
	Continuous improvement projects	No. & success	'Flexibility
	Response	Time	
	Resource	£	
Management	Policy documents	Rating	Qualifications
			Training
			Philosophy
	Continuous improvement	Rating	Ability to operate partnership
	Leadership		
	Safety	No. of accidents	Interpartnership personal/working relationships
	Environmental	Rating	
	Resouce allocation	£	

Note: This list of measures is not exhaustive.

- authority in principle to commit resources to developing partnerships
- evidence of acceptance of the long-term strategic view of supply and suppliers.

Failure factors:
- unwillingness to endorse supplier partnerships at board level
- imprecision, woolliness or 'weasel wording' of the policy statement
- no active deployment or follow-up of the policy.

2 A multidisciplinary internal working party should be formed to set the 'strategic vision', and thereafter to develop 'ideal' process maps, communication and control mechanisms, model documentation, charters etc. This activity should be set up as a clearly defined TQ project with deliveries, budget and timescale.

Success factors:
- a 'road map' to develop partnerships as straightforwardly as possible so that management can focus on content and expectations
- the optimization of the resources required to establish and maintain partnerships in the longer term.

Failure factors:
- a lack of ownership or maintenance of the process
- the adoption of a 'not invented here' syndrome
- perception of process and documentation as bureaucratic.

3 Strategic partnerships, possible partners and process owners must be identified.

Success factors:
- the development of a few strategic relationships with large demonstrable benefits
- the correct resourcing of the first few partnership initiatives.

Failure factors:
- a lack of willingness to acknowledge common interest.

4 The most promising strategic partnerships via joint steering group should be initiated.

Success factors:
- As (3) above.

Failure factors:
- short termism
- under-resourcing, either in quantity or quality
- a lack of clear process and timetable
- an inability to establish mutual trust.

Acknowledgements

The author is very grateful to the following for information used to form the basis of the proposed model of supplier partnerships: Dr Tony Heaney, Mr Alan Dunkley, Mr Neil Grocock, Mr Peter Jarman, Dr Bruce McAndrew and Mr Keith Sowley.

References

Christopher, M. (1990) Developing customer service strategies. In *Gower Handbook of Logistics and Distribution Management*, J. Gattorna, ed., Gower.

DTI (1994), *Building Competitive Advantage with your Suppliers. Improving Relationships – Why It's Important and How to Do It*. Supply Chain Management Group, Department of Trade and Industry.

Dyer, J. H. and Ouchi, W. G. (1993) Japanese-style partnerships: giving companies a competitive edge. *Sloan Management Review*, Fall, 51–63.

European Logistics Consultants (1995) *Survey into Developing Relationships throughout Europe*. European Logistics Consultants.

Gattorna, J. L. and Walters, D. W. (1996) *Managing the Supply Chain – a Strategic Perspective*. Macmillan.

Lamey, J. (1996) *Supply Chain Management, Best Practice and The Impact Of New Partnerships. Financial Times* Management Reports, FT Retail and Customer Publishing.

MacBeth, D. et al. (1989) Not purchasing but supply chain management. *Purchasing and Supply Management*, November, 30–2.

Ministry of International Trade and Industry (1987) *White Paper on Small and Medium Enterprises in Japan*. MITI, pp. 36–7.

P.E. Consulting (1996) *Logistics in Europe – The Vision and the Reality*. P.E. Consulting Service.

P.E. International (1994) *Supply Chain Partnerships – Who Wins?* P.E. International Logistics Consulting Services.

Pollock, A. (1995) Japan Incs' supplier firms get pummelled as yen soar. *International Herald Tribune*, 29 May, 11.

Stevens, G. C. (1989), Integrating the supply chain. *International Journal of Physical Distribution and Materials Management*, **19**(8).

Appendix 7.I: Supplier partnerships at Nissan Europe

SYSTEM AUDIT QUESTIONNAIRE

Report No.

Supplier Name:	Plant	Initial Audit New Supplier ☐	Initial Audit Existing Supplier ☐	Re: Audit ☐
Address:	Contact:	Quality System Overall Rating		
	Position:	Vital Part Supplier	Yes ☐	No ☐
	Tel:	Engineering Assistance Required	Yes ☐	No ☐
		Purchasing Assistance Required	Yes ☐	No ☐
	Fax:	Supplier Corrective Action Required	Yes ☐	No ☐

Concerns Identified During Audit:

....

....

....

....

....

....

A. MANAGEMENT	Auditor Comment	Rating	Supplier Reply	Countermeasure Implementation Timing
(1) How does your company promote a policy of employee/people involvement throughout the organisation?				
(2) How does your company promote continuous improvement as a philosophy?				
(3) How does your company promote pro-active concern analysis in all activities?				
(4) How do you ensure that responsibilities are defined and understood throughout the organisation?				
(5) How do you ensure that effective resourcing is provided for all tasks?				
(6) How do you as a company actively promote on and off task training?				

A. MANAGEMENT	Auditor Comment	Rating	Supplier Reply	Countermeasure Implementation Timing
(7) How do you as a company ensure that company, department and individual objectives are established and achieved?				
(8) How do you ensure that your company implements and operates effective workshop management?				

B. QUALITY MANUAL	Auditor Comment	Rating	Supplier Reply	Countermeasure Implementation Timing
(1) Does the Quality Manual contain policy statements and procedures?				
(2) Are the policy statements and procedures communicated to all personnel within the organisation?				
(3) How is the company organisation structured? (Please have an organisation chart available)				
(4) Is there a procedure for internal audits? Is this implemented and recorded?				
(5) What procedure is used to monitor quality costs?				
(6) How does your company measure plant quality and is the information used to bring about continuous improvement?				

B. QUALITY MANUAL	Auditor Comment	Rating	Supplier Reply	Countermeasure Implementation Timing
(7) Do your company quality plans define all relevant activities, responsibilities and resources?				
(8) What procedure is in place that ensures adequate resources are provided for inspection and verification?				
(9) Is there a project review procedure?				
(10) Is there a procedure in the quality manual which defines and maintains housekeeping standards?				
(11) Is there a procedure covering quality manual review?				
(12) What system is used to ensure that parts/process changes are communicated to Nissan?				

C. DRAWING/DOCUMENT AND SPECIFICATION CONTROL	Auditor Comment	Rating	Supplier Reply	Countermeasure Implementation Timing
(1) What procedure exists to control and verify Product Design?				
(2) How do you verify, control and issue drawings?				
(3) How do you control the issue of documentation?				
(4) How do you control and implement design changes?				
(5) Is there a procedure in the manual for the identification, collection and storage of Quality Records?				

D. CONTROL OF PURCHASED MATERIAL	Auditor Comment	Rating	Supplier Reply	Countermeasure Implementation Timing
(1) Does the Quality Manual have a vendor approval procedure?				
(2a) Does the Quality Manual have a vendor assessment programme?				
(2b) What methods are used to assure the sub-contractors produce quality?				
(3) What vendor improvement programme exists?				
(4a) Do Purchase Orders contain necessary technical and commercial data to ensure correct product is purchased?				
(4b) What system is used by purchase to control Drawings/Requirements of sub-contracted parts?				

D. CONTROL OF PURCHASED MATERIAL	Auditor Comment	Rating	Supplier Reply	Countermeasure Implementation Timing
(5) Is there a procedure for receiving inspection?				
(6) Is there a sampling plan which reflects the sub-contractors/suppliers current performance level?				
(7) Does the storage system adequately control parts storage and ensure stock rotation?				

E. CONTROL OF PROCESS/ FINISHED PARTS	Auditor Comment	Rating	Supplier Reply	Countermeasure Implementation Timing
(1) What department is responsible for quality during processing?				
(2) How is product quality assured?				
(3) How is material identified and controlled to assure that inspection status is known and defectives are segregated to prevent re-entry into the production process?				
(4) How are finished products evaluated?				
(5) What Department is responsible for conducting internal parts/process audits?				
(6) Do all processes have work instruction sheets available?				

E. CONTROL OF PROCESS/ FINISHED PARTS	Auditor Comment	Rating	Supplier Reply	Countermeasure Implementation Timing
(7) Is the operator aware of the contents of the work instruction sheets?				
(8) How is process capability assured, relative to customer requirements?				
(9) Is there a procedure for Lot Control/Traceability?				
(10) How are company wide housekeeping standards maintained and reviewed?				

F. CALIBRATION OF GAUGE AND TEST EQUIPMENT	Auditor Comment	Rating	Supplier Reply	Countermeasure Implementation Timing
(1) What is the procedure for calibration and maintenance of all measuring and test equipment, jigs and fixtures etc?				
(2) What system is used to recall and control gauge calibration and repair and how is this confirmed?				
(3) How is test/measuring equipment identified and referenced to the calibration system?				
(4) Do the equipment calibration records show records of action taken when required?				
(5) What facility is provided for the storage and protection of gauge and test equipment?				

G. CONTROL OF NON CONFORMING PRODUCTS	Auditor Comment	Rating	Supplier Reply	Countermeasure Implementation Timing
(1) Is there a procedure in the quality manual for the prevention, control, and rectification of non conforming products?				
(2) How do the operators know what to do when non-conforming material is identified?				
(3) Is there a troubleshooting procedure in the manual detailing responsibilities and communication channels?				
(4) What procedure is available to obtain Nissan authorisation for deviation/concession?				
(5) What system/procedure is used for the documentation of salvage/repair operations?				
(6) What procedure exists for the analysis and control of warranty/customer claims?				

H. MACHINE CONTROL	Auditor Comment	Rating	Supplier Reply	Countermeasure Implementation Timing
(1) Is there a procedure in the quality manual for preventative maintenance of machines, tools, jigs and fixtures etc.?				
(2) How are routine machine checks confirmed?				
(3) What type of machine instructions are displayed?				
(4) What type of corrective action programme exists for machines whose condition or capability is not satisfactory?				
(5) How is the machine tools status confirmed?				

Question Rating:

Excellent:	0	Excellent operation, Exceeds the level required
Good:	1	Working, performing well, Good
Marginal:	10	Barely satisfactory, some assurance of control
Non Effective:	50	A system exists but is not being followed or producing the desired effect
Non Existent:	100	Nothing currently exists

Nissan Audit Classification (NAC):

NAC Rating	Excellent 1				Good 2				Marginal 4				Unacceptable 4
	A	B	C	D	A	B	C	D	A	B	C	D	
Score Range Table	0	0.50	1.00	1.50	2.00	3.00	4.00	5.00	6.00	7.00	8.00	9.00	Above 10.00
	0.49	0.99	1.49	1.99	2.99	3.99	4.99	5.99	6.99	7.99	8.99	10.00	

Calculation chart:

Section	Total points scored/section	No. of questions assessed/section	Average Score	Quality Level	Quality Rating
A					
B					
C					
D					
E					
F					
G					
H					
Overall					

System Audit Classification Chart:

Overall

A Management of Quality
B Quality Manual
C Drawing and Spec. Control
D Purchased Material
E Control of Process/ Finished products
F Calibration of Gauge and Test Equip.
G Non-Conforming Materials
H Machine Control

Appendix 7.II: Supplier partnerships at Kodak Ltd

Establishing performance matrices for Q1 supplier programmes

The performance matrix is the primary means for tracking progress in a Kodak Quality First Supplier Programme (Q1SP). The matrix is intended to be the formal working document used for:

- benchmarking current position/performance
- establishing TEAM objectives and goals
- monitoring ongoing progress
- communicating progress within the TEAM and to Kodak/vendor management
- summarizing the programme for award nomination purposes.

The process for establishing the matrix is as follows:

1 Up to ten *pinpoints* (usually about six) are selected that collectively make up the performance the *team* wish to measure. Pinpoints should relate to issues of actual concern/opportunity and not be 'wish lists'.
2 Level 3 is designated as either the team's baseline reflecting the current position or the minimum acceptable level of performance for each pinpoint. Levels can be numeric or by description of a position.
3 Level 7 is what the team agree is the desired performance for each pinpoint and therefore represents their aim position. Such targets should be challenging but achievable.
4 Levels 8 to 10 are used to describe 'over' or 'stretch' achievements and levels 1 and 2 a deteriorated and probably unacceptable situation.
5 The intermediate levels are used for sub-goals. Not all levels need to be completed, although intermediate levels can be of value in tracking progress.
6 Weighting factors are agreed by the *customer team*. The weighting should add up to 100 so that the maximum matrix score will be out of 1,000.
7 Bonus points, usually in increments of 10 points up to a maximum of 100, are used to recognize one-off additional achievements that were not predicted or not covered by the pinpoints.
8 Each pinpoint is scored by the team at appropriate intervals, multiplied by the weighting factor and the bonus points added to give a total performance score.

9 Some pinpoints may be summary headings associated with a subgroup of other pinpoints that form a submatrix. The total scores of these are fed into the main matrix.

10 It is important that *all* in the team understand this process and feedback is provided to all involved. Although the matrix is the team's tool, it is recommended that each pinpoint has a specific owner.

11 Total matrix scores are related to recognition awards. The customer team will decide the score to be achieved for an appropriate award, usually a minimum of 700. Recognition should take into account that no individual pinpoint shall fall below level 5.

12 The matrix is updated at agreed intervals at team meetings and pinpoints and level aims are reviewed annually in the spirit of continuous improvement.

Characteristics of pinpoints

Pinpointing is the process of making performances SPECIFIC. They can refer to any action – a behaviour – or to an *outcome* – a *result*.

Pinpoints should be:

- measurable – countable or judgeable
- observable – visible
- reliable – verified by two or more independent observers
- controllable – the team must have a major influence over them
- active – if a behaviour, must be a doing action (impossible for dead person!)
- positive – stated in positive terms, which are more effective to reinforce.

Note: Pinpoints are not interpretations, beliefs or attitudes, and they are not abstract. Terms such as 'communication' represent a collection of behaviours or results and require pinpointing.

Checkist for evaluating pinpoints

To test the validity of a pinpoint, answer Yes or No to each question below. If you have an adequate pinpoint, all the answers should be Yes. Modify the pinpoint if there are any Nos. If you cannot, drop it and get a new one.

1 Is it a result or a behaviour?
2 Is it measurable?
3 Is it observable?
4 Can two independent counts agree?
5 Is it under the team's control?
6 Is it an active performance?

Measurement

Major techniques are *counting* and *judging*. Only when pinpoints selected cannot be made specific enough to permit counting should a judging technique be used. Judgement is by ranking or rating. Wherever possible, make rating specific by defining distinct criteria for different rating levels, e.g. by using the 'behaviourally anchored rating scale' (BARS) where each number on a scale represents a specific set of observable behaviours or activities. This is more objective than any other judging method.

Rankings should only be used when other measures of performance are impractical. Rating can usually be substituted for ranking. It also has more potential for reinforcement.

8 Customer management and development in retailing

Patrick Allen

This chapter examines the nature of relationships between retailers and their suppliers, and the effect these relationships have on customer management techniques. The chapter begins by introducing the retailing environment, and examining the types of relationships that can be formed. Contrast is also made with the Japanese practice of relationship building before drawing out key elements of relationship building and maintenance. Discussion of relationships within the context of category management is made in detail. The evolution of efficient consumer response (ECR) and its implications for current and future development of retailers is also covered. Case examples are provided to back up the discussion.

The purpose of industry is the conquest of nature in the service of man. (R. H. Tawney, economic historian)

Introduction

This chapter examines the nature of relationships between retailers and their suppliers and the effect that those relationships have on customer management techniques. Having outlined the relationship paradigm and its impact on new product development processes, it considers the implications for sustainable competitive advantage in retailing for the foreseeable future.

Collaboration produces the best outcome. This is the premise on which many companies are now developing customer management strategies. This concept is not particularly new in industrial arenas, where many firms work together to develop new processes and products to serve their markets. However, in the retailing environment, the situation is different. The large grocery outlets do not have the degree of sophistication found in their opposite numbers in industry – e.g. motor car manufacturers – when it comes to developing relationships with their suppliers. This is largely because of the buying power of retailers. Any industry analysis will quickly show that the buying power of retailers in the UK has risen dramatically over the past twenty years. This is due to industry concentration which, as Michael Porter (1985) points out, leads to increased buyer power. The increase in the market share of four major grocery retailers means that suppliers have fewer potential buyers and consequently become dependent on a few large purchasers (Emerson, 1962).

The intensity of retailer rivalry for market share is also increasing as the market matures. One way in which this rivalry now manifests itself is through a drive for efficiency in stocking policy. This means that techniques such as quick response (QR), just-in-time (JIT) and vendor managed inventory (VMI) are being used to reduce retailer inventory costs, all aimed at pushing the costs of stockholding down the supply chain. Herein lies the problem. Retailers are and have been for some time concerned with reducing costs (both direct – money off the product – and indirect – reduction in the cost of doing business). However, in a response to the concentrating retail market, suppliers have been placing emphasis on building relationships with key retail accounts (Lawrence, 1983; McCarthy and Perreault, 1993; Randell, 1990). Unfortunately for the suppliers, who would like to see the relationship as equal, the retailers see their role in the partnership as one of dominance as opposed to sharing and of conflict rather than co-operation.

The UK retailing environment

Before looking at the types of relationship in retailing and the importance they have for the successful implementation of ECR and category management, it would be useful to look briefly at the environment in which the firms, this chapter addresses, operate.

The retail food market in Britain was worth £59 billion in 1994 (retail market statistics taken from Keynote, 1995). This statistic becomes more meaningful when consideration is given to concentration of those sales. Seventy-seven per cent of sales went through supermarkets and superstores and these account for only 8 per cent of the total number of outlets. The market between 1990 and 1994 seems to indicate a strong growth rate (19 per cent). However, when this figure is adjusted for inflation it falls to a rather low 5 per cent. This situation has fuelled fierce competition within the industry causing some smaller firms to leave the market and has increased dominance of the four major players – Tesco, Sainsbury's, Safeway and ASDA.

On the supply side, a similar trend toward concentration appears to be emerging. Between 1986 and 1993 the number of supply firms fell by 14 per cent. As in the retail side of the industry, the suppliers are characterized by large multinational companies such as Grand Metropolitan and Kraft.

Given this situation, it is not surprising that the key trading driver has been price. But continuous margin erosion has given rise to supply side concentration. This, together with overcapacity in the market, has led stores to seek cost leadership positions that respond to consumer demand. These two critical factors for competitive advantage are forcing retailers (and suppliers) to re-evaluate their trading relationships and move toward partnerships that facilitate win-win scenarios.

Types of relationship

Quite obviously there are a multiplicity of relationship types in any industry, and retailing is no exception. They range on a spectrum from simple transactions to wholly co-operative ventures that seek win-win scenarios for the partners concerned. Webster (1992) plots seven broad categories of relationship (Figure 8.1).

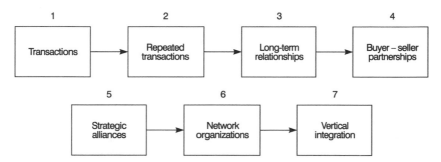

Figure 8.1 *The range of marketing relationships*

In the first two stages of Webster's model, the relationship is based around the transaction taking place. Economic factors of price and availability are the main drivers of exchange between the two parties.

In the third stage, the relationship has developed to a point where each company has a greater understanding of each other's goals, yet the interaction remains adversarial in nature. This is perhaps where most of the UK grocery retailers are currently positioned *vis-à-vis* their suppliers.

Stage four sees a move towards real partnerships underpinned by concepts of mutuality, trust and dependence.

Stage five is built on the trust elements of stage four and we begin to see commitment from both parties to achieving superordinate goals. The commitment is not just financial, in the form of budget provision, but in many cases a commitment of staff and skills (Marks and Spencer is a good example of this). It is not uncommon for collaborative efforts in, say, the area of new product development where teams from both supplier and retailer organizations meet to 'skill-pool'. This kind of activity has been taking place to greater degree of sophistication in the car industry where alliances are commonplace, e.g. Honda and Rover (before the takeover by BMW).

The next step on from alliances is a network organization. Again, this concept is not new, although in four years of research the author is yet to find evidence that this kind of organization exists in the UK. In Japan, where it does exist, the term given to network organizations is 'kieretsu'. Interestingly, not only do they have close relationships with suppliers and buyers but they also have relationships with companies not directly involved in the movement of goods and services from the point of production to the point of sale, e.g. advertising agencies, lawyers and, in some cases, banks. It is not just the number and diversity of relationships that is of interest, it is also the type of relationship. They are not 'loose-coupled' but are indeed tight relationships (Anderson, 1990). Often the relationship is financial as well as emotional and psychological. That is, the channel captain (the company with the most power in the channel) will invest in each of the satellite suppliers. The 'kieretsu' model is, however, difficult to imitate due to its complexity in terms of the trust, commitment, interdependence and power constructs that unpin its success.

Stage seven goes beyond the alliance to full vertical integration. This final stage has been the preferred option for many companies, particularly in the early eighties when merger and acquisition fever was high. The problem with acquisition is that firms need growth markets or larger shares of mature markets to cover the increase in fixed costs. Although margins may improve, any downturn in trading activity leads to diminished returns, particularly if the main measure of performance is return on assets.

Obviously, the best outcome for companies is a situation that delivers the benefits associated with vertical integration but without the risk of increased fixed costs. This scenario is found in partnerships. Marks and Spencer state that they are 'manufacturers without factories and their suppliers are retailers without shops'. And not all the advantage is to the retailer. Suppliers benefit from guaranteed outlets for their product and from the technical expertise that may exist in the retail company. In some cases the retailer can act as a mediator between two unrelated suppliers. For example, a high street retailer liked the design of a supplier's goods, but the supplier could not deliver the quantity. So the retailer introduced the design company to a production company who produced the required design in the required numbers. Thus the retailer creates a win-win-win scenario. Similarly, a high street retailer – noted for its quality – received substandard products from one of its long-time suppliers. Because of the nature of the relationship, the retailer not only helped the supplier solve its technical problems but carried on taking the substandard product (and paying for it) then discarded it, just to help the supplier's cash flow until they had solved the quality problem.

The degree of interdependence between companies in a network will characterize the relationship (Hogarth-Scott, Parkinson and Allen, 1994). Equally, the levels of power, conflict and co-operation (Reve and Stern, 1979) within the channel will determine the relationship functionality. What is important to note is that the degree of interdependence does not remain static; rather, it varies over time with changes in the market environment. Therefore, networks become akin to a living organism in a continual state of flux, and their management becomes difficult and time consuming. As a result, many firms do not invest in the relationship but merely exercise their power over other channel members. This leads inevitably to increased levels of conflict and a return to short-term transaction-based relationships. Williamson (1975) in his work on transaction cost economics (TCE) states that firms will act opportunistically. Transaction cost economics researchers operate on the assumption that managers of companies faced with achieving discrete sets of business objectives will be motivated by efficiency considerations where the maximum benefit can be gained at the minimum cost to the firm. This in turn leads to opportunistic behaviour and undermines the critical elements of a network – trust and commitment. Transaction cost economics is based on two polar forms of governance transactions – market-based discrete contracts and hierarchies. Market-based transactions are characterized by discrete contracts. These are relatively short-term, bargaining relationships between two autonomous buyers and sellers. The relationships are designed to facilitate efficient transfer of property rights. Hierarchical transactions usually deal with the production of wealth or the rationing of resources among superiors and subordinates.

If this is the case, then it is unlikely that any network organization will survive. Equally, if this statement is true, the unit of competition will remain at the product level. Thus a firm's competitive advantage (Porter, 1985) will be dependent on its ability to produce products that meet customer needs, and how it negotiates routes to market terms.

Unfortunately, we have already surpassed the product level of competition and moved to global organizational competitive units. The next step is, of course, the multiorganizational competitive unit (Figure 8.2).

Where there is such a development, the ability to manage conflict and encourage co-operation will become a critical success factor and a source of competitive advantage. As the Japanese have found, this multiorganizational model or 'kieretsu' cannot only provide a distinct competitive advantage but in the face of global competition can form effective barriers to market entry. In large kieretsu such as Mitsubishi, the routes to market for foreign competition can be difficult to find, as many suppliers are already committed to channel alliances.

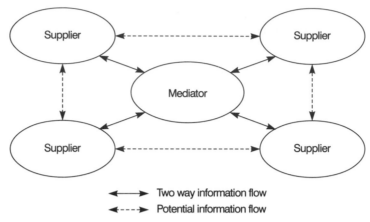

Figure 8.2 *The organizational unit*

Japanese-style relationships

For many years, the Japanese style of management has been a focus for academic researchers. However, the emphasis of this research has been in manufacturing, until recently, when the Japanese consumer society has come under closer scrutiny (Asmus and Griffin, 1993; Dwyer and Ouchi, 1993; Frey and Schlosser, 1993). The Japanese system is often referred to as best practice supply chain management, with firms investing in training their staff, developing suppliers and creating an environment of open communication and information sharing. This culture is not easily transplanted to the western method of trading, which is characterized by transaction-based relationships, little sharing of proprietary information and a general mistrust of suppliers. These characteristics only serve to reinforce opportunistic behaviour that exploit trading relationships for profit maximization. By its very nature profit maximization is short term – enticing competitors into an attractive market. Exacerbating this are the feelings of suppliers who may realize they are being exploited and display similar opportunistic behaviour when seeking buyers of their products or services. In contrast, the Japanese-style partnership nurtures an exclusive or semi-exclusive supplier–buyer relationship whose focus is on maximizing, not profit, but the efficiency of the value system (Hogarth-Scott, Parkinson and Allen, 1994). The benefits are reductions in the number of suppliers, transaction costs, production and inventory costs. Such activity increases margins and secures supply in the long term. The Japanese style of management recognizes that, in order to succeed in the long term, there must be a mutual dependence between the retailer and its suppliers built on trust and goal congruence. When this is achieved, such are the bonds which tie retailer and supplier together that an effective barrier to entry is formed.

IKEA has enjoyed success in the UK and other parts of the globe largely due to its supply chain management. (The company even includes the customer in the process – as delivery drivers and assemblers.) They have approximately 1,800 suppliers from over fifty different countries, each being subjected to a rigorous selection procedure before being taken on into a *long-term* relationship. The supplier part of the bargain is to offer low-cost, high-quality products and in return receive access to global markets and technical assistance from a number of nodal technical centres (Normann and Ramirez, 1993). This type of relationship is aimed at creating customer value at each point in the supply chain.

Risk

In addition to adding value and creating barriers to entry, there is another major driver of partnershipping that must be considered, that of risk reduction. The source of risk in all transactions is the need to make decisions in an environment where the outcome of an individual's or company's actions is uncertain. The author sees risk reduction and security as central elements that encourage companies to follow partnership strategies, especially in new product development areas. There are several forms of risk:

- commercial – will the market accept the product?; what will be the right pricing point to attract the desired level of sales and company profitability?
- technological – is the market ready to accept the latest technology?; is it capable of understanding it?
- scientific – is there a fundamental lack of knowledge?
- engineering – will the technology work?

Such risks encourage managers to follow risk-reducing strategies. One strategy is to develop links with other companies to form a network (i.e. a multidyadic system of exchange relationships) where risks are shared among the actors in the network. However, as we have already discussed, networks do not simply manifest themselves overnight.

Antecedents of networks

Before a network can exist, there has to be a number of antecedents in place (Figure 8.3).

Mohr and Spekman (1994) group these as follows:

1 Attributes of the partnership
  - *Commitment* – the willingness of members to exert effort on behalf of other members of the network.

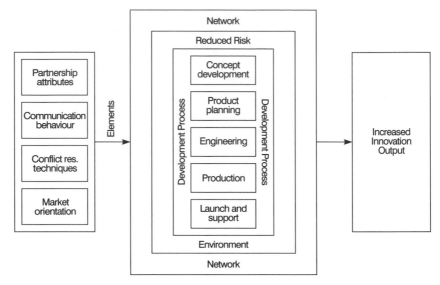

Figure 8.3 *A network model for new product development*

- *Co-ordination* – the defining of tasks each member expects the others to perform.
- *Interdependence* – the interaction of two or more members of the network where each is dependent on the other for perceived satisfaction of mutual goals.
- *Trust* – the belief that one party has that the other party in the relationship will act in a predictable way and fulfil its obligation in an exchange.

2 Communication behaviour
- *Quality* – the accuracy, reliability, relevancy and timeliness of the communication.
- *Information sharing* – the degree and frequency to which proprietary information exchanges are communicated between the participants in an exchange relationship.
- *Participation* – the extent to which partners are involved in joint planning and goal setting activities.

3 Conflict resolution
- *Joint problem-solving* – an integrative approach to problem-solving.
- *Persuasion* – the influence one party has over the other in persuading each other to adopt a particular solution to a conflict situation.
- *Domination* – the tacit exercise of power by one member of the network over another.
- *Harsh words* – the overt exercise of power by one member of the network over another.

- *Arbitration* – the intervention of a third party in a dyadic conflict situation.

In addition to Mohr and Spekman's antecedents the author would add:

- *Market orientation.*
- *Monitoring* – the monitoring of intra-industry activity and external environmental influences by all members of the network.
- *Analysis* – the interpretation and evaluation of market activity.
- *Reporting* – the dissemination of market information through the network.

If these antecedents are in place then it can be said that a true network has been formed. Figure 8.3 applies this theory to the high-risk activity of new product development and is presented as a model to show how the critical elements are needed to develop a network organization. If the supplier and retailers work together at an early stage in the development process – sharing the risk from the outset of the project – then each company's exposure to risk can be reduced. Lower risk would increase the propensity of each company to undertake more new product development activity.

The development of new product and processes is the lifeblood of companies (Zairi, 1995). However, it is how these products and services are managed that will provide the source of competitive advantage. The latest thinking draws upon the notion of partnershipping with all the attributes associated with it and tries to marshal the efforts of those involved in the supply chain towards meeting customer needs. This is no longer as simple as indulging product proliferation. It is aimed at developing a market orientation that views the consumer as not just a buyer of single product lines but a purchaser of a range of complementary products. Hence the premature death knell is sounded for the brand manager, while the appearance of the category manager is heralded (Dumaine, 1989). Changes in the retailing environment and increasing consumer sophistication have forced retailers and their suppliers to consider not only building brand awareness but also how they service the consumer at the point of sale. This has brought the actors in the supply chain closer together and the importance of trade marketing has increased.

Category management and efficient consumer response

Category management is consumer-based merchandising that manages categories of product consumers believe to be interrelated in meeting their demands. Thus, category management focuses on the demand side of the equation while ECR is concerned with the supply side. By careful monitoring of how consumers behave – in terms of their buying patterns – category managers can optimize their offering through improvements in new product development introductions, careful mixing of product range and promotion of the range and reduce costs of administration normally related to trade negotiations and high inventory levels.

What underpins the successful implementation of a category management system is effective supply of the right products at the right time to the right markets. The catalyst for this process is ECR. Efficient consumer response is a development of quick response, which merely functions around a transactional type of relationship, where goods are demanded and supplied in the quantities required when needed. The focus was around logistics and pushing inventory costs back down the supply chain. While efficiencies in the supply chain were welcomed, QR did not consider the consumer. Efficient consumer response has enhanced the process by recognizing the importance of the consumer and so links into the concept of category management.

Origins of efficient consumer response

Efficient consumer response was originated in the USA in 1993 (Coopers and Lybrand, 1996) as an integrated supply chain management system whose aim is to improve customer service and efficiency. Claims of supply chain savings in the region of 5 per cent of sales have been made. This equates to approximately £1 billion annually in the UK alone. Little wonder, then, that this system has attracted so much interest from all the major retailers and suppliers in the grocery industry. Ever-increasing competition in a mature market inevitably leads companies to seek cost savings to increase margins. Therefore, any system which claims savings of 5 per cent is bound to receive the attention of all the major players.

When Kurt Salmon Associates published their 'Black Book' (1993) they defined ECR as:

> . . . a grocery-industry strategy in which distributors and suppliers are working
> closely together to bring better value to the grocery consumer. By jointly
> focusing on the efficiency of the total grocery supply system, rather than the
> efficiency of individual components, they are reducing total system costs,
> inventories and physical assets while improving the consumer's choice of high
> quality fresh grocery products.

In order to achieve efficiencies in the 'total grocery supply system' it is necessary to take a holistic view of the process which delivers goods from the point of manufacture to the point of sale. Figure 8.4 shows the information

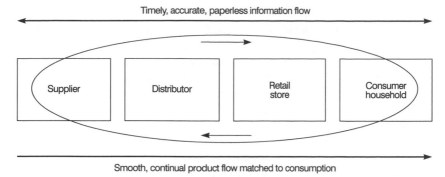

Figure 8.4 *The ECR system.* Source: *Kurt Salmon Associates (1993)*

and product flows, together with a holistic approach to meeting consumer demand.

The aim of this system is to create:

> ... a responsive, consumer driven system in which distributors and suppliers work together as business allies to maximize consumer satisfaction and minimize cost. Accurate information and high quality products flow through a paperless system between manufacturing line and check-out counter with minimum degradation or interruption both within and between trading partners. (Kurt Salmon Associates, 1993)

This aim is indeed a laudable one. In practice, however, getting channel partners to work together proves to be much more difficult than the quotation above would have us believe. The terms 'business allies' in the grocery industry is almost an oxymoron. The grocery retailers tend not to exhibit behaviour associated with building long-term relationships. What they have is long-term knowledge of supplier organizations with whom they trade on a regular basis. This is not a relationship that exhibits the critical elements for the kind of network we outlined earlier. Moreover, it has been known for a retail organization to make overtures towards partnershipping strategies, but when it comes to sharing information via electronic data interchange the relationship breaks down. At this point the retailer often exerts its buyer power and reverts to its trading routes and transaction-based negotiation, where a 'penny off a case' seems more important than consumer-based merchandising and building of long-term relationships.

This type of trading mentality is having an interesting effect on the industry structure. In a classic Porter (1985) 'five forces analysis' the concentration of retailers in the UK has given four major players immense buying power, to the point where even the supply side giants such as

Procter and Gamble and Unilever have perhaps felt under pressure to ensure their brands are price competitive if shelf space is to be secured. Adding to this pressure and again another manifestation of retailer power is the retailer's position on 'own-brand' products often supplied by the branded goods companies. However, the trading mentality of grocery retailers may yet be their undoing and force them down the path of partnershipping and ECR. If they continue to trade in a 'margin-bashing' manner we may see – and have to some extent already seen – a shake-out in the supply side with firms facing bankruptcy at worse and, at best, ceasing to trade with mass grocery outlets. If this occurs, the supply side will be concentrated, thus bringing the power base back to equilibrium. This scenario has not yet occurred but it might well do so, and its impact on the grocery industry could be dramatic. This is perhaps why some of the major high street retailers are actively pursuing long-term relationships that can lead to ECR systems working, and moving away from the old style trading behaviour, which revolves around the transaction not the consumer.

The cornerstones of ECR

It is widely accepted that there are four cornerstones of ECR:

- product replenishment
- new product development and introductions
- consumer and trade promotions
- merchandise management (Chain Store Age, 1995; Coopers and Lybrand, 1996).

Product replenishment

This concept aims to provide an answer to logistical problems of moving stock between manufacturer and retailer so that stock levels in the stores are kept at the optimum. The need for this becomes evident if we look at the stocking levels in the USA and Europe, where they can exceed 100 and 400 days respectively. The costs associated with carrying this amount of stock are immense. The aim of product replenishment is to reduce the stock days and this is effected by techniques such as vendor managed inventory and continuous replenishment to the warehouse. Electronic data interchange acts as the conduit that allows information to flow from the retailer to the supplier and vice versa. Information on stock levels is then tracked and replenished only when needed, thus improving the ordering/invoicing process and reducing the costs associated with handling and storing of inventory. Efficiency in the system is also gained as lead times are shortened. The benefits derived from product replenishment are not as great in the UK, however, because of existing trade efficiencies, which result in an average stockholding of only thirty days. Nevertheless, implementation of this process can still improve on thirty days.

If product replenishment is to meet its objectives – lower administration costs, shorter lead times and reduced stockholding – then it is of paramount importance that the relationship between the retailer and the supplier produces an effective working partnership. If this is to happen then the prerequisites for an effective partnership, outlined above, must be in place. In many cases this does not happen and firms try to partner without being fully cognisant of the constructs of partnershipping. Rather the focus is on short-term cost-cutting or 'margin-bashing'.

Consumer and trade promotions

These are used to stimulate interest in store. However, it is not always done well. Suppliers often have a greater understanding of their product and markets than the retailer, yet it is the retailer who promotes the product in store. This can be problematical. Recently, a major high street retailer introduced a range of kitchenware, supplied by a Dutch company. The range did not sell well, leaving the retailer with a large stockholding of product caused by forward ordering to support the promotional activity. This situation was reported to the supplier who then visited the London store to see how the product was being merchandised. Armed with greater customer knowledge than the retailer, the Dutch company remerchandised the product, sales were stimulated and the retailer was able to continue to stock the product. Thus collaboration between retailer and supplier can help improve the efficiency of consumer and trade promotions through: a better understanding of how promotions work, who they are aimed at and how best they can meet the consumer need; closer working relationships in the planning and execution of promotions and joint post-campaign analysis.

Merchandise management

This is simply about managing the range of product offering – amount, variation, packaging, size, placement and space allocation. But it is not as simple as it seems. The key to getting it right is to manage the merchandise from the consumer's point of view. Too often the merchandise is managed from the supply side – what is available and at what price. What creates effective product ranging is the store's ability to match the product offering to consumer needs; this will maximize the category performance by giving consumers what they want – and happy consumers buy again – while reducing the costs of stocking other items they purchase.

New product development and introductions

New product development is well documented as being a high-risk activity with up to 80 per cent of all new products introduced failing to achieve their predicted market penetration. However, innovation is a critical element in maintaining interest in the category and a stimulus for new sales. The dilemma for the stores is how to continually innovate, bringing new products to the shelves and keeping interest high, while reducing the risk and costs of new product development processes.

Supporters of ECR will claim that by making the consumer the focus of NPD rather than technology, the new introductions will have a better fit with the market and will therefore be successful. Again the key factor for success is developing the relationship between supplier and retailer so that information about the market is shared and both parties are involved in the development process at the idea generation stage (Figure 8.3).

The four elements above are said to produce substantial cost savings and produce a number of benefits for consumers, suppliers and retailers. Table 8.1 shows the breakdown of the estimated cost savings in the USA.

Total savings of 10.8 per cent represent some US$30 billion. But it is not only the retailer who benefits from ECR. The aim is to create win-win-win scenarios, so clearly a system which relies on interdependence must have benefit to more than one party; suppliers must also gain from the relationship. But perhaps more importantly, the consumer must benefit.

Table 8.1 *How ECR cuts costs in the USA*

ECR cornerstone	Total cost saving	How achieved
Product replenishment	4.1 per cent	Reduced stock levels EDI efficiencies in ordering and invoicing
Consumer and trade promotions	4.3 per cent	Reduction in forward orders, warehousing and mistargeted promotional activity
Merchandise management	1.5 per cent	Increased margins and improved stock turn
New product development and introductions	0.9 per cent	Fewer failures due to improved NPD processes

Source: Adapted from Kurt Salmon Associates (1993)

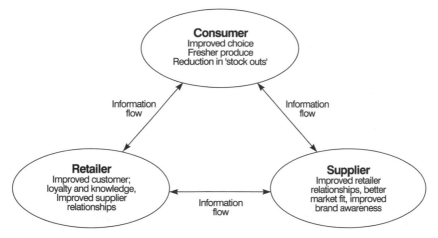

Figure 8.5 *ECR benefits*

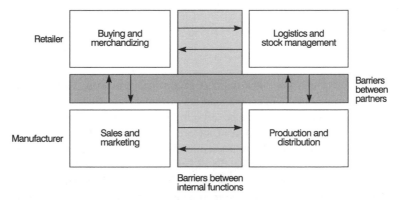

Figure 8.6 *Barriers to ECR effectiveness.* Source: *Coopers and Lybrand (1996)*

We can see the benefits of ECR quite clearly from Figure 8.5, but if ECR is to become profitably adopted in the UK then it is imperative that trading barriers between suppliers and retailers are removed for the greater good of the actors in the channel and the customer. Barriers not only exist between firms but also between functions (Figure 8.6).

The manifestation of these barriers is normally a conflict episode. Conflict occurs in all social systems and the interface between suppliers and retailers can be considered a social system. Conflict has a clear association with power and dependency and usually occurs when the attainment of one firm's goals is impeded by another firm in the channel. Conflict may be less when the level of dependency by one party on another is high because there is little the

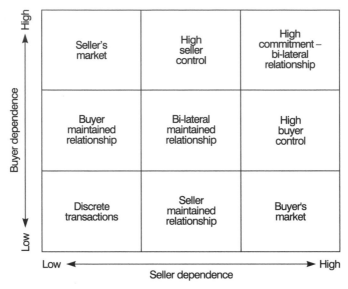

Figure 8.7 *Dependence grid.* Source: *Blenkhorn and MacKensie (1994)*

dependent firm can do other than to accept the situation. However, if the market environment changes, this can lead to opportunistic behaviour and the dependent firm can improve its position in another channel. The incidents that would normally have caused conflict are not forgotten but are suppressed because of the nature of the relationship and the imbalance in dependency.

Co-operation on the other hand is likely to occur when there is a mutual dependence between parties to achieve their goals. The balance between power/dependency and relationship management fluctuates as the environment changes from a seller's market to a buyer's market. Figure 8.7 plots the range of relationships associated with the varying degrees of buyer/supplier dependencies.

This grid can be used to aid managers in their relationship building. When this grid is used in conjunction with environmental analysis it becomes a powerful tool, helping to plot potential and real shifts in the company's power position and taking the appropriate relationship management action. The positioning on this grid will determine the effectiveness of ECR. If firms are positioned in the bottom left-hand corner where mutual dependence is low, then opportunistic behaviour may be exhibited and discrete transactions will form the basis of any relationship. If this is the case then little investment in shared goal setting, EDI and information sharing will be made. Where there is a high degree of power imbalance a similar situation may occur and one firm can exploit because of the dependency of the weaker firm. However, when environmental changes bring the power balances into equilibrium the conditions for relationship management and consequently ECR will be in place.

Examples of ECR application

Many firms in the retail grocery industry have at least considered implementing ECR management techniques, while some have tried to implement the system and some have discarded the idea altogether. Efficient consumer response is now in its fourteenth month of trial in the UK but many companies feel the system has failed to deliver the much talked about savings. In June 1997, 450 delegates from 170 companies attended a conference to hear how to turn the theory into practice. John Ballington of Unilever and David John of Kwik-Save introduced an 'enabling tool' known as the ECR UK process framework (*Supermarketing*, 1997) to help firms move from knowing the theory to implementing the system. The process has four elements – preparation, joint working and approach, planning and implementation. The conference highlighted companies that were already at the implementation stage and they included:

- Somerfield and Birds Eye Wall's
- Alldays and Bass
- Tesco and Bisto Foods.

Of the big four supermarket retailers, Tesco appears to be the company that is most committed to ECR. It has recently invited no fewer than 780 suppliers to take part in a supplier conference, the aim of which was to share information with suppliers so that they could help deliver Tesco's customer plan for 1997. They in return expect their suppliers to share technical and marketing information with them. In a show of commitment to partnership-ping, Tesco agreed to stop the launch of 'copy-cat brands' which hit at the very core of major suppliers' business.

Alldays and Bass have seen technological improvements in their businesses. Direct e-mail links and EDI have improved the communication between these two partners and they now have the ability to share information at random. The proof, of course, will be whether or not they commit to doing this.

In a survey of 200 companies carried out by the Institute of Grocery Distribution (IGD), concerns over trust and confidentiality were the main issues of companies involved in or considering the use of ECR systems. Most companies recognized the value of ECR with partners working together to solve demand side problems.

What ECR does not take into consideration is the history of these companies, which is rooted in trading. As such, trying to change the philosophy of a single point connection, where buyer deals with seller around price and delivery, to the 'bow tie' multiconnection model is proving to be difficult. This can be seen from the anecdotal evidence that states good intentions give way to harsh, short-term, transaction-based negotiations. As one delegate was heard to say in response to Tesco's claims on information-sharing: 'I've heard it but I haven't seen it yet . . .' (*Supermarketing*, 1997).

Somerfield Stores, on the other hand, have both seen and heard evidence of ECR success. In 1995 they trialled the co-managed inventory system (CMI), a key component of ECR. Twelve suppliers were given open access to CMI services and were given historical data on Somerfields' demand history. This allowed suppliers to model future demand patterns. In twelve months the system was able to reduce stock levels by 25 per cent while increasing service levels by 2.5 per cent. This was done without any detriment to customer service. However, it is the intangible benefits of improved communication and a fuller understanding of cultural issues surrounding re-engineering business processes that are perhaps the most valuable for long-term competitive advantage. The characteristics of a successful CMI programme are given in a article in *Partnership* (1996):

> [The] characteristics of a 'good' CMI programme are: top management commitment – a good relationship between manufacturers and retailers must already exist, based on trust and understanding; recognition that CMI and ECR are not primarily about technology but fundamental business issues shaping the organization's scope; cross functional team cultures . . . an electronic commerce infrastructure facilitates the exchange of information.

All these factors are underpinned by the research work of the IMP group et al., on relationships and their implications for the long-term success of companies. Any company considering the implementation of ECR pro-grammes should research their work for an insight into how to re-engineer their companies to meet the demands of a trading partnership based on trust, commitment and the sharing of information.

Conclusion

If ECR and category management techniques are to succeed, that is, be implemented in the supply chain and provide the acclaimed costs savings mentioned early, then the parties involved must receive mutual benefit. The difference between ECR systems and simple dyadic relationships is that everyone in the channel (including the consumer) must benefit. In dyadic relationships, win-win scenarios are easier to create: two players can manage others in the channel to deliver mutual benefit. In ECR systems, every participant in the channel looks for some benefit. Then, the need is for win-win-win-win scenarios. This requires the whole channel to work together and take responsibility for managing relationships within it. However, simple supply and demand economics dictate that a firm in a position of power will try to maximize its profit potential at the expense of other actors in the supply chain. This type of behaviour spells disaster for the success of ECR. It also encourages short-termism and a return to the Williamson (1975) transaction-based economic approach to business. ECR commits firms to long-term relationships. Direct investment in technology – e-mail links, EDI etc. – and indirect investment in relationship-building will ensure that there is a level of management information that provides advantages for all actors in the supply chain.

It is precisely this indirect investment that appears to be a barrier to successful implementation of ECR and category management techniques. Allied to this is the tension between the old methods of channel management, which focus on the transfer of goods from manufacture to point of sale with each shift in goods being the result of a dyadic process that *pushes* the goods from one channel member to another. ECR, on the other hand, focuses on the consumer and on the point of sale. From here a *pull* process is in place, where products and services are dictated by the consumer and pulled through the supply chain (Figure 8.8). The objective is improved customer satisfaction: happy customers buy again and thus the performance of all in the channel is improved over the long term.

If the partnerships are to work, then commitment from all parties must be in place. If only one player is committed, then actors in the channel will split into passive and active firms. The passive firms will merely react to demand from upstream channel members and will have less incentive to focus on the consumer. They will therefore add little value to the process of meeting customer needs.

The sole purpose of category management and ECR is to meet customer needs. However, it seems that many firms are using the systems to meet technology and product needs. Electronic data capture and transfer of information (EPOS and EDI) have revolutionized the retailing industry but the data captured is not being used to its full potential. This is because firms are more concerned with the 'how to' question of data capture rather than 'why' questions of consumer buying behaviour. Category management is consumer-based merchandising. Yet, retailers still talk in terms of product category when they should be talking about consumer category. Until this is realized and internalized the full power of ECR and category management will go unharnessed.

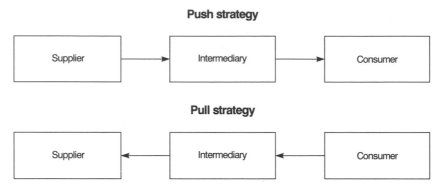

Figure 8.8 *Demand influences*

Key elements for the successful implementation of ECR

There are many benefits of ECR, including improved margins, effective use of promotional activity, efficient stocking policies and better responsiveness to consumer needs. But to realize these improvements, there are a number of critical success factors to consider:

- *Partnerships*: Throughout this chapter the link between successful ECR implementation and trading relationships has been emphasized. The system needs co-operation between channel partners to succeed. This means investment in relationship building, understanding cultures and the role they play and how to resolve conflict. ECR is a holistic system that includes many players and without giving the constructs of relationships (trust, commitment, power, dependency and conflict) due attention the system will inevitably fail.
- *Consumer focus*: ECR and category management are consumer-driven, merchandising systems. It seems obvious then, that the focus of a firm's attention should be on the consumer. However, this is not always the case and too much emphasis is given to the product and the technology. Important though these elements are, the system is there to manage customers, not products and technology.
- *Senior management commitment*: ECR is part of the overall business strategy of the firm; it should not be treated as a separate business function. Accordingly, it should receive attention from senior management in terms of how it fits with the overall business mission, how its performance can be measured, how it can be implemented via multifunctional teams and, ultimately, how it can sustain competitive advantage for the firm and the value chain as a whole in the long term.

The jury is still out on the success of ECR and category management. Some firms have embraced the system while others have merely paid lip service to it or have discarded the idea completely. Like most newly acclaimed saviours, ECR has its sceptics, quick to point out its shortcomings. What they fail to realize is that those shortcomings are the result of a wrong approach to implementation. Firms cannot simply invest in technology and products and still act opportunistically – changing suppliers at will or exercising coercive buying power over them. They must invest the 'softer' side of the system that accounts for corporate culture and relationship building. ECR and category management are in an evolutionary cycle. We have seen the enthusiastic introduction, we have moved through trial, with some failures and some successes; now is the time to evaluate and refine the system to reap the benefits, promised by ECR.

References

Anderson, P. (1992) Analyzing distribution channel dynamics: loose and tight coupling in distribution networks. *European Journal of Marketing*, **26**(2), 47–68.

Asmus, D. and Griffin, J. (1993) Harnessing the power of your suppliers. *The McKinsey Quarterly*, **3**, 63–78.

Blenkhorn, D. L. and MacKensie, H. F. The importance of buyer-seller relative dependence in relationship marketing. Paper presented to Relationship Marketing: Theory, Methods and Applications, Emory Business School, Atlanta. Georgia.

Chain Store Age (1995) February, 12.

Coopers and Lybrand (1996) *European ECR Study Summary Report.* Presented at the Geneva Conference, 26 January.

Dwyer, J. H. and Ouchi, W. G. (1993) Japanese-style partnerships: giving companies a competitive edge. *Sloan Management Review*, **35**, Fall, 51–64.

Dumaine, B. (1989) P & G rewrites the marketing rules. *Fortune*, 6 November, 34–42.

Emerson, R. M. (1962) Power-dependence relationships. *American Sociological Review*, **27**, 31–41.

Frey, S. C. and Schlosser, M. M. (1993) ABB and Ford: creating value through cooperation. *Sloan Management Review*, **35**, Fall, 65–72.

Hogarth-Scott, S., Parkinson, S. T. and Allen, P. (1994) Are retailers managing their channels of distribution effectively: the way forward. Paper presented to Relationship Marketing: Theory, Methods and Applications, Emory Business School, Atlanta, Georgia.

Keynote (1995) *Keynote Market Report: Supermarkets and Superstores.* Keynote, Middlesex.

Kurt Salmon Associates (1993) *Efficient Consumer Response – Enhancing Consumer Value in the Grocery Industry.* The Research Department Food Marketing Institute, January.

Lawrence, A. (1983) *The Management of Trade Marketing. Harvard University Press.*

McCarthy, E. J. and Perreault, W. D. Jr (1993) What retailers want. In *Applications in Basic Marketing*, 4th edn, 161–2.

Mohr, J. and Spekman, R. (1994) Characteristic of partnership success: partnership attributes, communication behaviour and conflict resolution techniques. *Strategic Management Journal*, **15**, 135–52.

Normann, R. and Ramirez, R. (1993) From value chain to value constellation: designing interactive strategy. *Harvard Business Review*, July–August.

Partnership (1996) 'Partnershipping' in distribution. August, 23.

Porter, M. (1985) *Competitive Advantage.* Free Press.

Randell, G. (1990) *Marketing to the Retail Trade.* Heinemann.

Reve, T. and Stern, L. W. (1979) Interorganizational relations in marketing channels. *Academy of Management Review*, **4**(3), 405–16.

Supermarketing (1997) 10 January, 15.

Webster, F. E. Jr (1992) The changing role of marketing in the corporation. *Journal of Marketing*, **56**, October, 1–17.

Williamson, O. E. (1975) *Markets and Hierarchies: Analysis and Antitrust Implications.* Free Press.

Zairi, M. (1995) Top down innovation for bottom up results. *World Class Design to Manufacture*, **2**(1), 6–12.

9 Auditing innovation through effective performance measurement

Mohamed Zairi

This chapter highlights the fundamental importance of continuously measuring and tracking innovation. It reviews various methodologies of measurement and presents a case for adopting an integrated perspective to the total process of innovation. Specific criteria of measurement are presented for both process and product-based assessments of innovation effectiveness. The chapter highlights best practice through discussion of Hewlett Packard, Exxon Chemicals, Rank Xerox, D2D, Kodak, Mercury, M&M Mars group, and others to highlight the form and format of assessment and audit. The chapter also indicates how QFD and the McKinsey 7Ss model can be used as holistic tools of measurement.

If you do things well, do them better. Be daring, be first, be different, be just. (Anita Roddick, founder and Managing Director, Body Shop International)

Introduction

Measurement in innovation is something of a necessary evil. We have all heard the expression 'innovate or you are dead' and this means that in order to spur innovation activity on an ongoing basis, there has to be a clear insistence from top management on continuous measurement, monitoring and improvement.

Measurement is the key trigger for action as it keeps people's minds and energies focused on adding value and is the best means possible for preventing complacency. This is even more true of innovation, since innovation is often associated with all the parameters that determine competitiveness (Plsek, 1997), namely:

- superior long-term financial performance is associated with innovation
- customers are increasingly demanding innovation

- competitors are getting increasingly better at copying past innovations
- new technologies enable innovation
- what used to work, doesn't work any more.

The reason why the issue of measurement in relation to innovation is more poignant is because it is an important core competence for business survival. This is recognized by Peter Drucker (1995), who says, 'Innovation [is a] . . . core competence . . . that every organization needs.'

The recognition that innovation is strongly linked to long-term financial performance has to come from top management. Plsek (1997) reports the following quotes from three leaders of very successful and admired organizations:

> If you think you are going to be successful running your business in the next ten years the way you did in the last ten years, you're out of your mind. To succeed, you have to disturb the present. (Roberto Goizueta, Coca-Cola)

> I'm convinced that if the role of change inside the institution is less than the role of change outside, the end is in sight. The only question is the timing of the end. (Jack Welch, General Electric)

> Swim upstream. Go the other way. Ignore the conventional wisdom. If everyone else is doing it one way, there's a good chance you can find your niche by going in exactly the opposite direction. (Sam Walton, Wal. Mart Stores)

One assumes, however, that, generally speaking, organizations are good at measurement and apply it effectively in relation to innovation. But is this really the case?

How effective are organizations at applying measurement?

A recent survey sought to establish answers to the following questions (Lingle and Schiemann, 1996):

- What are companies doing to increase results?
- Does measuring strategic performance make a difference?
- Is measurement being used to manage change?

The survey established that measurement is not widely pervasive as an integrated practice and its implementation is not a straightforward process. The value and impact of measurement is found to be significant and greatly distinguishes good companies from the rest. As Lingle and Schiemann argue:

For those executives who have gone beyond the given eyeshades and stopwatches to assess the pivot points of their company's strategy – from how well customer expectations are met to the ability to manage relevant environmentally and regulatory forces, to how adaptable the organization is – the measurement effort will yield ongoing results to the bottom line. (Lingle and Schiemann, 1996)

The survey represented the mailing of executives from a cross-section of industries in the USA. Responses came from 203 executives, 72 per cent of whom were top or senior executives. It is interesting to note that the answer to a question on the value of information in relation to innovation/change revealed this as a least important area and, further, that the quality of information is an issue, just as it is for the quality of the information on all areas of performance measurement (Figure 9.1).

Similarly, respondents have reported that the quality of measures related to innovation/change ranks the lowest when compared to areas such as financial performance, productivity, customer satisfaction and so on (Figure 9.2).

The respondents concerned also indicated that in most cases, measures on innovation are not included for management review and meetings, nor are they widely used for bringing about organizational change. They also reported that they are not linked to employee compensation (Figure 9.3).

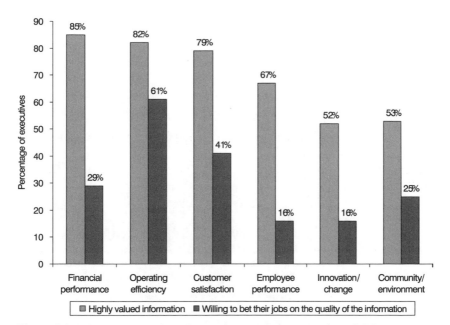

Figure 9.1 *Value versus quality of measurement.* Source: *Lingle and Schiemann (1996)*

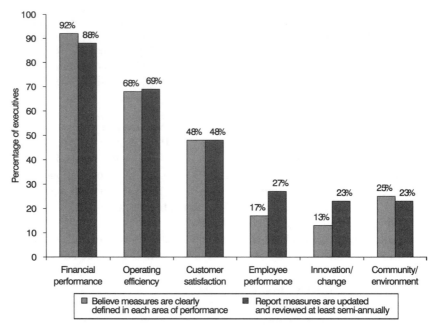

Figure 9.2 *Quality of measures.* Source: *Lingle and Schiemann (1996)*

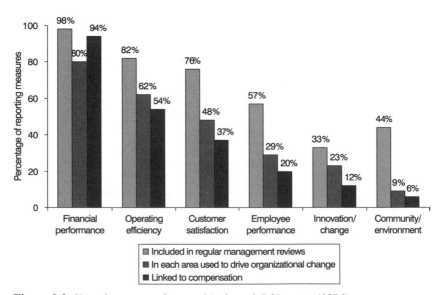

Figure 9.3 *Use of measures.* Source: *Lingle and Schiemann (1996)*

The survey concludes with some of the chief reasons for the lack of commitment to making measurement work in the area of innovation, as follows:

- Having fuzzy objectives without clear statements and no process for generating buy-in and commitments.
- Putting unjustified trust in informal systems, with many companies relying on feedback from informal, subjective sources. As the authors put it: 'Non-measurement managed companies often learn too late that an apparent problem which has absorbed resources is the concern of only a few squeaky wheels, while a more critical problem has gone unattended' (Lingle and Schiemann, 1996).
- Relying on entrenched measurement systems, with many companies ignoring the fact that measurement is closely associated with alleviating fear and inducing positive behaviour for making the system in question work.
- Being caught in the 'activity trap', sometimes referred to as measurement mania, where the focus is more on the measurements of activity than results.

Measurement in innovation: the integrated perspective

In order to truly and effectively measure the impact innovation can have on business competitiveness, the measurement activity has to focus not only on outputs of the products/services *per se* but also on the performance of the process of innovation itself. It is therefore extremely useful to examine the difference between two types of measures: process measures and product measures.

Process-focused measures

Process measures are concerned with speed, cost and quality in terms of, for example, the number of design changes. These measures are taken on a regular basis to address aspects of the innovation process that need optimizing so that costs are kept to a minimum, time is reduced and quality is enhanced.

Produce-based measures

Produce-based measures are concerned with the product's:

- performance in terms of market share
- worthiness in terms of leading to a competitive advantage – differentiation

- cost in relation to the benefits achieved
- financial worthiness.

Process-based and product-based measures are interrelated. The former are on-line measures and often lead to immediate action to deal with the problem, optimizing the innovation process and preventing bottlenecks. Product-based measures, on the other hand, tend to be retrospective in nature. They can be compiled only when the information is made available and the project is complete and performing in the marketplace.

Being too concerned with product-based measures too early in the innovation process will often distract teams from doing the right things (such as progressing the project). Imposing these types of measures earlier will encourage a 'let's work on less risky projects', or 'let's play safe' mentality, leading to small results with no significant leaps or real impact in the marketplace. The idea of focusing on the innovation process and its improvement is to allow:

- a continuous flow of projects
- a fast track development process
- low cost through improvements and optimizing (organizational entitlement) – capability of the process
- a mixture of large and small projects to reflect a healthy portfolio, which incorporates short-, medium- and long-term business needs.

It should also secure:

- profit improvement
- customer satisfaction (market share)
- consistent growth
- competitive supremacy in the business categories concerned.

Optimization of the projects internally to justify costs and make accurate financial predictions will lead to a product-based, 'play safe' culture. External optimization, on the other hand, is the most recommended route, and is based on the following motto: *Being first and good is better than being last and best.*

Being first means that there is:

- a time advantage
- cost advantage
- legitimacy in dictating premium prices
- flexibility to increase sales and achieve set targets.

Measurement in the context of 'hard aspects' of the innovation cycle are both well established and well documented. The following categories represent measures of ten found in the area of supply chain:

- quality
- delivery
- production process time
- flexibility
- costs.

Proposed performance measurement parameters for world-class manufacturers

The following is a compilation of measures found in world-class manufacturing organizations.

Quality

Accepted shipments = number of vendor shipments received that are accepted
number of vendor shipments received
= ____ %

Goal: To reduce rejected shipments with subsequent potential production delays.

Customer satisfaction = number of consumer complaints
= ____ % number of million units sold

Goal: To have no complaints over products.

Delivery

Vendor on-time delivery = number of deliveries early + late total number of vendor deliveries
= ____ %

Goal: All vendor deliveries to be on the day scheduled.

Schedule efficiency = number of item schedule changes greater than +10% on a weekly basis for all four weeks of a master schedule
= ____ %

Goal: To maintain and produce to the period schedule by week established before period started.

Plan service level = production schedule quantities – variance quantities
= ____ % production schedule quantities

Goal: To produce exactly to schedule each week.

Production process time

Pack availability ratio = number of different packs made/day averaged
over all days of the period
= ____ % number of different packs made during
period

Goal: To produce all packs every day. To have no changeovers or set-up time which leads to potential inventory build-up and out of inventory situations.

Changeovers = number of changeovers during period
= ____

Goal: To have no changeovers each period with their consequent cost and lost time.

Changeover lost time = production associated hours lost during all
changeovers for the period
= ____ AH number of changeovers during period

Goal: To minimize production lost time by having no changeovers or by making changeovers when production associates are not present, i.e. at weekends or other schedule down shifts.

Changeover recovery time = sum of hours of operation after each
changeover until process reaches expected
rate number of changeovers during period
= ____ %

Goal: To recover as fast as possible to expected rate after each changeover. To lose no production time after each changeover.

Line/process uptime ratio = weighted average over all lines of line/process
uptime for period
= ____ % weighted average over all lines of
scheduled operating time for period

Goal: To have 100 per cent line/process uptime.

Reliability ratio = preventive maintenance man hours + corrective
maintenance man hours
= ____ CV or plant M&E fixed assets

Goal: To balance both the preventive and corrective maintenance activity to give the lowest total maintenance cost/asset value ratio.

Stores inventory ratio = period end inventory of storeroom parts and
supplies ($)
= ____ % CV of plant M&E fixed assets

Goal: To reduce stores' inventory as equipment reliability improves.

Stores usage ratio = Maintenance repair parts used (Distributed) ($)
= ____ period end inventory of storeroom parts and
supplies ($)

Goal: To reduce consumption of spares as equipment reliability improves.

Flexibility

New pack introduction rate = number of new packs introduced
year-to-date
= ____ number of new packs introduced last
year for same time period

Goal: To understand the needs of the marketplace and bring products to market quickly and innovatively. To show ratios > 1.0.

Packing asset flexibility = CV of packing room fixed assets ($) number of
different packs made this period

Goal: To have flexible packing assets able to make a variety of different packs.

Costs

Raw materials days on hand = tonnes of raw materials on hand in
plant/company warehouse period end
= ____ days average tonnes scheduled/day
for following period

Goal: To reduce inventories and move toward just-in-time manufacturing.

Packing materials days on hand = units of packing materials on hand in
plant/company warehouse period end
= ____ days average units of packing
materials scheduled/day for following
period

Goal: To reduce inventories and move toward JIT manufacturing.

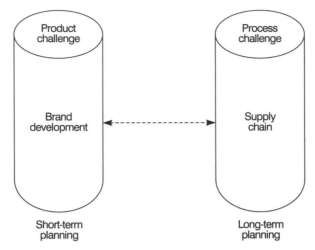

Figure 9.4 *Managing innovation through supply chain integration*

The challenge, however, tends to be more in this 'soft side' of the innovation cycle or what is referred to as the creative phase of innovation. There is a natural tension between the creative phase (brand development) and the productive phase (supply chain). As Figure 9.4 indicates, supply chain seeks stability, predictability and consistency, while brand development is more concerned with opportunity and speed. The tension in question can be better seen through Figure 9.5, where the outcome from the creative phase, if pushed without proper understanding of performance and capability, can lead to the breakdown of supply chain and result in poor performance in a variety of ways.

These tensions tend to be experienced by many organizations that fail to measure performance throughout the innovation process, by understanding, among other factors, processes and outcomes, capability and constraints opportunity and cost, quality and speed.

The most innovative organizations tend to be characterized by similar criteria:

- innovation is surgically defined
- the organization is serious about project management
- there is a wide spread of planning tools
- the organization uses a proper innovation process
- there is emphasis on *speed* (time to market)
- there is a culture of *measurement*
- there is a process of continuous learning and improvement.

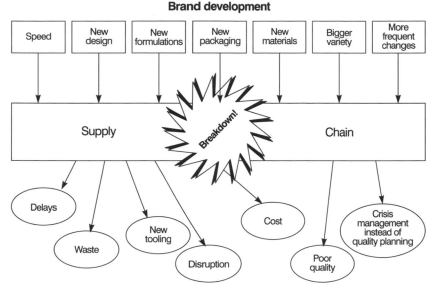

Figure 9.5 *Tension outcomes between brand development and supply chain*

The following section includes a series of case studies of best practice in the measuring of innovation performance.

Best practice in innovation performance measurement

Case study 1: Hewlett Packard

- Hewlett Packard (HP) realize that the biggest impact on customer satisfaction and return on investment comes from the time it takes HP to recognize the business opportunity to the time it takes to develop and introduce new products.
- The time line is measured through the innovation life cycle. The cycle begins when the opportunity for a new product becomes evident. *Produce innovation cycle time* is the interval between the moment the window of opportunity opens and the moment the first customers are satisfied.
- The opportunity occurs and is generally followed by some delay time until it is perceived. The goal is to reduce that delay to a minimum and get a product through that window as quickly as possible. *The cycle time begins when the opportunity occurs instead of when the project activity begins.*
- To reduce the dead time between opportunity and project initiation, HP uses a process of product development based on a principle called *information*

Table 9.1 *Hewlett Packard's nine steps to improve information processes*

The nine steps	Notes
1 Select the best available opportunity for project alignment	Considerable time needs to be spent on identifying and clarifying opportunities before projects begin
2 Provide visionary leadership	A visionary leader helps the project team to see the value their work has to the customer
3 Work on least probable, most valuable tasks first	Expected value increases when high-value outcomes with low priority of success are proven feasible
4 Strive for effective design of experiments	Experiments with multiple outcomes which probably yield, on average, the most information
5 Find ways to increase the rate of doing experiments	Information flow depends on the amount of information gained from each event and on the rate at which the events occur
6 Seek and use all information available from each experiment	
7 Minimize the time spent on non-value adding activities	Time spent on non-essential activities does not add value information. The project therefore loses forward momentum and increases the time factor
8 Provide information resources for engineers	A support organization should anticipate the information needs of development teams and make information available on a wide variety of topics
9 Design and manage project information flow	Companies need to put a product data management system in place which regulates the flow of and access to this information

Source: Marvin Patterson, HP's Director of R&D Operations (1993)

assembly line. The effectiveness of this model is heavily dependent on the robustness of the information processes available. Hewlett Packard recommends nine ways of improving information processes and these are listed in Table 9.1.

• Time to market can be made viable and reduced when time can be removed from the supply chain/manufacturing process and applied to brand development. The recommendations in Table 9.2 come from HP's experience.

Table 9.2 *Hewlett Packard's recommendations for reducing time to market*

Ways of reducing time spent	Notes
1 Implement concurrent processes	As in manufacturing, use parallel working for product development. Bring together as many people as possible to get the product to market in the shortest time
2 Improve the quality and timeliness of incoming materials	Just as JIT is used for materials supply and usage, so information needs a similar structure for the produce development process. The effect of poor quality or missing information is the same as that of inadequate supply on the shop floor
3 Streamline the flow of materials	Modern production lines take advantage of the well-planned flow of materials. Product-generation activity should be both well planned and efficient to move information from one development stage to another. For this smooth flow of information to occur, a consistent integrated set of information networks and tools must be in place
4 Minimize changeover time	Quick and speedy changeover time in production lines is a key challenge. The same phenomenon happens in NPD between the completion of one project and the initiation of another. The changeover process and design need to be carried out rapidly. The objective is to maximize the percentage of time that project teams spend adding value for customers
5 Eliminate bottlenecks	Production development bottlenecks occur when information flow is restricted or the rate of adding value to information is not keeping up with demand. Speeding up the development effort becomes a process of identifying and resolving these bottlenecks

Source: Marvin Patterson, HP's Director of R&D Operations (1993)

Examples of performance measures used for innovation at Hewlett Packard

Designer-customer interaction
Understanding customer needs = visits to customer
                                number of designers.

(This measure is to promote more interaction between designers and customers by calculating the amount of contact there is.)

Overall effectiveness of product development

Staffing level effectiveness = staff initially forecast as needed for project
staff actually needed by project.

(This measure monitors how closely the projections for the staff needed on a project match the staffing required by the project.)

Stability of the design = number of design changes in a project × 100
total cost of project.

(This measure tracks the number of design changes made. As large projects might need more changes simply because they are larger, by dividing by the project's cost, this metric adjusts for the size of the project.)

Overall effectiveness of the innovation process

Innovation effectiveness = number of projects finishing
development × 100
number of projects started development.

Other measures

Progress rate of project = months late
total months initially scheduled for project.

Cost estimation = actual cost of phase
projected cost of phase.

Milestone progress rate: number of milestones reached during
month × 100
number of milestones scheduled that month.

Case study 2: Exxon Chemical

The innovation process is based on *gates* and *stages*. Gates are key decision points aimed at moving good projects forward; stages are discrete groups of parallel activities occurring during the life of a typical innovation project. The various areas of activity generate information necessary to make a decision to proceed to the next stage. The various activities involved include:

- assessment of strategic fit
- determination of market attractiveness
- determination of technical feasibility
- determination of supply/entry route
- assessment of potential for competitive advantage
- treatment of legal/regulatory issues
- appraisal of financial attractiveness

- identification of killer variables
- development of a plan to proceed.

Idea	INITIAL SCREEN (start gate)
Preliminary assessment (stage 1)	Second screen (Gate 1)
Detailed assessment (stage 2)	Decision to develop (Gate 2)
Development (stage 3)	Entry to validation (Gate 3)
Validation (stage 4)	Launch decision (Gate 4)
Commercial launch (stage 5)	Post-launch review

Two examples of performance measures used for innovation at Exxon Chemicals are given below.

In-process measures

- Penetration: percentage of NPD budget utilizing innovation process.
- Percentage of new projects using the innovation process.
- Focus/culling: percentage of NO/GO of HOLD by gate 2.

Results-based measures

- Speed of innovation: elapsed time, stages 1 to 4.
- Performance: 2nd year IBIT vs. gate 4.
- Percentage of revenue from products up to five years old.

Definitions

- **Penetration**: the number of projects managed through the innovation process.
- **Focus**: reflected by early *culling*. Percentage of no-go or hold decisions made during a period of time by the end of stage 2 (detailed assessment).
- **Speed**: average period (in months) of average development time for projects approved for commercial launch (stage 5) during a specific year.
- **Performance**: NPD/NBD payout (NBD = new business development). Percentage of actual/protected IBIT ratio in a particular year for projects in their second full year of operation after their gate 4 'go ahead'.

Case study 3: Rank Xerox Group

Rank Xerox use an innovation process called product delivery process (PDP), which is defined as: 'the cycle of integrated Planning, Engineering, Manufacturing, Marketing, Launch and Management review activities which enables delivery of World Class Xerox products to end-user customers'.

The PDP has the following key components.

- *Management decision process* (MDP): This helps teams understand what needs to be accomplished and by when. The MDP provides guidance for product programme management and control by applying disciplined review and assessment – *Phase transfer review and major programme checkpoint reviews* – throughout the product life cycle.
- *Process elements*: Process elements identify what the teams need to do to get there, and when. These are the nuts and bolts of PDP, giving detailed descriptions of what needs to be done on a programme in a particular area of specialization from preconcept to maintenance.
- 'It is the integration of the Management Decision Process with the Process Elements that makes up the structure of the Product Delivery Process' (Rank Xerox).
- *Process enablers*: In order to implement any process successfully, there are enablers – information, skills and tools. The process enablers for PDP include documentation, organization effectiveness, training, and a network of computer systems.

The key features of the PDP include, among others, the following:

- integrates the work of all phases; the process is viewed as a whole
- front loads product delivery, putting people and resources into the early phases so that many activities can be planned early and in parallel
- provides a disciplined approach to managing product development delivery
- accommodates a full range of product programmes by enabling product delivery teams (PDTs) to customize the generic requirements and activities to reflect their programme specifications
- facilitates PDT planning and self-assessments and senior management reviews at major programme decision points
- captures and communicates lessons learned from programme experience
- provides training on process requirements and systems to meet programme needs.

Some examples of performance measures (product based) used for innovation at Rank Xerox are listed below.

Market share

Monitoring market share improvement is very important to Rank Xerox as it gives them a clear indication of how they compare with the competition. Through anonymous surveys, Rank Xerox benchmarks its market share against the top thirty of its competitors in Europe.

Revenue

Since the mid-1980s, Rank Xerox has consistently improved its revenue levels. The following aggressive programme was implemented in 1992 to enhance revenue levels:

1 Use new colour products to maximize new business opportunities.
2 Develop and implement specific plans to promote and reward new business.
3 Manage the business based on management dynamics measurement.
4 Accelerate implementation of concessionaires and added value sellers.
5 Use pilots and best practices to increase sales force effectiveness.
6 Develop and implement an integrated marketing programme with two major objectives:
   • to enhance strongly customer retention and annuity growth
   • to focus heavily on gaining new customers.

Case study 4: Design to Distribution (D2D) (now Celestica Ltd)

The innovation process at D2D is based on a four-phase and review system. This starts with the design phase and works through the process to volume manufacture. D2D reviews any non-compliances raised as part of the quality management system, which ensures collaboration between Design and Manufacturing.

Design for manufacture (DFM) is used extensively throughout the operation. It is based on understanding the process capabilities and ensuring that products are designed to suit these capabilities. Design for manufacture has now become fully integrated in the design process.

Process changes are formally communicated to the customer-supplier chains. This is to ensure that any enhancements to the process, which are to impact on customers, are thoroughly evaluated before deployment. Changes to products are formally communicated and agreed by the engineering change control process. No changes are allowed unless they are communicated to authorized personnel and have their support and approval.

Through the use of the appraisal system, all staff are trained to use the process. When changes to the process take place, the need for special training is highlighted before the introduction of the necessary changes. Changes to the process are reviewed to ensure that the predicted results are achieved. Reviews are carried out for:

• new requirements
• new equipment
• improvements.

New performance standards are reviewed and agreed at management level to ensure that the process is being operated for the required performance. Targets for improvement are also agreed and continuous reviews ensure that standards are met or exceeded.

Some examples of performing measures used by D2D for innovation are as follows.

Product-based measures

Cost reductions: D2D measures its performance in cost reduction by percentage and value added terms. Regular reviews are held monthly and involve customers. The products concerned are examined in relation to the following criteria:

- cost forecasts against targets
- impact of exchange rates
- material price changes
- joint activities to reduce cost by design changes.

D2D also uses value engineering workshops in the early stages of the product development process to examine the potential for reducing costs before production starts. The assumption is that at least 80 per cent of product costs should be designed before the manufacturing phase starts.

D2D has been setting itself a target of approximately 10 per cent cost reduction per year. This figure relied on two activities:

- the ability of the purchasing function to negotiate lower price contracts with suppliers
- the continuous effort to try and reduce manufacturing costs through innovation, quality improvements and other means.

Process-based measures

Time to market: D2D operates in a vulnerable market where in some categories product lifetimes could be as little as six months. In line with the company's vision, a process of reducing introduction times of new circuit boards was started in 1986.

Figures 9.6–9.10 illustrate the application of time to market measures at D2D. Figures 9.6 and 9.7 are concerned with design to manufacture cycle time. Figures 9.8 and 9.9 deal with engineering planning cycle time. Figure 9.10 illustrates engineering change cycle time.

Manufacturability assessment: Manufacturing and design engineers work together in the early stages of new product development using design tools

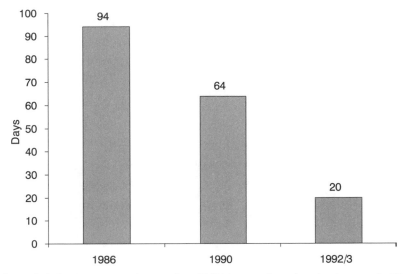

Figure 9.6 *Design to manufacture time (PCBs): manufacturing development build*

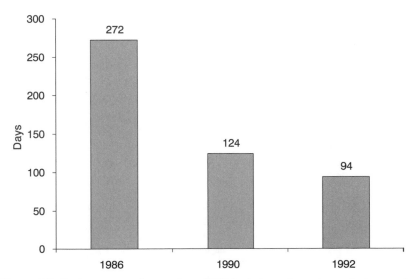

Figure 9.7 *Design to manufacture time (PCBs): design release to product general release*

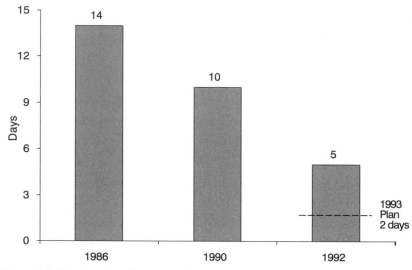

Figure 9.8 *Engineering planning cycle time: final product assembly planning*

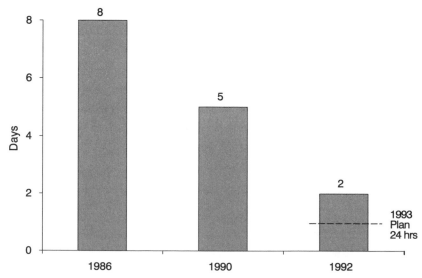

Figure 9.9 *Engineering planning cycle time: PCB assembly planning*

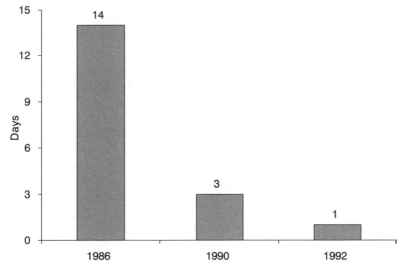

Figure 9.10 *Engineering change cycle time*

based on DFM principles. They can thus optimize design so that right first time can be achieved. No printed circuit board is allowed to go to production with attributes that would comprise quality or increase manufacturing cycle time.

The following are some of the benefits achieved from cycle time reduction:

- printed circuit product introduction cycle time reduced to three months
- high data integrity
- faster and automated take-on OEM design detail (electronic and data based)
- common standards between design and manufacturing
- electronic trading of design and commercial data
- automated processing of design information for manufacture.

Case study 5: Kodak Ltd

Kodak uses the following performance measures for innovation.

Process-based measures

- Product development cycle time.

Product-based measures

- The revenue from new products is counted as percentage of total sales, globally and regionally.
- Number of product firsts: breakthroughs and enhancements.
- Revenue, volume and share growth by channels and markets, globally and regionally.
- Superior sales and marketing productivity.
- Superior brand equity as measured by trends in: brand image by market and ability to sustain price premiums.

Case study 6: Mercury Telecommunications

Process-based measures

- Number of development projects with forecast first customer shipment in a quarter.
- Product and service development versus competitors.

Product-based measures

- Status of the brand.
- Customer acquisition.
- Customer retention.

Case study 7: M&M–Mars Group

Process-based measures

$$\text{New pack introduction rate} = \frac{\text{number of new packs introduced year to year}}{\text{number of new packs introduced last year for same period}}$$

Goal: to understand the needs of the marketplace and bring products to market quickly and innovatively. To show ratios >1.0.

$$\text{Packing asset flexibility} = \frac{\text{CV of packing room fixed assets (\$)}}{\text{number of different packs made this period}}$$

Goal: to have flexible packing assets able to make a variety of different packs.

Deming prize winners (Japanese company)

Product-based measures

- Market share.
- Market quality evaluation data.

Process-based measures

- New product sales (amount rate).
- Period for new product development.
- Number of design alterations.
- Enrichment of model assortment.
- Improvement in new product mass.
- Production start-up.
- Number of patent applications.

Case study 8: Measures in R&D at Dupont

Measures developed by the Imaging Systems Department (Research and Development Division) are based on a series of key processes:

1 R&D core processes
   - Human Development
   - Technology Planning and Development
   - Customer-Focused Innovation
   - Product and Process Design
   - Competitive Intelligence
   - Business Team Partnership.
2 Customer needs groups
   - people
   - standard R&D
   - OSHA
   - JIT manufacturing
   - process
   - product
   - innovation.

Measures related to the R&D process are referred to as *internal measures* while those related to customer needs are referred to as *external measures*.

Internal measures at Dupont

Human development: Dupont take into account the number of:

- courses taken per person
- accomplishment awards
- awards received (externally) organization's perception of appraisal system
- people actively involved in external professional organizations

- department and local initiatives
- people attending committee meetings
- courses approved compared with courses submitted
- degrees earned after employment
- formal university courses
- courses conducted on site.

Product and process design: yield

- number of vendors mill cost
- number of formal complaints
- number of raw materials/product type per cent of clean runs
- manufacturing cycle time (receipt of order to shipping)
- relative product quality = percentage of product line rated no. 1 or no. 2 by customers
- dollars sales new products last three years – profits
- time spent 'fire-fighting' new products and process ('hand holding')
- percentage coater downtime due to product/process problems
- number of process/product simplifications
- longevity of product versions
- effort before vs. effort after controlled sale
- shipping limits of material returned (how much was within specs vs. outside specs).

Business team partnership:

- number of people involved on business teams (horizontal integration)
- number of new product/process proposals
- number of team awards
- survey of business teams – how they value R&D participation.

Technology planning and development:

- number of long-term research programmes – need to define timing (active involvement in developing the programmes)
- number of patents issued
- number of 'core tech' programmes
- average time from idea conception (marketing/manufacturing request) to commercialization
- number of new or modified products and processes delivered
- number of technical publications and presentations external to IMG R&D.

Customer-focused innovation: laboratory programme cycle time

- number of SEED projects applied for
- number of successful SEED projects
- number of milestones achieved on time
- number of patent proposals
- number of new ventures initiated
- number of close customer partnerships
- number of new initiatives started
- number of differentiated products commanding price premium.

Competitive intelligence:

- number of competitive products analysed
- number products technology concepts
- number of patent and literature searches requested (need variable feedback loop)
- number of comprehensive competitive intelligence reports generated/ updated (business).

External key measures at Dupont

People:

- number of people actively participating in external professional societies
- number of external awards received (from groups outside IMG R&D).

Innovation:

- number of successful SEED projects
- number of new ventures initiated.

Product:

- number of raw materials
- number of vendors
- number of dollar sales of new products
- number of formal complaints.

Standard R&D:

- number of patents issued
- number of publications/presentations outside IMG R&D

- number of new products/processes
- time from product process conception to commercialization.

OSHA:

- volume of hazardous waste (solid, liquid, gaseous) plantwide.

JIT manufacturing:

- combined with process and product categories.

Process:

- yield
- mill cost
- manufacturing cycle time (raw materials shipping)
- percentage of clean runs (defect free).

Case study 9: Texas Instruments Europe

Texas Instruments uses a new product development process which has four main phases (Figure 9.11).

The process relies on the use of various tools to reduce the risk and help ensure that Designs are For Manufacturability. For instance, the use of feasibility studies and FMEA are quite common.

The process itself is streamlined to focus on the needs of customers and to meet requirements and expectations with great speed.

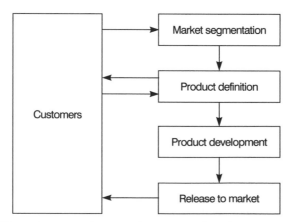

Figure 9.11 *Texas Instruments' approach to new product development*

The process relies on cross-functional team efforts. New products and new product families are defined by a global new product development team (NPDT).

Financial measures used in quantifying the contribution of innovation

Profitability ratios: Measure returns generated on sales or investment, often in comparison with industry standards. Examples include:

- profit margin on sales = net profit after taxes/sales
- return on total assets = net profit after taxes/total assets.

Activity ratios: These measure the use of resources and are best used in comparison with industry standards. Examples include:

- fixed asset turnover = sales/net fixed assets
- total asset turnover = sales/total assets
- average collection period = receivables/average sales per day
- inventory turnover = sales/inventory.

Project evaluation and comparison: These methods help to select among competing projects for the utilization of funds. They are particularly important to commercialization decisions as new products or processes are often easily conceptualized as the implementation of a project. The following are the two techniques used the most:

- The payback method calculates and compares the time to pay back initial investments for project alternatives. The more rapid the payback, the more desirable the project. The payback period is the time it takes a company to recover its original investment from net cash flows from the project.
- Discounted cash flow finds the present value of the expected net cash flows of an investment, discounted at the cost of capital. Net present value and internal rate of return project evaluation and comparison are types of discounted cash flow analysis. The advantage of these approaches is that they account for both the company's marginal cost of funds and the time profile of expected returns.

Auditing innovation for total effectiveness

There is a variety of tools that can be used for auditing innovation activity. This section discusses three specific tools which assess the effectiveness of innovation management in a pervasive and integrated manner. These are quality function deployment (QFD) and the 7Ss model.

Quality function deployment

Quality function deployment was developed in Japan in the late 1960s. Its purpose is to introduce quality in all aspects of innovation activity by starting with a clear understanding of customer wants.

Quality function deployment enables organizations to:

- deploy the 'voice of the customer' by specifically listing their wants and finding out what is important to them and in what order of priority
- translate customer wants and needs and ensuring that design parameters are up to set standards and target values
- optimize product and process design aspects to measure technical competitiveness and customer/market competitiveness
- feed back new learning and develop action plans for identified performance gaps.

As shown in Figure 9.12 (which relates to computer systems), QFD drills through the organization and drives the innovation process, from preliminary requirements all the way to product launch, support and post-launch review. At the heart of QFD is the building of the house of quality (Figure 9.13). The key elements of the house of quality (HOQ) include:

- the 'voice of customer' – wants list
- relationship matrix – interactions
- design requirements – 'hows' list

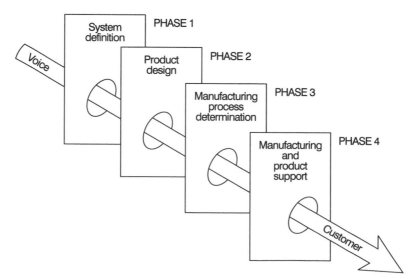

Figure 9.12 *QFD and value chain*

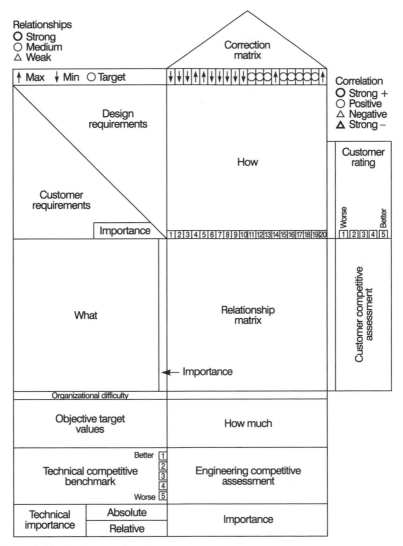

Figure 9.13 *The house of quality*

- technical comparisons – benchmarks
- target values
- market evaluation and benchmarking comparisons.

The roof of the house represents technical correlations between design parameters. The QFD houses can be replicated to cover other functional areas of innovation activity (Figures 9.14 and 9.15).

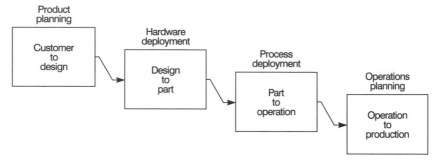

Figure 9.14 *QFD four-phase development*

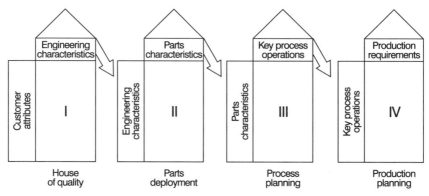

Figure 9.15 *Raked houses convey the consumer's voice through to manufacturing*

The benefits of QFD are very wide ranging. It helps to give feedback information on:

- customers' fulfilled and unfilled needs
- process strengths and weaknesses
- the level of innovating activity taking place
- competitor analysis
- achievements/performance standards.

Quality function deployment teaches people to start asking such questions as: 'Are we capable of giving customers what they want and need?' and 'How do we remain capable?' It also teaches people to stop saying: 'That is what we think the customer wants.' Quality function deployment stretches the quality standard to cover the following (Zairi, 1993):

- Expected quality: the bare minimum that the customer asked for and is willing to pay for. If undelivered, the customer will complain.
- Exciting quality: this is the aspect of quality that the customer wants but did not ask for. If delivered, the customer may not complain. However, if delivered, the customer will show delight and satisfaction.

See Chapter 5 for more information on QFD.

7Ss model

The 7Ss model, sometimes known as the McKinsey model, is based on the premise that for organizations to function effectively they have to rely on the interdependence of seven variables, all beginning with 's'.

- **strategy**: the plan leading to the allocation of resources
- **share values**: the goals shared by all employees
- **style**: the management style of the organization
- **structure:** the organizational map/chart
- **skills**: the strengths and capabilities of all employees
- **staff:** the people employed
- **systems**: procedures, guidelines and control mechanisms.

The seven variables are classified as *hardware variables* (strategy, structure) and *software variables* (style, systems, staff, skills and shared values).

The major contribution of the framework is the attention it draws to the less tangible, less visible aspects of organizational systems. As explained by Peters and Waterman (1982):

> In retrospect, what our framework has really done is to remind the world of professional managers that 'soft' is hard. It has enabled us to say, in effect, all that . . . you have been dismissing for so long as intractable, irrational, intuitive, informal organization can be managed. Clearly, it has as much or more to do with the way things work (or don't) around your companies as the formal structures and strategies do.

This was further explained by Waterman, Peters and Philips (1990):

> Our assertion is that productive organization change is not simply a matter of structure, although structure is important. It is not so simple as the interaction between strategy and structure, although strategy is critical too. Our claim is that effective organizational change is really the relationship between structure, strategy, systems, style, skills, staff, and something we call superordinate goals.

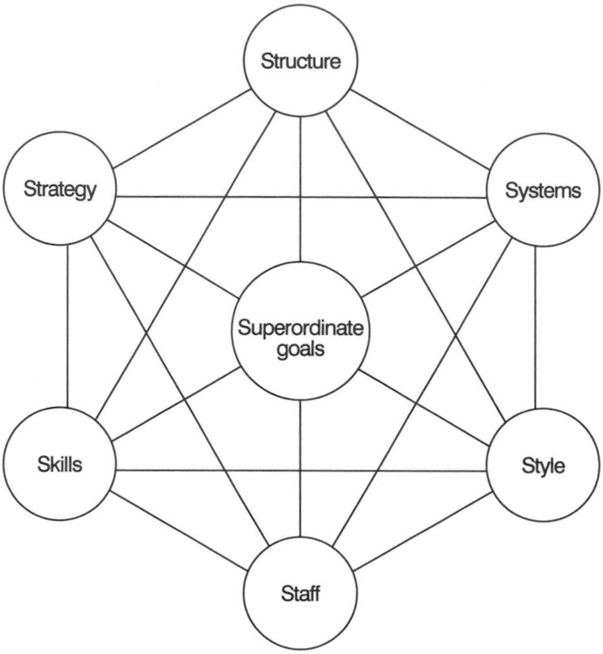

Figure 9.16 *The McKinsey model*

The McKinsey model (Figure 9.16) is sometimes referred to as the happy atom. It reflects the following characteristics:

- *multiplicity of factors* – they all influence how organizations behave
- interconnectedness of variables – progress can only be achieved by giving attention to all areas
- *all seven variables act as a driving force* – at particular points in time, one or more of the sevens will emerge as the most critical variable(s).

Applicability of the 7Ss model to the area of innovation

The 7S framework has been used very successfully in the area of innovation research. Work on innovation carried out by Pascale and Athos (1982) and later by Johne and Snelson (1988) was based on the 7Ss model. Indeed, innovation processes can be described by hard and soft organizational variables, as follows:

- *Strategy*: Is there a product development strategy that defines types of projects selected and the resources required?

- *Style*: Is there top management commitment and how much support is there from the top for new product development?
- *Shared values*: How much belief, enthusiasm and commitment is there for innovating activity?
- *Structure*: What lines of authority and responsibility are used for innovating activity?
- *Skills*: What specialist knowledge, tools and techniques are used for innovating activity?
- *Staff*: How much people involvement, empowerment, teamwork and degree of participation in decision-making is there in relation to product development?
- *Systems*: What procedures, guidelines and control mechanisms are used for managing innovation activity?

The Zairi benchmarking study of innovation processes

This study looked at innovation processes of twelve of the leading performers in European and world markets. An adaptation of the 7Ss model was used to develop a comprehensive benchmarking instrument (Zairi, 1994).

Using the 7Ss model criteria, a variety of good practices was identified covering many aspects of managing innovating activity:

1 Having top management playing a strategic role in directing, facilitating the allocation of resources and being active in reviewing and planning innovation activity.
2 Having innovation activity as an integral part of corporate strategy.
3 Top management commitment in creating a positive climate for innovation and activity supporting all the processes of innovation.
4 Having innovation as a voluntary activity, and a firm belief that innovation is vital to an organization's ability to remain competitive.
5 Having effective communication processes from the corporate level downwards, with clear objectives and a thorough understanding of the organizational goal. Communication also includes shares information on results and action plans.
6 Having a participative style of management, with a distributed approach to decision-making and full support from top management.
7 Having a project-based structure of managing innovation with multi-disciplinary teams, formal and informal reporting mechanisms and measurement.
8 Having project management driven by a thorough understanding of customer requirements, process capability and the organizational goal.
9 Organizations using all skills at their disposal effectively, as and when required.

10 Project management, not individually led, but driven by the creative contributions of all functions within the organization.
11 The use of modern tools and techniques in managing innovation activity.
12 Having systems that are vital to effective management of innovation activity and important for setting up the goals, managing the performance at individual project level and at business level.
13 Having systems in place to track down killer variables and to enable project leaders/teams/senior managers decide whether to terminate or proceed with projects.

The strategic deployment of performance measurement in innovation

Having covered the importance of applying measurement in the context of innovation management, the types of measurement to be used, how best in class organizations deploy measurement and examples of methodologies for auditing the process of innovation, it may now be worth putting together some guidelines on the effective cascading of measurement in the context of innovation.

When one refers to the application of measurement in relation to innovation activity, the type of measures to be used have to be:

• concerned with speed, cost and quality
• taken on a regular basis
• linked to innovation process rather than just concerned with outcomes only.

Outcomes have to be concerned with:

• the performance of products in terms of market share
• measuring worth in terms of differentiation/competitive advantage
• measuring cost in relation to the achieved benefits
• measuring financial worthiness.

The mix of performance measures that should be used can include the following areas.

1 *Time to market measures*: There are three recommended measures: the *speed* of innovation, carried out by monitoring the frequency of relaunches in each category; the *size* of the innovations, where the breakthroughs per period of time are measured, and the *effectiveness* of the various launches.

2 *Innovation impact measures*: These measures track the level of impact from each launch in terms of price premiums as a proportion of the total launches and also in terms of price premiums in relation to the total number of projects launched.
3 *Discipline of innovation*: These measures stop cannibalization and unnecessary launches (false innovation) through a clear demonstration of individual relaunch impact.

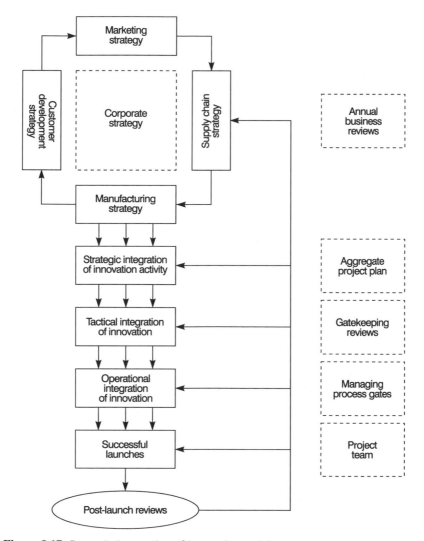

Figure 9.17 *Strategic integration of innovation activity*

4 *Cost management discipline*: Benefits to be passed on to the customer have to result from a commitment to continuous improvement and the use of quality tools and techniques to eliminate waste and optimize operations. Cost improvements per project will ensure that people will not carry on 'reinventing the wheel' and will seek to use new learning to be more efficient and effective.

5 *Advertising effectiveness*: This is to monitor the effectiveness of advertising by monitoring expenditure per brand and generated sales from each brand.

Table 9.3 *High-level performance measures for benchmarking*

Type of measure	Company I	Competitor A	Competitor B	Best in class
Percentage of sales from new products over past three years/total sales				
No. of relaunches/period time				
No. of breakthroughs/ total no. launches (per period time)				
Average time to market for a relaunch				
Average time to market for a breakthrough launch				
R&D yield = percentage of profit generated by amount of R&D investment/total amount of profit				
Resource allocated on R&D = percentage of expenditure on R&D/total amount of expenditure				
Rate of profitability by new products in a given period/total amount of profit in a given period				

6 *Resource implications of NPD*: This is to monitor the level of demand on resources at each stage of the innovation process.
7 *Work in progress*: This is to monitor the *flow* of innovation by monitoring work in progress and ensuring that bottleneck areas are dealt with.
8 *No project submissions per period of time:* This monitors the effectiveness of idea generation and the level of increase or otherwise of innovation activity.

Table 9.4 *High-level strategic measures*

Process	Measure	Frequency of reporting
Supply chain	• Capability improvement/target • Actual yield/planned • Cost improvement/target	Quarterly
Customer development	• New accounts/target • New business/target • Volumes	Quarterly
Brand development	• Brand performance/target • NPD rate/target	Quarterly
Human resource development	• No. trainee days/total no. employees • Total training budget/total employment expenditure • Total compensation cost/total revenues	Quarterly
Business performance	• Profitability • Growth • ROCE • ROI	1/2 yearly

Table 9.5 *Measures for project teams*

Measures for project teams

• Total cycle time (in months)
• Time/phase
• Time of approval at gates
• No. design changes cumulative cost of project/target cost
• Cost/phase vs. project cost

The effective deployment of the various categories of measures suggested must come through a proper framework, which links the translation of innovation activity from a strategic perspective (Figure 9.17).

The following stages would reflect a proper translation of corporate strategy and the carrying out of key activities supported by the most appropriate measures:

1 High-level (board level) measures for determining targets and developing the strategy.
2 High-level measures for innovation review group and the strategic planning group for tactical management.
3 Measures for the innovation process management to ensure that it gets improved and optimized.
4 Measures specifically recommended for project teams.
5 Audit reviews and regular benchmarking for measuring capability and competitiveness in relation to innovation activity.

Table 9.6 *Measures for innovation process*

Measures for innovation

- % NPD budget utilizing innovation process
- % New projects utilizing innovation processes
- % No/Go or hold between gates
- Project completion rate per period of time
- % Improvements in project lead time
- Number of new products released per period of time

Table 9.7 *Levels of ownership of measures*

Type of measures	Degree of reporting	Ownership level
Benchmarking	Yearly	Board
Business results	1/2 yearly	Board
Process measures (MACRO)	Quarterly	Board
Process measures (MICRO)	Monthly	Process director level
Project management measures	Bi-monthly	Innovation Review Group
Project management measures	Bi-monthly	Strategic Planning Group

Table 9.3 shows high-level performance measures for benchmarking, while Table 9.4 illustrates strategic measures. Table 9.5 lists measures for project teams, Table 9.6 measures for innovation processes and Table 9.7 the levels of ownership of measures.

References

Drucker, P. (1995) The information executives truly need. *Harvard Business Review*, **73**(1), 54–62.

Johne, A. and Snelson, P. C. (1988) Auditing product innovation activities in manufacturing firms. *R&D Management*, **18**(3), 227–33.

Lingle, J. H. and Schiemann, W. A. (1996) From balanced scorecard to strategic gauges: is measurement worth it? *Management Review*, March, 56–61.

Pascale, R. T. and Athos, A. G. (1982) *The Art of Japanese Management.* Penguin.

Peters, T. J. and Waterman, R. H. (1982) *In Search of Excellence.* Harper and Row.

Plsek, P. E. (1997) Creativity, innovation and quality. In *ASQC Quality Press*, Milwaukee,

Waterman, R. H., Peters, T. J. and Philips, J. R. (1980) Structure is not organisation. *Business Horizons*, June, 14–26.

Zairi, M. (1993) *Quality Function Deployment: a Modern Competitive Tool.* TQM Practitioner Series, Technical Communications.

Zairi, M. (1994) *Practical Benchmarking: the Complete Guide.* Chapman and Hall.

10 Being a world-class organization – what does it mean?

Kate Blackmon, Phil Hanson, Chris Voss and Frances Wilson

This chapter examines how the competitiveness of manufacturing companies has typically been assessed using high-level financial and economic measures, which are proxies for managerial inputs and outputs. An alternative method is to examine the operational practices and performances that are driving the competitiveness of individual manufacturers. These practices and performances need to be referenced to a so-called 'world-class' scale against which manufacturing companies can be benchmarked and towards which they must progress if they are to be competitive in the global market of the late twentieth century.

World-class manufacturing is considered as a point at which a certain standard of practice and performance has been obtained, equalling or surpassing the very best of the international competitors in every area of a company's business, such that the company has achieved international leadership and success.

The components of a model for benchmarking world-class status, developed by IBM and London Business School (LBS) and drawing on the ethos of the European Foundation for Quality Management (EFQM), Baldrige and so-called 'Japanese' manufacturing are presented, the central hypothesis being that the implementation of best practice leads to superior business performance and customer satisfaction.

The chapter illustrates how the technique of 'best practice benchmarking' can offer a significant insight into the workings of an individual site as well as the competitiveness of sector and national manufacturing capability, the latter through European manufacturing studies in which the model is applied. For individual sites, the critical factors necessary for achieving world-class status are dependent on a company's current practice and performance.

The chapter also shows that, because the goal of achieving and maintaining world-class manufacturing capability is a continuously moving target, it is essential to examine every element of the model of 'best practice' to ensure that it reflects the true state of the art.

Introduction

The competitiveness of manufacturing companies has typically been assessed using high-level financial and economic measures which are proxies for managerial inputs and outputs. An alternative method is to examine the operational practices and performances which are driving the competitiveness of individual manufacturers. These practices and performances need to be referenced to a so-called 'world-class' scale against which manufacturing companies can be benchmarked and towards which they must progress if they are to be competitive in the global market of the late twentieth century.

Such an examination of operational practices and performances forms the basis of the 'Made in Britain' and 'Made in Europe' studies undertaken by the LBS and the IBM Consulting Group. The goal was to test just how far European manufacturing companies had progressed in implementing 'best practice', and to see what results they had consequently achieved. Implicit in this was the assumption that the constituents of 'world-class best practice' could be defined. One source of such confidence was from the simple observation that the much documented picture of Japanese manufacturing practices is found on the book shelves of so many companies. Another source of confidence came from the internal benchmarking that has been common practice in the IBM plants.

These studies have subsequently expanded and have been branded as a benchmarking tool known as PROBE (PROmoting Business Excellence) which is offered by the Confederation of British Industry (CBI) as a service to its member and non-member companies.

The notion of world-class manufacturing

In recent years, manufacturing companies have had to change in order to compete in an increasingly global market in which manufacturing practices/techniques have become an important means of operating in order to reduce time to market (TTM), meet customer requirements, reduce/eliminate wastage and control and reduce costs. If companies are to compete successfully, implementation of so-called 'best practice' or 'world-class' manufacturing techniques is an essential, though not a sufficient, criterion for driving operational and ultimately business performance.

World-class manufacturing is the point at which a certain standard of practice and performance has been obtained, equalling or surpassing the very best of the international competitors in every area of a company's business such that the company has achieved international leadership and success. Companies that have not attained these standards will have varying difficulties in competing in the current global business environment.

With time, however, the definition of 'world class' and its component practice and performance standards will change as competitive advantage and differentiation will no longer be possible from the existing practices. The route from a company's current position to that of the moving and ever more demanding target of 'world class' may therefore be considered as a journey of continuous development and change. Determining a company's position on this journey in both absolute terms and relative to the rest of the manufacturing industry may be used to provide an agenda for the required change.

It should be considered that future world-class techniques will build on those of the past and present and will represent the foundations for future developments. Therefore it is inadvisable for a company to attempt to leap-frog existing practices in order to reduce the time taken to adopt future practices.

A model for benchmarking world-class status

It was not the intention of IBM and the LBS to create the definitive model for world-class manufacturing. Many perfectly sound conceptual models already exist in the publications of manufacturing authors, consultants and government reports. The high-level quality templates such as the Malcolm Baldrige American National Quality Award and the EFQM provide conceptual frameworks for world-class business operation.

The goal was to find a simple framework against which to test best practice but also one that would be consistent with the much published picture of Japanese manufacturing while fitting closely to the customer-driven quality ethos of Baldrige and EFQM. Indeed, it was planned that results from benchmarking specific manufacturing sites should be capable of use in the provision of trend data in any quality accreditation submission.

The key components of the model are characterized as follows (Figure 10.1):

- **Organization and culture**: with obvious leadership from the chief executive, a clear vision for the business is jointly developed and shared throughout the site. Employees are inspired to follow the direction set and are encouraged and trained to take responsibility for its achievement. The measurement of the business is displayed for all to see.
- **Logistics**: relationships with suppliers are built on the assumption of lasting partnerships. The benefits of joint activity leading to lower total supply chain costs are shared. Outbound logistics are capable of delivery into, for example, highly variable just-in-time retailers.

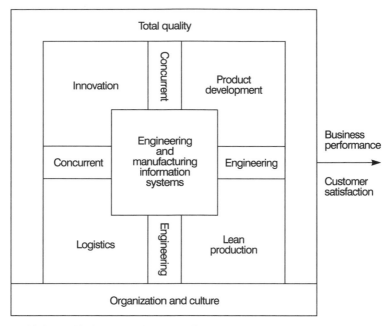

Figure 10.1 *World-class manufacturing, best practice model*

- **Manufacturing systems**: information technology systems are integrated so that the design process delivers a workable bill of materials to the planning process; for example, CAD and CAM can realistically be spoken of in the same breath. Business management system schedules are trusted and acted upon without need for local modification.
- **Lean production**: every aspect of the manufacturing process that adds cost but not value has been systematically eliminated (e.g. unnecessary movement, counting, inspection, paperwork etc.).
- **Concurrent engineering**: the design and development process involves suppliers and customers as well as manufacturing and sales teams. The product will not only meet customer requirements but will also enable optimum manufacturing and distribution.
- **Total quality**: with all business processes sharply focused on meeting and exceeding customer expectations, a spirit of continuous improvement pervades the entire business.
- **Product development**: occurs within empowered project teams using well-defined reproducible processes which incorporate continuous improvement achieving >20 per cent per annum cycle time improvements.
- **Innovation**: is considered as part of the organization's culture and is encouraged with customers being involved in the development of concepts.

Typically there have been significant/radical changes introduced into the product line with 50 per cent of sales from products in the first quarter of their life cycle.

The central hypothesis of this model is that the implementation of these best practices is linked directly to the attainment of improvements in process and business performance and also to increased customer satisfaction ultimately in the form of 'delighted' customers.

The model has been used to measure practice and performance of manufacturing sites against a world-class scale as part of the Made in Europe studies in which:

• Practices refer to the established processes that a company has put in place to improve the way it runs its manufacturing business. They range from organizational aspects such as empowerment to the use of techniques such as lean production.
• Performance may be defined as the measurable results of a company's processes, such as work in progress and production cycle time and also to the business impact such as market share and customer satisfaction.

It also enables the grouping of companies with similar characteristics in order to define 'generic' business agendas, which can assist and direct the change process necessary for attaining world-class status.

The Made in Europe study

The first phase of this project was undertaken in the UK and involved the benchmarking of approximately 200 manufacturing sites. The results of this phase were published in June 1993 in a report entitled *Made in Britain – the True State of British Manufacturing Industry* (Hanson and Voss, 1993). Subsequent phases in Germany and The Netherlands were similarly published during 1994. A consolidated report, a four nations study published in November 1994 (Voss et al., 1994), also incorporated the results from a smaller project in Finland. At the time of publishing the four nations study, over 700 site visits had been made across the four countries.

The initial manufacturing focus of the project was extended to include engineering and design issues resulting in the publication of another study in April 1996 (Voss et al., 1996a) in which the findings of visiting approximately 120 sites in each country were summarized. National, trade and local press coverage has been extensive following the publication of each phase.

Since the publication of the Made in Europe studies the coverage of the database has been extended. There have been more than 1,000 sites surveyed and additional projects are active in Canada, South Africa and India. Work is also planned in the USA and Asia Pacific regions so that the European results can be tested against this wider international context.

In addition, a separate but very similar initiative known as Microscope was developed in 1996 with European funding. In contrast to Made in Europe and PROBE, which are focused on companies with more than 100 employees, Microscope is targeted at companies with fewer than fifty employees. The project is administered by the West London Training and Enterprise Council (WLTEC) who together with an increasing number of Training and Enterprise Councils (TECs) and Business Links provide the channel to market for this tool. WLTEC is part of the Transnational Consortium, which comprises similar representatives from Belgium, Eire, Germany, Italy and Sweden. It is anticipated that by year end there will be a database in excess of 300 companies drawn from surveys in the five countries.

Motives and objectives

The objective of the study was to establish a large-scale benchmarking database that would enable the testing of best practice implementation and results against representative international samples. It was already clear in 1992 that benchmarking would become a widely used tool in business process improvement and that for this to be really valuable it must be conducted well beyond the UK boundaries of the first phase. Regular reference to the world-class statistics in the business press suggests that the benchmarking approach has filled a void in the measurement of industrial capability, enabling the focus to be moved away from macroeconomic indicators.

It has also been beneficial as a public relations vehicle increasing companies' awareness of the IBM Consulting Group and establishing relationships with manufacturing leaders.

In addition, identification of the real issues affecting manufacturing companies enabled the development and alignment of the capabilities of the IBM Consulting Group as closely as possible with the needs of the industry. This is interestingly different from the conventional view that a market-driven business listens and responds to the wants of its customers.

A further objective was the development of a diagnostic tool that would enable manufacturing sites to assess their starting point in the journey to 'world class'. An agenda for change must depend not only on a vision of the end point but also an understanding of the start point.

Project partnerships

In moving the study to other countries in Europe, academic partnerships similar to that between IBM and LBS have been established with the

Universities of Regensburg and Eindhoven, the Helsinki Institute of Economics and IMD in Switzerland.

As the project expanded in the UK it became necessary to establish a new channel to market with resources to meet the increasing demand for the benchmarking activity. This led, in November 1995, to the establishment of a partnership between IBM and the CBI who now market the project which they branded 'PROBE' to both their member and non-member companies. They undertake the benchmarking assessments and provide the results to IBM who maintain a current international database.

As the geographic coverage of the project extends, a similar model of IBM, the University and Trade Association is being applied in various forms in each country in which it operates.

Finding participants

Essential to the success of any project aimed at testing the state of the manufacturing industry was a sample both large enough and representative enough for meaningful conclusions to be drawn. The hypotheses established already pointed to the need for a mix of sizes, geographic location and industry sectors.

It was also important that the companies taking part should represent a typical mixture of maturity in best practice usage and therefore the use of IBM's customer base as a source of sample was rejected. Other parameters were emerging as important; in particular, many of the theories of industrial success were beginning to hinge on the supply chain in which companies were participating. A number of methods was used to ensure that a random sample was obtained and also that sector minimum sample sizes were achieved (Figures 10.2 and 10.3).

The benchmarking process

From the outset it was clear that the design of scripts would demand that the process of completing them would require facilitation. This ensures that:

- the subtlety of the questions could be described and explored
- the experience of taking part could be one in which there is inherent added value
- the context of the questions could be interpreted for the industry concerned.

The overall approach was therefore neither that of a widescale telephone survey of personal opinions nor that of a detailed process benchmark such as those that exist for comparing the performance of particular plant and machinery within an industry sector.

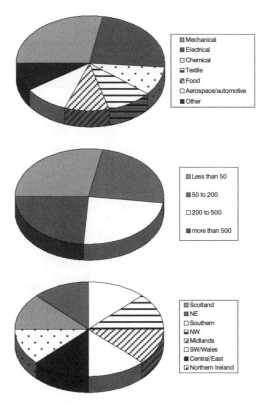

Figure 10.2 *Phase One UK sample sizes*

Since the goal was to test the implementation of best practice across industry sectors, it was assumed that there was potentially much to learn from experience which, while typical in one sector, was less utilized in another – for example, quick response logistics in the food and apparel industries or 'lean production' in electronic and motor industries.

Since implementation of best practice occurs at the site level, the focus of the study was at each site rather than at divisional or headquarters level. Initial targeting of the process to involve senior executives has been substituted by the involvement of a 'diagonal slice' of the organization in the form of a cross-functional, multilevel team. The latter is considered to balance the potential for a 'rose-tinted glasses' view, which the former could incur. Provision of the scripts to the team prior to the facilitation visit enables their completion. The subsequent visit incorporates a factory tour and group discussion to validate the results before the presentation of results and a discussion of an agenda for change (action plan) to address issues highlighted by the assessment.

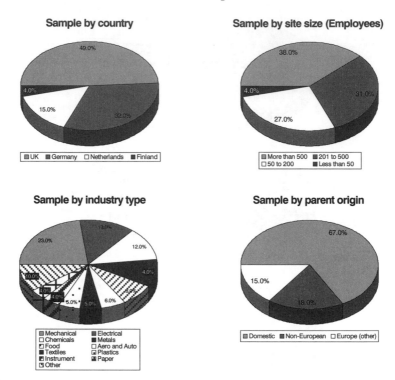

Figure 10.3 *European sample by nation, size and industry sector*

Benchmarking scripts

The scripts were designed to enable assessment by the company against each of the elements of the world-class model. Within each element of the model a series of questions, requiring a numeric response from one to five, test either the degree of implementation of best practice or the level of benefit/ performance achieved. The progress from one to five is characterized in three scenario descriptions representing the business journey involved in which typically a score of five will require measurement evidence. In addition, the scripts include questions that determine the site characteristics and opinions on associated issues (Figure 10.4).

It is important to note that with the exception of two questions relating to vision, the site is assessing its current status and not some desired future status.

The following extract from the 'Organization and Culture' section of the script offers an example of the scenarios:

1	Vision	Maximize product output; managers dictate direction; cost reduction key goal	Customer service, emphasis; employee involvement; quality and cycle times are key drivers	Leadership in quality and service; production balanced with customer needs; production cycle time less than order lead time
2	Shared vision, mission and goals	Insufficient direction; no shared plan or vision statement; employees do not understand goals	Management commitment to shared vision; written mission statement; some employee involvement	Total employee involvement; published improvement plan; individuals and dept's. have vision matching company's
3	Manufacturing strategy	Framed in Output and Cost targets, less than one year horizon	Functional strategy for manufacturing, 1–3 year horizon	Business led manufacturing strategy with strong links to corporate plan, 3–5 year horizon
10	Problem-solving	Crisis mindset, confusion, finger pointing	System for recognizing and responding to problems, emphasis on process not people, teamwork	Problems viewed as opportunities for further improvement, employees empowered to correct
11	Design process	Design department sole responsibility	Team-based involving Manufacturing	Customer driven including manufacturing, marketing and suppliers

Figure 10.4 *Benchmarking scripts*

The following questions ask you to position your site on a 1 to 5 scale against a variety of attributes. Three descriptions are provided, which characterize scores of 1, 3 and 5 respectively. If you are unable, or do not wish to answer, enter a '0'.

Where you see differences across the organization, where some areas are more advanced than others, it is best to assess an average position. For example, a pilot implementation does not warrant a score of '5'. We seek to assess the status today, not where it will be when current plans and projects deliver their expected results. Benchmarking will only ever be of value if the assessments are true reflections of the practices and performance of the organization.

Data analysis

The key question which the initial study sought to answer related to determining the proportion of British Manufacturing sites are employing world-class best practice.

Clearly, the sample was designed to enable comparisons by sector, geographic location and size of site. In addition, specific tests were devised to assess the effect of purchasing power, ownership, ISO 9000 implementation, export activity, breadth of best practice, MRPII usage and relationships with the Japanese and American transplants.

The scores from each question were used to construct indices, which measure different aspects of site practice and performance – for example, quality, lean production and logistics in addition to overall scores.

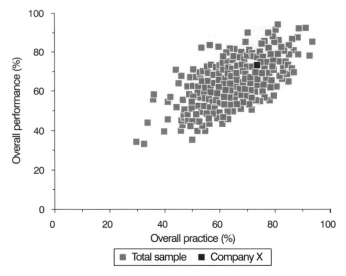

Figure 10.5 *Practice vs. performance scatter chart*

The basic test of validity of the model was to correlate those questions relating to implementation of best practice against the questions relating to performance, a technique used extensively throughout the analysis. Thus it was proved that more than 50 per cent of the variation in performance could be accounted for by variations in practice. The resulting typical scatter graph looks as shown in Figure 10.5.

The data was also tested by examining the distribution of the range of scores for each question to ensure that the expected normal distribution resulted. Additional rigorous statistical testing confirmed the reliability and validity of the model and its associated indices.

Is European manufacturing world class?

After examination of other international studies and a careful assessment of the question scripts, it was proposed that sites exhibiting better than 80 per cent practice and 80 per cent performance should be designated as 'world class'. As the study is extended into other countries so it is increasingly possible to assess just what it takes to be internationally ahead of the rest.

A boxing analogy was used to characterize the rough and tumble of industrial life and define companies by their practice and performance scores:

- **World class:** those with both practice and performance better than 80 per cent turned out to be just 2 per cent of the original sample. These companies have adopted a range of best practice and achieved high operational performance. They are capable of competing with the best of the world's manufacturers.

- **Contenders:** a healthy 46 per cent of the companies studied had practice and performance better than 60 per cent. This group, being well positioned to achieve world class, is clearly a source of optimism about the condition of European manufacturing. These companies have the potential to compete internationally.
- **Promising:** some 19 per cent of sites had put in place 60 per cent or more of the practices but had yet to enjoy performance benefits to the same level. This is, of course, entirely plausible in that the benefits of total quality management, for example, could take years to show in strong business benefits. None the less, these sites have the essential foundations for long-term competitiveness and could translate their efforts into results.
- **Will not go the distance**: these 9 per cent of sites have apparently better than 60 per cent performance scores but without the enduring best practice to the same level. It is possible, for example, to deliver quality output by inspecting every item that leaves the line. This is not, however, the basis of long-term competitiveness in many industries. They appear to be ahead of the game but may be vulnerable and unable to sustain the performance. In these companies insufficient time and effort have been invested in the training and practice development required.
- **Makeweights**: some 20 per cent of sites show both practice and performance in the 50–60 per cent range. They will struggle with real international competition and are typically in market niches that are in some way protected. These companies lack both the practice and performance needed to compete internationally and hence radical changes in management and practices will be required if they are to succeed.
- **Punchbags**: there were 4 per cent of sites showing practice and performance below 50 per cent, for whom the business strategy must be one of 'survival' (Figures 10.6 and 10.7).

The picture that emerges shows that approximately 2 per cent of European sites meet the world-class criteria and almost 50 per cent are well positioned to get there. This is a basis for optimism, although not complacency, as it should be remembered that the last part of the journey is the hardest and is towards a rapidly moving target.

Of particular concern in the UK is the long tail of low practice and performance sites (Figure 10.8). Much progress has been made, thanks to the positive effects of inward investment pulling best practice through the supply chain in the UK. However, the sites at the low end of the spectrum rarely see US or Japanese customers and as such never benefit from the best practice above them.

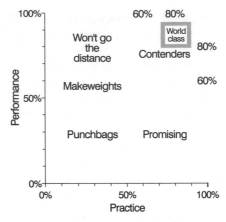

Figure 10.6 *Segmenting the sites by practice and performance*

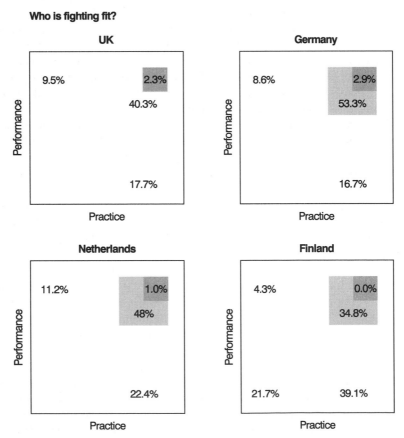

Figure 10.7 *European sites: who is fighting fit?*

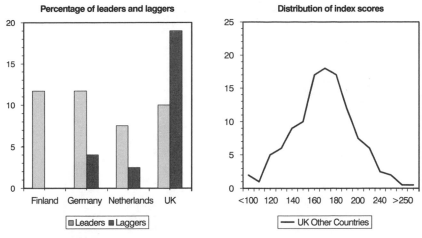

Figure 10.8 *The UK tail of low performers*

A sense of realism?

Participants were also asked for their personal views as to how close to being internationally competitive they perceived themselves to be and how long they believed it would take them to become world class. When asked a specific question on current international competitiveness, the results were strongly optimistic, as shown in Figure 10.9.

When these results are compared to their actual practice and performance results, there is evidently a higher level of self-opinion than the best practice levels suggest is reasonable. To test this picture further, the scores of the group who considered themselves to be already globally competitive were plotted according to their practice/performance scores, indicating that they were spread across the entire range of capabilities from punchbag to world class. This discrepancy between self-perception and reality clearly points to the need for the widescale use of benchmarking as a basis for objective comparison.

The other observation that can be drawn is that those who have already achieved high levels of practice are the most realistic about their position, while at lower levels the perception gap is most marked, as shown in Figure 10.10. In addition, these managers fail to realize that world-class status is a rapidly moving target.

National characteristics

By separating out those aspects of practice and performance that are more than 5 per cent different from the average, it is possible to indicate areas of national strengths or weaknesses. In the UK, for example, the management of

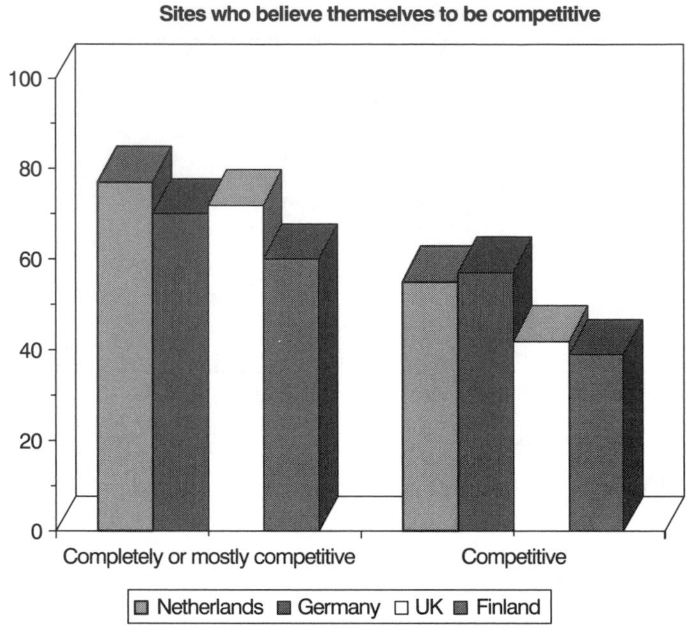

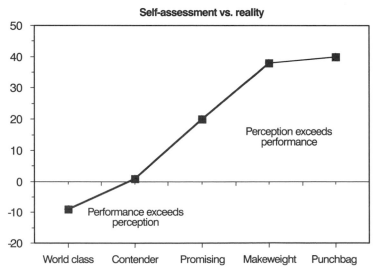

Figure 10.9 *To what extent to you consider yourself able to compete successfully with the best of your international competitors anywhere in the world?*

Figure 10.10 *Self-assessment vs. reality*

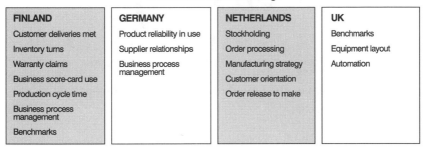

More than 5% above the average

FINLAND	GERMANY	NETHERLANDS	UK
Competitive cost	Benchmarks	Production cycle time	Supplier relationships
Equipment layout	Automation	Training	Business process management
Stockholding	Concurrent engineering	Warranty claims	Product reliability
Information systems	Equipment layout	Cash flow	
Preventive maintenance	Employee involvement		
Market share			
Manufacturing strategy			

More than 5% below the average

FINLAND	GERMANY	NETHERLANDS	UK
Customer deliveries met	Product reliability in use	Stockholding	Benchmarks
Inventory turns	Supplier relationships	Order processing	Equipment layout
Warranty claims	Business process management	Manufacturing strategy	Automation
Business score-card use		Customer orientation	
Production cycle time		Order release to make	
Business process management			
Benchmarks			

Figure 10.11 *National strengths and weaknesses*

supplier relationships may well have benefited from the Japanese and US inward investment; the highest national promotion of ISO 9000 may be the reason for a more widespread understanding of the management of business processes, while a high commitment to excellence in service may be related to the apparent strength in product reliability in service.

Interestingly, the German reputation for high-quality delivered products is not reflected in the views of manufacturing executives in this sample. In addition, German strengths and weaknesses are nearly the exact opposite to those in the UK (Figure 10.11).

When asked about their business priorities, it emerges that UK and Finnish sites are clearly customer service focused while German and Dutch sites are strongly product focused. In every country the availability of skilled manpower is cited as an inhibitor to achieving world-class status while commitment to investing in people as a business strategy is, on the other hand, often a medium or low priority.

The supply chain effect

In the UK sample, one of the areas explored was the hypothesis that there would be practice and performance differences between sites who are

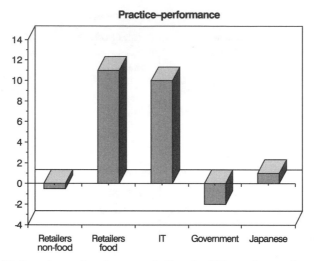

Figure 10.12 *Practice and performance indices for UK suppliers to large organizations*

suppliers to different major purchasers; this leads to the results depicted in Figure 10.12.

The companies in the information technology industry, typically US parented, who have been manufacturing in the UK for twenty years or more and who have adopted very open partnership sourcing strategies, have spawned a set of suppliers who exhibit both practice and performance that is almost identical to their customers.

That this is not yet obvious in the sites supplying the UK/Japanese inward investment sites is surely just a matter of time. It is salutary, however, to understand just how long these influences take to become evident.

Suppliers to the dominant food retailers show high performance but not the same apparent adoption of enduring best practice, perhaps due to the adversarial purchasing relationships that have existed. If the capability of the supplier is taken as the yardstick, it does appear that manufacturers can make better buyers than retailers. No wonder that the retail sector shows such strong interest in partnership sourcing procurement strategies.

The effect of site size

The practice and performance of different sizes of European site, in terms of the number of people employed on the site, shows an interesting pattern as outlined in Figure 10.13.

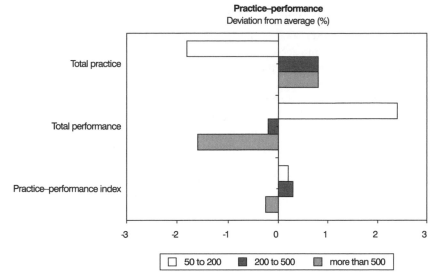

Figure 10.13 *Practice and performance indices for sites of different sizes*

Increasing size demands increasing process and procedures. Hence, in the smallest sites the need to establish company-wide processes to deliver best practice is typically unnecessary. As the site size increases above fifty employees, the data suggests they are increasingly likely to be adopting best practice. It also, however, suggests that the relative benefits being derived diminish as the site gets bigger.

In addition, as manufacturing site size increases, the numbers of management levels increase and organizational functions and departments gain increasing independence. These factors represent an inertia to change and an internal friction which must first be overcome by any attempt to implement best practice.

In the sites where world-class best practice has been established with faith and passion by executives who have discovered it for themselves and without corporate interference, the effect is inevitably far stronger than in similar sites where progress is driven by corporate energy from above. This, too, appears to favour the smaller, often independent sites.

In contrast, the subsequent Anglo-German design study (Voss et al., 1996b) indicated that design practice and performance are highest at sites with more than 500 employees, suggesting the existence of economies of scale in the overall design process. Small sites may therefore lack the human and technology resources necessary to manage world-class processes for innovation and product development.

ISO 9000 as a guide to quality practice

The promotion of ISO 9000 in the UK has been extensive with the numbers of companies achieving accreditation well ahead of the rest of Europe. Key to the hypotheses tested in the UK phase of Made in Europe was an understanding of the business benefit which has been gained in manufacturing sites by this clear time advantage.

When sites were listed in sequence of their overall practice and performance index, the top twenty were grouped and described as 'leaders', while the bottom twenty were similarly grouped and labelled as 'laggers'. Using the quality performance index as the vertical axis and a knowledge of which sites had achieved ISO 9000 accreditation as the horizontal axis, it was possible to plot the leaders and laggers into the four quadrants shown in Figure 10.14.

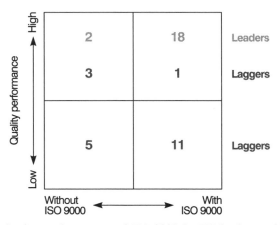

Figure 10.14 *Quality performance and ISO 9000 for UK leaders and laggers*

Of the top twenty sites, which all show high-quality performance, all but two have sought and achieved ISO 9000 accreditation. Among the twenty laggers, all but four have low quality performance. Of these sixteen low quality laggers, eleven have none the less achieved ISO 9000. It might then be concluded that ISO 9000 is perhaps necessary but not sufficient for quality performance.

Experience of those seeking to conform to ISO 9000 appears to include those for whom it has been a great voyage of discovery of the horizontal business processes that flow through the departments of the company and deliver customer service. For others it appears to have been a less inspiring experience of documenting procedures for the first time. What is clear is that sites who have high-quality performance and strong customer focus have done far more than simply meet ISO 9000 requirements.

Sector differences

A world-class site might be expected to represent electronics factories in green field sites with Japanese ownership and significant recent investment. In fact, as shown in Figure 10.15, world-class sites are found in every sector and with every nationality of ownership.

Chemicals	2
Electronics	1
Instruments	1
Machinery	4
Metal products	1
Plastics	2
Textiles	2
Food	1

Figure 10.15 *World-class manufacturers are found in every sector*

The idea that best practice can be learnt by one sector from another has often been argued and there are many intrepid benchmarking teams that make a positive virtue out of unlikely and unexpected sources of process comparison. In this project, the options were examined by listing the areas where sectors appear to have relative strengths and weaknesses. As well as confirming the potential benefits of the not uncommon practice of electronics sites benchmarking against food companies, for example Figure 10.16 suggests some rather less obvious places for benchmarking exploration.

Is manufacturing best practice enough?

One of the common observations offered has been that sites with world-class manufacturing best practice may not be internationally competitive if their products don't meet customer requirements in a cost-effective manner. Innovation – the generation of new product ideas – and product design and development – the conversion of the ideas into products ready for the

Sector	Relative strengths	Relative weaknesses	Benchmark sector?
Chemical	Training Product reliability Deliveries met	Cycle time Stockholding Design process	Textiles
Electrical	Preventative maintenance Information systems Equipment changeover	Deliveries met New product yield Cycle times	Food & drink
Food & drink	Cycle times Inventory turns Deliveries met	Batch sizes Business management Preventative maintenance	Electrical
Instrumentation	Equipment layout Stockholding Business process management	Order processing Warranty claims New product yield	Rubber & plastics
Mechanical	Stockholding Batch size Information systems	Warranty claims Product reliability Order processing	Paper & wood
Metals	New product yield Product reliability Order processing	Priority orders Cycle time Training	Chemical
Paper & wood	Order processing Supplier lead times Customer deliveries	Scrap/Rework Defects Batch sizes	Mechanical
Rubber & plastics	Warranty claims Order processing Priority orders	Cycle times Stockholding Scrap & rework	Aero/Auto
Textiles	Customer orientation Order processing New product yield	Defects Equipment layout Business process management	Instrumentation
Aero/Auto	Stockholding Kanban Supplier relationships	Cycle times Housekeeping Equipment changeover	Textiles

Figure 10.16 *Relative strengths and weaknesses by sector*

marketplace – are, of course, equally key aspects which were addressed in the Anglo-German design comparison undertaken in Made in Europe II.

An Anglo-German comparison of design

The long tail of poor performers existing in UK manufacturing does not appear to be present in design and innovation. It is evident, however, that in design, Germany has a lead over the UK (Figure 10.17), with 9 per cent of the German sites having world-class design practices and performances compared with only 3 per cent of UK sites in this category.

A number of areas deserve highlighting in terms of the gaps that exist between the practices adopted in the two countries. The widest gap is in monitoring the cost of developing new products. Given the high employment costs (wages plus social costs) that German firms face, it is not surprising that they have adopted practices to track design errors and rework costs. Conversely, UK firms, with lower labour costs, are under less pressure to

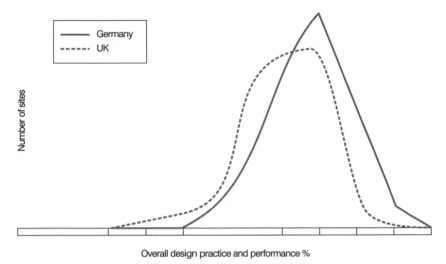

Overall design practice and performance %

Figure 10.17 *An Anglo-German comparison of design practice/performance*

understand exactly where costs are incurred in the product development cycle. German firms also place greater emphasis on allocation of resources and pay significantly more attention to design for production, providing another source of cost reduction.

German firms are significantly ahead in some aspects of applying new technology to the way they work. This lead is apparent in a wider use of computer-aided engineering and design tools and in the communication of data internally and externally via integrated systems.

The data did not support the statement that the UK does not value engineering enough. The great majority of UK manufacturers, 72 per cent, indicated that they consider engineering to be vital to innovation and only 7 per cent view engineering as just another overhead expense. This positive attitude is slightly stronger among German firms.

Additional questions were asked of the German managers concerning their perceptions of national strengths and weaknesses in design. They consider their key problem areas to be cost, labour flexibility, over-regulation and over-taxation. They see their strengths primarily in terms of the technology interaction and infrastructure available to firms in Germany.

The UK has been aggressively trying to create a more flexible, deregulated and lower tax environment than its counterparts in the rest of Europe. Despite British success in creating a positive economic climate, many organizations would like to see Britain copy Germany's infrastructure for developing and exchanging technical skills and knowledge.

Quality awards

The European and British Quality Awards (EQA/BQA) model is increasingly being used as a template for assessing a company's overall business excellence. Its fundamental premise is that excellence in the 'enablers' will lead to superior results in terms of employee and customer satisfaction, impact on society and business results, i.e. the same link between practice and performance that underlies the Made in Europe studies.

The processes examined by these studies include many of the key enablers in a manufacturing site, together with the key measures of operating and business results. It is therefore possible to evaluate the data collected using the EQA/BQA model, thus providing the opportunity to evaluate the model's effectiveness in manufacturing and design.

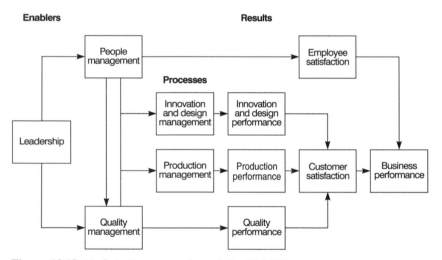

Figure 10.18 *Made in Europe results and the EQA/BQA*

The evaluation results shown in Figure 10.18 provide strong support for the EQA/BQA model. The lines illustrate where the relationships in the model are most strongly supported, with the width of the lines indicating the strength of the relationship. Overall, business performance is found to be strongly related to each of the enablers and performance measures.

Process excellence and performance were linked in both manufacturing and design. There was a clear relationship between leadership and both quality and people management – supporting the view that a lack of executive leadership often causes failure of total quality management.

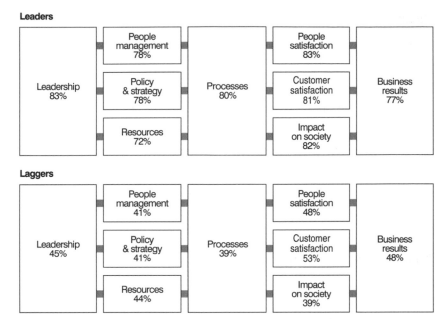

Figure 10.19 *Leaders (top 10 per cent of EQA/BQA score) and laggers (bottom 10 per cent of EQA/BQA score)*

There was a strong and important link between people management and quality management. In turn, quality management underlies both manufacturing and design performance. A key route to design excellence may therefore be via quality management.

The Made in Europe data can be used to measure both the enablers – in particular core processes – and their impact on manufacturing and design performance and subsequently to estimate a site's likely EQA/BQA standing based on manufacturing and engineering processes. The estimated scores for the leaders and laggers of the sample are shown in Figure 10.19.

The drivers of competitiveness

Figure 10.20 represents a model of international competitiveness with four of its key drivers – manufacturing capability, design, costs and investment.

As indicated previously, apart from the long tail, the UK's manufacturing capability is similar to Germany's but Germany holds a lead in design. Regarding investment, indicators such as the level of implementation of systems in both manufacturing and design point to a German lead. Finally, German companies report higher cost levels than those in the UK – any

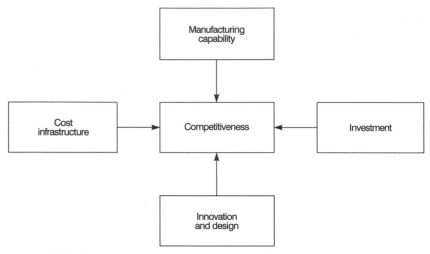

Figure 10.20 *Drivers of competitiveness*

productivity differences not being enough to overcome the high costs of labour.

Overall the UK leads Germany in one of the drivers of competitiveness, is virtually equal in one and behind in two. The relative competitiveness will depend ultimately on the markets in which a company operates. In some markets the key basis of competitiveness is price; in others it is manufacturing capability such as quality, responsiveness and service, while in others it is based on the technical performance of the products.

For companies in Germany, addressing costs is central to increasing international competitiveness. For UK companies, design is key to increasing competitiveness relative to Germany. In addition, UK companies need to raise levels of investment. In both countries, with most companies still far from world class, there is a need to improve practice and performance in all areas of design and manufacturing.

Critical factors for being world class

Interpreting the results for individual sites

In addition to the boxing analogy presented earlier, a rugby ball analogy can be used to describe the different starting points for the European manufacturing sites aiming to achieve a world-class position, depending on their current practice/performance positioning (Figure 10.21).

By examining each of these groups, it is possible to understand which agenda for change they should pursue in seeking to make the journey to a world-class position.

Different agenda for Change

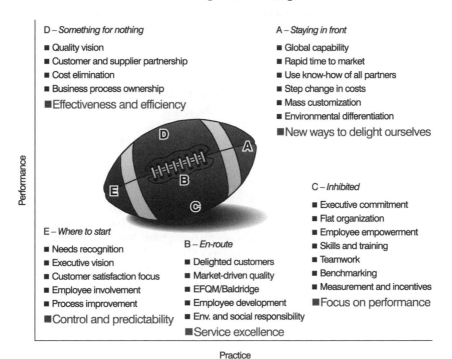

D – *Something for nothing*
- Quality vision
- Customer and supplier partnership
- Cost elimination
- Business process ownership
- ■Effectiveness and efficiency

A – *Staying in front*
- Global capability
- Rapid time to market
- Use know-how of all partners
- Step change in costs
- Mass customization
- Environmental differentiation
- ■New ways to delight ourselves

C – *Inhibited*
- Executive commitment
- Flat organization
- Employee empowerment
- Skills and training
- Teamwork
- Benchmarking
- Measurement and incentives
- ■Focus on performance

E – *Where to start*
- Needs recognition
- Executive vision
- Customer satisfaction focus
- Employee involvement
- Process improvement
- ■Control and predictability

B – *En-route*
- Delighted customers
- Market-driven quality
- EFQM/Baldridge
- Employee development
- Env. and social responsibility
- ■Service excellence

Performance / Practice

Figure 10.21 *Five different starting points*

Group E: 'Knowing where to start'

How come? It is possible to exist without long-term best practice or high performance if there is something unique about the product or if the market is in some way protected. There have been many such companies who have enjoyed a measure of financial success for long periods. For some it has simply been a case of not having attempted to change, while for others, the efforts to change have been unsuccessful. For example, some factories where TQM or JIT have apparently not worked they incorrectly deem such practices to be inappropriate.

So what? The point at which this situation breaks down is when the customer has a choice, an alternative supply source or a substitute product. Companies with quality and delivery capabilities that lack control and predictability will then rapidly lose market share.

Which way forward? Since there is no single universal solution, these sites face change on many fronts. The challenge is knowing where to start. What is clear is that rushing into automation or information systems at this stage is probably not where to begin, since there is no merit in speeding up poor processes. (Ironically it is much easier to get a board-room decision to buy a piece of software than to agree to tackle some fundamental aspect of business culture.) Equally, many sites in this group will be working with limited financial resources.

Highest priority must be the establishment of a clear and simple business vision with which employees can readily identify and through which they can be encouraged to take an active part in the improvement of customer facing business processes. There is much to be achieved at low cost. Changing business procedures will have limited impact if the attitudes and values of those operating them remain unchanged.

Group D: 'Something for nothing'

How come? Typical of this group are some of the suppliers to large retail stores. European retailers are often able to exercise significant purchasing leverage and, as a result, all their suppliers exhibit high performance in quality and delivery flexibility. The achievement of this performance has not always been an issue in which the retailer has been closely involved. It is always possible to provide such capability by extensive final inspection and high finished stock levels, for example, although this is far from world-class best practice.

This group may include very small sites where the labelling of instinctive good practice as a set of world-class processes simply is not necessary when so few people are involved. It could also be that there is something genuinely unique about the process that demands a quite different approach to the universal best practice model.

So what? This pattern of performance without best practice has a high product cost penalty. It is also something that some manufacturers achieve for their largest customers at the expense of their smaller customers. It ceases to be competitive as soon as other suppliers, through enduring best practice, can match the service levels at lower prices. Parts of the European automobile industry in the late 1980s were reported as spending more time in rectifying faults as their Japanese competitors did in assembling complete vehicles. The consequences can be measured in market share.

Which way forward? Increasing procurement based on 'high trust' partnership sourcing, instead of the strongly adversarial purchasing approaches, is already beginning to encourage best practice in first tier suppliers in the electronics and motor industries in particular. Retailers are recruiting skills from manufacturing industry to enable joint activity in cost reduction rather than purchasing by price negotiation. The challenge for sites in this group is to recognize the cost overhead they are unnecessarily carrying and with subsequent systematic simplification of manufacturing and business processes to enable high performance in quality and responsiveness at lower unit costs.

Group C: 'Inhibited'

How come? The companies in this group have invested in best practice but are yet to enjoy the benefits of their effort. Some time delay is inevitable and for any organization making change, performance that lags practice is entirely plausible.

There are many sites where the gap is not explained by time delay but by some inhibitors that are precluding performance gain. A change averse culture, poor project implementation, lack of real executive sponsorship or simply too many changes occurring simultaneously may all contribute to the problem. If much of the effort is expended in overcoming internal organizational friction, the gains in performance will be largely lost.

It is also not unusual to see world-class manufacturing lines alongside much less efficient, yet similar, manufacturing facilities in the same factory. The inability to translate learning across a site is sometimes also a trait of companies in this group.

So what? Not only is the operational performance impacted but seemingly failing approaches to competitive manufacturing will sometimes be abandoned, never to be revisited. Well-known and proven techniques become discredited as yet more fads and gimmicks while scepticism and resistance to change is reinforced.

Which way forward? In sports coaching it is sometimes argued that:

PERFORMANCE = SKILLS − INHIBITORS

For these companies the key issue is to recognize and remove the inhibitors rather than seeking yet more new skills and techniques.

A clear manufacturing strategy should seek to systematically introduce best practice with widescale employee involvement and training, well-understood measurement systems and strong customer focus.

Group B: 'En route'

How come? The majority of European manufacturing sites fall into this category. Employees will have been actively encouraged to take every opportunity to play their part in implementing a shared vision for the business. Working in teams they will be bringing efficiency and effectiveness to the design, manufacturing and commercial processes of the site. An ethos of continuous improvement will exist in all areas. Suppliers and customers will be active participants in new product introductions.

So what? These sites must begin to face the reality that the closer they get to being world class, the more difficult the rest of the journey appears to be. Most change programmes naturally decay and lose momentum; TQM initiatives will fade to nothing without being regularly re-energized. At this stage there is probably not much 'low hanging fruit' in terms of improvement opportunities. That which remains to be achieved in getting to be truly world class is by definition going to be difficult.

Which way forward? With by now reliable and efficient processes for quality and delivery, the task is to obsessively focus on exceeding customer expectations. Competitive differentiation will probably come from excellence of service more than product uniqueness. The adoption of high-level quality templates such as EFQM or Baldrige offer a basis for relentless pursuit of a market-driven strategy. Highly motivated and well-trained employees are an essential ingredient to achieving delighted customers.

Group A: 'Staying in front'

How come? These companies have achieved international market leadership through the adoption of all aspects of world-class best practice and enjoy performance levels that set them apart from the rest of their industry. They are able to deliver the performance, quality and cost-effectiveness of their entire supply chain to the benefit of their customers. Relationships with employees, business partners, customers and investors are built on a foundation of trust.

So what? The challenge for these companies is that there is no longer a road map to follow. The model of best practice, the high level quality templates and widescale benchmarking offer diminishing returns. What is required are innovative approaches to finding new ways to delight customers.

A constant search for 'breakthroughs' to new business concepts must be encouraged. Expectations of exemplar levels of social and environmental responsibility may also need to be accommodated.

Which way forward? Ever more demanding patterns of consumer behaviour are emphasizing the need to deliver individual products and services to meet individual personal needs. So-called 'mass customization' techniques must be explored with the goal of building tailored products at mass-production economies of scale. Already evidenced in sports goods, apparel, personal computer and cycle manufacturers, for example, the elimination of finished goods stocks can more than offset customization costs.

World-class suppliers must seek to provide global capability. New product introductions must constantly outperform the industry. These sites must capture and exploit their own intellectual capital and manage their organizational learning process. Competitive edge must be maintained by continuing to invest in relationships with suppliers, employees and customers.

Notwithstanding a relentless continuous improvement ethos, these sites will be seeking significant step function change in product costs, for example (especially in higher wage economies).

While not every initiative will work, there will be no let up in the search for ways to set new standards in best practice.

A long-term programme

What has been achieved so far is to show that the technique of best practice benchmarking can offer a significant insight into the workings of an individual site as well as the competitiveness of sector and national manufacturing capability.

The goal of achieving and maintaining world-class manufacturing capability is, of course, a continuously moving target. It is essential to examine every element of the model of best practice to ensure that it reflects the true state of the art. The winners will be those who can stay ahead of the model.

For those who have already participated in this particular programme there is a stake in the ground against which to test their rate of improvement and indeed it is hoped that they will have been able to identify the business processes they should systematically examine and benchmark against the best they can find.

Finally, no amount of benchmarking alone will improve any business. It is the vision, energy and teamwork of the entire organization that will deliver the improvement.

References

Hanson, P. and Voss, C. (1993) *Made in Britain – the True State of Britain's Manufacturing Industry.* IBM Consulting Group.

Voss, C., Blackmon, K., Hanson, P. and Claxton, T. (1996a) *Made in Europe II: an Anglo-German Design Study.* IBM Consulting Group.

Voss, C., Blackmon, K., Hanson, P. and Claxton, T. (1996b) Managing new product design and development: an Anglo-German study. *Business Strategy Review,* **7**(3), 1–15.

Voss, C., Blackmon, K., Hanson, P. and Oak, B. (1994) *Made in Europe – a Four Nations Best Practice Study.* IBM Consulting Group.

11 Sustaining a culture of discontinuous innovation

Pervaiz Ahmed

This chapter focuses upon the 'softer' dimension of innovation, namely that of innovation cultures and innovation climates. The chapter presents a case arguing that, despite the fact that the softer side of innovation is often ignored, possession of a culture and organizational climate of innovation underpins long-term competitive success. The chapter looks at how climates and cultures of innovation can be built and sustained. Evidence is also presented to define the parameters necessary for organizational cultures to be effective, and the types of norms that need to be put in place to create innovative behaviour by employees.

Individual motivations and characteristics are also discussed in relation to their impact upon innovation and creativity within the organization. The key role that leadership and employee empowerment play within innovation is also highlighted, while characteristics that define innovation climates and cultures are identified. The theoretical discussion is supplemented by case studies to illustrate theoretical issues.

Introduction

Virtually all companies talk about innovation, and the importance of 'doing' innovation. Many try to 'do it', but only a few succeed in doing it. The reality is that innovation for the most part frightens organizations because it is inevitably linked to risk. Many companies, therefore, pay only lip service to the power and benefits of innovation, most of them remaining averse to the aggressive investment and commitment that innovation demands. Instead they dabble in innovation and creativity. Even though innovation is debated in senior level meetings as being the lifeblood of the company, with occasional resources and R&D funds diverted to it, the commitment usually ends there. However, becoming innovative demands more than debate and resources; it requires an organizational culture that constantly guides organizational members to strive for innovation and a climate conducive to creativity.

Innovation is holistic in nature. It covers the entire range of activities necessary to provide value to customers and a satisfactory return to the business. As Buckler (1997) suggests, innovation 'is an environment, a culture – an almost spiritual force – that exists in a company' and drives value creation.

Innovation can be viewed as three fairly distinct phases. These are often seen as sequential but in reality are iterative and often run concurrently. The first is the idea generation phase, typically the fuzzy front end. A lot of the ideas from this stage often do not proceed to the second stage because numerous problems can occur, ranging from feasibility to compatibility with strategic direction. The second stage is usually the structured methodology phase, and is often a 'Stagegate' system (a series of 'hoops' through which the new idea must pass in order to demonstrate its feasibility and compatibility with the organization's objectives – see Chapter 3, section 'From idea to implementation'). Most large companies deploy some variation of a structured methodology. The third stage is commercialization, where the idea becomes operational. In others words, the product is produced so as to allow extraction of value from all that has been created in the earlier phases.

Although innovation cannot be smelt, touched, heard, tasted or seen, it can be sensed. It is probably best described as a pervasive attitude that allows a business to see beyond the present and create the future. Innovation is the engine of change and in today's fiercely competitive environment, resisting change is dangerous. Companies cannot protect themselves from change regardless of their excellence or the vastness of their current resource basin. While change brings uncertainty and risk, it also creates opportunity and the key driver of the organization's ability to change is innovation. However, simply deciding that the organization has to be innovative is not sufficient; that decision must be backed by actions that create an environment in which people are so comfortable with innovation that they create it.

Culture is a primary determinant of innovation. The possession of positive cultural characteristics provides the organization with the necessary ingredients to innovate. Culture has multiple elements that can serve to enhance or inhibit the tendency to innovate. Moreover the culture of innovation needs to be matched against the appropriate organizational context. To examine culture in isolation is a mistake, and to simply identify one type of culture and propose it as the panacea to an organization's lack of innovation is to compound that mistake.

Innovation cultures and innovation climates

Visiting organizations such as 3M, Hewlett Packard, Sony, Honda and The Body Shop leaves one with a feeling not often encountered in ordinary companies. This 'feeling' often defies definition, yet despite its intangibility, contains organizational concreteness as real as the machinery on the shop floor. This feeling is usually found rooted in the prevailing psyche of each organization. A company such as 3M feels dynamic, while some of its counterparts feel rather staid and unexciting. The feel of the organization reflects both its climate and culture.

The term climate originates from organizational theorists such as Lewin (leadership styles create social climates) and McGregor (theory X and Y), who used the term to refer to social climate and organizational climate respectively. The climate of the organization is inferred by its members through the organization's practices, procedures and rewards systems, and indicates the way the business runs itself on a daily and routine basis. In one sense it is the encapsulation of the organization's true priorities.

Humans are active observers of the environment in which they live. They shape the environment and are themselves shaped by the environment in which they exist and from which they assume organizational priorities. From this understanding, they align themselves to achieve their own particular ends. These personal ends may coincide with those of the organization or they may conflict. Understanding and perceptions therefore act as guiding mechanisms. The practices and procedures that define these perceptions are encompassed by the term 'climate'. Schneider, Brief and Guzzo (1996) define four dimensions of climate:

1 Nature of interpersonal relationships
   - Is there trust or mistrust?
   - Are relationships reciprocal and based on collaboration, or are they competitive?
   - Does the organization make newcomers welcome and give them support, or does it allow them to achieve and assimilate simply by independent effort?
   - Do the individuals feel valued by the company?
2 Nature of hierarchy
   - Are decisions made centrally or through consensus and participation?
   - Is there a spirit of teamwork or is work more or less individualistic?
   - Are there any special privileges accorded to certain individuals, such as management staff?
3 Nature of work
   - Is work challenging or boring?
   - Are jobs tightly defined and routine, or do they provide flexibility?
   - Are sufficient resources provided to undertake the tasks for which individuals are given responsibility?
4 Focus of support and rewards
   - What aspects of performance are appraised and rewarded?
   - What projects and actions/behaviours get supported?

- Is getting the work done (quantity) or getting the work right (quality) rewarded?
- On what basis are people hired?

The parameters listed above help to define climate. It is primarily from these sources that employees draw their inferences about the organizational environment in which they find themselves, and understand the priorities accorded to certain goals that the organization espouses.

Closely allied to the concept of climate is culture. Organizational culture refers to deeply held beliefs and values. In one sense, therefore, culture is a reflection of climate, but operates at a deeper level. Where climate is observable in the practices and policies of the organization, the beliefs and values of culture are not, but exist as cognitive schema that govern behaviour and actions to given environmental stimuli. To illustrate the interlinkage, 3M has adopted the practice of setting aside a certain amount of time for employees to do creative work on their own initiative. To support this, specific seed funding is provided, and the individuals are encouraged to share and involve and become involved each other's projects. This environment of support (climate) makes individuals believe that senior management values innovation (culture). Culture thus appears to stem from the interpretations that employees give to their experience of organizational reality (why things are the way they are and the how and why of organizational priorities).

If the notion of innovation culture is to be useful, it is important to be clear what we mean by the term. Failure to specify it clearly leads to confusion and misunderstanding. The question 'What is innovation culture?' is pertinent, yet complex, partly because of the way the concept has evolved and partly because of the inherent complexity within the concept itself. It is perhaps important to remember that the concept of corporate culture has developed from anthropological attempts to understand whole societies. The term came to be used to describe other social groupings, ranging from nations down to corporations and departments and even teams within businesses.

There are many definitions of culture but most describe it as the pattern of arrangement or behaviour adopted by a group (society, corporation or team) as the accepted way of solving problems. As such, culture includes all the institutionalized ways and the implicit beliefs, norms, values and premises that underline and govern behaviour.

Furthermore, culture can be thought of as having two components: explicit or implicit. The distinction between the terms 'explicit' and 'implicit' in this sense is important in that it allows a better understanding of how to analyse and manage it. Explicit culture represents the typical patterns of behaviour by the people and the distinctive artefacts they produce and live within. Implicit refers to the values, beliefs, norms and premises which underline and determine the observed patterns of behaviour (i.e. those expressed within explicit culture).

The distinction is necessary because it serves to highlight the fact that it is easier to manipulate explicit aspects when trying to fashion organizational change. For example, in trying to make the company customer orientated, it may be possible to elicit certain actions and behaviour from employees through relatively simple training in customer satisfaction techniques, but at the same time, not necessarily effecting a change in implicit culture. A change in implicit culture would mean altering the value set of the individual members to the extent that it became an unconscious action, rather than guided by procedural or other organizational control routines. The degree and extent to which this happens is dependent on the strength of the culture.

The strength of culture depends primarily on two things:

1 Pervasiveness of the norms, beliefs and behaviours in the explicit culture (the proportion of members holding strongly to specific beliefs and standards of behaviours).
2 The match between the implicit and explicit aspects of culture.

Another way of looking at culture is in terms of cultural norms. Essentially norms vary along two dimensions:

1 Their intensity: the amount of approval/disapproval attached to an expectation.
2 Crystallization: the prevalence of the norm.

When analysing an organization's culture, it may be that certain values are held widely but without intensity – for example, everyone understands what top management wants, but there is no strong approval/disapproval. By way of contrast, it may be that a given norm such as innovation, is positively valued in one group (marketing and R&D) and negatively valued by another (say manufacturing). There is intensity but no crystallization. It is only when both intensity and consensus exist concurrently that a strong culture develops. This is why it is difficult to develop or change culture.

Strong cultures score highly on each of the above attributes. Moreover, really strong cultures work at the implicit level and exert a greater degree of control over people's behaviour and beliefs. Strong cultures can be beneficial as well as harmful, depending on the circumstances in which the organization finds itself. The value of strong cultures is that, by virtue of deeply held assumptions and beliefs, the organization is able to facilitate behaviour in accordance with organizational principles. A company that can create strong culture has employees who believe in its products, its customers, and its processes. They sell its philosophy willingly because it is part of their own identity.

However, organizations also need to be wary of a *strong* culture; this can be a hindrance as well as a strength. To effectively use culture over the long term, organizations need also to posses certain values and assumptions about *accepting change*. These values must be driven by the strategic direction in which the company is moving. Without these a strong culture can be a barrier to recognizing the need for change, and to the ability for reorganization if the need is recognized. Supporting this apparently contradictory facet of culture, Denison (1990) in a longitudinal study found evidence that suggests incoherent and weak cultures at one point in time were associated with greater organizational effectiveness in the future, and that some strong cultures eventually led to decline in corporate performance. Clearly, balance and understanding of context are important. Cultures with a strong drive for innovation and change can lead to problems when market circumstances and customer requirements demand predictability and conformance to specifications. John Scully's rescue of Apple Computers from the innovative but less predictable culture created by Steve Jobs is a good example of the weakness of a strong culture.

Generally we can say that because culture can directly affect behaviour, it can help a company to prosper. An innovative culture can make it easy for senior management to implement innovation strategies and plans. The key benefit is that often it can do things that simple use of formal systems, procedures or authority cannot. Moreover, given the nature of culture and climate, it is clear that senior managers play a critical role in shaping culture, since they are able to give priority to innovation, as well as take efforts, in terms of rewards, for instance, to guard against complacency. Employees take the priorities set by what management values, and use these to guide their actions. The challenge for management then is to make sure that the employees make the right type of attributions, since any mismatches or miscommunication easily lead to confusion and chaos.

Organizational culture and effectiveness

Having tackled the issue of defining culture, it is necessary to check the attributes that make for its effectiveness. The topic of culture and effectiveness is of central importance, yet the area is beset by formidable research problems. For example, any theory of cultural effectiveness must encompass a broad range of phenomena extending from core assumptions to visible artefacts, and from social structures to individual meaning. In addition, the theory must also address culture as symbolic representations of past attempts at adaptation and survival, as well as a set of limiting or enabling conditions for future adaptation. Even though attempts at integration have been made, there is still very limited consensus regarding a universal theory, and a great deal of scepticism exists about whether culture can ever be measured in a way that allows one organization to be compared with another.

Empirical evidence: culture effectiveness

The empirical work on organizational culture can be traced back to the early work of classical organization theorists such as Likert (1961), Burns and Stalker (1961), or Lawrence and Lorsh (1967). In more recent times, a vast base of popular literature on the subject was started by writers such as Peters and Waterman (1982) in espousing a theory of excellence, which purports to identify cultural characteristics of successful companies.

Numerous studies have produced evidence highlighting the importance of culture to organizational performance and effectiveness. Wilkins and Ouchi (1983), for example, discuss the concept of 'clan' organization and explore the hypothetical conditions under which clans would be more efficient organizational forms, while Gordon (1985) observes that high and low performing companies in the banking and utilities industries have different culture profiles. Kotter and Heskett (1992) present an analysis of the relationship between strong cultures, adaptive cultures and effectiveness and most recently, Deshpande, Farley and Webster (1993) link culture types to innovativeness. Deshpande, Farley and Webster used a synthesis of over 100 previous studies in organizational behaviour, sociology and anthropology to define four generic culture types: market culture, adhocracy culture, clan culture and hierarchical culture. Their study appears to suggest that certain cultures are more able to enhance innovativeness than others. Market and adhocracy cultures score highly for high-performance companies, exhibiting a statistically significant relationship. A study by Goran Ekvall (1991) in Sweden further supports the link between culture and innovativeness.

More generally, Dennison and Mishra (1995) identify four cultural traits and values that are associated with cultural effectiveness. These are briefly defined below:

1 *Involvement is a cultural trait which is positively related to effectiveness.* Involvement of a large number of participants appears to be linked with effectiveness by virtue of providing a collective definition of behaviours, systems, and meanings in a way that calls for individual conformity. Typically, this involvement is gained through integration around a small number of key values. This characteristic is popularly recognized as a strong culture. Involvement and participation create a sense of ownership and responsibility, out of which develop a greater commitment to the organization and a growing capacity to operate under conditions of ambiguity.
2 *Consistency is a cultural trait that is positively related to effectiveness.* Consistency has both positive and negative organizational consequences. The positive influence of consistency is that it provides integration and co-ordination, while the negative aspect is that highly consistent cultures are

often the most resistant to change and adaptation. The concept of consistency allows us to explain the existence of subcultures within an organization. Sources of integration range from a limited set of rules about when and how to agree and disagree, all the way to a unitary culture with high conformity and little or no dissent. None the less, in each case, the degree of consistency of the system is a salient trait of the organization's culture.

3 *Adaptability, or the capacity for internal change in response to external conditions is a cultural trait that is positively related to effectiveness.* An effective organization must develop norms and beliefs that support its capacity to receive and interpret signals from its environment and translate them into cognitive, behavioural and structural changes. When consistency becomes detached from the external environment, firms will often develop into insular bureaucracies and, as such, are unlikely to be adaptable.

4 *A sense of mission or long-term vision is a cultural trait that is positively related to effectiveness.* Interestingly, this contrasts with the adaptability notion, in that it emphasizes the stability of an organization's central purpose and de-emphasizes its capacity for situational adaptability and change. A mission appears to provide two major influences on the organization's functioning. First, a mission provides purpose and meaning, and a host of non-economic reasons why the organization's work is important; second, a sense of mission defines the appropriate course of action for the organization and its members. Both of these factors reflect and amplify the key values of the organization.

Denison and Mishra (1995) propose that for effectiveness, organizations need to reconcile all four of these traits. Together they serve to acknowledge two contrasts: one between internal integration and external adaptation, the other between change and stability. Involvement and consistency have as their focus the dynamics of internal integration, while mission and adaptability address the dynamics of external adaptation. This focus is consistent with Schein's (1985) observation that culture is developed as an organization learns to cope with the dual problems of external adaptation and internal integration. In addition, involvement and adaptability describe traits related to an organization's capacity to change, while the consistency and mission are more likely to contribute to the organization's capacity to remain stable and predictable over time.

The individual and innovation culture

People play a role in organizational culture and organizations need to recognize the type of employees that can most effectively drive innovation. From a diverse range of research (psychology to management) it has been found that a core of reasonably stable personality traits characterize creative individuals. These personality traits for innovation are listed below:

- high valuation of aesthetic qualities in experience
- broad interests
- attraction to complexity
- high energy
- independence of judgement
- intuition
- self-confidence
- ability to accommodate opposites
- firm sense of self as creative (Barron and Harrington, 1981)
- persistence
- curiosity
- energy
- intellectual honesty (Amabile, 1988)
- internal locus of control (reflective/introspective) (Woodman and Schoenfeldt, 1990).

Although it seems to be generally agreed that personality is related to creativity, attempts to try and use this inventory type of approach in an organizational setting as a predictor of creative accomplishments is fraught with dangers, and is hardly likely to be any more useful than attempts at picking good leaders through the use of trait theory approaches. Nevertheless, it does highlight the need to focus on individual actors, and to try and nurture such characteristics or at least bring them out, if necessary, in an organizational setting.

Cognitive factors and innovation

Research indicates a number of cognitive factors associated with creativity. For example, medical psychology indicates differences in cognitive processing, ascribing the left of the cerebral cortex to rational thinking, and the right brain to intuition.

Cognitive parameters affecting idea production are given below:

- associative fluency
- fluency of expression
- figural fluency
- ideational fluency
- speech fluency
- word fluency
- practical ideational fluency

- originality (Carroll, 1985)
- fluency
- flexibility
- originality
- elaboration (Guildford, 1983).

Personal motivational factors affecting innovation

At the individual level, numerous motivation-related factors have been identified as drivers of creative production. The key ones are presented below:

1 *Intrinsic versus extrinsic motivation.* Intrinsic motivation is a key driver of creativity (Amabile, 1990; Barron and Harrington, 1981). In fact, extrinsic interventions such as rewards and evaluations appear to adversely affect innovation motivation because they appear to redirect attention from 'experimenting' to following rules or technicalities of performing a specific task. Furthermore, apprehension about evaluation appears to divert attention away from the innovation because individuals become reluctant to take risks since these risks may be negatively evaluated. Contrarily, in order to be creative, individuals need freedom to take risks, play with ideas and expand the range of considerations from which solutions may emerge.

2 *Challenging individuals.* Open-ended, non-structured tasks engender higher creativity than narrow ones by virtue of the fact that people respond positively when they are challenged and are provided with sufficient scope to generate novel solutions. It appears that it is not the individual who lacks creative potential but the organizational expectations that exert a primary debilitating effect upon the individual's inclination to innovate (Amabile et al., 1991; Shalley and Oldham, 1985).

3 *Skills and knowledge.* Creativity is affected by relevant skills such as expertise, technical skills, talent etc. However, such domain-related skills can have both positive as well as negative consequences. Positively, knowledge enhances the possibility of creating new understanding. Negatively, high domain relevant skills may narrow the search heuristics to learnt routines and thereby constrain fundamentally new perspectives. This can lead to functional 'fixedness'.

At a more macro level, Schneider (1987) suggests that organizations may attract and select persons with matching styles. Organizational culture, as well as other aspects of the organization, may be difficult to change because people who are attracted to the organization may be resistant to accepting new cognitive styles. When a change is forced, the people attracted by the old organization may leave because they no longer match the newly accepted cognitive style. Among other things, this culture-cognitive style match suggests that organizational conditions (including training programmes) supportive of creativity will be effective only to the extent that the potential and current organizational members know of and prefer these conditions.

Structure and innovation

Although most research appears to agree that innovation is influenced by social processes, research in this area thus far has taken a back seat to research on individual differences and antecedents. Generally it can be said that innovation is enhanced by organic structures rather than mechanistic structures. Innovation is increased by the use of highly participative structures and cultures (e.g. high performance-high commitment work systems (Burnside, 1990)). For instance, an idea champion must be made to feel part of the total innovation; at the very least he or she must be allowed to follow the progress of the innovation. This builds involvement via ownership and enhances attachment and commitment at the organizational level. There is also a strong case here to let the individual lead the project in a total sense from beginning to end.

Organic structures that promote innovation

- Freedom from rules.
- Opportunity for participation, and informality.
- The chance to air views, with the knowledge that they will be considered.
- Face-to-face communication and a lack of bureaucracy.
- Interdisciplinary teams and the breaking down of departmental barriers.
- An emphasis on creative interaction and aims.
- The willingness to look outwards and take on external ideas.
- Flexibility with respect to changing needs.
- Lack of hierarchies.
- Information that flows downwards as well as upwards.

Mechanistic structures that hinder innovation

- Rigid departmental separation and functional specialization.
- Hierarchies.
- Bureaucracy.
- Many rules and set procedures.
- Formal reporting.
- Long decision chains and slow decision-making.
- Little individual freedom of action.
- Communication via the written word.
- Much information flows upwards, while directives flow downwards.

Cultural norms for innovation

Since the external context impacts heavily upon innovation and the intrinsic creativity inherent in the organization defines its ability to adapt to, and even shape the environment, the question might be asked, can culture promote innovation? Indeed, does culture hinder or enhance the process of creativity and innovation? The answer is that it simply depends on the norms that are widely held by the organization. If the right types of norms are held and are widely shared, then culture can activate creativity. Just as easily, if the wrong culture exists, then no matter how much effort is put into promoting innovation or how good people's intentions are, few ideas are likely to be forthcoming.

A variety of researchers (Andrew, 1996; Filipczak, 1997; Judge Fryxell and Dooley, 1997; Picken and Dess, 1997; Pinchot and Pinchot, 1996; Schneider, Gunnarson and Niles-Jones, 1996) appear to point to the same set of critical norms involved in promoting and implementing innovation and creativity.

Norms that promote innovation are presented below.

Challenge and belief in action

The degree to which employees are involved in daily operations and the degree of 'stretch' required.

Key attributes are:

- obsession with precision
- emphasis on results
- meeting your commitments
- timeliness
- knowing the value of getting things done
- realization that hard work is expected and appreciated
- eagerness to get things done
- ability to cut through bureaucracy.

Freedom and risk-taking

The degree to which the individuals are given latitude in defining and executing their own work.

Key attributes are:

- freedom to experiment
- willingness to challenge the status quo

- expectation that innovation is part of your job
- freedom to try things and fail
- acceptance of mistakes
- willingness to discuss dumb ideas
- lack of punishment for mistakes.

Dynamism and future orientation

The degree to which the organization is active and forward looking. Pace of work is 'full speed', 'breakneck' etc.
   Key attributes are:

- ability to forget the past
- willingness to focus on the long term
- drive to improve
- positive attitudes towards change
- positive attitudes towards the environment
- empowerment of people
- emphasis on quality.

External orientation

The degree to which the organization is sensitive to customers and the external environment.
   Key attributes are:

- willingness to adopt the customer's perspective
- the ability to build relationships with all external interfaces (supplier, distributors etc.).

Trusts and openness

The degree of emotional safety that employees experience in their working relationships. When there is high trust, new ideas surface easily.
   Key attributes are:

- willingness to have open and shared communication
- the ability to listen more effectively
- open access
- acceptance of criticism
- encouragement of lateral thinking
- intellectual honesty.

Debates

The degree to which employees feel free to debate issues actively, and the degree to which minority views are expressed readily and listened to with an open mind.

Key attributes are:

- expectation and acceptance of conflict
- acceptance of criticism
- lack of sensitivity.

Cross-functional interaction and freedom

The degree to which interaction across functions is facilitated and encouraged.

Key attributes are:

- willingness to move people around
- teamwork
- management of interdependencies
- flexibility in jobs, budgets and functional areas.

Myths and stories

The degree to which success stories are designed and celebrated.

Key attributes:

- symbolism and action
- the building and dissemination of stories and myths.

Leadership commitment and involvement

The extent to which leadership exhibits real commitment and leads by example and actions rather than empty exhortation.

Key attributes are:

- senior management commitment
- walking the talk
- declaration of mission/vision.

Awards and rewards

The manner in which successes (and failures) are celebrated and rewarded.
   Key attributes are:

- valuing of ideas
- top management attention and support
- respect for beginning ideas
- celebration of accomplishments, e.g. awards
- implementation of suggestions
- encouragement.

Innovation time and training

The amount of time and training employees are given to develop new ideas and
new possibilities and the way in which new ideas are received and treated.
   Key attributes are:

- built-in resource slack
- adequate funding
- time
- opportunities
- promotions
- tools
- infrastructure, e.g. rooms, equipment etc.
- continuous training
- encouragement of lateral thinking
- encouragement of skills development.

Corporate identification and unity

The extent to which employees identify with the company, its philosophy, its
products and customers.
   Key attributes are:

- sense of pride
- willingness to share the credit
- sense of ownership
- elimination of mixed messages
- shared vision and common direction
- a building of consensus
- mutual respect and trust
- concern for the whole organization.

Organizational structure: autonomy and flexibility

The degree to which the structure facilitates innovation activities.
   Key attributes are:

- decision-making responsibility at lower levels
- decentralized procedures
- freedom to act
- expectation of action
- belief that the individual can have an impact
- delegation
- quick, flexible decision-making to minimize bureaucracy.

Corporate missions, philosophy statements and innovation culture

Having a clear corporate philosophy enables individuals to co-ordinate their activities to achieve common purposes, even in the absence of direction from their managers (Ouchi, 1983). One effect of corporate statements is their influence in creating a strong culture capable of appropriate guiding of behaviours and actions. However, there is also a degree of doubt as to whether statements of credo have any value in driving the organization forward. Most statements encountered are often of little value because they fail to grab people's attention or motivate them to work toward a common end (Collins and Porras, 1991).

   Despite these concerns, Ledford, Wendnhof and Strahley (1994) suggest if correctly formulated and expressed, philosophy statements have three advantages:

1 The statements can be used to guide behaviour and decision-making.
2 Philosophy statements express organizational culture, which can help employees interpret ambiguous stimuli.
3 They may contribute to organizational performance by motivating employees or inspiring feelings of commitment.

It is worth bearing in mind that the statement does not have to move mountains to make a cumulative difference in firm performance. If individual employees become just a little bit more dedicated to innovation, exert just a little bit more effort towards creativity goals, care just a little bit more about their work, then the statement may produce a positive return on the investment needed to create it.

So what makes a statement effective? According to Ledford, Wendnhof and Strahley (1994) four basic guiding principles are needed to bring a statement to life:

1 Make it a compelling statement. Avoid boring details and routine descriptions.
2 Install an effective communication and implementation process.
3 Create a strong link between the philosophy and the systems governing behaviour.
4 Have an ongoing process of affirmation and renewal.

Leadership and innovation culture

Leading edge organizations consistently innovate, and do so with courage. It is the task of organizational leaders to provide the culture and climate that nurture and acknowledge innovation at every level. However, notwithstanding the fact that leadership is critically important, it is nevertheless insufficient on its own to build a culture of continuous improvement and innovation. To do this, many innovation champions must be identified, recruited, developed, trained, encouraged and acknowledged throughout the organization.

In order to build a successful and sustainable culture of innovation, leadership needs to accomplish two broad tasks. First, leaders need to be acutely sensitive to their environment and acutely aware of the impact that they themselves have on those around them. This sensitivity enables them to provide an important human perspective to the task at hand and is critical because it is only within this awareness that the leader can begin to bridge the gap between 'leaderspeak' and the real world of organizational culture. The second factor is the ability of leaders to accept and deal with ambiguity. Innovation cannot occur without ambiguity, and organizations and individuals that are not able to tolerate ambiguity in the workplace environment, and relationships reproduce only routine actions. Innovative structures, for example, cannot have all attendant problems worked out in advance. Leaders need to build a deep appreciation of this fact, otherwise there is a simple tendency to create a culture of blame. Tolerance of ambiguity allows space for risk taking, and exploration of alternative solution spaces which do not always produce results. This hedges against constant deployment of tried and tested routines for all occasions. In fact, as Tom Peters suggests, most successful managers have an unusual ability to resolve paradox and to translate conflicts and tensions into excitement, high commitment and superior performance.

Mills and Delbecq (1996) identify characteristics that distinguish highly innovative firms from less innovative ones:

- Top management commits both financial and emotional support to innovation, and they promote innovation through champions and advocates for innovation.
- Top management has to ensure that realistic and accurate assessments of the markets are made for the planned innovation. Highly innovative firms are close to the end users, and are accurately able to assess potential demand.
- Top management ensures that innovation projects get the necessary support from all levels of the organization.
- Top management ensures that structured methodology/systems are set in place so that each innovation goes through a careful screening process prior to implementation.

The above suggests that senior management play a pivotal role in enhancing or hindering organizational innovation. If senior management are able to install all of the above types of procedures and practices, they effectively seed a climate conducive to innovation. It is important to note that it is not sufficient to emphasize only one or a few practices. Climates are created by numerous elements coming together to reinforce employee perceptions. Weaknesses or contradictions along even single dimensions can quite easily debilitate efforts. For example, if rewards are not structured for innovation but are given for efficient performance of routine operations, then no matter how seductive the other cues and perceptions are, employees are likely to respond with caution and uncertainty. This is particularly the case because perceptions of the climate are made on aggregates of experience.

Additionally, managers create climate not by what they say but by what they do. It is through visible actions over time rather than through simple statements that employees begin to cement perceptions. It is only when employees see things happening around them, and do things that push them towards innovation that they begin to internalize the values of innovation. At innovative companies, the whole systems of organizational function is geared up to emphasize innovation (who gets hired, how they are rewarded, how the organization is designed and laid out, what processes are given priority and resource back-up, and so on).

Leadership, innovation and empowerment

Empowering people to innovate is one of the most effective ways for leaders to mobilize the energies of people to be creative. Combined with leadership support and commitment, empowerment gives people freedom to take responsibility for innovation. Empowerment in the presence of strong cultures that guide actions and behaviour produces both energy and enthusiasm to consistent work towards an innovative goal. Employees themselves are able to devise ways that allow them to innovate and accomplish their tasks. The only serious problem with empowerment occurs when it is provided in a organization without a strong value system capable of driving activities in a unified manner aligned to the superordinate goals of the organization. In these conditions, empowerment is little less than abdication of responsibility, and when responsibility and power is pushed downwards, chaos typically ensues.

Even with empowerment, innovative actions can be incapacitated. Often people encounter organizational barriers that inhibit innovation. Creativity blockers come in all shapes and forms. Some common ones are listed below:

- self-imposed barriers
- unwarranted assumptions
- thinking there is only one correct answer
- failing to challenge the obvious
- pressure to conform
- fear of looking foolish.

Killer phrases also abound:

- 'It will cost too much.'
- 'We have never done things that way.'
- 'If it's that good, why hasn't someone thought of it before?'
- 'Has it been done somewhere else?'
- 'Yes, BUT . . .'
- 'It CAN'T be done that way.'
- 'Its impossible.' etc.

Actions that need to be addressed so that empowerment can contribute to innovation are listed below.

Establish a meaningful 'actions' boundary

For employees to be creative and innovative they need to understand the primacy of the innovation agenda, and understand how far they are being empowered to achieve these ends. Successful companies need to draw an 'actions' boundary by explicitly defining the domain of action and the priority, and the level of responsibility and empowerment provided to reach these ends. This usually occurs through mission and vision statements. Devised correctly, these statements can act as powerful enablers; used incorrectly, they can be powerful disablers, breeding cynicism and discontent.

Define risk tolerance

Employees need to know the level of risks that they can safely take. This helps them to define the space within which they are allowed to act in an empowered manner, and the occasions when they need to approach someone more senior. For example, employees need to understand how much time they can spend on their pet projects, and how much effort they need to ensure that their 'routine' operations are not made suboptimal. They need also to understand the penalties if inefficiencies creep into aspects of their task. In this way, understanding of risk provides clear definition of the priority and space for innovative actions. Without knowing the risk tolerance that exists within the organization, employees tend to be unwilling to try to innovate, or to engage in activities that depart from tradition.

The best way for leaders to define the action space is not to discourage innovation, but to stipulate a broad direction that is consistent and clear. This means that as leaders they must be capable of accepting ambiguity, and be able to place trust in employees' ability to stretch out to goals rather than prescribe details of specific actions that stifle creative actions.

Structure involvement

Involvement does not occur on its own; senior management need to design into their organizations ways of buying involvement. Involvement requires emotional encouragement, as well as an infrastructure to create possibilities of involvement. Organizational design and layout can be used to create a physical environment to enhance interaction. Awards and special recognition schemes are also mechanisms to encourage 'buy-in' into innovation as a philosophy and a way of organizational life; establishing specific mechanisms such as quality circles is yet another. Without direct structures to induce innovation, leadership commitment to innovation remains an empty exhortation and produces empty results.

Accountability

A very common problem in empowered innovation is that everyone is encouraged to participate in cross-functional process involvement, to an extent that almost everybody loses track of who is accountable for what. The result of unrestricted and uncontrolled empowerment is chaos. As new processes are put in place, new forms of behavioural guidance must be provided and must be accompanied by redefinitions of responsibility. While empowerment on the surface looks like an unstructured process, it is anything but that. In reality, it is a clear definition of domains in which the individuals are allowed to exert creative discretion, and the responsibility that they must execute while engaging in their total task as employees of the organization.

Action orientation rather than bureaucracy orientation

To ensure that innovation occurs, leaders must ensure that there are no bureaucratic bottlenecks that suffocate attempts at innovation. One primary culprit of this is overly bureaucratic procedures for rubber-stamping approval or reporting requirements. Faced with such obstacles, a lot of employee initiatives fail. In fact, a large proportion of suggestion schemes appear to fail, not because there is a lack of ideas but because of the protocols, and the failure of the protocols to process with sufficient speed a favourable or unfavourable response. Clearly employee innovativeness is not always the stumbling block; often the organizational processes and structures are so burdensome and unwieldy that they create a high level of unresponsiveness. Through leadership commitment to re-engineer out unfruitful elements of bureaucracy, processes and structure can lay the foundation for a climate of innovation.

Characteristics of innovation climates and cultures

Despite the interest in the field of innovation, much of the research evidence concerning management practices about innovation cultures and creative climate remains unsystematic and anecdotal.

As mentioned earlier, the importance of culture has been emphasized by organizational theorists such as Burns and Stalker, who present a case for organic structures as opposed to mechanistic ones. In popular literature, Peters and Waterman (1982) present similar arguments, which suggest that in order to facilitate innovation, work environments must be simultaneously tight and loose. Burgleman and Sayles (1986) highlight the dependency of innovation with the development and maintenance of an appropriate context within which innovation can occur. Judge, Fryxell and Dooley (1997) in presenting findings from a study of R&D units, compare cultures and climates between innovative and less innovative firms, and argue that the key distinguishing factor between innovative and less innovative firms is the ability of management to create a sense of community in the workplace. Highly innovative companies behave as focused communities, whereas less innovative companies units behave more like traditional bureaucratic departments. They suggest four managerial practices that influence the making of such goal directed communities.

Balanced autonomy

Autonomy is defined as having control over the means as well as the ends of one's work. This concept appears to be one of central importance. There are two types of autonomy:

- *strategic autonomy*: the freedom to set one's own agenda
- *operational autonomy*: the freedom to attack a problem, once it has been set by the organization, in ways that are determined by the individual.

Operational autonomy encourages a sense of the individual and promotes entrepreneurial spirit, whereas strategic autonomy is more to do with the level of alignment with organizational goals. It appears that firms that are most innovative emphasize operational autonomy but retain strategic autonomy for top management. Top management appear to specify ultimate goals to be attained but thereafter provide freedom to allow individuals to be creative in the ways they achieve goals. Giving strategic autonomy, in the sense of allowing individuals a large degree of freedom to determine their destiny, ultimately leads to less innovation. The result of strategic autonomy is an absence of guidelines and a focus on effort. In contrast, having too little operational autonomy also has the effect of creating imbalance. Here the road maps become too rigidly specified, and control drives out innovative flair, leading eventually to bureaucratic atmospheres. What works best is a balance between operational and strategic autonomy.

Personalized recognition

Rewarding individuals for their contribution to the organization is widely used by corporations. However, while recognition can take many forms, there is a common distinction: rewards can be either extrinsic or intrinsic. Extrinsic rewards are such things as pay increases, bonuses and shares and stock options. Intrinsic rewards are those that are based on internal feelings of accomplishment by the recipient, for example being personally thanked by the CEO, being recognized by the peer group or being given an award or trophy.

Innovative companies appear to rely heavily on personalized intrinsic awards, both for individuals as well as groups. Less innovative companies tend to place almost exclusive emphasis on extrinsic awards. It appears that when individuals are motivated more by intrinsic desires than extrinsic desires, there is greater creative thought and action. Nevertheless, it has to be stated that extrinsic rewards have to be present at a base level in order to ensure that individuals are at least comfortable with their salary. Beyond the base salary thresholds, it appears that innovation is primarily driven by one's level of self-esteem rather than external monetary rewards. It appears that extrinsic rewards often yield only temporary compliance. Extrinsic rewards promote competitive behaviours which disrupt workplace relationships, inhibit openness and learning, discourage risk-taking, and can effectively undermine interest in work itself. When extrinsic rewards are used, individuals tend to channel their energies towards trying to get the extrinsic reward rather than unleashing their creative potential.

Integrated socio-technical system

Highly innovative companies appear to place equal emphasis on the technical side as well as the social side of the organization. In other words, they look to nurture not only technical abilities and expertise but also to promote a sense of sharing and togetherness. Fostering group cohesiveness requires paying attention to the recruitment process to ensure social 'fit' beyond technical expertise, and also about carefully integrating new individuals through a well-designed socialization programme. Less innovative firms, on the other hand, seem more concerned with explicit, aggressive individual goals. Less innovative firms tend to create an environment of independence, whereas innovative ones create a much more co-operative environment. Highly innovative companies also appear to place much more reasonable goal expectations, and try not to overload individuals with projects, the prevalent belief being that too many projects spread effort too thinly, leading individuals to step from the surface of one to the next. These conditions create time pressures, which militate strongly against innovativeness.

Continuity of slack

Slack is the cushion of resources that allows an organization to adapt to internal and external pressures. Slack has been correlated positively to innovation. Judge, Fryxell and Dooley (1997) note that it is not just the existence of slack but the existence of slack over time that appears to have positive impact upon innovation. They find less innovative firms have slack but these firms appear to have experienced significant disruptions or discontinuities of slack in their past or were expecting disruptions in the future. Therefore innovativeness seems to be linked with both experience and expectations of slack resources. It can be hypothesized that slack, and future expectations of uninterrupted slack, provide scope for the organization and its members to take risks that they would not do so under conditions of no slack, or interruptions in slack. Organizationally this would appear to indicate the need for generating a baseline stock of slack in a variety of critical resources (such as time and seed funding for new projects).

We move on now to illustrate salient points of the foregoing discussion by presenting case experiences of international companies.

Case study 1: Sony Corporation – leadership involvement and commitment

Small groups and a culture of innovations ingrained by top management is the winning formula at Sony. While like many companies Sony has an eye on bottom-line results, what seems to make Sony stand out from the others is the emphasis its executives appear to place in the details of innovation. Executives keep a close eye on the ideas and how they came about. Sony executives appear to have input into the process, and even become part of the working team for brief periods, actively contributing to the idea creation process.

Organizationally, Sony avoids creating huge structures and heavy control mechanisms which inevitably suffocate innovation. It prefers small independent teams that are able to take risks.

Team formation at Sony is also slightly unusual. Instead of the usual procedure of management simply assigning individuals to specific projects, there is more of a 'selling' process with employees. Often it takes some time for the people to catch the spirit of the project and subsequently to buy into it. The formation of teams appears more *ad hoc* than those initiated through management edict. This is not to say that Sony does not have a formal innovation process with all the usual milestones, but simply that it is not the key to successful development of ideas time and time again. Many of the very successful innovative products at Sony emerge from the periphery, from under the table and from skunkworks. These often are the sources of something radical and different to the world, and often they are derived from small, apparently independent teams. Simple modification innovations typically emerge from the normal routine structured process of innovation.

To harvest the benefits of radical innovation, Sony recognizes that it has to have a willingness to experiment in the marketplace. Many of Sony's competitors are reluctant to introduce products unless they are virtually certain of success. Sony is much less conservative. Sony sends a large number of products into the marketplace knowing that not all will succeed. The company operates on the principle that, while it may be much more comfortable to select two or three products that you are 100 per cent sure of, this forces you to kill some innovative products that you do not know whether the market will accept or not. However, if you don't take a risk with these, then you will never know. The Sony Walkman is a perfect example (*IW*, 1996a).

Case study 2: AT&T Paradyne Corporation – structure as a force of innovation

Innovation cultures do not – indeed, cannot – work in isolation. Cultures need to be supported by correct processes and structures in order to be effective in promoting effective innovation.

Many companies track projects as they move from idea to final launch though a funnelling system of gates that maintain linkage and timing between different functions. At each gate, the project status is assessed against prespecified criteria before being allowed to move to the next stage. Such evaluations are used by many large companies to provide the basic structure to induce cross-functional integration and interaction. Companies such as

Unilever, Ford, Dupont, AT&T all use a stage system of one form or another to aid their innovation process.

AT&T Paradyne Corporation, a manufacturer of modems and multimedia access devices, has used a structured approach to raise its new product development productivity.

AT&T Paradyne uses the stage gate system to track time to market, on a monthly basis to enhance the product realization process. A group committee is dedicated to the tracking task. Results of time-tracking are presented to executives as a management tool. The tracking and reports have helped identify 'hand-offs' that do not dovetail. Identifying the source of disconnects is used to rectify the problems. Structuring the process has meant that a much higher degree of alignment occurs. Before this innovation, projects were frequently off target by a long margin, creating situations in which sales didn't believe manufacturing, who didn't believe engineering. In the end, nobody really believed anybody else. People were not being assigned, parts were not being ordered, and so on. By getting everyone to believe in the launch date, and following the progress by a tight tracking, many of these problems were identified and weeded out of the system (*IW*, 1996b).

Case study 3: Lucent Technologies – heritage and mission of innovation

Lucent Technologies emerged from the split up of Bell Laboratories from AT&T on 1 February 1996. By this date AT&T Bell Laboratories had left an indelible mark in the history of modern technical invention, changing the fabric of modern society through its continuous commitment to R&D. Its legacy is a history full of successes. It was the birthplace of the transistor, the communications satellite, laser, solar cell, cellular telephony and stereo recording. Lucent Technologies recognizes that the engine of innovation is to be derived from the Bell Labs' formula for invention. However, Lucent Technologies is not looking simply for successful invention, it is wanting more; it wants successful innovation. The difference is important for Lucent Technologies. Lucent Technologies want to move beyond the concept of invention, which is closely synonymous with idea generation to innovation, which is about taking the ideas and converting them into a market reality. On the surface, this could be seen as a move away from the tradition of pure research which led Bell Labs to add seven Nobel prize winners to its history of success.

However, simply accepting this would be to ignore the fact that ever since the 1960s, Bell Labs have explicitly acknowledged and accepted the basic tenet that a fundamental responsibility of research is to be a window to the outside world. The belief is clearly that basic research is vital. The Labs' mission is to lead Lucent Technologies in creating and obtaining technology that it needs, and in getting that to the marketplace. The vision is to make Lucent Technologies the first choice in both existing and new businesses.

With the split from AT&T into AT&T Laboratories and Lucent Technologies, the total investment in research has gone up. The major change has come in the way of refocusing Bell Labs' efforts. Following its mission, Lucent Technology has made a policy of committing 1 per cent of the previous year's revenues to basic research, with a total R&D spend of around 11 per cent. With buoyant revenues, exhibiting growth rates of around 15 per cent per annum, this spells major growth in both research and development. The investments are indicative of other initiatives to support the new drive. The Labs have been reorganized and restructured. Engineers and scientists working on projects directly related to product development are aligned with Lucent Technologies' businesses, and therefore its customer teams who will sell the commercial fruits of these developments. Supporting these projects are a second level of projects, which provide centralized competency centres, such as, for example, in design automation. Underpinning both of these are basic sciences such as engineering, computing, mathematics and communications sciences.

In addition to this are a select number of new ventures, which don't necessarily line up with existing Lucent Technology businesses. Inferno (a newly announced network operating system) is a good example of an area which did not fit, and a new business was created to go with this product. Other areas such as fingerprint recognition, internet telephony and billing software also fall in this category.

The company is also taking a much more systematic approach to planning. Business units use technology and product road maps which help to bring together researchers, engineers closer to sales and the needs of the marketplace. This form of structure heightens the level and type of participation, and is particularly useful in making researchers part of the product team, and therefore key inputs in producing and maintaining the product plan.

These new initiatives are carefully dovetailed to the original strengths of Bell Laboratories. The company still remains committed to technical excellence, and recruitment is made to ensure that best technical expertise and talent is captured. In fact, part of the mission still remains 'to hire the best, develop the best and retain the best'.

Leadership has played an active role in the company's attempt to combine technical excellence with market responsiveness. Soft actions are intermeshed with hard targets. Lucent Technologies drives itself forward by setting innovation benchmarks to attain. One such innovation metric is the percentage of revenue that must be derived from new products in the last three years. This stipulation not only provides the Labs with a clear business aim but also serves to assure Lucent Technologies' customers that the company will continue to lead the way in technology.

At the strategic level the company is attempting to become much more geographically diverse. For example, it is increasing its presence in China and Japan. Hitherto work was primarily instinctive and intuitive but with the globalization of operations a much more systematic approach of working, learning and dissemination is needed. In response to this the company has started to institute a certification process which ensures that there is a worldwide excellence. Principles of total quality management have found widespread use to assess and continuously improve every aspect of R&D. The Labs have at the moment fifteen sites around the world, and there is a tendency to localize particular types of expertise in specific areas. The typical process is that if someone starts off some good work in a particular field, this attracts others to the same geographical area, and the whole thing grows by feeding itself. What management do is cultivate this natural tendency and dramatize 'innovation as a team sport'. In this way, natural communities of excellence spring up. The challenge is to align and channel employee energies to business goals.

The third part of the Labs' strategy is based on creating the right environment for people to work in. Bell Labs, because of its historical legacy, obviously has its own special kudos. The initiative to create the right environment is encapsulated by an approach called 'Brand and Spirit'. Robert L. Martin, Director of Lucent Technologies' technology strategy, states about the Brand and Spirit approach: 'A key part of research is creating the right environment for the people to work in. In itself the process is not so tidy. You want world leaders. For instance, the Inferno project has its own directors and runs as a stand-alone venture. That gives the people involved control of their own destiny.' The Inferno model is increasingly being followed worldwide. Researchers are given the resources to develop their ideas, but also the responsibility to innovate and realize the potential of those ideas (Anon., 1996).

Case study 4: Pacific Western Airlines (PWA) – culture of empowerment and creativity

To be successful in today's environment requires the qualities of innovation and creativity. The two are intertwined – creativity involves ingenuity and imagination in problem-solving, while innovation takes the creative idea and puts it into practice.

Much of PWA's success can be attributed to corporate culture that encourages creativity and innovation. Only this environment enabled PWA to weather the pressures of deregulation. PWA survived and grew by virtue of being more creative and innovative than any of its major competitors. PWA's success was due mainly to its ability to create a climate that encourages risk taking, finding opportunities in failure, permitting failure, and having an action-orientated perspective. All these characteristics are the reverse of traditional organizations where work activities remain well within 'safe boundaries', which are often themselves cocooned within a bureaucratic environment. In stark contrast, PWA managed to avoid these cultural characteristics and in so doing moved from being a small regional Canadian airline in the 1960s to one of the top twenty-five airline companies in the world.

The development of the Chieftain shuttle is a good illustrative example of the innovative culture of PWA. PWA's identification of the need for quick, inexpensive and convenient service between two points led eventually into one of the most successful Canadian air services. At the time, PWA was based in Edmonton, the centre of the oil and gas industry, while Calgary housed most corporate head offices of the oil companies. This created a need for frequent and reliable travel in the shortest time possible. The Chieftain airbus was based on Eastern Airlines' air shuttle service between several major US cities. The airline issued tickets on board the flights and guaranteed seating, even if another back-up aircraft was required. Business executives and government officials on tight travel schedules needed such level of service. The image of the Chieftain was created on a disparaging statement made by a competitor, Trans-Canada Airlines, that the PWA aircraft looked like a covered wagon. PWA responded by taking the negative comments and building positively, creating a western theme, and appropriately furnishing the interior of the aircraft with Native American motifs.

While this service was being developed, a slot between Alberta and Vancouver became available. PWA seized the opportunity. The route was dubbed the 'Stampeder' and was introduced with great ceremony and fanfare. Flight attendants were allowed to design their own special western outfits, catering was encouraged to create innovative in-flight service, and everyone became part of the sales team. In sum, employees were freed from the restrictions of a tight structure and allowed to take risks in shaping and implementing a new product.

Despite intense competition from national airlines, which made the whole venture extremely risky, PWA succeeded beyond its expectations. The 'Stampeder' service proved that if the organization can differentiate itself from competitors in significant ways then there was potential to be successful. Projecting an image of being feisty, innovative and safe, and offering competitive fares with friendly and enthusiastic staff was all that was required to lay the foundation of success. This example serves to illustrate that innovation does not have to be original to succeed. An old idea can be developed, and it can take on its own identity.

From these early beginnings both employees and management became caught up with the entrepreneurial spirit, and innovation and creativity thrived. Employee and management teams travelled the globe on the lookout for potential opportunities. Everything from airline operations in South East

Asia to hotels in the Caribbean were investigated. The entire organization became entrepreneurial and alert to their own creative potential. Employees were given flexibility and were challenged, and failure was tolerated. The result was the development of one of the most successful airlines of the time. The airline thrived on its ability to innovate. What made the success possible? The answer is in the culture that PWA was able to create. The characteristics of the success are listed below.

- innovation was encouraged by top management
- failure was not career-ending
- task forces developed creative ideas
- thinking was global
- problems were viewed as opportunities
- nothing was impossible
- corporate structure encouraged creativity and innovation
- a feeling of excitement and challenge prevailed
- there were no limits to opportunities
- risk-taking was encouraged
- an action-orientated environment existed
- people and skills were carefully selected
- the company was proud to go back to the basics.

It was primarily through the creation of an environment which created an atmosphere of fun, freedom and empowered action that PWA managed to successfully mould a culture supportive of innovation. The success was through the ability of the organization to develop behavioural characteristics and reflexes that were never apparent in the traditional outfit. Employees understood the safety of the environment and undertook their duties with a sense of fun and enthusiasm to make the airline highly customer focused and operationally efficient. Although creativity and innovation may not be all that were needed to be successful, certainly they formed the basis of success. It is obvious also that creating an exhilarating environment brings out the best in people. Successful companies are those that bring out the best in their people, and are able to capitalize on their strengths (Rhys, 1996).

Summary

In attempting to build an enduring company, it is vitally important to understand the key role of the soft side of the organization in innovation. Companies like IBM and Apple saw their fortunes overturned because of their inability to focus upon innovation, and more importantly to understand the importance of culture and climate in innovation. Apple Computers, after the departure of Steve Jobs, encountered dramatic failure despite its focus upon innovation. One of the reasons for this was that their leaders narrowly focused their efforts in trying to come up with the next great innovation. Instead, their time would have been better spent designing and creating an environment that would be able to create innovations of the future. Companies aspiring towards innovative goals need to learn from the examples of highly successful companies like 3M and The Body Shop, whose leaders spend their energy and effort in building organizational cultures and climates which perpetually create innovation.

In accepting this viewpoint, the key question in innovation begins to change from the traditional issue of focusing effort on the next great innovation to one which asks whether you are creating an environment that stimulates innovation. Are you simply focusing on your product portfolio or are you focused on building a culture that cannot be copied? Are you busy inventing a narrow base of products, or are you experimenting with creating *innovativeness*. Without doubt, the most innovative companies of the future will be dominated by those that do not simply focus energies upon product and technical innovation, but those who have managed to build enduring environments of human communities striving towards innovation through the creation of appropriate cultures and climate. This will be the energy of renewal and the drive to a successful future.

References

Amabile, T. M. (1988) A model of creativity and innovation in organizations. In *Research in Organizational Behaviour*, B. M. Straw and L. L. Cummings, eds, vol. 10, JAI Press, pp. 123–67.

Amabile, T. M. (1990) Within you, without you: the social psychology of creativity and beyond. In *Theories of Creativity*, M. A, Runco and B. S. Albert, eds, Sage Publishing, pp. 61–91.

Amabile, T. M. et al. (1991) Social influences on creativity: evaluation, co-action and surveillance. *Creativity Research Journal*, **3**, 6–21.

Andrew, C. A. (1996) The peopleware paradigm. *Hospital Materials Management*, **18**(1), 47–60.

Anon. (1996) Ideas plus application equals innovation. *Guidelines*, Autumn, 26–31.

Barron, F. and Harrington, D. M. (1981) Creativity, intelligence, and personality. *Annual Review of Psychology*, **32**, 439–76.

Buckler, S. A. (1997) The spiritual nature of innovation. *Research-Technology Management*, March–April, 43–7.

Burgleman, R. A. and Sayles, L. R. (1986) *Inside Corporate Innovation: Strategy, Structure and Managerial Skills*. The Free Press.

Burns, T. and Stalker, G. M. (1961) *The Management of Innovation*. Tavistock Publications.

Burnside, R. M. (1990) Improving corporate climates for creativity. In *Innovation and Creativity at Work*, M. A. West and J. L. Farr, eds, Wiley, pp. 265–84.

Carroll (1985) *Domains of Cognitive Ability*. Paper presented at the meeting of the American Association for the Advancement of Science.

Collins, J. C. and Porras, J. I. (1991) Organizational vision and visionary organizations. *California Management Review*, **34**, 30–52.

Denison, D. R. (1990) *Corporate Culture and Organizational Effectiveness*. Wiley Press.

Denison, D. R. and Mishra, A. K. (1995) Toward a theory of organizational culture and effectiveness. *Organization Science*, **6**(2), 204–23.

Deshpande, R., Farley, J. U. and Webster, F. E. (1993) Corporate culture, customer orientation and innovativeness in Japanese firms: a quadrad analysis. *Journal of Marketing*, **57**, 23–7.

Ekvall, G. (1991) Creativity in project work: a longitudinal study of product development project. *Creativity and Innovation Management*, March, 17–26.

Filipczak, B. (1997) It takes all kinds: creativity in the work force. *Training*, May, 32–8.

Gordon, (1985) The relationship between corporate culture to industry sector and corporate performance. In *Gaining Control of Corporate Culture*, R. H. Kilman, M. J. Saxton, R. Serpa and associates, eds, Jossey-Bass.

Guildford (1983) Transformation abilities of functions. *Journal of Creative Behaviour*, **17**, 75–83.

IW (1996a) Sony Corporation. *IW*, 3 June, 16–17.

IW (1996b) AT&T Paradyne. *IW*, 3 June, 9–12.

Kilman, M. J. Saxton, R. Serpa and associates, eds, Jossey-Bass.

Judge, W. Q., Fryxell, G. E. and Dooley, R. S. (1997) The new task of R&D management: creating goal directed communities for innovation. *California Management Review*, **39**(3), Spring, 72–84.

Kotter, J. P. and Heskett, J. L. (1992) *Corporate Culture and Performance*. The Free Press.

Lawerence, P. R. and Lorsch, J. (1967) *Organization and Environment: Managing Differentiation and Integration*. Harvard University Press.

Likert, R. l. (1961) *New Patterns of Management*. McGraw-Hill.

Ledford, G. E., Wendnhof, J. R. and Strahley, J. T. (1994) Realising a corporate philosophy. *Organizational Dynamics*, Spring, 5–19.

Mills, P. and Delbecq, A. (1996) Managerial practices that enhance innovation. *Organisational Dynamics*, Summer, 24–34.

Ouchi, W. (1983) *Theory Z: How American Business can Meet the Japanese Challenge*. Addison-Wesley.

Peters, T. and Waterman, R. (1982) *In Search of Excellence: Lessons from America's Best Run Companies*. Warner Books.

Picken, J. C. and Dess, G. G. (1997) Out of (strategic) control. *Organizational Dynamics*, Summer, 35–48.

Pinchot, E. and Pinchot, G. (1996) Seeding a climate for innovation. *Executive Excellence*, June, 17–18.

Rhys, W. (1996) Making innovation fly. *Executive Excellence*, February 11–14.

Schein, E. H. (1985) *Organizational Culture and Leadership*. Jossey Bass.

Schneider, B. (1987) The people make the place. *Personnel Psychology*, **28**, 337–53.

Schneider, B., Gunnarson, S. K. and Niles-Jolly, K. (1996) Creating the climate and culture of success. *Organizational Dynamics*, Summer, 17–29.

Schneider, B., Brief, A. P. and Guzzo, R. A. (1996) Creating a climate and culture for sustainable change. *Organizational Dynamics*, Spring, 7–19.

Shalley, C. E. and Oldham, G. R. (1985) Effects of goal difficulty and expected evaluation on intrinsic motivation: a laboratory study. *Academy of Management Journal*, **28**, 628–40.

Wilkins, A. and Ouchi, W. (1983) Efficient cultures: exploring the relationship between culture and organizational performance. *Administrative Science Quarterly*, **28**(60), 468–98.

Woodman, R. W. and Schoenfeldt, L. F. (1990) An interactionist model of creative behavior. *Journal of Creative Behaviour*, **24**, 279–90.

12 Concluding remarks

Why process innovation?

The approach adopted in putting together this text represents a major departure from other books written on the subject of innovation management. Most texts seems to represent innovation management from a project/product stance and tend to focus more on micro aspects of new product development. *Best Practice: Process Innovation Management* does, however, emphasize the need for considering the activity of innovation from a corporatewide perspective, in its totality and through demonstrating clear linkages between various functional disciplines.

Innovation and its management does, in reality, affect several stakeholders. Deschamps and Nayak (1995), for instance, refer to the concept of *balanced satisfaction* and operating in a way so as to create the *high-performance business*. Process innovation management delivers outcomes through a virtuous circle:

> satisfied owners will make the necessary investments in terms of pay and benefits, productivity improvement, and work environment to increase employee satisfaction. Satisfied employees will work hard to provide the goods and services that increase customer satisfaction. Satisfied customers will provide the loyalty, higher sales and profits that will boost owner satisfaction even further. (Deschamps and Nayak, 1995)

The purpose of this book was not to prove that innovation management is a new concept. The endeavours for improving the quality of life generally speaking have always been with humankind through different eras. As Mitchell (1998) argues: 'If innovation means "to seek, continually, new ways to run businesses differently and better", that is something that generations of managers have done.'

What is important, however, is to present the management of innovation processes in a wider and new context which considers the following questions:

- How to build innovative capabilities for repeated superior performance?
- How to continue to replenish customer/consumer needs and act as preferred supplier?

- How to create consistency and effectiveness in managing innovation projects?
- How to innovate through mass customization?
- How to create a culture of sustainable innovativeness?

As Mitchell (1998) argues, culture is at the heart of sustainable innovation. The more we understand it and learn how to manage it the more successful we can expect to be in the marketplace: 'Culture is concerned with how people work when no one is telling them how to work. Get that right and sustainable competitive advantage, by innovation and other means, will emerge.'

The challenge for the future of innovation management

A holistic approach to the management of innovation is perhaps a prerequisite in the 1990s for a wide variety of reasons. Unless the array of critical factors is considered carefully, the notion of world class will always remain elusive. The evolution in our understanding of the term 'innovation' itself has moved gradually from a 'product push' to a 'market pull' perspective; 'technology driven' to 'customer driven'; 'product focus' to 'process focus'. As Williams argues: 'Technological Innovation is the result of a highly complex chain of events, of which the science or technological aspect is one of the least crucial' (Williams, 1996a).

Williams believes that, apart from R&D, the most critical factors to competitive success include manufacturing and marketing skills, as well as financial acumen. This argument is shared by many. At a recent forum of senior executives, discussing the future of manufacturing and technology management for the year 2005 (Williams, 1996b), it was unanimously agreed that the future of competitiveness in manufacturing will not depend on technology but on knowledge-based management and the harnessing of people's innovativeness and creativity. The executives agreed that the key elements to look out for include:

- The focus on process knowledge and the understanding of core manufacturing processes.
- Moving away from the conventional definition of process knowledge (which tended to encapsulate technical and physical activities) to cover social activities of production.
- The encouragement of learning as a core competence. Companies have now shifted their 'faith' from harnessing technological options to a new approach, which mainly encourages the use of people by implementing the most effective ways for involving people in optimizing the so-called technological options. It was, on the whole, agreed that: 'Technology

confers agility and speed. But that agility and speed, in turn, requires a workforce with greater latitude to act and therefore more skills and a greater understanding of the company's overall direction (Williams, 1996b).

- Having a committed workforce. This is to assist organizations in achieving and sustaining superior performance.
- The ability to use change as a stimulus for growth.

In all, it is predicted that by the year 2005, world-class manufacturing organizations will be characterized by the following attributes (Williams, 1996b):

- Understanding processes deeply and being able to manufacture without any disruptions.
- Employing a multiskilled and committed workforce.
- Integrating seamlessly with customers and suppliers.
- Designing and manufacturing with a full understanding of the cost savings and environmental benefits of eliminating waste and pollution.
- Moving information and production quickly around the globe and giving leverage to technology and capacity.
- Growing and competing on learning and knowledge as well as speed, quality and price.

The arguments presented in the previous discussion about the future of the manufacturing industry and the contributory role of innovation management are supported more widely. It is popularly regarded that technological evolution and its diffusion, together with the level of sophistication the former introduces on the way innovation management takes place, will have a lasting effect on the way organizations shape up their competitiveness.

Arthur D. Little Consultants (*Technology Strategies*, April 1996) have facilitated a forum to gather the views of companies in the USA and Europe on the impact of shifts in technology and innovation management and also to highlight and propose some best practices. A number of factors were put together, covering core aspects related to the appraisal and exploitation of technology, and aspects of innovation management, project management resource management global competitiveness, among others.

1 It is widely suggested that technological benefits can come only from using integration and fusion through the reliance on many diverse technologies, rather than seeking to reap out major benefits from a single source. It was suggested that organizations would need to develop a portfolio of technology-related competencies. It will then be left to individual companies to opt for the right mix and approach for determining how they would play the game, thereby establishing their competitiveness.

2 There is a need to drive the harnessing of technology and innovation for profitability and growth by perhaps placing emphasis on adding value, optimization and performance from a wide variety of perspectives.

3 There is a need to drive innovation in a seamless way by co-ordinating all key activities, integrating all the necessary key players' contributions, providing adequate support and resources and capturing the potential of working in partnerships.

4 Cross-functional approaches must be used for project management and an insistence on measurement, in such a way that they start to drive positive behaviours and attitudes and, in turn, linking these to the right incentives and reward schemes.

5 Organizations must be globally focused through being 'smart'. They have to have outreach mechanisms and a clear appreciation and understanding of the global market.

This debate, facilitated by Arthur D. Little, has concluded by getting all the delegates involved to agree on the following sets of best practice for effective competitiveness in the future to come:

- To have a mix of strong, empowered teams for driving core processes related to product development and technology development.
- To have a well-defined and aligned technology vision and strategy.
- To have a well-balanced portfolio of key technology application platforms in order to enable the launch of a regular stream of exciting product and process innovations.
- To have a robust innovation process stretching from concept to customer. Essentially, this aspect would rely on the effective integration of brand development with the supply chain: 'The seamlessness achieved through effective integration of the supply chain is a critical pathway to future breakthroughs in time to market, product performance, product cost and risk management' (*Technology Strategies*, April 1996).
- To have a well-defined, effectively leveraged sourcing and partnering strategy.
- Fostering a market-oriented, customer-driven culture conducive to creativity, innovation and managed risk.
- Maintaining and sustaining a culture of innovation.
- Having an effective budgeting and resource management process.
- Having a global intelligence network for harnessing technology and innovation competence.
- To have inspired, committed, technology leadership.

There appears to be a general consensus on the direction of technological and innovation developments in the future. It is very clear that the effective management of innovation is going to be heavily dependent on a mixture of hard systems and processes. This will have to be supported by good infrastructures and information technology, and reliant on the harnessing of people's creativity and synergy levels. But above all, the future of innovation management will be heavily dependent on:

- good leadership
- vision/strategy for exploitation of technology
- effective technology maps and innovation mixes which will deliver competitive advantages
- insistence on measurement and continuous improvement
- the development of a positive culture and a climate conducive to sustainable innovation.

Some likely developments for the management of innovation process in the future

While it will always be very difficult to predict the future in so far as the management of innovation is concerned, none the less there are many emerging factors both as opportunity and issues to be dealt with, that can be discussed.

Integration

One of the key learning in the extended concept of innovation management is the adoption of principles which rely on contributions coming from a wide variety of stakeholders and therefore deal with issues associated with integration and linkages. Some of the most critical aspects include:

- internal linkages through the application of internal marketing
- external linkages through the integration of suppliers and customers
- interorganizational linkages for shared innovative benefits.

Harmonization

The notion of the global customer is well accepted now and many innovative organizations are reaching out to global markets through the adoption of the *mass customization* principle by using:
- new structural approaches based on process orientation
- new strategic approaches based on market orientation

- globalization approaches through the adoption of economies of scale and scope
- building regionally based centres of excellence through the transfer of key core competencies.

Smart partnerships

In many industries the process of innovation will become an extended concept relying more on collaborative efforts and networks of relationships. It is more and more likely that organizations will focus only on their core competencies if these are in the area of:

- developing technological inventions and innovations
- translating technological inventions/innovations into commercial opportunities
- providing resources and means for innovating
- providing access to global markets.

The level of synergy between these various core competencies will provide a powerful innovative approach for impacting continuously on global customers (Figure 12.1).

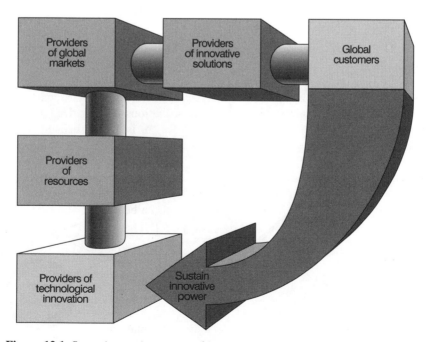

Figure 12.1 *Smart innovation partnerships*

Global extended innovation process

The principles of process orientation are going to affect each aspect of innovation management. This will mean that there is going to be a radical shift from one-off projects more into the continuous approach of innovativeness. For instance:

- The cycle of inventing and developing new technologies and prototypes is a continuous process and yet everyone's focus has been hitherto on *outcomes* (i.e. singular technologies). It would therefore be more appropriate to start re-focusing on the process of inventing and developing and to measure several outcomes and a continuum of technical solutions.
- The cycle of translating customer/consumer needs into innovative solutions is a continuous one and yet in many instances the focus has always been project-based, focusing on singular products/services. As discussed in the book, the approach to be adopted has to be on optimizing the process of innovation and the delivery of a wide range of customer solutions.
- The cycle of delivering value to customers and consumers has on the whole been through a transactional approach focusing on whether the newly launched product or service is satisfying customer/consumer needs. The more appropriate approach is of course to work beyond the immediate

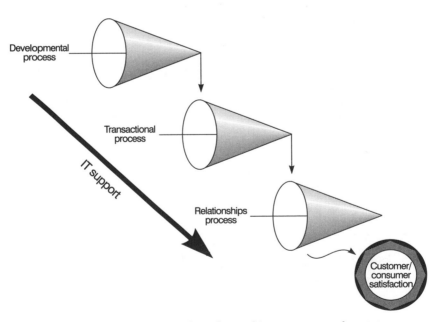

Figure 12.2 *Managing innovation through a multiprocess approach*

needs and to develop long-term partnerships in a multi-faceted, multi-level relationship mode (Figure 12.2).

- Information technology and the opportunity for sharing information will enable organizations to link-in through an extended innovation process approach. The principles of process orientation are generic in nature and can be adopted for each stage of the extended innovation chain (Figures 12.3, 12.4 and 12.5).
- The extended innovation process will, however, become effective only through a global innovation deployment process. The latter is meant to scan, stir and support innovation activity for a global impact. Such a process, as illustrated in Figure 12.6, addresses *why*, *what* and *how* aspects

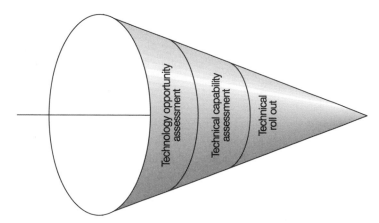

Figure 12.3 *Managing through a multiprocess approach: R&D chain*

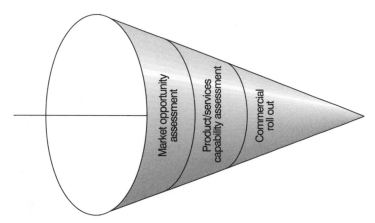

Figure 12.4 *Managing through a multiprocess approach: extended supply chain*

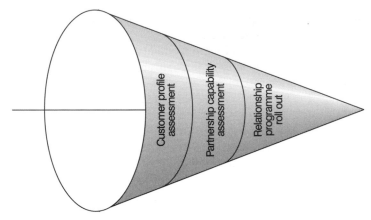

Figure 12.5 *Managing through a multiprocess approach: customer development and management chain*

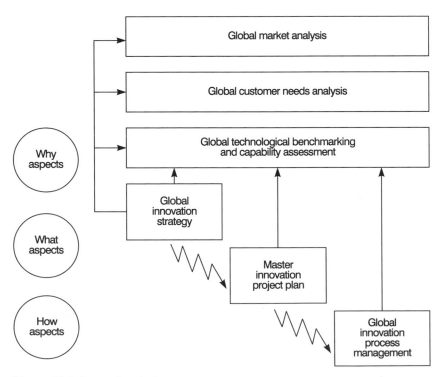

Figure 12.6 *Innovation deployment process*

of global innovation and has the ability to generate global alignment and focus on global customers.

References

Deschamps, J. P. and Nayak, P. R. (1995) *Product Juggernauts: How Companies Mobilize to Generate a Stream of Market Winners*. Harvard Business School Press.

Mitchell, P. (1998) Innovation in its right place. *Financial Times*, 17 April, p. 12.

Technology Strategies (1996) April (122), MCB University Press.

Williams, P. (1996a) Technological innovation needs the support of the business backroom boys. *Technology Strategies*, May, 10.

Williams, P. (1996b) The future of manufacturing. *Technology Management*, May, 20.

Index